THE NEW
SINGLE MALT
WHISKEY

CIDER MILL
PRESS

BOOK
PUBLISHERS

KENNEBUNKPORT, MAINE

13-Digit ISBN: 9781604336474
10-Digit ISBN: 1604336471

This book may be ordered by mail from the publisher. Please include $5.95 for postage and handling. Please support your local bookseller first!

Books published by Cider Mill Press Book Publishers are available at special discounts for bulk purchases in the United States by corporations, institutions, and other organizations. For more information, please contact the publisher.

Cider Mill Press Book Publishers
"Where good books are ready for press"
PO Box 454
12 Spring Street
Kennebunkport, Maine 04046

Visit us on the Web! www.cidermillpress.com

Design by Jaime Christopher

Typography: Warnock Pro, Old Barrel, Source Sans Pro, Sackers Antique Roman

Printed in China

1 2 3 4 5 6 7 8 9 0
First Edition

— CONTENTS —

INTRODUCTION

COCKTAILS

Original Chatham Artillery Punch, by David Wondrich
The Big Bash

WHISKEY AROUND THE WORLD

INTRODUCTION

— FOREWORD —

BY CHIP TATE
HEAD DISTILLER, TATE & COMPANY DISTILLERY

In 1976, Stephen Spurrier accidently turned the wine world up side down. In what has now come to be known as "The Judgment of Paris," French wine experts came to the shocking conclusion that not only were many of California's wine just as good as the best France had to offer—some were better. Considering many wine experts thought wine-making outside of France was a pointless enterprise, the news shook the wine world and changed the enological landscape forever.

I am embarrassed to admit it, but I was entirely unfamiliar with the Judgment of Paris and the epic milestone it represented until just a few years ago. Perhaps it is because I was quite young when it happened. But perhaps it is because, some forty years later, it is almost hard to imagine that the world of wine had been so different such a short time ago. That milestone event in Paris fueled a revolution in wine that has resulted in wonderful wines not only from California, but also from around the world, which grow and shine like never before.

My introduction to this story came through whisky. One of my proudest moments happened in 2012. I received a call from Neil Ridley in London. He and several other whisky

writers and critics had organized a clandestine competition they called "Best in Glass." In brief, these UK whisky judges organized a whisky competition on their own UK turf focusing around single malt whisky, a traditionally product, and picked my American single malt as their favorite. I was shocked. Part of the shock could be attributed to the fact that I did not even know my malt was in the competition, no doubt. But even more shocking was that UK whisky critics had organized a UK whisky competition and chosen an American single malt as their favorite.

Once several journalists drew parallels between the 2012 Best in Glass competition and the 1976 Judgment of Paris, I began to understand that the most important victory was not a personal one, as gratifying as it was. I realized in that moment that new things were possible for malt whisky around the world. Not just American single malts, but for single malts from South Africa, continental Europe, India and other parts of Asia, and anywhere else in the world that distillers were bold enough to try their hand at what had been assumed to be an exclusively Scottish enterprise until the recent past.

This quiet malt whisky revolution has been going on for decades. But only now are the malts of these labors becoming more known to the broader whisky world. Not so long ago, Americans could not even buy malt whisky in the US. Now, not only can we buy a wide array of the Scottish single malts that have set the bar for decades, but also Americans and distillers around the world are producing single malt whiskies that rival and even surpass the Scots'. It is an exciting time to be a malt distiller and, perhaps, an even more exciting time to be a single malt enthusiast. This book, The New Single Malt Whiskey, is another landmark moment in that revolution. With viewpoints from writers around the world, it is an important first attempt at providing whisky enthusiasts with a rubric for interpretation of an ever-fluid movement.

Explore boldly, without bias or reserve. A new chapter in single malt whisky is unfolding for us all.

EDITOR'S NOTE

BY CARLO DEVITO

This is the most widespread and ambitious whiskey project the industry has ever seen undertaken. We have assembled whiskey writers from around the world—more than forty writers from over a dozen countries have contributed to making this the most complete and definitive research on the New Single Malt Whiskey.

What is the New Single Malt? More than anything there are two things that help define it. Firstly, it is single malt whiskey made anywhere in the world. It does not need to be made in Scotland. That was the first criteria. The craft movement around the world is striving to compete at the top, most epic level. These men and women are pushing the envelope of our knowledge of the industry. Using new oak finishes, such as wine casks from Bordeaux, Sauternes, Porto, Cognac, and many other types, they are experimenting with local barleys, oak, and wine barrels, and working with local brewers who use local ingredients. This leads to our next point.

The New Single Malt, secondly, is about style as well as place. Ten years ago, the few small craft distillers that took on this idea wanted to make something comparable; they wanted to emulate and be considered "just as good." While they made the whiskey outside of Scotland, they used enough parts to re-create the same flavor profiles. But now there is a new gen-

eration that thumbs their collective noses at this notion.

Terroir has worked its way into the lexicon of whisky. Because terroir in whisky began in Scotland, single malt was Scotland's claim to such a thing. The New Single Malt is about distillers creating single malt whiskies that reflect the terroir of THEIR region. They want to make a German single malt. They want to make a Canadian single malt. They want to make a Japanese single malt. They want to make a Texas single malt. Copying the four regions of Scotland isn't good enough anymore. The mold has been broken, and now the believers are running things.

Did we exclude Scotland? No! How could one exclude the point of origin? Sure, traditional single malts made the same way they have been made for generations, for centuries, can still be obtained. They are the classics. But complacency has no place in distilling any more. Nor does stasis. The seeds of the revolution were sewn there. The New Single Malt revolution started in Scotland itself with the bottling of The Balvennie DoubleWood. Seen at the time by some as more of a gimmick than anything else, it touched off a vertible revolution, like a stone in a still pond, the ripples went out, and bounced back from the shore.

Now in Scotland, there are distillers who have engaged, who have picked up the gauntlet, who are rising to the challenge. Super, triple-peated whiskies, or those whose parts flew into space, those who are trying new wood finishes, and experimenting just like their brethren across any number of oceans or ponds (whichever you prefer). If they were embracing the spirit of the new movement, we did our best to acknowledge their participation.

Thus, you will not find classic single malt Scotches in this collection. Just because they released a five, ten, twelve or fifteen year old expression doesn't get them into the club. Those who are pressing the envelope in Scotland we have counted among the members of the new movement.

We have not attempted to note every expression nor every release from every house. It would be a fool's errand. The list is way too fluid, if you will pardon the pun. Distilleries, labels, and bottlers are issuing new releases in record numbers. The list would be way too long and incomplete. Instead, we attempted to find the releases that best exemplified the new movement, and expressed the terroir or the style of the producer.

When at all possible, we tried to find local writers who had visited the producers themselves, who could best translate the reasoning behind the craft distiller's intentions. This was not always possible, since some labels or producers are so remote or the release so small. Regardless, we attempted to turn over even the smallest of stones, no matter how far flung.

One of the other things we did not include were expressions that claimed to be single malt products but did not print that statement on their labels. No ticket, no shirt.

You may note different spellings of whisk(e)y throughout—here we matched the standard across that particular country or the individual distillery. We're following these movers and shakers to the tee—or rather the "e."

We also attempted to include articles on woods, ice, tasting, and the like, trying to explain wherein this new vision emanates from. The New Single Malt drinker is a classicist, but he or she is also someone who likes pressing the boundaries. They are not such snobs that they won't try their single malt in a mixed drink. They'll make a punch from it. They'll have it over ice. They'll have it with a steak… or with sushi!

The New Single Malt Whiskey revolution is an exciting place right now. The wave has been building for sometime. Here is the first snapshot of that wave. Taken and offered by those who stand there on the shores to witness it!

Enjoy!

— INTRODUCTION —

BY CLAY RISEN
AUTHOR OF *AMERICAN WHISKEY, BOURBON & RYE*

Can the phrase "the new single malt whiskey" be anything other than a blatant contradiction in terms? After all, malt whiskey has been made in more or less the same fashion for 400 years. It is all about tradition, about mossy glens and wind-battered tairns, about the Sixteen Men of Tain who have been making Glenmorangie since 1842. It's not the same sixteen men of course, but you'd be forgiven for thinking otherwise for all the ritual and heritage piled chock-a-block around them.

But in fact single malt, as a viable, sellable, respectable category, didn't emerge until the last few decades. For most of their existence, the great distilleries of today—Glenfiddich and Glenfarclas and GlenDronach, and even a few non-Glens—were feeders, selling their stocks to blenders. Bottles of single malt were rare, and by and large drinkers didn't seek them out.

That began to change in the 1970s and 1980s. An oversupply of whiskey stocks—the infamous "Whiskey loch"—forced producers to find new ways to market their spirits. They began emphasizing all those things that we take for granted today, but were revolutionary at the time: instead of blending to produce smooth uniformity, the component whiskeys in a blend—the all-malt spirits coming from single-source distilleries—would be singled out for their idiosyncrasies, their small-batch inconsistencies, their robust nobility. Instead of praising suave blenders, rough-hewn distillers—those Sixteen Men of Tain—would get top billing. They called it "single malt," made by a single producer from a single grain malt.

Along with these new spirits came a new generation of whiskey advocates, led by the incomparable Michael Jackson, who explained to a curious global audience how to drink them. It helped enormously that all this happened during the booming 1980s, when young people flush with cash grabbed onto single malt as an express ticket to respectability.

The 1980s were a long time ago, or at least they seem that way. And through the 1990s and 2000s, even as single malt sales rose, the category began to show its age. Skyrocketing auction prices and the growth of exclusive scotch clubs gave single malt an air of unattainability. "Single malt" remained a mark of prestige to some, but a mark of impossible refinement to others. There is a scene in the 1996 film Swingers in which Mike, played by Jon Favreau, asked for a scotch on the rocks. What kind? He's at a loss. "Any scotch will do. As long as it's not a blend, of course. Single malt, Glen Livet, Glen Galley, perhaps, any Glen."

He can pretend to be sophisticated—dress in a suit, go to fancy parties—but single malt, so the joke went, was out of his league.

And then, in the mid-2000s, came bourbon—again. One reason single malt could thrive in the United States was that American drinkers had long since given up on their homegrown brown spirits as uncouth. But a broad turn toward American-made, homegrown retro flavors made bourbon once again desirable—and its low price point made it an easy sell against single malts.

Headwinds like this have forced other spirit trends to ground. And yet today, the outlook for single malt whiskey couldn't be better. Sales of single malt scotch in the United States grew by 13 percent in 2015, almost twice as fast as bourbon. Growth is even faster in the developing economies of Asia,

Russia, and India. From 2004 to 2014, global exports rose 159 percent. Auction prices for extremely old and rare bottlings are rising at nearly vertical rates, while the supply of well-aged stocks is dwindling. New distilleries are opening across Scotland to meet demand, and international investors are swooping in to buy existing facilities or start their own.

But, as this book's breadth attests, the real story today isn't the growth of sales, but the growth of the category—it's not your grandfather's single malt. Yes, the Glens are still going strong. But so is Bastille in France, and Nikka in Japan. The United States has a robust single malt scene along the West Coast (which isn't to slight the great single malts coming out of New England and Texas and various points in between). Name a country, and these days there's probably a single malt distillery somewhere. And not just the obvious, temperate, and culturally British places like Australia and South Africa, but places like Taiwan and Italy as well.

And in the same way that American craft brewers began by aping British and German beer styles before cultivating their own weird and delicious categories, single malts today come in varieties no man of Tain would approve of. In the United States, a subset of single malts are made by distilling and aging commercial beer so that the hops, transmogrified through the still, impart a lusciously sweet, fragrant tang. In a riff on Scottish peat, Corsair, a distillery in Nashville, malts some of its barley over native hickory wood; Balcones, in Texas, uses local scrub brush. Lost Spirits, from Salinas, California, uses peat gathered from the slopes of Mt. Diablo to create Leviathan, a whiskey so dankly peaty that Lagavulin tastes like seltzer water beside it.

Outside Taipei, the King Car distillery, home of award-winning Kavalan single malt whisky, adjusted its distilling and aging process to account for the brutally hot and humid Taiwanese summers. The result is an aggressive yet sophisticated quaff, a brooding bruiser in a tuxedo; if Scottish single malts are Sean Connery, Kavalan is Daniel Craig.

Perhaps the most exciting aspect of all of this change is that it is still in its infancy. In Scotland, the concept of terroir is well understood—the same whiskey made in the Highlands will taste different from an identical expression made along the Lowlands English border, thanks to differences in climate, water, even the soil the barley is grown in, and not to mention the different hands that make it. It's still too early to define single malt regions outside Scotland, but they're coming. Already people talk about the single malt distilleries concentrated in the American Pacific Northwest as a distinct category; in 20 years, we may well be talking the same way about French single malts clustered around Brittany or Cognac.

And it may be even longer before many of these new single malts reach the stratospheric acclaim and prices that currently surround Scottish single malts. Though Japanese whiskey is enjoying a prestige boom, it may be a while before the same acclaim (and demand) visits India or South Africa. But that's a good thing: It means that, at least for now, intrepid drinkers can tour the world for a song. Many of these new lands are open for exploration—but not for long.

WHISKEY VERSUS WHISKY

BY ERIC ASIMOV

I'm looking out there for the one person who apparently was not offended by the spelling of "whiskey" in my column on Speyside single malts. If you are that person, allow me to explain.

Whiskey is a word with an alternative spelling, *whisky.* Or maybe it's the other way around. Dictionary.com seems to prefer *whiskey. The New York Times* stylebook definitively prefers whiskey:

> *whiskey(s). The general term covers bourbon, rye, Scotch and other liquors distilled from a mash of grain. For consistency, use this spelling even for liquors (typically Scotch) labeled whisky.*

But clearly, definitively, and somewhat aggressively, people from Scotland and many fans of Scotch have informed me of their preference for *whisky* over *whiskey,* judging by the flood of comments and emails I [received]. Here is a brief sample:

Graham Kent of London wrote: "I cannot pass over the unforgivable use by a serious writer on wines and spirits of 'whiskey' to refer to Scotch whisky." He goes on to say: "I am afraid I found the constant misspelling of the product made your article quite unreadable. It is exactly the same as if you had called it 'gin' all the way through or were to describe Lafite as Burgundy. It is simply a basic

error that a reputable writer should not make."

Well, allow me to say in my defense: I never claimed to be reputable!

Meanwhile, Margaret Tong wrote: "Last year I sent you an email to inform you that Scotch whisky has no 'e.' Irish whiskey has the 'e.' Yet, this year you continue your indifference. What a great disappointment that you think so little of the world's greatest drink, 'The glorified yellow water!'"

"Glorified yellow water?" I've never heard that before. Margaret Tong, allow me to introduce you to Frank Zappa.

I shall spare you the other email comments I've received, except this one, from a gentleman in Scotland: "Sadly the word 'whiskey' conjures up a very different brew here in Scotland. Scotch Whisky it has ever been, and 'Scotch Whiskey' an embarrassing solecism unworthy of *The New York Times*."

By "solecism," he means, according to my dictionary, a nonstandard usage or grammatical construction and a violation of etiquette.

Let me say that it is not now nor has it ever been (rarely been, at least) my intention to offend. And while I may appear to be enjoying this—well, why not?—I have not meant to behave solecistically.

Look, I could not work at a place like *The New York Times* if I didn't love language and take it seriously. I know that the vast majority of Scots and partisans of Scotch prefer the e-less whisky. Knowing how they would react, I tried to preempt it in my column with a little disclaimer. Obviously, it was not enough to stem the tide.

I decided to check in with my favorite word authority, Jesse Sheidlower, editor-at-large of the *Oxford English Dictionary*, and this is what he said:

"As an aficionado of whisky and whiskey, I do have deep feelings on the usage, which is pretty much that the *Times* style should be changed. This isn't a case where a small group of fanatics are insisting on some highly personal interpretation of an issue that is not adhered to by anyone outside their cult. It's almost universally the case that the word is spelled 'whisky' in Scotland and Canada, and 'whiskey' [in Ireland and the United States], and that, as you have seen, people really do care about this as an important distinction. I'd also observe that the O.E.D. points this out in its entry. So I would encourage you to adopt this distinction in the style book. I have no problem with using 'whiskey' as the main generic form, if there's no indication of location."

Thanks, Jesse! I will discuss this usage issue with my editors and the editors whose job it is to make stylistic decisions for *The New York Times*. Your opinions will be heard.

— HOW IS WHISKY MADE — AND WHERE DOES ITS FLAVOR COME FROM?

DISTILLING AND MATURING WHISKY

BY ANGELO CAPUANO

Whisky is defined in the *Oxford Dictionary* as "[a] spirit distilled from malted grain, especially barley or rye." There is more to it than that, of course. Making whisky is complex. Whisky is not "made" into a finished product, it takes time. The spirit that becomes "whisky" is clear as water when it is distilled. To become whisky, this clear liquid (which is called "new make") needs to mature in oak. This piece will show you how this "new make" is distilled, and then matured

into whisky. It explains how different types of whisky get their distinct flavors, and from where.

It should be noted here that this piece is about how whisky (without the "e") is made. It will therefore focus on the typical production of Scotch style malt whisky, and not Canadian whisky, American whiskey (such as bourbon or Tennessee whiskey which is made from a mash of at least 51% corn, and which needs to mature by law in new charred oak barrels) or Irish whiskey (which tends to be made from malted and unmalted barley, and is usually distilled three times; though this is a generalization as I am advised that whiskey distilled at the Cooley distillery in Ireland is distilled twice and some Irish whiskies are made purely from malted barley). Now, let's begin the story by introducing you to the grain that tends to be used to make whisky: barley.

IN THE BEGINNING, THERE IS BARLEY.

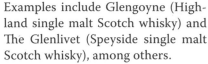

In the beginning, there is barley. This barley is malted (for malt whisky), and then dried. It is dried either with air or smoke from burning peat ("peat smoke"). Peat is a spongy material, which, put simply, is an organic fuel formed by the partial decomposition of organic matter—usually plant matter—in wetlands. The creation of peat is the first step in the formation of coal.

Many distilleries do not use peat when drying the malt used to make their whisky; this means the natural flavors and aromas of the malt are likely to be pronounced in the "distillery character" of these distilleries.

Examples include Glengoyne (Highland single malt Scotch whisky) and The Glenlivet (Speyside single malt Scotch whisky), among others.

In contrast, many distilleries on the Isle of Islay—Ardbeg, Laphroaig, Caol Ila, Lagavulin, Bruichladdich, Bowmore, etc.—and other islands—Talisker, Highland Park—use peat to dry the malt used to make many of their expressions. As the malt is dried with peat smoke, it absorbs phenols from the smoke. This means that natural flavor of the malt is paired with the vegetal and earthy peat smoke (resulting whisky is sometimes described as medicinal, tarry, earthy, carbolic, etc.). Some of these expressions are also coastal or maritime in flavor, with sea spray and salt. More lightly peated whiskies tend to have a mossy character.

The level of peat in a whisky depends on the whisky's "Phenol Parts Per Million" (PPM). A number of factors can determine a malt's PPM, including how long it is exposed to peat smoke, the type of peat used, and the density of the smoke. Different distilleries produce whisky with different PPMs; the higher the PPM, the more "peaty" the whisky is likely to be.

THE MALT IS USED TO MAKE WORT (MALT/GRAIN-INFUSED WATER).

The dried malt is then cracked or ground into a grist ("milling"). It is then steeped in hot water (usually from 145°F) for a while in a process called *mashing,* when the enzymes convert the starches to sugars. The mashing process involves putting the malt and water in a machine called a *mash tun,* which stirs the mixture; this process develops enzymes that convert the starch in the grain to sugar. Now, the resulting sugary water, called *wort,* is ready to be converted to an alcoholic *wash* (what is essentially a simple beer).

WORT IS FERMENTED AND MADE INTO A WASH (A SIMPLE BEER).

To make the wash, yeast is added to the wort when it reaches somewhere between 64°F to 82°F (depending on the kind of yeast that is used). The yeast converts the sugars in the wort to alcohol while adding flavorsome impurities called *congeners.* This process is called *fermentation* and occurs in vessels called *washbacks.* It usually takes a few days. The wash tends to be around 8–9% alcohol by volume (ABV).

Many different types of yeast are used to create alcohol of different flavors, from bakers' yeast used by many moonshiners, to the more sophisticated ale yeasts that tend to be used by artisan distillers. You will find that every distillery has a particular strain of yeast they prefer to use, and this yeast contributes to their distillery character. Sometimes the batch is spoiled by wild yeast hanging around, eager to ferment any sugary liquids into a foul-smelling (and no doubt foul-tasting) wash.

The race to beat that pesky wild yeast from spoiling the show requires a clean work area and getting the wort down in temperature as quickly as possible to add the nice, friendly yeast—the longer it takes, the more time the wild yeast has to ruin the batch, but if the wort is too hot the nice, cultured yeast will die. Once the yeast is placed into the wort, the wort begins to slowly ferment into a wash—a form of beer. The wash neither looks nor smells palatable, having a layer of foam and scum on the top.

THE WASH IS DISTILLED.

The wash, now containing alcohol, is placed in a "copper still." Copper stills are used because the copper helps remove sulfides in the wash and it can also accentuate esters and aldehydes. A still allows alcohol

vapor to travel up its neck and then be converted to liquid at the top when it reaches a condenser (which is usually a coil with cool water running through it).

Once in the still, the wash is heated. Because alcohol evaporates at a lower temperature than water, it can be separated from the water in the wash by heating the wash to a temperature above 173°F but below 212°F.

As the wash reaches around 150°F, a liquid clear as water begins to travel up the still as vapor. Acetone, a ketone, and methanol boil at the lowest temperatures—real nasty smelling and poisonous—and this, fortunately, comes out of the still first. The small portion of alcohol that comes out of the still first is called *foreshots*. It is collected and discarded by a distiller. Then, when the wash reaches 173°F, that is when the good drinkable alco-

hol—ethanol—boils and travels up the still as vapor to be condensed into liquid and collected by the distiller. As the wash heats up, though, higher alcohols such as fusel alcohols (2-Propanol/rubbing alcohol at 180°F and 3-Methyl-1-Butanol at 211°F) also begin to boil and then follow the ethanol up the still.

A distiller using a "pot still" needs to typically undertake two distillation runs—first distilling the wash to produce "low wines" (usually 18–25% alcohol by volume) and then re-distilling the "low wines" to get a stronger alcohol usually between 60–70% alcohol by volume. Sometimes, to get a lighter spirit, a distiller might want to run it through the still again (as is typical with triple distilled Irish whiskey, or Auchentoshan, which defies the Scotch industry standard of distilling twice).

Other types of stills can include reflux stills, which can distill a wash multiple times in one cycle by using packing or bubble-plates (these kinds of stills are mostly used to distill vodka because with each distillation the alcohol is stripped of some flavor and it becomes purer and more concentrated with ethanol—this is why whisky is usually distilled only two or three times to keep the flavor of the barley and fermentation). These reflux stills sometimes have a condenser at the top of the still neck with cool water running through it, and this cool water blocks heavier vapors so that lighter vapors can pass through to be collected, thereby producing a very fine spirit.

A DISTILLER NEEDS TO MAKE "CUTS" AND CHOOSE WHAT DISTILLATE TO TURN INTO WHISKY.

During distillation a distiller needs to make what is known as "cuts" after discarding the foreshots. As just noted, foreshots come out of the still first at the start of a distillation run because it comprises mostly of volatile acetone and methanol, which boil at low temperatures. It is important to emphasize that the alcohols in foreshots are poisonous and must be discarded.

The first part of the run is the *heads*. Heads comprise of acetone, acetaldehyde and abetate; these alcohols smell bad and taste very harsh on the palate. Consuming them will likely give you a killer hangover. They smell like nail polish and nail polish remover.

As the amount of ethanol flowing out of the still increases, the drinkable spirit emerges in the form of *hearts*. Hearts comprise predominately of ethanol and the most desirable congeners; they have a rich, pleasant aroma and flavor, with sweetness and much more smoothness than heads. Hearts are more expressive of the raw ingredients used to make the wash. They smell and taste like something you would want to drink—often quite fruity, sweet, and malty. This alcohol can also smell yeasty from the fermentation process, much like sake, Chinese rice wine, or Shōchū made from grain.

After a while, the hearts begin to fade into the *tails*, which smell very much like wet cardboard, baby sick, and wet dog. It's not poisonous; it just smells and tastes strange and undesirable. Tails may sometimes add some congeners and flavor compounds not found in hearts, and they are sometimes very important ingredients to a distillery's character.

The unused heads and tails tend to be recycled, and used in future distillation runs to squeeze any ethanol out of them.

Once the distiller makes all the desired *cuts*, you have whisky in its infancy—*new make*. The important thing to remember is that different distilleries tend to produce new make that taste different to one another.

THE DISTILLED "NEW MAKE" IS PLACED INTO OAK BARRELS TO MATURE.

People figured out a long time ago that even the best new make can be improved. In days now long passed, oak barrels were used to store and transport almost everything—fish, meat, and even new make spirit. Before placing the new make in the barrel, traders would burn

and char the insides of the barrel. What they probably didn't realize, but what they found out later, is that this charring actually unlocked a lot of the sugars and flavors in the oak that could then be infused into the new make. People found that after spending time in these

charred oak barrels, the new make began to not only change color but also smell and taste better. People noticed that the kind of color, aroma, and flavors that developed relied very heavily on what type of oak the new make was stored in. Distillers now use oak casks to add flavor to their new make over the course of many years, and rightly so because it is estimated that a whisky gets upwards of 60% of its flavor from oak.

When new make sits in oak barrels, the pores in the oak expand when it is warmer, soaking up the new make, and close when it is colder, squeezing the new make back out into the cask. Over time, from being soaked up and squeezed out over and over from the oak, the new make slowly begins to take on color, aroma ,and flavors from the oak casks in which it matures.

Because the casks are often charred (burnt on the inside) the new make also gets filtered by the oak, in a similar process to carbon filtration, which removes some of the more undesirable compounds in the new make. The alcohols that boil at low temperature sometimes evaporate away as the new make rests in the casks, especially in hot summer months, escaping through the pores in the oak or the bunghole as it is opened. By far, however, the new make gets most of its flavor from the oak itself.

AMERICAN OAK

The most popular cask in which to mature whisky, at least in Scotland, is American oak. American oak (or Quercus alba) is an oak tree that grows in North America. As new make rests in American oak, the new make tends to draw out oils from the wood called "vanillins," which typically resemble the aroma and taste of vanilla. American oak also offers compounds that smell or taste like caramel, coconut, butterscotch, fudge, and, particularly with older whisky, ginger. When a whisky is matured in American oak that has never been used for anything else before, it is called "virgin wood" or "virgin oak."

This typically gives a whisky a "bourbon-y" character (think pancakes, brown sugar, and syrup), because bourbon is matured in new oak barrels that have been charred (although bourbon must be made from at least 51% corn so it is different from malt whisky, which is made from barley). Using virgin wood to mature malt whisky is not very common, though it does increasingly now occur, and this practice is seeing what many call the "bourbonization" of malt whisky.

FRENCH OAK

Whisky can also be matured in French oak, which, broadly speaking, tends to give a whisky subtle spicy notes, clove, and a satiny texture. The main French oak forests are Allier, Limousin, Nevers, Tronçais and Vosges. Oak from each oak forest is thought to be distinctive.

OTHER TYPES OF OAK

Whisky can also be matured or finished in Spanish oak, Hungarian oak, Swedish oak—which is used quite extensively by Swedish distilleries—or Japanese oak (also known as Mizunara). Japanese oak tends to have strong notes associated with cinnamon and a distinct spiciness.

EX-BOURBON, EX-SHERRY, EX-WINE, EX-BRANDY CASKS

Whisky not only derives its flavor from the oak, but also whatever the oak barrels held before it stored the whisky. Malt whisky distilleries tend to mature new make in casks that have already matured something else—bourbon, sherry, and wine are the most common examples. This means that not only does the new make draw out flavor from the American oak or French oak, but it also becomes infused with the flavor of the previous contents of the oak, whether that was bourbon, sherry, or wine. Increasingly, distilleries are also using barrels that have held rum, brandy or Cognac. Jameson has even finished one of its expressions in barrels that have been seasoned with craft stout beer.

WHISKY MATURED IN AMERICAN OAK EX-BOURBON BARRELS

It is estimated that about 90% of Scotch malt whisky is matured in American oak casks that previously held bourbon. By spending time in American oak that has previously held bourbon, a malt whisky tends to draw out some distinct "bourbon-y" notes alongside the American oak influence—common notes include raisins, honey, sultana, vanilla, cereal notes (such as rye, depending on the type of bourbon barrel used), and raw sugar. Bourbon-matured whiskies also tend to have a golden color, noting of course that caramel may be added to enhance color.

WHISKY MATURED IN EX-SHERRY BARRELS

Contrary to what you might think, not all sherry is stored in Spanish oak. Some sherry makers store their sherry in American oak, and then pass on the used sherry casks to whisky makers who put their whisky in those used sherry casks. Apart from flavors from the American oak, ex-sherry American oak casks can give a whisky a more fruit cake and chocolaty flavor profile with peel and spice, though the flavors do seem to vary depending on the type of sherry that was used; whether that is Oloroso, Pedro Ximénez, Fino, etc.; the interaction between the sherry used; and the distillery's malt charac-

ter. It might offer nuts, prune, cherries, Christmas cake, raisins, sultana, or dried fruit. It might be dry (Fino), medium-dry (Oloroso) or sweet (PX). Sherry-matured whiskies also tend to have a reddish or brown hued color, noting of course that caramel may be added to enhance color. This is not always the case, however.

Whisky can also be matured in ex-wine, ex-port, ex-brandy, or ex-rum barrels—basically any oak barrel that has previously held something delicious. The two most popular ones are, however, ex-bourbon and ex-sherry barrels.

BRINGING IT ALL TOGETHER: DISTILLERY CHARACTER + OAK INFLUENCE OVER TIME = WHISKY.

As discussed above, it is clear that a whisky's flavor profile is made up of two different main elements: (1) distillery character; and (2) oak influence. Let's further explore these two concepts.

DISTILLERY CHARACTER

Distillery character from the distillate makes up the first main element in a whisky's flavor profile. That flavor comes from the kind of malt that is used to make the wort, whether or not the malt is dried using peat smoke, the kind of yeast that is used to ferment the wort into a wash, and the cuts that are made when distilling the wash into new make spirit (all explained above).

Typical distillery characters would mainly be made up of the sweet fruity esters that are produced when fermenting wort into wash, and then concentrated by distilling the wash into new make spirit. Let me give some examples, by referring to the distillery character which I tend to perceive in some expressions of three Scotch whisky distilleries: Glenfiddich, Glengoyne, and, Bruichladdich.

Glenfiddich tends to have (in my opinion) a distillery character that is dominated by apple and pear flavors. Glengoyne, however, tends to (in my opinion) tailor its new make to have more toffee and honey characters alongside the fruity esters and resinous cereals. The distillery character of Bruichladdich is very hard to pin down because the distillery uses different types of barley (such as barley from Islay as opposed to barley from the mainland of Scotland, for example). However, when we look at the flavor profile of the Bruichladdich Islay Barley, we can see that the new make seems to have drawn out not only sweet honeys but also earthiness and coastal salinity (or something that tastes like salt). So, what we have here is the "bare bones" of the whisky—the distillery character—before the new make is placed into oak.

OAK INFLUENCE FROM TIME IN OAK

Oak influence makes up the second main element in a whisky's flavor profile. As explained above, a whisky gets most of its flavor from the oak in which it matures (conservative estimates would be that whisky gets upwards of 60% of its flavor from oak). So, when new make rich in certain flavor compounds that tend to make up a distillery character are put in oak, the new make begins to draw out even more flavor from the oak.

The more time a whisky spends in oak, the more likely it is that its distillery character will gradually fade to the flavor of the oak and whatever was stored in the oak before.

THE ANGEL'S SHARE
BY CARLO DEVITO

Every master distiller and distillery owner must suffer the theft of his or her whisky on a regular basis. As whisky matures in the cask, a portion of the liquid evaporates. Over the centuries, this has come to be known as The Angel's Share.

According to the distillers at Bruichladdich, "As much as 5% of the volume of the new spirit we put into a cask will be quickly absorbed into the thirsty wood when it is initially filled—but it does not stop there. A smaller proportion, up to 2%, will go right through the grain each year and out into the atmosphere to be lost forever (unless you are an angel). It is therefore not uncommon for a cask that is fifteen years old to be half empty by the time it is bottled." In warmer climates the Angel's Share may be as high as 5% per year.

There are numerous factors that play a part including temperature and moisture (or lack thereof).

WHY BOURBON BARRELS DOMINATE NOT JUST AMERICAN WHISKEY, BUT IRISH, SCOTCH AND JAPANESE TOO

BY RICHARD THOMAS

When it comes to whiskey and wood, two basic facts stick fast. The first is that barrel maturation, that intricate dance of cask, climate, and clock, often accounts for half, or more, of how a whiskey tastes by the time it reaches the bottle.

The second is that when it comes to those casks, the 53-gallon (200-liter) American Standard Barrel (ASB) dominates. This barrel type is the bedrock of the American whiskey industry, where smaller barrels are the province of the craft sector and larger barrels almost unknown. Once the U.S. is done with them, those ex-bourbon barrels travel in thousands to Scotland, Ireland, and Japan where they go on to become the bedrock for those whiskeys as well. The predominance of the ASB in world whiskey is so overwhelming that the next most

common cask type, the hogshead, is usually built using ex-bourbon barrel staves.

Although some Europeans claim the ASB is an evolution of the hogshead, any brief study of American whiskey history reveals this not to be the case. Instead, the ASB evolved hand in glove with the American whiskey industry itself, because, as with so many things, it was a product of experimentation, accident, and meeting particular demands. Indeed, the barrel was still changing as recently as the mid-twentieth century.

In the earliest days of whiskey making, barrels traveled infrequently, and when they did travel it was rarely for long distances. As a result, they were all manner of shapes and sizes. Two events in Thomas Jefferson's presidency started the process towards a handy, standardized barrel: the end of Alexander Hamilton's whiskey tax and the Louisiana Purchase.

"Kentuckians had access to the Ohio and Mississippi Rivers and no financial penalty for storing whiskey in barrels for long periods of time," said Chris Morris, Master Distiller at Woodford Reserve. "So, now barrels began to be moved, and guess what, the bowed shape of today's ASB was the best for rolling and turning corners."

With mobility being an issue, size became one as well, and coopers began turning out barrels that balanced size and volume against ease of handling. Other early nineteenth century experiences in the whiskey industry also contributed, such as the widespread adoption of charring the insides of whiskey barrels.

"During the charring process, the interior temperature becomes very hot," said Morris. "This allows for the formation of a rich layer of caramelized oak sugars just under the char. Small barrels will not reach the same temperature levels and will not have the same level of flavor developed."

Next, whiskey-makers discovered the merits of air circulation, which led Frederick Stitzel of Stitzel-Weller fame to patent the rickhouse design for whiskey warehousing in 1879. As it turns out, barrels need to be roughly the size of the modern ASB to make a rickhouse function as intended. Too big and the barrels are not just hard to handle, but also heavy enough to reduce the maximum height of the warehouse (today this would pose a problem for all the major distilleries save Four Roses, who uses one-story warehouses). Too small and the rickhouse loses its storage efficiency.

Yet, it was not the modern 53-gallon barrel that emerged from this process, not at first. Instead, the 48-gallon barrel was the original ASB. According to bourbon historian Michael Veach, it was the pressure of the Second World War that forced the change. The war made white oak a scarce commodity, and larger barrels made better use of the rationed wood. The 53-gallon size was about as large as the existing rickhouses. Coming hard on the heels of the disruption of Prohibition and the Great Depression, the wartime change to 53 gallons was made, and it has stuck ever since.

Since the modern ASB developed as a key feature of American whiskey, distillers in the U.S. naturally look at it as the ideal vessel for aging whiskey. "The barrel fits our needs as an efficient way to utilize cooperage and warehouse space," said Michael Nelson, Brown-Forman's Cooperage Plant Director. "We have also perfected the toast and charring process for the current sized barrel."

Yet a major feature of the ASB as it is used at home is that it is made with charred, new white oak. What is more, the Kentucky and Tennessee climate of warm, humid summers and freezing winters speed the absorption of the big wood flavors, such as vanilla.

Neither of these things are true in Scotland, Ireland, Japan, and often in other countries that make whiskey and rely heavily on used ASBs for aging their spirit, with over 90% of the whisky aging in Scotland resting in ex-bourbon wood. Instead, for these

whiskey industries it is the ubiquity of the ASB that attracts them. Very little American whiskey is aged in used barrels (such as Early Times), so the main resale markets must necessarily lie elsewhere.

An important, illustrative point is that when it comes to ex-bourbon barrels, only a very modest amount of the Scotch made is matured using first-fill ASBs, and this whisky generally finds its way into the premium blends and single malts. Whiskey industries around the world might reuse ASBs two, three, or even four times, and with each use there is progressively less flavor left in the wood. The vast bulk of Scotch whisky made is for mass-market blends and comes from those much-recycled ASBs.

Once transatlantic shipping became cheaper, a huge supply of relatively inexpensive, used American barrels became available to Scotland, Ireland, Japan and other spirits industries as well, making them a very affordable option for an aging vessel. By contrast, a used sherry butt usually costs ten times as much as a used ASB, while holding just slightly more than twice as much, so the sheer economic logic of using ASBs in quantity is obvious.

BUT WHY USED WOOD?

Whiskey industries outside the United States use new oak to a certain degree, but are heavily reliant on casks already used to make other booze, whether it be bourbon, sherry, port, wine, Madeira, or rum. While cost is part of the reason this came to be, another reason comes back to the climate American whiskey-makers work in compared to that of their Irish and Scottish counterparts.

"The warmer temperatures in the US in summer compared to Scotland [...] help produce a quick extraction," said Stuart MacPherson, Master of Wood at The Macallan. "The style of straight whiskey, including bourbon, is very much this dark intense woody character, whereas Scotch whisky maturation, at much lower temperatures, and sometimes in bigger casks, is a slower process with the contribution from the oak being less intense."

Because of the climate, maturation processes based on time grow in importance relative to those based on wood. A case in point is the hogshead, which today is almost invariably built by taking five ASBs, breaking them down, and using the old staves to build four slightly larger hogsheads (225-liters), each with new barrel heads added. After the ASB, the most common whiskey cask used in Ireland and Scotland is the hogshead, often using ex-bourbon wood. Given the fiercer climate and faster maturation time in the US, the 12% increase in volume in a hogshead would significantly alter the maturation of the whiskey within, but in Scotland it makes only a slight difference.

"The only difference from a cask perspective is the addition of new ends," said MacPherson, "which will impart slightly more color and flavor, but this will once again depend on the toasting levels of the new wood [used in the] ends."

AMERICAN STANDARD

Bourbon whiskey has enjoyed new heights in recent years, with exports topping $1 billion. However, that success underscores just how parochial the bourbon industry is, as the Scotch industry has exports valued at six times this figure. Underscoring both industries, however, is a key and common commodity, the foundation for whiskey-making around the world: the American Standard Barrel. For largely separate reasons, whiskey-makers around the world are dependent on American timber, coopering, and the barrels these produce.

How Old Is Your Whiskey?
Are You Sure?

BY STEVE URY

Here's a quiz. Let's say you have a bottle of whiskey that says "Distilled June 12, 1996 and Bottled December 5, 2015." How old is the whiskey in that bottle?

The answer is: you don't know. The label has not given you enough information to determine the age of the whiskey. How so? Well, the age of a whiskey is the time spent in a barrel. According to the Federal regulations, "Age" means:

The period during which, after distillation and before bottling, distilled spirits have been stored in oak containers. "Age" for bourbon whisky, rye whisky, wheat whisky, malt whisky, or rye malt whisky, and straight whiskies other than straight corn whisky, means the period the whisky has been stored in charred new oak containers. [27 CFR §5.11]

Even if you know when a whiskey was distilled and when it was bottled, you don't know how much time it actually spent in the barrel. It is not uncommon for whiskeys to be transferred to stainless steel containers before being bottled, sometimes for years. Some brandies spend decades in glass containers. Steel and glass are considered neutral containers that don't impact the flavor of the spirit. While some would certainly argue with that statement, I doubt anyone would argue that their impact is anywhere near as strong as that of an oak barrel.

In contrast to a vintage date or distilled and bottled dates, an age statement (e.g. "10 years old") represents the amount of time that the youngest whiskey in the bottle spent in the barrel (and the proper type of barrel). On brandies, however, even those age statements are often incorrect, but that's a story for another time.

The moral of the story is: unless there is an actual age statement on that whiskey, you don't know how old it is.

— HOW THE WOOD MAKES — WHISKEY GOOD

BY RICHARD THOMAS

Whenever the subject of why a given whiskey tastes the way it does arises, my favorite statistic is that, depending on who made it, barrel-aging contributes between 40% and 80% of the flavor. Barrel-aging itself breaks down into several factors, but the oak used in making that barrel, cask, butt, hogshead, or pipe is of clear importance.

Underscoring just how important oak is to maturing whiskey is how the different types of oak each have their own particular influence on flavor. The world is home to over 600 species of oak tree, but only a handful are currently in use by whiskey-makers around the world.

AMERICAN WHITE OAK

Whether it be bourbon, rye, malt, or Tennessee whiskey, the bedrock of American whiskey-making is new Quercus alba, or white oak. Once cured, toasted, and charred, this oak provides the vanillin, lactone, and wood sugars that give American whiskies their characteristic caramel and vanilla flavors, as well as their amber color.

Chris Morris, Master Distiller at Woodford Reserve, said, "These and other compounds will be extracted by the spirit as it penetrates up to half the depth of the oak barrel stave and heading during maturation. Over the many years that Woodford Reserve is matured in the barrel, it will extract on average 85% of these desirable heat derived oak components."

Remember that statistic of wood giving whiskey 40% to 80% of its flavor? Aging in white oak provides "Woodford Reserve with 100% of its color naturally, and approximately 50% to 60% of its aroma and flavor," said Morris.

One interesting development that has come out of the craft whiskey movement in America is the use of unusual, regional white oaks, such as what Few Spirits does in relying on oak from Minnesota. The shorter growing season of Minnesota, relative to more traditional cooperage timber areas, such as Ohio or Alabama, makes for a tighter wood grain. While this doesn't change the elements the whiskey derives from the wood, it should slow the process of extracting those elements.

EUROPEAN OAK

Until recently, European oak meant one of two types: Spanish or French.

Both are frequently consolidated into the single species Quercus robur, but

that simplification isn't entirely accurate.

"Three main species of [Spanish] oak can be used in cask making," says Kevin O'Gorman, Master of Maturation at Midleton Distillery, makers of Jameson. "The most common would be Quercus robur, followed by Quercus petraea and finally, Quercus pyrenaica."

In Ireland and Scotland, Spanish oak is prized as the wood used in aging sherry, which is then reused for making whiskey. The flavor derived is sometimes simplified as being just the result of the previous seasoning with sherry, but the cask wood itself makes an important contribution.

O'Gorman explained, "American oak contains higher amounts of odorous compounds such as vanillin and oak lactones than European oak. On the other hand, Spanish oak contains more total extractables and particularly twice the amount of extractable phenols than American oak." This combination of native Spanish oak flavors and seasoning with sherry contributes the dried fruit, nut, fig, and date flavors characteristic of sherry wood-aged whiskies.

Even in the case of French oak, the simplification to just the one species of oak tree isn't accurate, as Quercus sessilis sometimes appears as well. In the Irish and Scottish context, French oak typically indicates a used wine cask, but some small forays have been made with Scotch and American whiskey using new French oak. Combined with a wine seasoning, French oak can contribute ripe berry flavors and enhanced spiciness, while the use of new French oak (such as in The Spice Tree or Maker's 46) is known predominately for the latter quality.

BARRELS OF SCOTCH

"In general, French oak has a good, tight grain structure and is favored by many wine producers in France," says O'Gorman. "We observed higher levels of whiskey lactones from the French oak in comparison to Spanish oak. We also established that there were slightly higher levels of syringic acid, vanillin, syringaldehyde, and coniferyl aldehyde due to the French oak contribution."

One new type of European oak has joined this traditional pair, and that is Irish oak. Midleton launched a new expression this year partly aged in new Irish oak. As in the United States, this should prove but the initial foray into the use of regional, non-traditional timber.

Where Irish oak differs from its Spanish and French cousins is in that it is exactly the opposite of the Minnesota white oak described earlier. Ireland's mild, wet climate makes for an expansive growing season, giving the wood a wider grain and making it less dense and more porous. These factors accelerate the extraction of flavor elements from the wood, a feature that when combined with Irish oak, also carrying many of the desired chemicals, becomes something of a "super" whiskey oak.

JAPANESE OAK

Quercus mongolica is usually referred to as Mizunara within the industry. The wood is now found in Scotland as well as Japan, starting with Bowmore making a Mizunara-finished single malt whisky. Currently, the Scots follow the Japanese practice of relying on their native oak for finishing, due to Mizunara's specific characteristics.

Japanese oak is particularly porous, so much so that it lacks the sturdiness of other kinds of oak and staves of this wood are prone to leaking. However, the wood is also heavily laden with vanillins, which when combined with its wide open structure (recall the Irish oak above) makes it a very flavorful wood.

Even as a finishing wood, Mizunara is "subtle, but has a big impact on the final blend," says Mike Miyamoto, Suntory's Global Brand Ambassador. "It has tastes of sandal wood, spicy, even cinnamon-like flavor."

IS IT THE WOOD THAT MAKES IT GOOD?

Even at a distillery that says 80% of what its whiskey tastes like comes from the cask, it's not so simple as to quote Kenny Rogers and say it's the wood that makes it good. Just with the cask itself, elements such as the size of the barrel, time, climate, and the warehouse the casks rest in all contribute to that 40% to 80% number. Yet when the range of how much time served in the barrel contributes to flavor starts at nearly half, the choice of oak and how it is used are at least as important as any other factor in whiskey-making.

Whiskey Law:
Barrels New and Used

BY STEVE URY

Most American whiskey drinkers know that according to U.S. regulations, bourbon must be aged in new, charred oak containers. But did you know that American rye whiskey, wheat whiskey, malt whiskey, and rye malt whiskey must also be aged in new charred oak? In addition, any whiskey labeled "straight," with the exception of straight corn whiskey, must be aged in new charred oak. (Want proof? See the US Code of Federal Regulations, 27 CFR § 5.22(b)(1)(i) and 5.22(b)(1)(iii)).

A distillery can make a whiskey and age it in used barrels but they cannot call it bourbon, rye whiskey, etc. Some such whiskies are just labeled generically, such as Early Times' "Kentucky Whiskey." The TTB also recognizes the categories of whiskey distilled from bourbon mash, rye mash, wheat mash, etc. If you see that designation, it means that the whiskey was stored in used oak.

The new oak requirement presents a problem for American distilleries that want to make Scotch-style single malt whiskey. Scotch single malts are almost always aged in used barrels (often bourbon barrels), but an American distillery can't call its spirit "malt whiskey" if it's aged in used oak.

SMALL BARREL AGING

BY RICHARD THOMAS

Renewed interest in small barrel aging has come up hand-in-hand with the micro-distilling boom, causing even big distilleries to get in on the act. Proponents of small barrel aging claim the use of smaller barrels allows them to create a superior product in a short space of time—an attractive proposition for a small start-up who would otherwise need to wait at least a few years before they could even begin to sell any product.

Yet critics claim small barrel aging accelerates only some of the benefits of oak barrel maturation, so the whiskey produced is left somewhat lacking. Even many whiskey-lovers do not really understand what happens inside an oak barrel over the months and years of primary and secondary maturation (or "finishing," as the latter is often called), and therefore wonder what the advantages and disadvantages of using a 53 gallon barrel vs a 5 or 10 gallon barrel really are.

IT'S ALL ABOUT SURFACE AREA

Aging in a smaller barrel increases the proportion of interior barrel surface area to stored volume, putting more wood surface into contact with the whiskey within. It is a proven and demonstrable fact that this increased contact accelerates the rate at which the whiskey absorbs characteristics from the wood, such as color and an aged whiskey's oaky and vanilla notes.

According to the American Distilling Institute, using a small barrel can turn out "an excellent product in only three to six months." With such a quick turnaround time, it's obvious why a new distillery might start with small barrel products, since it allows them to put something on the market in as little as half a year. The speedy maturation of small barrel aging is also a big plus for experiments, since it allows a distiller who is trying something new to see what the results might be much sooner.

What is true for micro-distillers and modern whiskey pioneers is doubly true of home distillers, for whom small barrel aging is usually the only practical choice. Few home distillers produce in the sheer quantity necessary to merit even one or two 53-gallon barrels, or have the patience necessary to wait many years to have a drinkable homemade whiskey.

THE DOWNSIDE

The key problem with small barrel aging is that it accelerates the absorption of everything else from the wood as well. A common misconception is that the longer a whiskey stays in the barrel, the better it gets. Nothing could be further from the truth.

Aging in oak is a delicate three-way dance between the climate, the whiskey, and the wood. While the exact line is hard to determine with any specificity, aging a whiskey for too long imparts a nauseating astringency, especially if the wood in question is new oak.

This effect places a time limit on how long whiskey can sit in a barrel without "going bad," and that limit comes much sooner for small barrels than big barrels. One or two years seems to be the most a whiskey can profit from being in a small barrel, and therein lies the problem. Many whiskey qualities come from esterification, or the reactions between wood acids, alcohol, oxygen, and various other chemicals, and those reactions take time. If you bottle your whiskey after 15 months, very little of that has happened, so critics of small barrel aging aren't wrong when they say the processing choice "leaves something out."

The decades-long aging periods that are a fixture of scotch-making produce such fine results in part

because scotch-makers rely almost entirely on used bourbon, sherry, and port casks for their primary maturation. Some of the oak's less desirable qualities have already been used up during the first round of aging.

All bets are off for a small barrel finishing, as is the case for Laphroaig Quarter Cask. Finishing a whiskey in a second set of barrels is always meant to be a short term thing by its very nature, rarely lasting more than a year. For secondary aging, it's hard to see what drawbacks small barrel use might have, if any.

OPEN MINDS

Small barrel aging might not produce "traditional" whiskey, but what is traditional whiskey anyway? Even the products of a big, well-established label like Jack Daniel's have changed periodically in ways that some found objectionable. Many whiskies made today are quite different from what was being made a century or more ago, even for the big old names in Scotch, Canadian, and Irish whiskey that have been in continuous operation all that time.

Furthermore, more goes into an enjoyable bottle of whiskey than the oak it's aged in. The size and nature of the barrel is just one factor, and while I can't deny that small barrel aging leads directly to a more circumspect maturation period, that doesn't mean it's bad. Some whiskies clearly come out very well indeed after only several months in a small barrel, in much the same way that some come out very poorly after several years in a big barrel.

The important thing to keep in mind about small barrel aging is that what matters is what you want from your whiskey. The proliferation of small barrel whiskey is a good thing in my book, because it means an experimentation boom in whiskey-making, and it's great that American whiskey laws and organizations are liberal enough to permit such things. No one is telling Ranger Creek they can't make mesquite-tinged bourbon in small barrels in the same way the Scotch Whisky Association (SWA) told Compass Box they couldn't make The Spice Tree with French oak staves. Think about that the next time a whiskey-snob scoffs at small barrel aging on the basis of "tradition."

— BOB HOCKERT AND HIS — OLD-SCHOOL COOPERAGE

BY MARIA BUTEUX READE

No wonder coopering is a lost art. It takes a hell of a long time to make a wooden barrel. But the explosion in craft spirits has created a dire need for these containers. So Bob Hockert, founder of US Barrel, located outside of Lake Placid, heeded the signs around him and became a master cooper known for his premium-quality casks made of sustainably-harvested New York white oak. Without such vessels, we'd all be sippin' moonshine instead of barrel-aged bourbon. And that's no slam on un-aged white whiskey either.

"I can't keep up with demand! Unlike the big guys, we build each barrel to spec, one at a time," Hockert says. Call it the slow barrel movement perhaps. And that's the way he likes it.

Up until the early twentieth century, every town, ship, and railroad had their own dedicated cooper. So did breweries, distilleries and wineries. (In fact, my own great-uncle used to be the cooper for West End Brewery in Utica, now known as Saranac.) Different disciplines of coopers knew how to match the wood with the product to be shipped or stored.

Knowledge and skills were passed down through generations. Wooden barrels were the ideal shipping container because they kept liquids in, materials dry, and moisture out. Their durable construction ensured longevity if well maintained. It's amazing to think they're still crafted with just two materials: wood staves and metal hoops. Not a nail, no glue. The process can be sped up with machines and manufactured assembly-line style, or they can be crafted by one person using only hand tools. Down in Kentucky, one industrial cooperage cranks out thousands of barrels daily. Up in the Adirondacks, at the base of Whiteface Mountain, Hockert and his two employees, Justin Bidelspach and his dad, Chris, are pleased if they produce two or three casks a day.

US Barrel is New York State's oldest cooperage and the first since the Prohibition. It began in … 2004. Hockert started out building enormous barrel-shaped cedar saunas popular with the winter crowd. Two years later, a distiller in the area asked if Hockert could make some barrels for his spirits. Always up for a new challenge, Hockert readily agreed. US Barrel now manufactures a broad array of items including wooden casks from 650 milliliters to about 1,500 gallons, brining tubs, rain barrels, fermentation tanks, mugs, sauna barrels, whatever someone wants. "We love special projects that allow us to create and innovate," Hockert says. "If it's round and made of wood, we're up for it!"

Hockert spent his first career on Wall Street but moved permanently to Wilmington, New York, in 2004 where he and his wife, Sue, had a home for 20 years. His engineering degree now comes in handy as he operates his business, designing and building many of the machines himself. He also works closely with a talented machinist in town. "Up here in the Adirondacks, we need to be self-sufficient, fabricating and fixing our own equipment."

Just like his predecessors, Hockert matches wood to project. Sugar maple, cherry, yellow birch, fir—each imparts unique characteristics to the vessel underway. But white oak remains his primary material for whiskey barrels with its tight grain, durability, and resilience. He sources the majority from western New York, the Finger Lakes, and the Hudson Valley. White oak also grows well in southern Vermont, Massachusetts, and Pennsylvania.

"We look for old-growth oak, 90 to 100-plus years old. Trees that grow deep in the forest compete for canopy and therefore grow straight and true to get the most sunlight for photosynthesis. Those trees will have the longest and straightest grain," explains Hockert.

A barrel's journey begins in the woods. A logger fells the trees, a sawyer cuts them into manageable lengths, and a miller saws them into rough-cut boards. "Quarter-sawn oak is labor-intensive," says Hockert. The boards are carefully stacked in ricks to ensure air circulates between the boards and left outside to dry for six months to a year.

Fresh cut oak contains 85% moisture, so it seasons as it dries. Think of a thick slab of prime beef aging in a butcher's meat locker, with all manner of flavor-enhancing molds and bacteria penetrating the surface. As the oak decomposes, spores help to oxidize the natural sugars. (Ya never thought about wood containing sugar, eh?) Nature cleanses the boards with her cycles of rain, sun, and wind, softening the harsh tannins and eliminating odors or impurities. Kiln drying is great for firewood but that process actually kills all the desirable molds and bacteria that lend flavor and complexity to the finished barrel.

So how does a cooper build a barrel? First step is to joint, or shape, the staves, which are tapered at the ends and beveled so they "keystone" together when formed in an upright circle. Then he raises, or assembles, the barrel, setting the staves by hand into a metal raising hoop. After the staves are in place, one or more additional raising hoops are put in place to firmly bind the cone and help it maintain its shape.

Next, the open-ended cone is steamed, soaked, or heated to soften the wood for drawing, or shaping. A cooper has three choices: heat it over a small fire, steam it or soak it in a tank of hot water. The combination of heat and steam softens the lignin (fibers) of the wood and allows it to stretch. "We choose to steam it because we want as pure an oak flavor as possible," Hockert says. "Soaking is a very

fast way to soften the lignin and can help remove some of the tannin from the wood as well, but it also removes some of the water-soluble heartwood extractives (natural flavorings) we feel should be in the whiskey. This is arguably the greatest latitude the cooper has in influencing the flavor profile of the barrel, and cooperages are generally known for their individual handling of the barrel and resulting flavor imparted in the spirit."

The cooper then draws the barrel into its classic shape, looping a metal cable over the top end and slowly cranking it tight with a windlass. Next comes the fun part: charring the interior. The distiller selects the desired depth of charcoal and amount of crinkling and crackling he wants on the inside of the barrel. A #3 char is pretty common for most whiskies. That's when the wood starts to get cracks and bumps.

After the barrel has cooled, the cooper cuts the croze, or the notch, into which the head fits, and fits the heads into the top and bottom of the barrel. He sands down the barrel body and hammers the permanent galvanized steel hoops in place. He cuts the bung hole (the entrance point for the whiskey) and cauterizes it to seal the pores of the wood. The final step is pressure-testing the barrel and ensuring it's watertight. Quick and easy, right?

A full 100% of a whiskey's color and up to 75% of its flavor derive from the barrel. Storage conditions impact a whiskey's profile as well. If a barrel of whiskey ages in a room with fluctuating temperature and humidity, it will develop far more complexity than whiskey aged in a climate-controlled facility. If the room gets hot and humid in summer, then cold and dry in winter, the atmospheric pressure will push the spirit through the charcoal layer and into the wood where it picks up rich vanillins and pleasant tannins. As the whiskey passes back and forth, the charcoal acts as a natural filter and smoothes out any harshness. That's why a barrel stored at consistent 72°F and 40% humidity will produce a boring whiskey.

Size matters. The smaller the barrel, the faster the whiskey ages. The ratio of volume to charred surface area changes with the size of the barrel. More access to charred oak means deeper flavor and richer hue.

Ideally, whiskey production is a collaborative effort between cooper and distiller. "Every step of the process, from how we raise and toast each barrel, has a huge impact on how the spirit evolves," Hockert says. "A whiskey is the end result of marrying the distilled spirit with the unique characteristics of the barrel."

He continues, "I prefer working with several smaller distillers rather than commit to one big name. It's fun to be a part of a new business getting off the ground." Case in point: Coppersea Distillery in West Park, NY. "They're the reason we got into the whiskey barrel business." Hockert had been delivering a cedar sauna to the Hudson Valley back in 2012. "This enormous barrel was strapped down on the back bed of my truck. When I stopped at a red light in some town, this guy literally chased me down and grilled me with questions about the sauna barrel. Turns out it was Coppersea's chief distiller, Christopher Briar Williams. He persisted with phone calls and I could see he was serious, so I decided to work with him. Thus it began. Chris convinced us to develop our product line and we helped launch his."

Coppersea's "Excelsior" bourbon was released recently. It's the first bourbon made with 100% New York State product, from the Hudson Valley grains to the barrels made in the Adirondacks of New York white oak. Chris Williams explained: "Everything we do is geared toward increasing the elements of terroir to reflect the region. There's no point in going to the effort to produce a whiskey made with 100% New York grains and then age the spirit in a barrel from the Midwest. Bob's a pleasure to work with and his barrels are beautifully crafted."

Gristmill Distillery in Keene, NY, right down the road from Hockert's workshop, opened in October 2014. Owner Keith Van Sise first produced "Rusty Piton," an un-aged white whiskey. Then, he rolled out his first bottles of Black Fly bourbon, which had aged in Hockert's barrels for five to seven months. Van Sise and his partner, Steph Hadik, toured almost every distillery in New York and a few in Vermont. "We volunteered at some as well, picking up tips from all the places we visited and studying the equipment," Van Sise says. "We do a lot of reading and learn from trial and error. Steph introduces the whiskey to the public at farmers markets, and three

other buddies make the corn mash and run it through the still. I oversee the final distilling." They already have plans for future expansion.

Hockert also works with Hudson Valley Distillery in Germantown, known for its applejack whiskey aged in special barrels made with a unique combination of woods. Down at Plan Bee Farm Brewery in Poughkeepsie, Evan Watson uses honey for his lambic beer, which he ferments in one of the tanks Hockert made. Other partnerships include Last Shot Distillery in Skaneateles, Spring Brook Hollow in Queensbury, and Glenrose Spirits in the Finger Lakes, where Matt Slobado, a chef, makes absinthe.

"It's a symbiotic rapport; we all learn together," Hockert says. "Everyone comes to the table with distinct

resources and abilities, then we put together the puzzle."

Prohibition might have killed the cooperage industry, but the resurgence of craft distillers and wineries is reviving the art. "We could actually use more barrel makers to help meet the demand," Hockert says. In fact, he would love to share his knowledge with people and train them to start up cooperages in their own locale. "It doesn't make sense for people like us to be making and shipping barrels off to Alaska or other far-flung places. One hundred fifty or two hundred years ago, breweries and distilleries used to have their own cooperages on-site as part of the whole business. It may be time to return to that practice."

While Hockert loves producing barrels for his distillers ("We get a little more efficient with each barrel"), the engineer in him clearly relishes tackling the unusual projects.

"If someone told me I'd be a cooper at this point in my life, I'd have written him off as a lunatic! I just wanted to get out of the city and come up here to lead a simple life. But it's been a serendipitous trip with the right people and opportunities coming along at the right time. Whenever we hit a dead end, somehow the right solution shows up in our path. It happens constantly. We just have to be attuned and open to the new idea."

Simple life, maybe not. Richly rewarding and pretty darn fun? Hockert will drink to that.

PEAT: THE GREAT SMOKY DIVIDE

BY AMANDA SCHUSTER

Whiskey enthusiasts agree on many things, but they love to argue about peat smoke. As chili peppers are to spicy food, peat is to whiskey. Just as people boast of their tolerance for hot peppers in, say a bowl of chili or a fiery vindaloo, whiskey drinkers and producers enjoy out-peating each other. All the while other whiskey connoisseurs prefer their unsmoked dram, thank you very much. Many whiskey fans enjoy both, of course. But they will always inevitably meet the staunch defenders of both sides of the smoke line.

Why is peat in the whiskey in the first place?

Peat is a type of soil consisting of partially decayed vegetable matter, found in wet, boggy areas known as 'peatlands' or 'mires.' The predominant component of it is a type of moss called Sphagnum, which gives it that characteristic sort of rubbery smell, especially when burned. Dried peat has been used as an effective fuel and heat source in place of wood for centuries, particularly in Ireland, Scotland, England, and Russia.

Two of the biggest misconceptions for novice whiskey drinkers are that all Scotch is peated, and that it's only found in Scotch. Peat comes into whiskey production as the fuel source for drying barley or other grains (but mostly barley) for malting. However, the grains can be dried without the use of peat, either simply by letting them air dry, which takes quite a long time, or using unpeated fuel such as certain types of wood.

Furthermore, not all peated whiskey is the same. You might have rolled your eyes a few times hearing a wine enthusiast use the term "terroir" to describe the differences between grape varieties in different regions and how that affects the characteristics of specific wines. The same holds true for whiskey. Aside from the type of oak used to age a whiskey, the other factors that shape the flavors of whiskey are the water source, the soil, and how the grain was processed, i.e. whether it was peated, which, by the way, is not restricted to Scotland, although that is where the style is most prevalent.

The Islay region of Scotland is known for a particularly fierce style of peated whiskey, and this is the variation that earned peated whiskey its reputation, with devoted fans and those with a searing intolerance. Thanks to the tempestuous weather conditions and proximity to the sea, Islay whiskies such as Lagavulin, Laphroaig, Bowmore, Ardbeg and Caol Ila tend to taste like the fiery aftermath of a maritime battle, sometimes with rather pronounced elements of seaweed, brine,

fish oil, iodine, and rubber tire. (One of the more hilarious descriptions of Laphroaig found in their "Opinions Welcome" campaign is that it tastes like "burning hospital.")

In the Highlands and other parts of Scotland, if used in production (there are many who don't), the peat, which is found farther inland, lends more of a rich, sweet smoke, more reminiscent of pipe tobacco and even smoked or barbecued meat. Some of the peated Highland malts to look out for are Oban, BenRiach, Benromach, Old Pulteney and Clynelish. Highland Park from Orkney has a very subtle charcoal smokiness, while Talisker

from the Isle of Skye uses peat smoke as a more dominant element.

Even some distilleries and regions who are known for peat-free maltings release peated expressions. Irish whiskey is traditionally unpeated, but now producers such as Connemara are going peat-crazy. The English Whisky Company has peated and non-peated styles. Any Glen Garioch Scotch that is older than 1995 hails back to a time they used peated malt, and they are now releasing bottlings such as the 1994 as a peat-nostalgic time capsule. Bruichladdich also reopened as a mostly peat-free distillery, yet you wouldn't guess it after tasting the Port

Charlotte releases. And let's not leave out the blended Scotches that use peaty single malts for everything from gentle flavor enhancements (Johnnie Walker Black) to creating big in-your-face expressions like Compass Box Peat Monster.

Single malt whiskey production is catching on outside the UK and Ireland too, even in nations that don't use peat as an everyday heating source. McCarthy's out of Clear Creek Distillery in Oregon uses peated barley sourced from Scotland to produce single malt whiskey on American shores. Corsair Triple Smoke incorporates peat-smoked barley with cherry wood and beech wood-smoked barleys for just a waft of peaty funk. Indian whiskey company Amrut is also in on the peat game. Peated Japanese whiskies are, of course, a thing too.

So just because you might have tried a peated whiskey and not fallen madly in love, it's worth tasting others. It's like saying you don't like Chardonnay because it's too "oaky." No. Oak is oaky. Peat is peaty. It's all in how a producer chooses to showcase it and which one works with your palate. And you can't argue that.

How a Master Distiller
Noses a Single Malt
with Dave Pickerell

BY CARLO DEVITO

I sat in the Hillrock Estate tasting room one day with Master Distiller Dave Pickerell, and tried six or eight single malts from around the world. Dave had time to explain a great many things. What almost seemed like a throw away to him was a HUGE revelation.

"Never stick your nose directly into a glass of whiskey. The alcohol will burn out your olfactory system," he said. "Firstly, hold the glass slightly away and breathe in through your mouth. You'll be able to pick up a lot more."

The former West Point chemistry professor (and graduate, I might add, who also played offensive tackle back in the day), who has nosed thousands of drams in his time and created some of the world's best whiskies, went onto explain the second part of nosing. Next, put the glass all the way to one side of your nose, and "roll" or wave it slowly and completely to the other side of your nose. Slowly. "Your olfactory glands are not equal. They work differently, pick up or sense different things. So roll the glass from one side to the other. That way you have the best chance of picking up the nuances of the whiskey."

THE RISE OF FAKE WHISKEY

BY RICHARD THOMAS

If you mention the term "fake whiskey" in American whiskey circles, more likely than not you'll find yourself in a conversation about labeling issues and so-called "Potemkin distilleries." Yet, to a broader set of whiskey fans, the term might refer to a far more disturbing trend in the rise of truly questionable, and in some cases, downright fake whiskey products.

FAKES FROM DOWN UNDER?

On the questionable side, Australia's plunge into whiskey-making has taken some producers away from their Scottish and Irish roots, and towards American methods, with some producers experimenting with rye, bourbon, and sour mash whiskey. Yet some of these American-style products are released at a proof lower than what is legally acceptable in the United States, raising the question of whether it is "fake" American-style whiskey.

The problem with applying that label to Australian bourbon is that said watered down whiskies are merely following the pattern established by American whiskey imports. Jim Beam White is cut to 37% ABV (74 proof) in Australia, below the US statutory 40% minimum. Maker's Mark also cuts its whiskey for the Australian market, from the American standard of 45% ABV to 40%.

So long as the underpowered American-style Australian whiskey stays in Australia and is otherwise made in the American style, it seems unjust to call it fake merely because some of it follows in American footsteps.

INDIAN NON-WHISKY IN EUROPE

Far more alarming than the minor quibble over Australian ABV levels is the way products labeled "whisky" in India are finding their way onto European shelves, despite the European Union officially upholding Scottish definitions for what whisky is supposed to be.

Although India draws a whisky-drinking tradition from the days of the British Raj, the country has no legal definitions for what whisky is or how it is made. Because of this, most Indian whisky brands are usually a blend of a rum-like distillate with a small proportion of imported Scottish malt whisky. With just a few exceptions, such as Amrut, most Indian whisky would never pass muster in Europe, Japan, or North America.

This would be only slightly disturbing if the Indian non-whisky stayed in India. Yet according to the Scotch Whisky Association (SWA), the trade group that represents Scotch industry interests, the last several years have seen a growing amount of Indian "whisky" imported into Belgium, France, the Netherlands, and Spain, where it is blended again with more grain and/or malt whisky from Scotland. It is then sold in a variety of cheap supermarket brands, sometimes claiming to be "Scotch" and sometimes merely as "whisky," when at least a hefty proportion of the product is neither Scotch nor whisky.

WHAT'S IN A NAME?

If Americans think they have a labeling problem, they should look at some of the labels going on bottles in India and China, designed to fool drinkers into thinking the contents are pricey Scottish imports. Last year the SWA filed 103 trademark disputes, with 19 in India and 17 in China. Other major offenders included Nepal, Nigeria, and South Africa.

The typical offense is a brand name using the word "Glen," which according to the SWA is strongly suggestive of a Scottish origin. Falsely labeled, non-bourbon products are beginning to appear abroad as well, complete with fake names conjuring images of the Bluegrass.

BOOM DARKSIDE

Although it has brought shortages and rising prices, overall the world whiskey boom has been a good thing for drinkers, since it has also brought with it a wave of new products and a spirit of innovation. At the same time, a big chunk of that boom has taken place in foreign markets where whiskey laws are weak or non-existent, and trademark protections are only slightly better. Low standards have given rise to a crop of frauds producing non-whiskey products under misleading names, and now some of those fake whiskeys are starting to find their way onto store shelves in places where drinkers expect better.

— WHISKEY GLASSES —

BY CARLO DEVITO

There are really only two glasses where single malt whiskey or single malt Scotch are concerned. One is for tasting. The other is for drinking. Let me explain. No, that would take too long. Let me sum up. There are hundreds of single malt whiskies around the world. You are only one person. You have a nose, eyes, mouth, and your wits. On the other hand, the whiskies have hundreds of layers of scents and flavors and, of course, lingering aftertastes. You, on the other hand, just want a drink. One does not accommodate ice or rocks. The other does. But why two glasses?

Okay. For tasting you really only need one kind of glass—a single malt whiskey or a whiskey tasting glass.

Now, without sounding elitist, many other beverages have their own glass that accentuates that beverage's highlights. The champagne flute allows the effervescence to show itself off and to keep a narrow liquid column, thus keeping your bubbly, well, bubbly longer. The brandy snifter helps draw out the aromas of that fine elixir. Heck, even beer has special glasses for special styles. It was Raymond Davidson who finally decided whiskey had suffered long enough. The design is based on the traditional glasses valued by master blenders and professionals around the world, used for nosing and tasting. The bowl at the base is wide, and makes it easy for the taster to swirl their product and mix it with air to get the maximum oxygen to liquid ratio, and get the aromas flowing. A narrowed, fluted rim focuses the bouquet, so that the taster will get the full aromatic expression of the spirit. The rest is left up to your taste buds.

Why do we taste? Because sometimes you want to get all the nuances of the expression. You want to experience all those layers of fruit and nuttiness, and caramel and toffee and honey, and vanilla and spices that you keep hearing about. That's what it's all about. It's about learning to understand the nuances of the product, and appreciating the work these craftsmen put into their whiskey. The Glencairn Whisky Glass is the most common one of these glasses. And there are a dozen nice and similar ones made around the world. Find them, buy a set of two or four, and have some fun.

Second is the whiskey tumbler or Old Fashioned glass. Now, you can have a set of tasting glasses so that you and your friends can explore the multifaceted world of whiskey and Scotch. But sometimes, you just want to crack the seal on a bottle, clink some ice in a glass, kick back with a few friends, and have a drink. That's when you call on a 10oz or 12oz whiskey tumbler or old-fashioned glass. They are usually fairly simple in design. The cut glass and Waterford crystal ones are generally the same size and shape as their less expensive Libby counterparts. Doesn't matter. A good set of six of any of these straight up and down, squat cylindrical glasses will more than do the trick! Sip, laugh, enjoy!

And that is all you need to know about glasses.

TO ENHANCE FLAVOR, JUST ADD WATER

BY HAROLD MCGEE

When fine-tuning the flavor of dishes and drinks, I've always turned to the usual bench of taste and aroma boosters: salt and pepper, lemon juice, herbs and spices, this or that condiment. One ingredient that never, ever came to mind was water. Water has no flavor to give. It doesn't boost, it dilutes.

[Then] the London bartender Tony Conigliaro told me that weak cocktails can be more aromatic than stronger drinks. That observation provoked me to play with the proportions of alcohol and water in spirits and wines. [A month later], a barista showed me that I could make tastier coffee by brewing it with less ground coffee and more water.

It's true, as it turned out: Water is indeed a useful flavor enhancer, exactly because it dilutes other ingredients and can change their balance for the better.

It's no secret that the alcohol in drinks can get in the way of our enjoying their flavors. When alcohol makes up more than 10 to 12 percent of a liquid's volume, we begin to notice its irritating, pungent effects in the mouth and in the nose. Spirits like whiskey and gin are 40% alcohol or more, and very pungent indeed.

Fans and judges of Scotch whiskies often sample their flavor by "nosing" them, or sniffing the aroma that gathers in the glass. Nosers have long known that diluting the spirit with roughly the same amount of water reduces the alcohol burn. And at the same time, strangely, amplifies the aromas.

How can water reduce one sensation and amplify another? Both alcohol and aroma molecules are volatile, meaning they evaporate from foods and drinks and are carried by the air to the odor receptors high up in the nasal cavity.

Aroma molecules are also more chemically similar to alcohol molecules than they are to water, so they tend to cling to alcohol, and are quicker to evaporate out of a drink when there's less alcohol to cling to.

This means that the more alcoholic a drink is, the more it cloisters its aroma molecules, and the less aroma it releases into the air. Add water and there's less alcohol to irritate and burn, and more aroma release.

The same principle explains why stiff martinis and Manhattans can be less aromatic than lower-proof cocktails, as many bartenders know. Audrey Saunders of the Pegu Club in New York told me that realizing this led her to develop a series of what she calls "inverted drinks," in which spirits play a supporting role to vermouth or other low-alcohol ingredients.

Her Madeira Martinez combines

one part gin (40% alcohol) and two parts Madeira (20 percent) for a drink that starts at around 30 percent alcohol before ice dilutes it further. The Intro to Aperol, with two parts of the 11% aperitif wine to one of gin, comes in around 20%. With drinks like these, Ms. Saunders said, the goal is to highlight the flavors of the weaker ingredient.

Just to see what spirits themselves are like with no alcohol burn at all, I diluted a number of them with plain water by three to one, to cut their alcohol levels to the equivalent of a low-alcohol wine. All of them remained plenty aromatic, a couple of English gins spectacularly so. With a bit of lemon juice and sugar, they made an odd but pleasant drink: an aqua-gin.

High-alcohol wines, those that exceed about 14% alcohol, are often described as "hot" and unbalanced. Alcohol's irritating effects account for the heat. And flavor chemists have found that high alcohol levels accentuate a wine's bitterness, reduce its apparent acidity and diminish the release of most aroma molecules. Alcohol particularly holds down fruity and floral aromas, so the aroma that's left is mainly woody, herbaceous and vegetal.

I couldn't find any recent trials of wine dilution, but it's been practiced since the days of ancient Greece, so I went ahead and tried it on a California zinfandel with 14.9% alcohol. I poured a partial glass of the wine and added about a quarter of its volume in water, to get it down to 12%.

A glass of the full-strength wine tasted hot, dense, jammy, and a little sulfurous, while the diluted version was lighter all around but still full of flavor, tarter, more fruity than jammy, and less sulfurous. It was no substitute for a true 12% wine, made from grapes harvested with less fermentable sugar and a different balance of flavors that we taste full-strength.

But the watered-down wine was surprisingly pleasant, and maybe more suited to summer evenings than the intense original. I ended up alternating sips and enjoying the contrast.

There's even a place for more water in coffee. I learned this from James Hoffmann, a 2007 winner of the World Barista Championship whose passion for flavor has led him from espresso to brewed coffee and its less concentrated but more diverse aromas.

Mr. Hoffmann is the proprietor of Square Mile Coffee, a roasting company in London, and a six-stool, espresso-less coffee bar that [closed after] a temporary residence in the Shoreditch district. At the bar, named Penny University for the term applied to the first London coffeehouses, he and his colleagues offered a revelatory short course in the possibilities of brewed coffee. They presented a menu of three contrasting kinds of beans, brewed them using any of three methods, and chatted with their customers about the fine points of the ingredients, process and flavor.

Earlier, I enrolled in a tasting of coffees from Kenya, Ethiopia and Guatemala, all roasted lightly to avoid losing their distinctive qualities in the intense but more generic flavors of a dark roast. Each cup was less concentrated than I'm used to making for myself, yet delicious and distinctive.

Mr. Hoffmann explained that industry standards for brewed coffee strength vary a great deal, from around 1.25% extracted coffee solids in the United States to something approaching 2% in Brazil and in specialty coffeehouses. He aims for 1.5%, and gets it consistently with the help of a precision water boiler and a digital scale on which he does the brewing, pouring water to the gram.

"It seems silly, debating decimals," Mr. Hoffmann said, "but it makes a big difference to the flavor." A tablespoon of water more or less can shift the extracted solids by a perceptible amount. It also matters how the coffee solids are extracted. Mr. Hoffmann told me that concentrated brews are often made palatable by using a lot of coffee and reducing the brewing time or the temperature to extract only the easy-going portion of its flavor materials. The result is intense but one-dimensional. More fully extracting a smaller amount of gently roasted, high-quality coffee, as Mr. Hoffmann and a number of new-wave brewing

advocates are doing, brings out its full range of tastes and aromas.

"When I drink coffee I'm looking for clarity, by which I mean distinguishable, characterful, interesting flavors," Mr. Hoffmann said. The lightness of his brews did seem to highlight their very different aromas, which changed but remained enjoyable even as the remains cooled to room temperature. "No other liquid I know evolves as much as you drink it," he said.

I brought home some of Mr. Hoffmann's Yirgacheffe, an Ethiopian coffee that I love for its unusual blueberry aroma, and measured my brewing against his with the help of a refractometer, a device that measures dissolved solids. (Refractometers are sold [online at around $40-50]). I made a cup at my standard strength, which turned out to be 2.2% coffee solids.

When I dropped the strength close to Mr. Hoffmann's preferred 1.5% by using a third less ground coffee (about 12 grams of coffee to 180 grams, or 6 fluid ounces, of water), the fruity aroma was much more evident, and the flavor generally brighter and more lively. Clarity is a good word for the overall impression.

So I'm making my coffee with more water now, and getting many more cups from a bag of beans.

You don't need a refractometer to explore the power of dilution, though a scale is advisable for getting close to Mr. Hoffmann's sweet spot for coffee, since volume measures are unreliable and the decimals count. If you're in the habit of brewing strong cups from premium beans, then give his proportions a try, weighing out both coffee and water. Or, later in the day, pour a glass of strong spirits or a big wine and try adding some water. Or make one of Ms. Saunders's inverted cocktails. And see whether the flavor you get is not so much watered-down as opened up, and good.

ROCKS DON'T MELT, NOR DO THEIR FANS

BY CATHERINE SAINT LOUIS

When whiskey stones first showed up on store shelves five years ago, they seemed destined to be another fleeting oddity, perhaps an upscale version of the Pet Rock fad of 1975.

After all, it's tough to persuade drinkers they need soapstone rocks—stored in the freezer—to chill their whiskey instead of ice, which eventually dilutes it. Purists think single malts should be savored neat or with a splash of water. The stones have never caught on in bars, either. "It's idiotic," said Dale DeGroff, a noted mixologist who is partial to Glenlivet 12 with big square ice. "You won't see them at the bar unless they are making fun of them."

Even so, the fad is proving remarkably resilient, and even expanding, with more than a dozen competitors promoting their unique artisanal twist. There are Sipping Stones and Chilling Rocks, and different sizes of cubes and disks, and one-upmanship over whose stones are the best.

"I have no idea what the counterfeiters would be saying to you, if they are being honest, other than 'we copied that guy,'" Andrew Hellman wrote in an e-mail. His Teroforma Whisky Stones are cut and tumbled in Vermont by a bearded craftsman named Glenn Bowman, and are now sold by more than 1,100 retailers nationwide.

Some makers of soapstone countertops even turned to fashioning cubes for imbibers when their home-remodeling businesses slowed. In 2010, Barry Dresen of Brookings, OR, started shaping scraps from kitchen countertops that his business installs into what he called Italian Ice. He sold imported soapstone for $16.95 for two bags of nine cubes on Amazon. Soon, his leftovers weren't enough to keep up with demand, and he bought full slabs.

Last year, he started sourcing his soapstone from a quarry in the Blue Ridge Mountains of Virginia, changed the name to Ice Breaker, and increased the price by a dollar. "I sell a lot to military bases," said Mr. Dresen, who dreams of giving up countertops in favor of making stones exclusively.

Jesse Billin of Chocorua, NH, has already reached that goal. "I wish I had done this 20 years ago, and saved myself 20 years of chiseling stone on my knees," he said. After decades as a high-end masonry contractor for multimillion-dollar homes, Mr. Billin began selling Hammerstone's Whiskey Disks two years ago. He started making the disks, which resemble elegant hockey pucks, only for relatives. "It was a family thing," he said. "No one thought we could sell these things."

Single Malt Scotch Prophet:
Honoring Michael Jackson

BY CARLO DEVITO

Michael Jackson was a complicated man. And a talented one. I first met Michael when I was the Associate Publisher at Running Press, and we published several of his books. He had long been involved in the publishing industry. It is little known that he was one of the founding partners of Quarto, one of the world's largest illustrated book publishers.

Michael was already a popular figure in the beer and single malt Scotch world when I first met him. He was a television star, the beer world adored him, and he was already considered the grand wizard of the single malt Scotch universe. He was a disheveled looking chap in gray trousers, a rumpled corduroy jacket, and hair that looked like a wilting afro. He looked like an English professor who'd failed the audition for Grand Funk Railroad.

He wore his classic befuddled English professor demeanor well. He was quiet, unassuming, and slightly suspicious of people. He was always peering over his glasses at you. He was not entirely chatty. Yet, get him in front of a crowd, and he was fantastic.

Regardless of whether it was a beer or whiskey crowd, he was an amazing person to watch and listen to. And his understanding of the two elixirs was unmatched. He had a terrific memory, and could relate vast sums of knowledge about many brewers around the world and distillers in Scotland. He could explain the flavors you were tasting, how they had achieved them, what the components were, and who the distiller or brewer was and the name of their underlings. He did not speak quickly or loudly. And you found yourself trying very hard to listen.

He traveled extensively, and I heard from him (or someone in his office, or his agent) at least two or three times a year. He would come to the U.S. from the U.K. for a series of tour dates. I always knew when he was in town, because we would get an irate call, asking why there weren't enough books in the stores. Of course, he never told us when he was going to be in the country. This was back in the days before social media, when everything was communicated by fax or phone. We would argue. I would argue, pleading with him to let us know in advance when he was coming, that we might load the markets where in he would appear. He'd come in for lunch, or into town for a tasting, and by the next day, he would leave. We were all friends again. Of course, even after he agreed to keep us abreast of his next tour, he absolutely never did.

The first single malt tasting I ever went to was with Michael Jackson. As we entered the large banquet room, he was mobbed and glad-handed by at least a hundred admirers. He shook hands, peered over his glasses, and nodded his head a lot. But once all the hoopla died down, he began in earnest, and I was amazed at how complicated it all was, and how he attempted to simplify it. He was a proselytizer and a prophet all in one, who foretold the world of the greatness of single malt scotch. They agreed, and they listened. It was amazing, and I will never forget that first experience. And there are thousands more just like me. The single malt Scotch world, and by extension, the single malt whiskey world owes Michael a huge debt of gratitude.

He spent a lifetime educating the public on beer and single malt. His influence on each industry, especially single malt Scotch, was powerful and undeniable. And His presence in a room was mesmerizing to those who wanted to learn. He was never loud. People quieted down to listen to him. He educated thousands of people during the course of his career personally, and millions more via his written word. Despite many who would attempt to fill the vacuum he left when he departed, there is no one who ever can. Single malt whiskey today enjoys a new explosion, a new birth, the world over. It would have been interesting to see his reaction to it, peering over the rims of those glasses. Regardless, he would have complained there were not enough books in the stores.

COCKTAILS

TAKE A SIP OF HISTORY

BY ROBERT SIMONSON

The old-fashioned may finally be earning its name.

One of the most venerable of whiskey-based cocktails, it has a history that stretches back farther than the martini's. For decades it has suffered under the reputation of something your grandmother drank—overly sweet, fruit-laden, and spritzed-up. But grandma wouldn't recognize what's happened to it lately.

The old-fashioned is one of the most requested mixed drinks at some of New York's newest and most self-consciously artisanal drinking dens, including [Prime Meats in Carroll Gardens, Brooklyn; Rye in Williamsburg, Brooklyn; and Jack the Horse in Brooklyn Heights].

Cocktail aficionados say it couldn't have happened to a nicer drink.

"The old-fashioned is one of the original cocktails, in the true sense of the word," said Damon Boelte, bar director at Prime Meats. "It's kind of like having a Model T on your menu."

It's so old that it was called a "whiskey cocktail" until late-nineteenth-century parvenus like the martini and Manhattan forced purists to order an "old fashioned" whiskey cocktail. But while the martini and the Manhattan came through the cocktail dark ages of the 1970s and 80s with much of their dignity, the old-fashioned developed a personality disorder.

Its majestically austere profile (basically a slug of rye with minuscule touches of water, bitters, and sugar) was tarted up with a muddled orange slice and maraschino cherry, and a diluting dose of soda water. This rendition has its advocates, and remains popular in supper clubs across America. But it sends shudders down the spines of the new breed of cocktail classicists.

"A bastardization of the original drink," said Kevin Jaszek, a bartender at Smith & Mills in [TriBeCa].

Disciples of the cocktail renaissance, like Mr. Boelte and Mr. Jaszek, have restored the old-fashioned to what they feel is its rightful form— "back to integrity," as Julie Reiner put it. The Clover Club, her Boerum Hill bar, [has] an entire menu section devoted to the old-fashioned and its variants.

Yes, variants. Devotees are not completely doctrinaire in their recipes, varying the type of bitters or sweeteners used.

And old-fashioneds built on bourbon (PDT in the East Village), rum (the Oak Bar) and tequila (Death & Company in the East Village) are not unheard-of. Just keep that maraschino cherry well away.

RYE OLD FASHIONED

ADAPTED FROM RYE, BROOKLYN

1 tsp Demerara sugar
2 ounces rye whiskey
1 or 2 dashes Angostura bitters

1 to 2 dashes orange bitters
1 strip lemon peel

Spoon sugar into a shaker and add about a teaspoon of very hot water for a simple syrup. Stir until dissolved, adding a little more water if needed.

Add whiskey and bitters, and stir again. Add several ice cubes and stir well to chill.

Strain into an old-fashioned glass, add 2 or 3 big ice cubes, twist lemon peel over the top and drop in.

DRINKING LIKE A POET

BY ROSIE SCHAAP

One chilly evening more than a decade ago, my Glasgow-born-and-bred friend Angus Robertson greeted me at his Brooklyn Heights doorway in his kilt and sporran and welcomed me to my first Burns supper, the Scottish celebration on Jan. 25 that honors the poet Robert Burns. About 20 of us gathered around the haggis (nothing to be afraid of, basically a big mealy sausage), neeps and tatties (that's turnips and potatoes), and whisky-fortified gravy. Then the time arrived

for dessert, poetry, song, and whisky. Lots of Scotch whisky, selected with care by our hosts.

Up to that night, I had nostalgic associations with the blended Scotches favored by my grandfather — Dewar's especially—but I attached a little latent class rage to single malts. Scotch, I thought, was a rich man's game: the sort of thing that might be found in a still life, in a cut-crystal glass beside a leather-bound book that might never be read. Burns night, then, created some cognitive dissonance. If any writer can be regarded as a poet of the people, it's Burns— "the Ploughman Poet," a farmer's son—who taught us that freedom and whisky go together. The best Burns suppers "are the home kind, without any pomp or pretension whatsoever," says another Glaswegian and an artist, Lex Braes, who always includes a group reading of Burns' "Tam O'Shanter," which, he says, is "a great cautionary tale of the demon drink." (Braes' and Burns' tongues were at least partly in cheek.)

Burns night is the perfect opportunity to consider Scotch's tremendous variety, from mellow and gentle to vegetal and even barnyard-y, and up through to the big, peaty, smoky numbers that many people think of first when they think Scotch (see below for a range of recommendations). While the evening highlights whisky served neat—but with a pitcher of water alongside it, which often helps to open up its flavors — there's no reason not to kick the festivities off with a Rabbie Burns cocktail, which adds vermouth, Bénédictine and a bit of citrus. A Rob Roy (a variation on the Manhattan, with Scotch) is also a fine choice. It's worth noting, however, that the Rob Roy was created not on a windswept Hebridean isle but at the Waldorf Hotel in New York City in 1894.

RABBIE BURNS COCKTAIL

BY ROSIE SCHAAP

What's not to love about a holiday that celebrates a poet? Or one that demands generous quantities of whisky? Burns might have answered the latter question long ago: "O thou, my muse!/guid auld Scotch drink!/Whether thro' wimplin worms thou jink,/Or, richly brown, ream owre the brink." Got that? Me, neither. But that won't stop me from raising a [glass].

1 one-inch strip of orange peel
1½ ounces Dewar's White Label

½ ounce Carpano Antica sweet vermouth
3 dashes Bénédictine

Rub the rim of a cocktail glass with the orange peel. Shake the other ingredients in a glass with ice.

Strain into the cocktail glass and garnish with the reserved peel.

BURNS SUPPER SINGLE MALT RECOMMENDATIONS

I asked my two favorite Scotsmen, Lex Braes and Angus Robertson, to tell me their favorite whiskies for their Burns suppers (and I added my own choices).

• Ardbeg 10: Complex, peaty, a little oily, tinged with sea salt and a honeyed sweetness.

• Glen Garioch 12: Earthy, laced with smoke and toasty barley.

• Glenfarclas 12: Bright and friendly, with hints of vanilla and brown sugar.

• Lagavulin 16: Smoky and ashy, with a burst of dark spice.

THE HIGH-ALTITUDE HIGHBALL

BY ROSIE SCHAAP

This excellent highball was created at the San Francisco bar ABV. If your favorite after-work bar doesn't have Génépy, ask them to get it. It's not crazy expensive, it plays well with many spirits, and it's also delicious on its own. Your favorite single malt whiskey can be substituted for the Hakushu (even if it doesn't come from an equally high altitude).

1½ ounces Hakushu single malt whiskey
½ ounce Dolin Génépy des Alpes

3 ounces club soda
Lemon slice

Pour all ingredients into tall glass.

Add ice, and stir gently.

Garnish with a lemon twist.

— SHINE AND POLISH — FOR BARROOM STAPLE

BY JONATHAN MILES

Duane Fernandez lost a job because of a Rusty Nail. This was [years] ago, when Mr. Fernandez was starting his first solo shift as a bartender at a Greenwich Village restaurant.

Noting his manager's new hire, the restaurant's owner asked Mr. Fernandez if he knew how to make a Rusty Nail, a Scotch and Drambuie cocktail that, like the Rat Pack members who favored it, had its ring-a-ding-ding heyday in the 1960s. Mr. Fernandez, far more attuned to the vodka drinks then in vogue, drew a blank. "I was fired on the spot," he said. "That was it."

Mr. Fernandez—a 33-year-old Brooklyn native who can now be found behind the bar at Entwine, [a restaurant on] Washington Street in the West Village—loves telling that story, even the part about being unemployed for a month and a half afterward.

That's because there's a happy ending. It's served in a highball glass, with a basil leaf draped over the ice, and goes by the name Scotland Yard. The drink's flavor, owing to a fragrant dose of basil and a syrup made with lemon grass and ginger, is herbal, sweet and summery. But there's a Rusty Nail buried deep inside.

"When I went home that day, after being fired, the first thing I did was look up the recipe for a Rusty Nail," said Mr. Fernandez, whose neck is tattooed with the Chinese symbol for longevity. "It stayed in my mind for-ever." Long enough, anyway, for basil and lemon grass to sprout from it.

Mr. Fernandez's tweak may be a personal rebuttal to a quick-tempered former employer. But it's also a riposte to the perception that Scotch, mixed with anything besides soda, must be brooding, autumnal, and masculine.

The Rusty Nail has always had a grizzly reputation (there's that name, for starters), as portrayed by this description from the blog Barfly's Beat: "a quintessential 'old man' drink that sounds like it will knock you in the gulliver and send you on a third-class trip to guttersville." Whatever your gulliver is, the Scotland Yard won't assault it, and unlike many Scotch drinks, which seem to bloom best by the glow of a wood fire, this one thrives in sunlight. And as Mr. Fernandez noted, "the basil and ginger give it a very feminine twist."

He's not alone in reclaiming the Rusty Nail from the gnarled, liver-spotted hands that have been tending it since the 60s. At the Raines Law Room, which [is] in the Flatiron District, muddled ginger is added to the Scotch and Drambuie formula, along with the fizz of club soda, in a drink called a Rusty Collins. The Highland Cooler, at the Brandy Library on Moore Street in TriBeCa, is a Rusty Nail leavened with ginger beer.

"Who drinks Rusty Nails in 2004?" Mr. Fernandez remembered grumbling, on his way home from being fired. [Years] later, he's happy with his answer.

AMERICAN 25

BY ROBERT SIMONSON

This drink, intended as a holiday season quaff, is a simple riff on the French 75, a Prohibition-era Champagne cocktail that includes lemon juice, simple syrup and—depending on which scholar or bartender you consult—gin or Cognac. (Both versions taste good.) Substituting for the traditional spirit is flavorful, fruity apple brandy (make certain you get the bonded version), and peaty Scotch (either single malt or blended will do, as long as there's plenty of smoke on it). The two are natural liquid partners. The aromatic, effervescent result is as pleasing to the nose as it is to the tongue. The name is a nod to the provenance of the primary spirit (apple brandy is as old as the republic) and the day of year it's meant for, Christmas.

1 ounce bonded apple brandy, preferably Laird's
¼ ounce smoky Scotch (Peat Monster and Laphroaig 10-year-old are good options)

½ ounce fresh lemon juice
½ ounce simple syrup (see note)
3 to 4 ounces Champagne
Lemon twist

In a cocktail shaker filled three-quarters with ice, combine the apple brandy, Scotch, lemon juice and simple syrup. Shake until chilled, about 30 seconds. Strain into a flute.

Top with chilled Champagne. Squeeze the lemon twist over the glass, rub it across the rim, then drop it into the drink.

To make simple syrup, warm 1 cup sugar in 1 cup water in a saucepan over low heat until dissolved. Cool to room temperature before using. (There will be extra syrup; refrigerate if not using immediately.)

— WHISKY, SUMMER STYLE —

BY JASON ROWAN

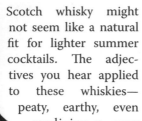

Scotch whisky might not seem like a natural fit for lighter summer cocktails. The adjectives you hear applied to these whiskies—peaty, earthy, even medicine-y—may not immediately suggest beach-ready drinks. But in fact the smokiness or salinity of Scotch whiskies is the very reason they can do so well in citrus-infused drinks with a bit of sugar: they stand up to the sweetness. And just as the complex layers of flavors and aromas of straight whisky open up when you add water, they also sing when combined with the ingredients in these three warm-weather Scotch drinks, created by bartenders from Glasgow, New York City, and Los Angeles.

The refreshing American Smash cocktail features mint, honey, and lemon, which complement a bright Scotch whisky.

AMERICAN SMASH

Angus McIlwraith, barman for Badaboom, a Glasgow-based event bar company, created what is essentially a Scotch-y Southside for warm-weather gatherings. Built around the bright, light, zero-peat Auchentoshan American Oak, with lemon juice, honey syrup, and mint served over crushed ice, it's highly restorative after a long day in the summer sun. A key aspect of preparing the drink, says McIlwraith, is in the treatment of the mint: "The trick is to have a gentle hand with the mint. It's better to lightly bruise it clapping it in your hands to release the minty oils. Crushing it releases grassy and vegetal flavors, which can ruin a cocktail."

1½ ounces Auchentoshan American Oak
¾ ounce fresh lemon juice

½ ounce honey syrup (1 part honey, 2 parts water)
4–5 mint leaves

Shake the ingredients together, and strain into a glass filled with crushed ice.

Garnish with a mint sprig.

SAVANNAH MULE

Dan Sabo, the beverage manager for the Ace Hotel Downtown Los Angeles, explains the origins of this savory cocktail: "We like to play with variations on classics, and the Moscow Mule is the ultimate L.A. classic to modify. I was focused on the combination of ginger and peaches for summer, so the drink grew from there. The Scotch started as a small float for aroma, but became an increasingly important part of the drink to add a complexity of smoke on both the nose and the palate."

3 sage leaves
1 ounce Laphroaig 10 (or other smoky Islay Scotch)
1 ounce vodka

¾ ounce Giffard Crème de Pêche de Vigne
½ ounce lemon juice
4 drops Bittermens Orange Citrate
Ginger beer

In the bottom of a cocktail shaker, muddle 2 of the sage leaves.

Add the remaining ingredients (except ginger beer), add ice and shake.

Double strain the liquid into a rock glass or copper mug filled with ice.

Top with ginger beer.

Garnish with the remaining sage leaf.

CATHOLIC GUILT

At Highlands, a Scottish gastropub in the West Village, NY, the beverage director Andrey Kalinin built the devilishly refreshing Catholic Guilt around the richly peated Black Grouse expression of The Famous Grouse. The result is something savory, tangy, a wee spicy, and sweet. It's a drink designed to assuage the guilt sometimes associated with enjoying a cocktail. "If you are Catholic, you'll understand," explains Kalinin.

2 ounces Black Grouse Blended Whisky
¾ ounce ginger syrup
¾ ounce lemon juice

Dash orange bitters
Dash fig bitters
Fernet Branca

Shake the first five ingredients together.

Pour them into an ice-filled rocks glass.

Float the Fernet Branca on top.

— ORIGINAL CHATHAM — ARTILLERY PUNCH

THE BIG BASH

BY DAVID WONDRICH

Times are hard, yes, but hard times require respite all the more urgently. The office party has been downsized to a sad little gathering in the conference room; friends are mostly seen as little boxes on Facebook. The big holiday party, the December blowout—someone has to do it.

That someone, whoever it is, would be well advised to mix a copious quantity of punch, something strong and serious, unfussy yet with a sense of luxury. A nineteenth-century recipe for Chatham Artillery Punch, unearthed by the cocktail scholar David Wondrich, would do the trick nicely. Mixing a bowl of it—about 25 servings—is no more complicated than opening a bottle (or, to be a stickler about it, six bottles). It is highly potent, a punch that packs a punch, but it goes down easy. The someone who serves it will earn a year's worth of gratitude.

8 lemons
1 pound superfine sugar
750-ml bottle bourbon or rye
750-ml bottle Cognac

750-ml bottle dark Jamaican rum
3 bottles Champagne or other
   sparkling wine
Nutmeg

Squeeze and strain the lemons to make 16 ounces of juice. Peel the lemons and muddle the peels with the sugar. Let the peels and sugar sit for an hour, then muddle again. Add the lemon juice and stir until sugar has dissolved. Strain out the peels.

Fill a 2- to 3-gallon bucket or bowl with crushed ice or ice cubes. Add the lemon-sugar mixture and the bourbon, Cognac and rum. Stir and add the Champagne. Taste and adjust for sweetness. Grate nutmeg over the top and serve.

WHISKEY AROUND THE WORLD

AUSTRALIA

BY ANGELO CAPUANO

Whisky has been produced in Australia for a very long time, and in fact in the 1890s the illicit whisky production in the state of Victoria produced a whisky that was affectionately called "new milk" and "mountain dew." For most of Australia's history, whisky production was underground and illegal, or seriously hindered by burdensome regulatory requirements. The early whisky trade in Australia resembles something from a Wild West movie with illicit stills, whisky smuggling, illegal moonshining, and rugged gun slinging outlaw bushrangers.

The law in Australia was designed to crack down on backyard moonshiners, and protect the public from harm that could result from the unregulated distillation of whisky (such as whisky with acetone or methanol, and not just the safe-to-drink ethanol). No one was distilling whisky, because the law—specifically as provided by the Distillation Act 1901 (Cth)—required licensees to have large capacities that may simply have been unfeasible for smaller (or start-up) commercial ventures. The law's requirements were seen to be highly prescriptive and interventionist in terms of how a person conducted their business. The Australian whisky industry, led by Bill Lark, refused to follow the Tasmanian Tiger to extinction. A number of issues relating to this law were brought to the attention of the government, including members of Parliament, and eventually the law was changed. The Distillation Act 1901 (Cth) was eventually repealed and ceased on July 1, 2006. It was repealed by the Excise Laws Amendment (Fuel Tax Reform and Other Measures) Act 2006 (Cth).

In 1992, about 150 years after the last licensed Tasmanian distillery closed its doors, Bill and Lyn Lark obtained their General Distiller's License. The Lark Distillery commenced production, and other distilleries began to sprout, mostly in Victoria and Tasmania. Released from the shackles of previous regulation, Australian whisky producers now flourish. The trailblazers were followed by other whisky producers and the rest is history. Now, we can all start to enjoy the magnificent whisky that is flowing out of Tasmania, and, more generally, Australia.

Most of the whisky distilleries in Australia are located in Tasmania, and include Tasmania Distillery (Sullivans Cove), Overeem Distillery, Hellyers Road, Nant, and Belgrove. Victoria is home to Bakery Hill, New World Whisky Distillery (Starward) and Timboon Railroad Shed Distillery, and Western Australia is home to the Great Southern Distilling Company. The Australian whisky industry, now in boom times, is seeing an unprecedented increase in distilleries. Joining the ranks of Australian distilleries are Redlands Estate in Tasmania, Applewood Distillery in South Australia, Archie Rose Distilling Co. in Sydney, and Whipper Snapper distillery in Western Australia, among others.

Existing Australian distilleries are now spearheading a renaissance in Australian whisky-making and rising from the ashes is whisky that many think is world class whisky; in 2014 Sullivans Cove French Oak won the honor of the world's best single malt whisky in the World Whiskies Awards. Since then, Australian whisky has been in extremely high demand.

Australian whisky tends to be made in the Scottish tradition; that is, distilleries tend to distill spirit from a wash of malted barley and then age the spirit in used barrels that have previously held bourbon, sherry, Apera (Australian sherry), port, wine, etc. There are exceptions. Belgrove makes rye whisky while Whipper Snapper uses a mash bill of corn, wheat, and malted barley. The grain used in Australian whisky tends to be locally sourced, and this adds to the uniqueness of Australian whisky.

Australian whisky does not merely aim to replicate Scotch whisky. The warm and dry Australian climate may allow the spirit in oak barrels to draw out wood flavors more rapidly than in Scotland. A number of distilleries also use specific strains of barley and yeast to create distillate that has a certain character and flavor profile. Additionally, most Australian whisky is quite young and below 10 years old (though, there are notable exceptions, including Hellyers Road and Sullivans Cove, which each offer whisky aged at least 12 years).

BAKERY HILL DOUBLE WOOD 46%

Bakery Hill Distillery is located in Victoria, Australia, and produces a variety of whiskies, including cask strength whiskies. After sampling the Double Wood, I am very keen to try the cask strength Bakery Hill whiskies, which would have some more flavor and clout (more alcohol = more flavor!). Power and kick is something I think this whisky lacks, but it is incredibly smooth, so I can only imagine it at cask strength—a strength that would probably rectify the lack of power and kick!

Nose: A little alcoholic on the nose, this whisky releases some wood (obviously!), caramel, toffee, lemon, and subtle hints of vanilla. After resting for a while, raspberries float up with cherries, some peach, and mango.

Palate: With a light kick, this whisky offers a sensationally smooth delivery with wood and notes of citrus and lime. A lovely dry smokiness coats my tongue and bitter fruits add a sharp crispness; delightful. Tart, the sweet raspberry on the nose morphs to bitter blackberry. Beautiful! Excellent work Bakery Hill! I can taste a distinct sweetness in this whisky, either bourbon or sherry. A respectable intensity of warmth lingers on my tongue, with that lovely bitter fruit smokiness radiating from the middle.

This Australian whisky is excellent! Laid back, it delivers a youthful glow in a silky smooth package. I think this whisky is very good, so any improvement would make a good whisky excellent!

AC

BAKERY HILL DOUBLE WOOD 46%

Nutmeg weaves around honeyed dried apricots as alcohol adds a bitter cloud that evaporates.

Nose: The aroma of nutmeg sprinkled over overripe apricot is first noticeable with a mild hint that this whisky could have used a bit more time in the barrel. The new spirit is a presence in the glass, almost doughy, but the sugary fruit adds some nice vitality with the alcohol.

Palate: An immediate surge of bitterness takes hold, not quite oak-dominated but more resembling the bitterness of alcohol. Some notes of creamy porridge emerge with wisps of dry smoke and dried apricot drizzled with some honey. There are sparks of nutmeg and spicy oak. The finish is moderate with a lingering dryness lifting off the base of the tongue as a dull bitterness replaces the vibrant dried fruit sweetness.

Nice sweet complexity with decent spiciness. Bitter notes, and this whisky seems a little immature on the nose.

AC

BAKERY HILL CLASSIC CASK STRENGTH 60.1%

A dry burst of alcohol is accompanied with tart fruit and a similar alcoholic fume of a cask strength British-style pot still rum.

Nose: Strangely conjuring memories of chlorinated swimming pools, the alcohol spearheads the assault with dry ethanol alongside dark, but tart, berry fruits and a sweet burst of tinned apricots in syrup.

Palate: A big burst of dry alcohol smacks against the palate. The theme in this whisky, I think, is a tart fruiti-ness that is lacking in a much needed sweetness to balance the experience. The taste of this whisky seems to be dominated by the alcohol, which adds a dry bitterness and seems to over-power the influence of the oak. The finish is dry and, strangely, very simi-lar to a cask strength British-style pot still rum!

I actually enjoyed the dry finish. The alcohol seems much too dominant.

AC

BAKERY HILL PEATED
CASK STRENGTH 60.002%

This fairy tale involves Australian peat and creamy layers of complex fruit living happily ever after under the thunderous clouds of spicy oak, which also sprays down a gentle salty rain. It is complemented with notes of salted pistachio and the bite of anise seed—breathtaking stuff and a work of art by David Baker! This world whisk(e)y now joins the league of some others in my Top Spirits, because in my view, it offers a magical complexity, superb quality, and a truly distinctive Australian whisky experience.

Nose: This is a very mild, almost unnoticeable, peat on the first sniff. It is there, but hardly plays a strong role as some notes of freshly cut dry grass mingle with stone fruit (apricot and plum in particular). Let the whisky rest in the glass, and the peat develops a little more potency...but not much. I would describe this whisky as lightly peated as it delivers a fruity heart with a peat that gets stronger and stronger with each nosing. The distinct mild peat, a freshly cut dry grass with an earthy aspect, merges nicely with the alcohol and offers some licorice and under-ripe blackberries.

A few drops of water releases the magic. The sweetness of banana chips fills the glass with creamy white chocolate as anise seed adds an earthiness and mild licorice. The sweetness of freshly picked berries develops as the grain from the distillate and creamy alcohol shines through an herbaceous fog of grass and sweet fruit notes. Just as the whisky seems to settle, it performs a final twist in its stellar performance, releasing bread and butter pudding as the grainy bread mingles with sweet sultana and butter. There are few peated whiskies that release a nose as complex as this one. Pure magic.

Palate: The peat is much more noticeable on the palate, as a big surge of lush and dry grass hits the palate with a burst of yellow plum picked from the tree too soon; there is some bitterness and sourness that counteracts the notes of sweetness that develop in the middle of the tasting. The peat lingers on the base of the tongue with some grassy notes; typically dry and Australian.

The oak is spicy and the creaminess fades to dry burnt grass with shimmers of sweet candied plums. The most interesting note is the nuttiness of this whisky, which resembles salted pistachio and the bite of anise seed. Dry grass lingers on the palate with a surge of bitterness that retreats and gives way to shimmers of fruity sweetness. The distinct sweetness of toffee remains with praline and hints of something medicinal; perhaps the unique peat interacting with the alcohol.

Get to know this whisky and be prepared to be blown away. Be patient and savor it with a few drops of water.

AC

BLACK GATE DISTILLERY

BLACK GATE 520S
SINGLE MALT WHISKY 67%

I was blown away when I recently tried the latest release from the Black Gate Distillery, the 520s. The "520s" refers to the five casks that were blended together by Brian Hollingworth at his distillery in Mendooran, half way between Dunedoo and Gilgandra, nearly five hours north-west of Sydney.

At a whopping 67% ABV, you'd think it would be an absolute behemoth. Well, it is, but it still achieved a remarkable balance: heavy sherry and port characters come together with that classic burnt toffee and brown sugar note you often get with Brian's spirits. It's big, fat, oily, and fruity, but an undercurrent of smoke and earthiness provide plenty of structure. Worth every dollar.

LM

AWC SINGLE MALT WHISKEY 40%

Castle Glen Distillery is a massive winery/brewery/distillery housed in a real life castle (albeit built in 1994) in Queensland. The Master Distiller there oversees an empire where they make more than 500 different kinds of beverages. They make rum, corn spirits, vodka, gin, grappa, absinthe, strega, brandy, schnapps, and as well as a host of Eaux de Vie including: Mandarin Eau de Vie, Cherry Eau de Vie and Strawberry Eau de Vie. Many of these products are made from the numerous fruits and grains grown in the region and are 100% natural.

The label is named for the Australia Whiskey Company brand. AWC Single Malt Whiskey is aged for two years in oak. It is bottled at 40% ABV. Dark fruit overtones (think Christmas fruitcake and plum pudding).

CD

GREAT SOUTHERN DISTILLING COMPANY

BY LUKE MCCARTHY

Following more international awards, it's a great time to get acquainted with the Limeburners single malts from the Great Southern Distilling Company in Albany, Western Australia. Limeburners roughly splits into two camps: cask strength expressions at around 61% ABV, and non-cask strength expressions, which have been diluted to 40–48% ABV.

All of these whiskies come from single casks, mainly ex-Australian fortifieds. But an intriguing peated expression is also available, where local West Australian peat has been used to incense the malted barley the distillery mashes, ferments, and distills.

There's already a slight salty note to the Limeburners spirit, possibly due to its proximity to the sea, which is just across the road from the distillery—although how a whisky acquires a salty character is a contentious topic. So if you're into the peated stuff from the Scottish west coast, you need to give this a try. Just clear a space in your wallet.

LIMEBURNERS BARREL M98 60%

The Limeburners M98 is a whisky from the Great Southern Distilling Company, located in Western Australia. It is a single cask barrel strength whisky that is matured in 100 liter ex-Bourbon American oak casks and then finished in ex-Sherry casks.

This whisky struck me with its peculiar character, and I could not quite put my finger on it at first. On the nose I could detect something that I felt was not quite right, and at first it resembled the glue and plastic of duct tape. As the whisky rested in the glass, it developed into the musty smell of wet raw dough; wholemeal in fact. What I notice with this whisky is that it has quite a rummy feel to it; it feels young, sweet, yet wood influenced. It certainly packs quite a punch at 60% ABV, but this is one of those whiskies that I think is either liked or not liked because of its odd character.

Apart from that strange duct tape/ raw dough character, I got a lot of lovely notes shining through the strangeness. That strangeness was more pronounced because I blind tasted this whisky alongside other whiskies.

Nose: Sweet sherry bounces up from the glass with layers of vanilla drenched over dried apricot and malt, but that raw dough/duct tape continues to smack against my nostrils, unsettling the experience.

Palate: The sweet sherry moves from the nose to the palate with some vanilla and apricot, but on the palate comes bursts of dry grapefruit and prune with spicy peppery ginger and the zest of lime. Whatever buttery oiliness that is noticeable, though, is stripped away by the artificiality of that glue I can detect. The finish on this whisky is decent, though it loses its puff quite quickly.

AC

LIMEBURNERS M90 "DIRECTORS CUT" 61%

Limeburners is produced in the southern tip of Western Australia, in a place called Albany. Limeburners M90 "Directors Cut" is a single cask offering that is bottled at a ferocious 61% ABV. The M90 was matured in an American oak barrique and finished in an old in-house brandy cask.

On the nose, the whisky offers undertones of doughy wholemeal loaf shining through vanilla, buttery herb bread, chocolate-coated raisins, Christmassy fruit tart, herbal notes, celery, nuts, satay, water chestnuts, strawberry seeds, red candy, glazed cherries, and the burn of wasabi. The palate presents with a surge of crystalline brown sugar, very rummy and herbal in character, with a big hit of medium-dry brandy and underlying notes of luscious malt, vanilla, butter, toffee and raisins that gradually dry into the finish. The Limeburners Distillery character comes out in the finish with a malty note that underpins sweet pastry and lingering vanilla, caramel, and raspberry-flavored candy as the burn of wasabi peas and that delectable dry brandy are a praiseworthy finale.

Overall, Limeburners M90 "Directors Cut" is an Aussie dram with a rumbling fire in its belly—the drying kick of an old in-house brandy cask is cushioned by soft vanillas from the American oak, and all the while the distinctly malty (and downright delicious) Limeburners Distillery character shines through it all. The age of the brandy cask Limeburners used to finish this whisky is unknown, but it certainly seems "old" given the curious herbal rancio notes that glow on the nose and the palate. Those herbal notes add a different dimension to this whisky that, together with a nice solid kick in the teeth by an old brandy cask that is softened by vanillas, fruit, and a rich underlying juicy malt, makes the Limeburners M90 one of the most enjoyable Australian whiskies to pass my lips—not only is it lip-smacking whisky, but also it is distinctly Australian lip-smacking whisky. Its price of $350 (AUD) is perhaps some indication that this whisky was made with little expense spared—the most selective cuts and casks seem to have been used, and the result, as the director already knows, is pretty darn special whisky. It is expensive whisky though, perhaps a little too expensive one thinks.

AC

HELLYERS ROAD DISTILLERY

BY ANGELO CAPUANO

Hellyers Road is a distillery in Tasmania, the apple island off the south coast of Victoria. It is the most southern state in Australia, very lush and beautiful. I have been fortunate enough to work in Hobart and attend a conference in Launceston, both of which are in Tasmania.

Tasmania is famous for many things, and very slowly whisky is creeping into that list. It produces oysters, salmon, and beer, so this might allow for good whisky because Tasmania has access to crisp, clean water and high quality barley.

HELLYERS ROAD PINOT NOIR FINISH 46.2%

This whisky inspired a poetic mood, and as cheesy as that sounds, the mood rubbed off while writing this review. Here's to words, and, trying to make them rhyme—a dying Australian tradition.

A long time ago, in 1825 to be exact, a man named Henry Hellyer set food on very alien-looking tract. A far cry from Hampshire in England, his place of birth, this new land was rugged and had waters that did not much look like an English firth. As Chief Surveyor for the Van Diemen's Land Company, he was there to make the wild land more tame, but took his own life in 1832; some think because people tried to blacken his name. On lives his legacy though, with a Tasmanian malt named Hellyers Road. The Betta Milk Company, with some nervous cows probably on the brink, decided that Australians were thirsty for a different kind of drink. So they decided to make whisky, Tasmanian whisky to be

precise, but they don't seem to be milking consumers and blaming the big Australian tax excise. Hellyers Road whisky sells for a good price, and aren't we all lucky; their whisky usually tastes so nice. Here's to an Australian distillery that makes me very proud, for making malt whisky that is good value and stands out from the crowd. One whisky they've produced is my favorite Australian booze, having drawn most of its flavor from being placed in American white oak and then French oak pinot noir barrels and taking a six-month snooze. It tastes of berries, orange, and spice, and when I reach for another Australian whisky, I always seem to think twice.

Nose: On the nose—which is sweet, dusty, and granular—find caramel, lemon, and floral-scented soap, orange zest, dry oats, vinegar, pear salad, vanillas, pine wood, woodworking glue, and saw dust.

Palate: On the palate, the whisky

is winy, with a dry yet sweet flavor profile. Find orange peel and blood orange, mixed fresh berries, and a gentle flurry of spice. There is also the taste of crushed wedges of lime soaked in cola and dark chocolate towards the finish. A bitter floral hue, somewhat being a trademark of Hellyers Road it seems to me, glows softly. The finish offers flavors of chocolate, dried cranberries, cold drip coffee, wood, and a lingering sweetness in the form of reduced berries.

Buy it. Rarely do you see an Australian whisky of this quality finished in Pinot Noir barrels, and even more rarely do you see such whisky below $100 (AUD)! The Hellyers Road Pinot Noir Finish is a vibrant, smooth, and drinkable dram that sells for a very reasonable price for an Australian whisky. It offers a very distinct style though, so be on alert. Do not expect big oak-driven notes, or a malt hijacked by sherry or port. Expect subtle shades of flavor from that American white oak, re-shaped by the extra time the whisky spent in Pinot Noir barrels. The result? Berries, citrus, and spice with some tones of chocolate and cold drip coffee.

AC

HELLYERS ROAD THE GORGE HENRY'S LEGACY LIMITED EDITION 59.4%

Memories conjured: Tasting red wine from the oak barrel, eating Billy Tea chocolate, smoking the last third of a cigar, standing in the citrus section of the fruit market, eating honey.

Nose: Fresh citrus peel, mainly orange and mandarin with bursts of pink grapefruit, combine with vanilla, rapadura sugar, dried figs, natural lemonade, fizzy sherbet, effervescent fruit salts, splints of wood, and cinnamon.

Palate: A sweet entry of tropical fruit, papaya, apple, rock melon, and honey is short-lived, as heavier citrus and then big wood notes take hold on the palate with lots of spice, pepper, and cinnamon; a real treat for those who appreciate the layers in a woody cigar or mouth-puckering Shiraz. A bitter floral and chicory finish with oak tannin, black tea, tobacco, tar, and dark chocolate dominating over soft bursts of fresh almond, herbaceous notes, honey, and melon.

Buy it! Finally, rather than a replication of typical Scotch flavors, we have an Australian whisky in its own right; initial sweetness is swept away by oak and tannins, which evolve into a deep, complex, and balanced finish. Overall, this is a distinctive Tasmanian whisky that brings to life that heaven-sent ingredient that is integral to whisky: oak. Oftentimes whisky marketers equate woody whisky to chewing wood, but this is an oversimplification of wood notes in whisky. It misses one of the main delights of drinking whisky or any oak-matured alcohol—exploring the layers and flavors that oak imparts into alcohol (whether it is wine, whisky, Cognac, etc.). Granted, like the beaver, I like the taste of wood. Apart from chewing pencils beyond recognition, I savor the pronounced wood flavors in some wine, cigars, chocolate, and coffee. So, if the smell of these woody delights gets you salivating like Pavlov's dogs (or me), then the complex Hellyers Road The Gorge may be for you.

AC

LARK DISTILLERY

BY ANGELO CAPUANO

One evening we had the pleasure of attending the Tasmanian Pavilion VIP Party for the Taste of Melbourne, a festival that takes place every year in Albert Park.

Tasmania is an apple-shaped island that lies off the southeastern tip of Australia. It was once home to the now extinct Tasmanian tiger and the now endangered Tasmanian devil, and it has been, for as long as I can remember, the Australian heartland of oysters, salmon, and brie. The VIP event was designed to show off what Tasmania has to offer.

The event that evening showcased produce from Tasmania, a pristine part of the world that I have seen for myself having worked in both Launceston and Hobart—just imagine crisp, fresh, lush, green, and clean! That evening, we mingled with a number of business owners and tasted the delights of Tasmania—oysters (natural,

tempura, etc.), salmon, white and red wine (pinot noir), sparkling wine, beer, wagyu, beef tartare, lamb belly, apple and pear cider, and, of course, Tasmanian single malt whisky. The island even produces whisky-cured Tasmanian salmon, which is marinated in Lark whisky for two days—it is packed with flavor, sweet zing and a salty kick.

Bill Lark is hailed as the "godfather of Australian whisky," having started the Lark Distillery in 1992. Apart from being the trailblazer of the Australian whisky renaissance (and a very friendly person!), Bill is extremely knowledgeable and passionate about whisky. He is keen to give the world the finest quality Tasmanian whisky.

That's TASMANIAN whisky. Sure, Scotch whisky is sublime when made correctly, but the Tasmanian barley and unique climate of Tasmania offers something distinctly, well, Tasmanian! From what I tasted that evening, the Lark distillery is certainly hitting the mark with its 46% ABV (Cask No 393, Port Matured) single malt whisky—big rich fruitcake notes with dark cherries, chocolate and heavy in port on the nose, lashing the palate with the distinct whip of Tasmanian barley (I will not review this whisky here as I was chatting while tasting it, but the character of the whisky was beautiful!).

LARK PORT WOOD DISTILLER'S SELECTION 46%

The Distiller's Selection does not provide an age statement, but as it is aged in ex-Port wood quarter casks, the maturation process is accelerated and the flavors speak for themselves.

Oranges. The true heart of the Lark flavor, a view endorsed by Bill Lark himself (we asked him in person). The nose provides a zesty citrus burst with smooth caramel undertones. This is a big whisky across the palate; full bodied and complex. The finish leaves a memorable taste of

dark chocolate and orange rind, with a spicy zing from the 46% alcohol specific to this Lark release.

Across the range of Tasmanian whiskies you may find smoother, richer or more complex drams, but you would be hard pressed to find one that you could honestly describe as better. The Lark Distiller's Selection speaks for Tasmania, and represents the start of a new chapter in the evolution of world whisky.

NT & AM

MACKEY TASMANIAN SINGLE MALT WHISKY 49%

This compelling single malt was released in late 2015. Unlike other Tasmanian distillers, though, Hobart-based maker Damian Mackey decided to triple distill his whisky following the Irish method, and has created a lighter, more purified spirit.

But we're a long way from the delicate Irish whiskies produced at Midleton (Jameson) or Bushmills. Each expression Mackey has released, all from single casks that have previously held Australian fortified wine (port), have shown rich, toffee, camphor, raisin notes similar to the top Overeem and Lark expressions of a comparable ilk.

But the extra distillation has wrought an additional subtlety and refinement. It's a fascinating approach, but stock is limited, so you'll have to move fast to try one of Tasmania's most impressive new whiskies.

LM

THE BIG BLACK COCK SINGLE MALT

Crikey! Now I know whisky is made in some pretty far out places but leaning towards the more radical end of the scale would have to be Mt. Uncle Distillery in North Queensland. Despite the immense heat and being located on the outskirts of woop-woop, they have managed to produce a grouse little drop.

The 5 Year Old single malt has one of the more dinky-di whisky names going around. The drinks menu I had a gander at when first sampling it read BBC. However, the large rooster on the front of the bottle makes it clear: this whisky is called the Big Black Cock. It is fair dinkum [Aussie for genuine] outback whisky. And strewth [Aussie for God's truth]: it tastes the part.

Nose: On the nose, there are faint hints of malty Arnott's biscuits—quickly drowned by whiffs of recently slashed sugar cane and Arnott's double coat Tim Tams.

Palate: On the palate, there is vanilla—perhaps a little too much—accompanied by Anzac biscuits and cherry ripe. There are also some bitter fruit elements—possibly created by the ex-red wine barrels they were matured in: American oak staves with French oak lids. The finish is warm and a little rough with spicy, meaty notes, like snags [Aussie for sausages] on a barbie.

If you ever come across the BBC in a whisky bar down under, it is certainly worth ordering—if only to be forced to say the name out loud—but also because of the beaut, uniquely Australian flavors to be found. This is true blue outback whisky. It's unrefined. But a ripper.

NT

NANT PORT WOOD 43%

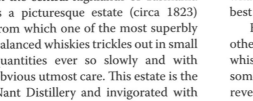

In the central highlands of Tasmania is a picturesque estate (circa 1823) from which one of the most superbly balanced whiskies trickles out in small quantities ever so slowly and with obvious utmost care. This estate is the Nant Distillery and invigorated with

what in my view is among the world's best whisky.

Blind tasting this whisky alongside other Australian and New Zealand whiskies, and then again alongside some of my favorite Scotch whiskies revealed a Tasmanian whisky with impeccable balance. This whisky is 43% alcohol volume, but there is no shortage of spark as it ignites on the palate an explosion of diverse favors.

It is clear that the ingredients used to produce this whisky are first rate, from pristine water and the finest port casks, to the highest quality barley; the water and barley are sourced from the highland lakes surrounding the distillery.

This whisky washes against the palate gently, releasing a complex character that shines with the sweetness of exceptional quality port as the oak weighs in to impart delightful flavors that balance against it to create a superbly balanced whisky.

Nose: The nose on this whisky is light and fresh, like the gentle breeze on a fresh spring morning in the hills of the wine-producing Tamar valley in Tasmania's north. Sniffing this whisky brings back fond memories of sitting in a Tasmanian winery, patiently waiting for a tasting of red wine, as the aroma of wine stained wood would perfume the air.

Palate: The creaminess of whipped cream coats the tongue as

bitter oak and the dry sharpness of red wine cuts through the sweet shine of maple and honey. Vanilla develops on the tongue, as that whipped cream thickens with sprinklings of anise and shavings of dark chocolate. That red wine is distinctly sweet with bursts of dryness, almost like Lambrusco. A subtle earthiness also develops, as gushes of chocolate milk wash up against tobacco leaves and the herbaceous notes of basil and spicy nutmeg. The finish on this whisky is initially light but gains on intensity as the taste buds scream out for more excitement.

AC

BY ANGELO CAPUANO

Starward whisky is made by the New World Whisky Distillery in Melbourne, Australia. More specifically, the distillery is located in an old Qantas hangar in Essendon airport, which is in the western part of Melbourne.

The whisky is made from barley, which is grown in Victoria (Melbourne is the capital city of the state of Victoria in Australia, like Chicago is to Illinois, for example). Once the barley is made into wort and fermented into a wash with yeast, that wash is distilled and then put into aged Apera casks to mature. Apera is a sherry produced in Australia. Therefore, what we have in Starward whisky is an unpeated whisky made of barley, and aged in Apera (i.e., Australian sherry) barrels.

Starward whisky is, relatively speaking, a fairly new brand of Aus-

tralian whisky. It was released a few years ago, and, to be honest, at that time I did not much like it. Neither did a number of Melbourne bartenders and bar owners with whom I have had the pleasure of discussing whisky. The last time I tried Starward, or discussed it with a bartender, was in 2014 (and that was about old batches). As a whisky is the product of different processes, such as fermentation, distillation, and maturation in different casks, a whisky will likely vary from batch to batch, though most distilleries have measures in place to try to obtain consistency in their products. So, it seemed high time to try a more recent batch of Starward whisky, to see how the whisky is going now that it has been commercially available for a while and now that the distillery is in full flight.

STARWARD SINGLE MALT WHISKY 43%

What struck me first was the array of fruit on the palate—apple, tropical fruit (banana, slight pineapple), and orchard fruit were particularly notable. We know that, for example, abundant esters that develop when fermenting wort into wash and in a subsequent distillation run include Ethyl hexanoate (which has an apple character) and Isoamyl acetate (which has a fruity, banana character). It is not easy (as any home brewer or moonshiner will no doubt attest) to,

firstly, produce (through fermentation) and then concentrate (through distillation) those lovely fruity characteristics. A job well done to Starward's distillers and brewers.

In addition to these fruity characteristics, the oak influence began to add some lovely layers and depth to the whisky, introducing vanillas, sugary caramels and toffee, and, of course, the Apera with its fruit cake and gentle toasty notes (because oak barrels tend to be toasted before they age whisky). The oak also gave the whisky a slightly woody kick. Much improved from a couple of years ago, in my opinion.

There is also a candy note, shining, and I also get some slight rummy tones with cereal and mild ethanol.

The oak seems to play a bigger role on the finish. There are hints of spice and sugary/honey tones lingering with the taste of the wood, which seems to resemble very dark chocolate.

Overall, Starward struck me as a young whisky that is jam-packed with delicious fruity esters (which come from the distillate). That alone is reason to try it. The oak provided some depth and contributed nicely to the finish, though for me what I loved about this Starward was its fruity distillery character. While it is not the most complex malt around, it is very drinkable. With company, when it is antisocial to engage in a private one on one rendezvous with your whisky, Starward was dangerously drinkable; I stopped at two, but wanted more. Good sign. Rarely do I drink (or want) more than two measures of whisky in one night.

Starward isn't some meeting point between Scotch and bourbon,

as some people suggest. It is young, sweet, vibrant, and fruity Australian whisky—pretty good Australian whisky—and at $80(AUD) a bottle, it is reasonably priced too.

AC

NEW WORLD PROJECTS PORT DOUBLE CASK #1 48.6%

The Australian whisky industry experienced a big moment in late 2015 when a subsidiary of Diageo, the world's largest spirits company, pur-

chased a stake in Melbourne's New World Whisky Distillery, producers of the popular Starward Malt Whisky. The move certainly quelled any doubt

about Australian whisky having a future on the international stage.

Full control still rests with the board at New World Whisky, so their innovative approach to whisky-making will continue to thrive. Which is great news, because under their New World Projects (NWP) label, there are plenty of interesting releases well worth your hard-earned.

A recent stunner was their New World Projects Port Double Cask #1—a marriage of two barrels of whisky that had both been resting in ex-Australian tawny casks. It's a softer, less emphatic whisky than other NWP releases, and much more refined than its counterparts here. But it still offers up plenty of floral and fruity complexity. And it's reasonably priced, too, a welcome achievement.

LM

Interview with David Vitale, CEO and Founder of New World Whisky Distillery, about Starward Whisky

BY ANGELO CAPUANO

New World Whisky Distillery is a Melbourne, Australia-based distillery that produces Starward whisky. Starward was released to the market and it hit the ground running, taking out first prize in the Single Malt category at the 2013 Australasian Whisky Awards and appearing on the shelves of Australia's largest liquor retailer.

AC: Why did you start production? Did you see a gap in the market or was it to fulfill some passion?

DV: Starward was actually started by accident. I moved to Tasmania with my then-fiancé (now wife), and had a chance meeting with Lark Distillery. I wasn't much of a whisky drinker then, but everything about whisky captivated me. The opportunity to create an iconic Australian whisky that we could offer the world with pride was the dream, and is what gets me up every morning.

AC: Do you think that your product is distinctive? If so, what makes it distinctive from other whiskies on the market?

DV: We operate in a very competitive and crowded market. It was really important to me that we justified our existence on the shelfs of bars and homes by creating something distinctive—not just a product from Australia or Melbourne. For us that means looking at every part of the production process and exploring how we can add something to it and make it our own. Every part of our process has been tweaked (either slightly or significantly) to create our unique and distinctive whisky. It is unique in that it is very young, yet complex and approachable. In the Australian whisky context it is also affordable.

AC: For those who do not know, Starward is matured in Melbourne, Australia. The weather in Melbourne can fluctuate from a low of 46°F to a high of 95°F (some nights I've worn a coat and others I've worn a t-shirt and shorts). Do you think the weather fluctuations in Victoria contribute to Starward's character? Do you take advantage of these weather fluctuations to give Starward a particular flavor profile?

DV: There is no doubt in my mind that we could not make Starward anywhere else in the world. Our weather plays a huge part in our maturation process and we use this to our advantage. Our approachability and complexity comes about through the time the spirit spends in the barrel. That is not really that different to any distillery (whisky, rum, or brandy)—but we measure the progress of our whisky in days, not years. That is unique.

In terms of flavor profile, we were very cautious of releasing a young spirit, which in our environment could have the potential to be one-dimensional—completely wood-focused and harsh. So, we've got a very structured wood policy, which provides us with barrels that have a broad spectrum of characters—some highly focused on extractive wood characteristics (raisins and dried figs from the Apera, caramel, vanilla, and marzipan from the oak), others that focus on the tropical & orchard fruit (banana, apples, and pears) and malt characteristics, which come from the spirit, and others that provide mouthfeel and finish.

AC: Starward won first prize in the Single Malt category at the 2013 Australasian Whisky Awards. What processes do you follow to ensure that your whisky is high quality?

DV: We are fortunate to have a group of brewers and distillers that have worked in large—and small—breweries, wineries, and distilleries. This has given us the opportunity to really learn from the best when it comes to quality systems. Everything we do is tracked and monitored online. The benefit to me is that I can have confidence in the consistency and quality of each part of the process. Each bottle is uniquely identifiable and gives us the ability to trace right back to the barley used in the brew. Our goal with Starward was always to create a consistent whisky from each bottling we do. We limit our bottlings to four batches per annum and our hope is that those four batches will just get bigger and bigger each year until the bottling line doesn't have any downtime!

AC: Is there a flavor profile that you aim to achieve when distilling? Do you select casks to achieve this flavor profile? When blending casks for your final product, what flavors, texture, and character do you aim to achieve?

DV: Yes, upstream of the barrel, we focus on three things: Barley, fermentation, and our cuts. These are done with very minimal variation between each brew. Each batch of barley is tested in our lab so we have an idea of what we need to do to manage extraction of sugars and optimize fermentation. Our fermenters are temperature controlled to ensure we get a consistent fermentation throughout the year. We have them working overtime now, to maintain the temperature we are looking for during fermentation. And our cuts—particularly between hearts and feints—is something that is critical for us to ensure we can come to market with a dynamic and complex spirit that doesn't need to spend years in a barrel to "clean it up." In terms of spirit flavors, we look for the following: orchard fruit, butterscotch, anise, biscuity sweetness, and an oily note from the barley.

Downstream—in the barrel—we almost exclusively use Apera casks for Starward. We have a 13-point sensory checklist that every shortlisted barrel goes through before being considered as part of a release candidate. While not statistically significant, we have at least four team members—typically six work through our sensory program. The results fall into three categories: Starward candidates, Future Starward candidates, Not Starward. The "Not Starward" barrels are really strange and exciting. Some have phenolic (smokey) characteristics, others are floral and light (think Glenmorangie); they are great and interesting whiskies—but they just don't meet our specification.

There shouldn't be any surprises with Starward. A good balance of extractive wood and dried fruit characters, alongside our signature spirit: Banana, apple, and pear, pepper, sweetness, and spice. A rounded mouthfeel and lingering taste that invites you back for more.

AC: Apart from the weather (if relevant), why did you set up a distillery in Melbourne?

DV: Weather was a part of it, but there are a few reasons. Melbourne is the food capital of Australia. We have the most restaurants per capita in Australia. We have a great cultural diversity, which has of course influenced the food and drink scene. I also wanted the best team available to make our whisky, and situating ourselves in the far-flung corners of Australia would have compromised my ability to get—and keep—the best talent. We are also a modern distillery. I didn't feel the need to try and play the heritage card and come up with some sort of historical connection to a place. We are a company that started in 2007—there is nothing old about us! Scotland will always capture people's hearts with the romantic notions of rolling hills, rock filtered springs, and windswept mountains. I want to capture people's minds and challenge their perceptions of what whisky can be. We do this by being equally passionate as any other distiller in the world, but apply a good dose of analysis and innovation to the way we approach things.

AC: Why did you choose to bottle Starward at 43%?

DV: It tasted better (to us) at 43% than it did at 40-46% ABV. Having said that, my personal preference is a dash of water.

AC: The vast majority of Australian whisky from operating distilleries was around $100 or more until Starward came on the scene. Other Australian whisky also bottled at 43% retails for around $50 more than Starward. Why release Starward with a price tag of around $80?

DV: $80 for a single malt whisky is a lot of money. At home, I have two sections to my collection. My "standards," and the "rotation." Glenmorangie 10 Year Old, Balvenie 12 Year Old, Laphroaig 10 Year Old, Bruichladdich 10 Year Old, Buffalo Trace, and of course Starward are my standards. These are the whiskies that I always have at home and form the basis of either the whisky cocktails I make, or the whiskies I have for a mood I am in. I then have my "rotation whiskies." This is the section of guilty pleasures that I have and will spend any amount on—depending on the budget I have available. I think once you start approaching $100 and above, it is difficult to justify being in people's bars as a fixture –as a "standard." And that is our goal. I want to build a loyal group of drinkers that come back to Starward for the unique qualities it has and its ability to work well either neat or in a cocktail.

AC: Why do you think people choose to buy Australian whisky, including Starward?
   DV: I think there are lots of reasons. I buy Australian whisky because I am curious about the category and understanding why people have bothered to make whisky. It's bloody hard work and very risky! I want to understand what story lies behind the whisky. What philosophy does the distillery have towards the spirit.

AC: What is your favorite way to enjoy Starward? Do you find that Starward matches particularly well with anything?
   DV: I can't get enough of our own take on a Manhattan. We call it the Ned Kelly (i.e., an Aussie Rob Roy).
   60ml Starward
   30ml Maidenii Sweet Vermouth
   A healthy dose of orange bitters
   A slither of orange peel

AC: What three words do you want people to associate with Starward?
   DV: Unshackled from tradition.

OVEREEM DISTILLERY

BY ANGELO CAPUANO

On rare occasions, a blind taste of a whisky and the first sip releases very little, if any, of its true quality. Then take a second sip a few minutes later and it is as though a gremlin cheekily replaced the whisky with some magical elixir that epitomizes everything I have come to appreciate in a whisky: depth, complexity, power, balance, flavor, elegance, smoothness…you get the point I'm sure. Its magic is not unlocked just yet…abracadabra add water! POW! With a trickle of water, this whisky unleashes an abundance of diverse character that retains a violent potency that enters the palate smooth as silk, like a good Tasmanian oyster. This is exactly what was experienced during a blind tasting of the Overeem Port Cask Matured Cask Strength Whisky.

This whisky is a powerful cask strength whisky that, with the addition of water, unlocks even more magic while retaining potency and flair. It has an exceptional balance one can particularly enjoy. I highly recommend this whisky because it is not overly sweet, with lots of dryness and bursts of saltiness that all balance nicely against the bright shimmers of fruit and port sweetness.

OVEREEM PORT CASK MATURED CASK STRENGTH 60%

This is the first cask strength Australian whisky I have tasted, and it blew my socks off! Jim Murray agrees, classifying this whisky as "liquid gold" in his *Whisky Bible 2013.* What I especially enjoy about this whisky is that it has a crisp ferocity and unleashes a well-balanced diversity of flavors. Superb!

Color: The color of this whisky is a light amber with shimmering gold.

Nose: On the nose, this whisky releases gusts of acidic lemon and white pepper with spicy wood. With water, this whisky opens up considerably, with shimmers of honeydew, cantaloupe, mango fruit, passion fruit, and bitter dense oak. After letting it rest in the glass, its playful side comes out to play, releasing marshmallow, licorice, aniseed, whipped cream, and mint!

Palate: On the palate, this whisky has a lovely soft texture with bursts of energy and burning fire that emits orange peel and zest with dried mango. Towards the end, the whisky releases on the back of the palate sea salt and iodine. With water, a strong forceful blast of flavor that starts very dry, like a chardonnay, leaves a crisp dryness on the tongue with very light smokiness evaporating off it. As the whisky settles, this dryness is met with flurries of sea salt and iodine that add saltiness to the sweet mango and honeydew as an alcoholic bitterness sets in. Then a sharp jab of energetic spice slaps the tongue, as tangy lime and red wine add an interesting twist. The finish is exceptional. This whisky leaves flavors that radiate from the tongue for a long time with intensity and consistency.

AC

OVEREEM SHERRY CASK MATURED CASK STRENGTH 60%

The high-quality sherry shines through in this whisky, as it releases bursts of dryness in a dense fog of sweet yet heavy red wine illuminated with flashes of Moscato, fig, and prune. It is also silky smooth on the palate. All this points to the use of great quality ingredients and sherry casks, as well as excellent distillation skills. The only negative is a nagging new spirit stench,

indicating to me at least that this whisky is a tad immature.

I had tasted the Port Cask before, whereas this is the Sherry Cask. What is the difference between port and sherry? Both are fortified wine, but port is originally from Portugal, whereas sherry is originally from southern Spain.

Color: This whisky has light tinges of brown and red in a sea of gold.

Nose: On the nose high-quality sherry wafts into the air, with hints of cherry and a dusting of icing layered over Christmas cake. Vanilla develops on the nose, with more subtle notes of walnut and pumpkin seeds as mineral water provides a welcome breeze of freshness. Shavings of dark chocolate and some orange extract bring bitterness, as the unmistakable smell of Black Forest cake with sour cherry and cream wafts up from the glass. I can go on for hours. This has shimmers of sweetness (fig, prune, Moscato grape), but it is not overly sweet. As it rests, a mild honey lifts from the nose. The new make smell taints the whisky a little, detracting from the experience.

Palate: The sweetness on the nose does not overwhelm the palate, and it balances beautifully with the bitterness of the dark chocolate, the sweetness of the Black Forest cake, and the sourness of the cherry. It moves from the nose to the palate almost seamlessly and without disruption. What I particularly love is that while there are undertones of sweetness, there is a burst of bitterness and sourness; a sourness that is distinctly Overeem whisky! (I got this with the Port cask too.) That dry note is a heavy red wine, like a grenache/cabernet sauvignon that is sensationally dry with sparks of sweetness and an almost chewy Moscato grape with undertones of prune and fig. Lovely balance, with extremely high-quality sherry as the foundation. The lusciousness of crème brûlée with its crisp bitterness intermingling with the sweet sugar is sensational. It is a powerful whisky with bursts of flavor. The finish is sensational. It is long, strong, and lasts a while.

AC

TASMANIA DISTILLERY

BY ANGELO CAPUANO

Sullivans Cove produces single cask whisky, which means that each of its whiskies expresses the particular character of the cask from which it was taken. That is just the nature of single cask whisky; some casks may contain the right mix of phenolic compounds that allow the whisky to develop into a magical whisky while other casks may have the wrong mix of phenolic compounds so the whisky does not develop in the same way. It just comes down to the cask, and the particular way the whisky has soaked up the character of the oak cask. Oak has hundreds of phenolic compounds that whisky soaks up while it matures in a cask, so it is pretty easy to see how the character of a whisky depends to a large extent on the oak cask.

Oxidization, climate, and distilling are other factors, though you would expect the quality of distilling by Patrick McGuire and Co at Sullivans Cove to be top notch. As for the oxidization and climate, well, this should also be consistent with other casks, give or take some different weather patterns during different maturation periods.

SULLIVANS COVE AMERICAN OAK (HH0211) 47.5%

This beauty makes the other Sullivans Cove expressions seem clumsy, with its refined elegance and heavenly balance that offers no big ripples, just sipping pleasure with a lovely citrus theme interlaced with chocolate fudge cake and helpings of vanilla.

Put in the barrel in 2000 and bottled in 2013, this whisky offers a citrus theme alongside bitter oak and showcases a mature whisky bursting with complexity and fresh vibrancy.

Nose: Fresh and crisp, this whisky offers crushed lemon leaves with Terry's Chocolate Orange and nutmeg-coated dark chocolate fudge cake. The oak influence is beautiful, with spicy notes intermingling with the sweet fruity heart; nutmeg and cloves in particular as notes of vanilla smooth the flecks of barley that radiate from the bright distillate shining with its delicate fruitiness (green mango, ripe banana, paw paw). The sweetness is also herbaceous and complex, like manuka honey and the slightest shimmers of maple.

Palate: The lemon leaves on the palate morph into varied citrus fruits, with orange and grapefruit rind taking a leading role. There is a dry bitterness and sourness that hits the palate with bitter dry wood and the sweet shimmer of toffee alongside a distinct bitter-sweetness, almost like lime in bourbon and cola.

The entry is smooth and deliciously vibrant, with an intensity that builds on the palate and retains impeccable balance: a haze of oak-laden smoke carries the bourbon cask influence that intermingles with the sweet distillate. Sensational work by Sullivans Cove to produce a whisky that is crisp, vibrant, youthful, and yet complex. A sugary sweetness remains on the tongue with the bitter citrus theme that draws in the lovely oak.

AC

SULLIVANS COVE AMERICAN OAK (HH130) 47.5%

Yogurt coated raisins with bourbon theme but less intense and offering its own distinct style as the spices develop with the distillate.

Put in a barrel in 2000 and bottled in 2013, this whisky offers a bourbon-based theme but with a flavor profile with notes that are distinctly Sullivans Cove HH130!

Nose: Creamy berry fruit yogurt is noticeable with shavings of lemon zest and white chocolate praline layered with crushed cinnamon sticks. The sweetness and creaminess develops into yogurt raisins, as a sugary sweetness is intertwined with a milk-based sourness and layered with caramel. The yogurt resembles the sweeter variety or the yogurt coated nuts/fruit.

Palate: Sweet! Wonderfully sweet, reminding me of a great American bourbon but without the burst of dry, bitter, toasted wood. Toffee develops on the palate, as it releases its burnt bitterness and a wave of buttery creaminess that quickly vanishes into a cloud of dry wood. This whisky is sharp and crisp rather than luscious and oily, and its flavors energetic and thin rather than dense and rich. A lingering dry bitterness with the spicy oak putting on quite a (late) show! Glad it decided to join the party.

AC

SULLIVANS COVE AMERICAN OAK HH537 47.5%

Sweet winy theme on the palate with mixed berries, vanilla, spice, and a drying finish with a dry herbaceous twist.

This single cask offering from Sullivans Cove is very easy drinking whisky and extremely enjoyable. Initially skewed to the sweet side with a burst of winy themed fruit, it then balances out with a drying finish and very spicy/dry herbaceous twist. I have been slightly disappointed with previous offerings from Sullivans Cove, but the HH537 hits the nail on the head in terms of enjoy-ability and distinctiveness. It also explains why this Tasmanian distillery is making a bigger splash in the whisky world with each passing year.

Nose: Light, fruity (apple, green pear), delicate and floral with hints of chocolate (dark chocolate with mint comes in waves), vanilla fudge, caramel, sweet watermelon and raspberry infused white wine—strange how some whiskies share a similar bouquet to some wines, but this offers dry white wine on the nose with a herbaceous twist with mixed berries and oozing vanilla. The herbaceous twist is pretty fascinating actually, with dried parsley and oregano coming in flashes with wood spices (nutmeg especially) and wet bark/forest undergrowth.

Palate: The sugars hit the palate and then die down as the oak acts as a counterweight to the sweetness, which gradually recedes into a drying finish. This whisky is such a curiosity. The wine theme continues on the palate, but it is much sweeter and resembles Moscato or a noble Riesling with spearmint and mild notes of vanilla, cloves, cardamom, nutmeg, and cinnamon. The wine theme represents a fruitiness often found in white wine, with citrus notes accompanying the berries, for example—this is very interesting whisky! The herbaceous notes on the nose have fallen away, and on the palate the spices take over.

Sweet pear cider with a continu-ing white wine theme continues with the spices gradually taking on that dried herb theme on the nose. Would I have another dram? Yes. Would I buy a bottle? Yes. Unique, spicy/her-baceous twist, sweet yet drying.

AC

SULLIVANS COVE DOUBLE CASK 40%

The Sullivans Cove Double Cask is like a beautiful and delicate flower; be patient and nurture it to let its beauty unfurl. It has many components but it requires careful attention to hear it. While the Sullivans Cove Double Cask plays hard to get, it is well worth the chase, trust me.

Congratulations to Sullivans Cove, a Tasmanian distillery, for producing a sensational whisky. It takes a long while to unpack and get to know, but once you break the ice, expect quite an experience. The only problem is while there is a lot happening, I found it was hard to detect a lot of what was happening and it needed careful con-centration. This made it a little dull, unfortunately.

This is a single cask whisky, from cask DC 58. Its youngest barrel date is 2000 and its bottle date is 2012 (according to the sample bottle). There were 943 bottles in this batch. Two American oak barrels and one French oak barrel was used to pro-duce this particular cask, and well done to Sullivans Cove for doing this! It has a spectacular character after getting acquainted with it.

Nose: The light waft of watermelon fills the glass with sweetness, as hon-eyed oats add substance to sprinklings of cocoa. A mild bitterness is present in the form of oak. Among the oak are sweet lemon drops and a fresh country breeze carrying with it floral notes. I

am taken back to my visit to a lavender farm in Melbourne on a sunny spring day. Fresh and light, this nose still has a splashing of rainfall and lush green with some fresh peach and apricot. Beautiful whisky! Creamy—though not oily—with different flavors grappling with one another, and that flickering light in the room has suddenly started to shine! Great balance, and because its character is coming out it puts on a pretty interesting show! Initially, it was slightly uninteresting but now my tongue seems to have caught up and the layers are peeling away beautifully. I better stop or else I will be here all night!

Palate: There are some characters that remain locked away behind a door, cloaking their personality. This whisky was very shy at first, but now it softly drapes the tongue like velvet and releases bursts of oak and honey, with a sensational bitterness that is like a dense poppy seed orange cake smothered in brandy and the finest of dark chocolates. It has a youthful spark that I absolutely adore now, as a dense cloud of that sumptuous orange cake tantalizes the tongue. It is fresh and light, with a lot happening. Please, Sir, can I have some more? Long and enjoyable, though it loses some puff towards the end.

AC

SULLIVANS COVE FRENCH OAK HH524 47.5%

The Sullivans Cove French Oak HH524 is a superbly balanced whisky that bursts with varying shades of sweet stone fruit as the bitter oak and cocoa moderate it to allow spicy raw ginger and rich gingerbread to shine on the palate just as it is swept away by creamy vanilla, which evaporates into a cloud of dry grapefruit that radiates off the base of the tongue. It is a great balance, lovely texture, and some spark too!

I cut the whisky down to about 30% alcohol volume, which releases a sumptuous fruit basket of flavor—basket and all—pulsating with fructose, lush green leaves, earthiness, and the smell of fresh spring water.

Nose Neat (47.5%): The nose on this whisky is incredibly diverse, as the smell of vanilla and orange are carried with creaminess of couverture chocolate. The cocoa bursts with bitterness and explodes with bright orange zest and dry dense oak. The wood on the nose is solid and fragrant. Then that sweet fruit cake develops, but the sweetness is tamed by the wholemeal holding together the raisins and dried apple. The gentle breeze of spring water is also present, along with an abundance of character. That pavlova is interesting, as beaten egg white merges with sugar and whipped cream to hold together the zing of lemon and buzz of licorice. All the while the floral notes chime gently in the breeze. I can keep going…

Nose With Water (about 30%): It is amazing how much this whisky opens up with a splash of water. Nosing this whisky is like having a picnic under a peach tree when flowers are in full bloom on a lovely warm spring day. The gentle waft of lush cut grass merges with a diverse bouquet of floral notes as the aroma of peaches freshly fallen from the tree mix with common picnic fare, apples, pears, and luscious cream. Dense cheesecake also develops, as its crumbly biscuit base brings buttery shortbread and vanilla with notes of lavender.

Palate Neat (47.5%): If I could describe the taste as one thing, it would be a dark chocolate and ginger tart topped with stone fruits (apricot, peach, cherries), some banana chips, and shavings of licorice, orange zest, and smothered with cream and vanilla. That oak is just right, too.

Palate With Water (about 30%): Still sporting some kick even with water, the bitterness of dark chocolate and oak grapples with sweet stone fruits such as cherries, as the layers of peach and apple begin to unfurl on the palate. This is sensational because not only can I taste the crisp freshness of apple and peach, but also the sugary softness of baked apple and peach crumble topped with dark chocolate and served in a lovely wooden dessert bowl. Rich custard also forms on the tongue, with creamy helpings of vanilla and sprinklings of aniseed. Strong and powerful, the finish tingles the tongue as powerful bursts of dry grapefruit and oak merge with bitter dark chocolate and spicy gingerbread. The finish is fabulous, lasting a long time but not overstaying its welcome.

AC

SULLIVANS COVE FRENCH OAK HH0423 47.5%

This whisky is drawn from cask HH0423, which was made of French oak and previously held fortified wine. This whisky is balanced and elegant, yet assertive with beautifully integrated flavors showcasing dense Christmas cake, malt loaf, dark chocolate, caramel, sticky date pudding, surges of barley, and a rounded warming glow on the finish, especially of gingerbread, mild menthol, and sweetened pickled spice.

Nose: Lashes of barley are softened by layers of caramel, sticky date pudding and hints of vanilla spiced English-style pot still rum. Flecks of cocoa and freshly polished wood balance against that sweetness, which begins to thicken into dark chocolate, rich dense fruit-packed Christmas cake and shards of toffee with a slice of malt loaf. The bright caramel and vanilla-infused sticky date pudding flickers on and off randomly, giving way to the other characters, then returning at unexpected times with the occasional sprig of mint and burst of menthol. Such a complex bouquet, and one that radiates all the classic aromas of ex-fortified wine matured whisky with a distinctive Sullivans Cove twist.

Palate: Thick, mouth-coating, viscous, and rich. This whisky offers a beautiful balance. The nose suggests sweetness will flood the palate, but once this whisky hits the tongue, the flavors balance out. The initial burst of winy sugars are moderated by the oak, which are then whipped into line by the flash of barley. An initial wave of thick honey, caramel, and vanilla cake merges with dried dark fruit (dates, raisins, fig), and as the whisky rests on the palate, the sugars recede into malt loaf with mild hints of filtered coffee and the buzz of barley, which are accompanied by dense dark chocolate-coated Christmas cake that is packed with dried fruit. The finish is long and progressively showcases sweet, rounded spiciness. Gingerbread and mild menthol drops glow on the palate with very mild notes of sweetened pickled ginger, but acting as a counterbalance to that spicy sweet "heat" on the tongue are soothing waves of vanilla and that BIG, RICH, DENSE Christmas cake that bursts with cocoa and cereal notes.

AC

An Interview with Marketing Director Bertie Cason at Sullivans Cove

BY ANGELO CAPUANO

Sullivans Cove is a brand of Australian whisky produced by the Tasmania Distillery in Hobart, Australia. Once the whisky has served its time after being "distilled with conviction," it is released from the confines of its oak cask and bottled for us incredibly thirsty mainland Australians. Some of it escapes our clutches and it finds its way to the United Kingdom, Europe, US, and Canada but, the truth is, we don't let much escape. We know a good thing when we taste it, and Sullivans Cove makes some spectacular whisky—my favorite Sullivans Cove (and Australian whisky!) is the French Oak HH0423.

With this most recent taste of liquid heaven, I set out to ask the distillers at Sullivans Cove a few questions about its whisky. Thanks very much to Bert at Sullivans Cove for taking the time to answer my questions.

AC: Why did you start production? Did you see a gap in the market or was it to fulfill some passion?

BC: Bit of both. The market was growing, and making whisky in Tasmania seemed like a hell of a good idea at the time!

AC: How long has Sullivans Cove been producing whisky?

BC: Since 1994.

AC: Do you think that your product is distinctive? If so, what makes it distinctive from other whiskies on the market?

BC: As a Tassie malt, it is already different from any other malts on the market, given that it is made in Tasmania from Tasmanian ingredients, including Tasmanian barley and water. It is different from the other Tasmanian malts in that Sullivans Cove has the oldest whiskies on the market due to using 200 and 300 liter barrels. Most 2014 bottling will be between 12 and 14 year old with the odd 15 and 11 year old.

AC: Sullivans Cove has won a number of prestigious awards for some of its expressions, including Jim Murray's Southern Hemisphere Whisky of the Year in his *Whisky Bible 2013*. What processes do you follow to ensure that your whisky is high quality?

BC: Cascade and Moo Brew are highly experienced breweries that make our wash to a specified recipe and this ensures consistence of the wash. In the distillery, the run is cut very short to ensure that we only keep the cleanest and sweetest ethanols in the heart of the run. We make sure that our barrels are of high quality and finally, we taste every single barrel that gets bottled and nothing makes it into a bottle if we believe that it is not of the right quality.

AC: Is there a flavor profile that you aim to achieve when distilling? Do you select casks to achieve this flavor profile? Do you tailor different products for different palates?

BC: Not really, we simply aim to keep the cleanest part of the run and make sure that the wash from the brewery is of the correct standard. This translates into the typical sweet, complex, malty Sullivans Cove flavor.

AC: Why do you bottle the American oak and French oak expressions at 47.5%?

BC: Over many months of testing, we found that this strength was the best overall for enjoying our single casks neat.

AC: What do you look for when "hand selecting" (as noted on your bottles) oak casks? Can you let us know where you source your French and American oak casks?

BC: For French oak we look for the following: 200-300 liter barrels, emptied most recently to avoid mold build up. French or European oak, we look at the general quality of the build, no leaks, etc. and importantly we look at the smell, no off notes to the nose, etc. American oak: 200-225 liter, well built, ex-bourbon, and again no off notes, good smelling. French oak we get from McWilliams in New South Wales, and American oak from a variety of distillers. The current American oak barrels are from Jim Beam, and we have some Jack Daniels and Heaven Hill in the background, waiting.

AC: Sullivans Cove is known for offering whiskies from single casks, which in turn means that the character of your whisky depends on the cask from which it is taken. Why not blend casks for a (more) consistent product?

BC: It is more interesting to have a different whisky every time. The French oak and American oak both have a distinct flavor profile, and the single casks allow us to have a breadth within that.

AC: Why do you think people choose to buy Tasmanian whisky, including Sullivans Cove?

BC: Because it tastes damn good.

AC: What is your biggest export market? Can you give us an idea how much whisky you export and to where?

BC: Mainland Australia gets about 90% of our product and about 7% goes to the rest of the world. Mainly to Europe and the UK, then US and Canada.

AC: Can you give us an idea of how much whisky you produce per year at Sullivans Cove?

BC: Currently enough for about 20,000 bottles per year.

AC: Are there any plans for any new expressions in the pipeline?

BC: Yes, very limited release full cask strength called the Ballbreaker.

AC: Do you have any other comments for readers?

BC: Thanks for the support and drink Tassie whisky, doesn't matter which one, just support the locals. All of your support has meant we now have a proper industry with a tourism trail.

The Timboon Distillery is located in Timboon, Victoria, Australia. It brings to life the fascinating history of illicit whisky production in Victoria, and inspired by this history, the owners of Timboon Distillery have, I think, produced an iconic Australian whisky that carries with it the feel of 1890s "mountain dew" (the name given to whisky produced in the Timboon District in the 1890s) and the precision of modern whisky-making. Just like the 1890s mountain dew, the Timboon whisky is as smooth as new milk but with some ferocity and fire.

TIMBOON SINGLE MALT WHISKY 40%

This whisky brings to mind "Mad Dog" Morgan, famed Australian bushranger. Bushrangers are Australia's answer to outlaw cowboys. Like outlaw cowboys in America, most

bushrangers enjoyed whisky (possibly a little too much!) and some even distilled whisky. They also enjoyed lots of other things, but best to keep this MA-rated! (Just think Roy O'Bannon from *Shanghai Noon*.)

The Timboon Single Malt Whisky is a friendly mild mannered whisky that is easy to drink, but it has flurries of anger, just like "Mad Dog" Morgan. In folklore, "Mad Dog" Morgan is known as the traveler's friend, and he was protected by many against the long arm of the law. He was not all cuddles and smiles though, because he is described as a man who would, without hesitation, shoot down two men. He died in Peechelba, Victoria, on 8 April 1865, so he would never have tasted the "mountain dew" from Timboon. Pity!

Nose: The nose is incredibly light and fresh, with whiffs of pinot gris, almond extract, and very light sprinklings of cardamom. Mild notes of orange flesh are accompanied by a light wine dryness and gusts of freshness, spring water, rainfall, winter morning dew. Sensational! It is very complex for such a young whisky.

Palate: On the palate, as expected, this whisky begins light and fresh. It has a luscious oily texture that delivers an array of flavors gracefully, but with spark and bravado. This is a deceptive character, so mild mannered on the nose but then delivering a burst of flavors on the palate while retaining a polite demeanor....the traveler's friend who would without hesitation shoot down two men in a blaze of fury!

This whisky glides against the glass beautifully, as its lusciousness meets the tongue and coats it smooth as new milk! The whisky hugs the side of the glass like a long lost friend.

The distinctive flavor of maple and oak is first noticeable, with helpings of thick cream. Wedges of fresh mandarin pieces with a dusting of cocoa are brought together with a lovely maple syrup and rich oak, mahogany in fact. It is not all mild, with sparks of bakery spices—cinnamon and chewy gingerbread—adding some more character. All this is accompanied with dry chardonnay, which strikes the palate a little drier than the pinot gris on the nose. Towards the end, the taste of raisins develop with very ripe baby figs, almost like a sticky date pudding with shavings of almond and dashes of port. This whisky dances on the tongue softly and quietly, with developing flavors as that lovely fruit morphs into dried apricot, bursts of toffee, and candied apple. Throughout the whole experience, there is a bitterness, but it is almost perfectly balanced.

AC

TIMBOON CASK STRENGTH 64.7%

While the 40% ABV Timboon was the "Mad Dog" Morgan of whisky with its friendliness and sparks of rage, the cask strength Timboon, to keep the bushranger theme, is definitely the Ned Kelly of whisky: it bursts out iron plated and with guns blazing, hitting the right notes with each blast. An immediate firestorm of dense Port and piercing creamy alcohol electrifies the taste buds with the buzz of malt; an energy develops into dark chocolate layered over raisin-dense Christmas cake as the snap of dry wood adds some spice, and leaves the palate with a smoky haze of Port-stained wood tannins while the earthy bite of wood spices flood in and out like a gentle tide.

Move over Tasmania. First it was Starward and Bakery Hill, and now it is Timboon that confirms to me that Victoria is fast becoming the new heartland of Australian whisky. It may be the four seasons in one day, the extreme weather fluctuations or a magic spell, but the people at Starward, Bakery Hill, and Timboon appear to have attracted the favor of the oak gods as their superbly crafted distillate mature in what are clearly high-quality casks. All this means that what we have in Victoria is a rebirth of the whisky industry, a renais-

sance from the old days of illicit "new milk" and "mountain dew" that used to trickle down in the 1890s to quench the insatiable Australian thirst for booze.

Timboon Cask Strength boasts an elegant maturity and youthful aggression that makes it, in my opinion at least, one of the very best "world whiskies" (from outside Scotland, Ireland, or the US) I have tasted. This whisky also has a genuine uniqueness and originality about its character that in

my view is in the same league as two other exceptionally crafted non-Scotch whiskies: Kavalan Solist Sherry Cask & Hicks and Healey Cornish Whiskey. "World whisky" tends to be quite young and, unfortunately in my experience, much of it is tainted with the undesirable aspects of new spirit. The Timboon Cask Strength has none of this, and it radiates with the crisp flecks of malt within its Port rich fiery core. One possible reason for the rapid maturation of the spirit may be that the area around Timboon in Victoria reached 109°F in January that year, which explains a lot about weather patterns during the time this whisky matured in country Victoria; weather patterns that may have, I imagine, caused the oak pores to expand and contract more often than in other regions with more stable weather, thereby allowing lots of interaction between the oak and the spirit.

Do not let the age of this whisky fool you, because the distiller at Timboon has absolutely nailed this one. Congratulations Tim, a job very well done.

Nose: Rich dashes of sweet Port intermingle with dry oak tannins as the gust of raisin-dense Christmas cake and dark chocolate carry granular grain and the gentle glow of the distillate. The distillate continues to retain its heart of earthy grain, but without the undesirable aspects that are commonly associated with new spirit. As the whisky rests, dried fruit develops, in particular dried fig and banana chips, and a luscious creaminess fills the glass. This is a Christmas cake layered with shavings of dark chocolate, dried fig, and dashes of Port. Within that foundation are flashes of something different with each nosing, banana chips, crushed mint, and an alcohol drenched orange dusted with cocoa.

Palate: An immediate surge of bitter dryness floods into the palate, stinging with the bite of creamy alcohol, the burst of dry wood, and the sweet moderating force of sugary sultana that carries the Port-stained character of wood tannins. The sultana develops bitterness, morphing into raisins, and then dried fig as dates linger with the spicy wood. The smoky haze of grape tannins and the bite of earthy anise seed lingers, with the gentle glow of the grainy distillate shining within the lingering Port, now dry and steaming off the tongue as the aroma of nutmeg and bark spices moves from the nose to the palate.

Powerful and supremely complex, this masterstroke is also incredibly smooth for a whisky bottled at 64.7% ABV. It offers rich Port-stained wood tannins and the snap of an angry Australian tiger snake. Please be wary of the alcohol volume of this whisky, and note that it is quite dry and piercing at first.

AC

BY ANGELO CAPUANO

William McHenry & Sons distill-ery is located in the southern parts of Tasmania, and while it is called a "distillery," its Three Capes signature brand is comprised of whisky from the Tasmania Distillery that has been aged in American oak bourbon bar-rels for at least ten years. The whisky is then cut down to 43.5% ABV and bottled as "Three Capes Single Malt Tasmanian Whisky." The whisky in this review was bottle 250 taken from barrel 5.

This whisky is seriously good.

It is a sensationally smooth whisky that is dangerously "more-ish" and yet deceptively quiet, because it bursts with dry spicy character in the middle to the end as the unexpected shine of menthol/eucalyptus radiates on the finish.

THREE CAPES SINGLE MALT TASMANIAN WHISKY 10 YEAR OLD UNPEATED 43.5%

Nose: Creamy, light, and elegant, the aroma of sour berries wafts up with wet bark and wood sap as sweet honey mingles with the solid buzz of spice, nutmeg, and anise seed in particular. The sweetness is complex, with green underripe strawberries, and layered over some light cream and sour lollies.

Palate: Light jabs of bitter berries morph into green grape as a tart sourness is washed away by dry wood and yellow plum sprinkled with nutmeg and raisins. The bitter-dry character is almost like a thick cloud that has the shine of sweet bourbon flickering in the darkness.

Finish: The finish is long and lingering, as the very Australian taste of menthol and eucalyptus glows on the tip of the tongue within that bitter-dry cloud of wood, bark and green grape.

This whisky is light and fresh with a character that quietly whispers with bitter fruit and sour lolly/candy as complex spice (nutmeg) and wood SLAP the palate, and just as things risk getting boring, the glow of menthol/eucalyptus shines.

AC

AUSTRIA

BY CARLO DEVITO

A ustria has had a long love affair with all the beverages of the spirit world. Wonderful wines are made there, both red and white, dessert wines, and beer. Schnapps especially, or strong fruit-infused spirits, have always been popular in this country. And there is a long history of distilling. There has also long been a love of whisky in Austria as well. With the edict of the EEU's deregulating (if you will) the restrictions on single malt whisky, an explosion of whisky-making happened throughout its rich distilling industry. Here, local distillers with proud histories, in the main, are trying to create single malt whiskies that express the terroir of their own regions. The results have been surprising and delicious!

KECKEIS SINGLE MALT WHISKY 43%

Harald Keckeis loves the finer things in life, especially food and beverages. He had a yen for developing distilled spirits from fruits at an early age. Keckeis' distillery has become known for producing quality product with a unique flare. Harald founded the distillery in 2005. Keckeis makes fruit brandies, gin, and rum, and produces about 20,000 liters of distillate a year. Keckeis is considered one of the best distilleries in Austria. Keckeis decided in 2008 to make whisky 80% of their production. Their first release was Cask No. Forever 1, which produced 625 bottles. Since then, their business has grown substantially. Their single malt starts with barley that is kilned with beech wood smoke. Then it is stored in sherry casks and made with crystal clear Alpquellwasser (Alp spring water) from the Silvretta-Arlberg mountain ranges, making for a unique whisky. The whisky is matured for five years. The result is a single malt with hints of fruit up front and slightly smoky notes. Smooth sherry, vanilla finish.

Johann Haider and his family were farmers in Austria. In 1995, they set a course for a new future in distilling. They wanted to create a distilling business that was an experience of all the senses. Whisky would be the ultimate prize. They called their whisky business Waldviertler Whisky J.H. Soon, they started distilling whisky. By 1998 they had introduced their first whisky, their highly acclaimed rye.

Waldviertler Whisky J.H. is Austria's first whisky company. Under Johann's hand, Haider has attempted to create a unique whiskey experience. Johann's mantra from the very beginning was not to produce an imitation of America or Irish or especially Scottish whisky, but rather to create a new product with its own very special character. A product of place. "Scots were the model but not the template," claimed Johann.

J. HAIDER SINGLE MALT 46%

Haider makes three different rye whiskies, all of which have been very successful. They make two single malts. J. Haider Single Malt Whisky 46% is made from 100% barley malt. Johann reasons that lightly roasting the malt allows caramel tones to emerge, while coffee-caramel tones emerge when the malt is dark roasted.

This barley is light roasted and subsequently smoked with peat. The whiskey is then aged six years in Austrian Manhartsberger summer oak, non-chill filtered. Smoke and light caramel tones come through. Tasting notes include "slightly tart, malty caramel on the palate."

J. HAIDER DARK SINGLE MALT 41%

The other single malt they produce is J. Haider Dark Single Malt Whisky 41%. On this whisky. Haider roasts the barley longer, looking for more of the chocolate and coffee flavors. And then this whisky is aged for six years in Austria oak formerly used to store sweet white wines. Not filtered cold. "Smoky and very intense caramel notes."

BY ANGELO CAPUANO

REISETBAUER Brand

Reisetbauer is a distillery in Austria that produces brandy and whisky. Nein, that is not typo, I did say Austria! In 1995, Reisetbauer started distilling malt whisky that was designed to be (and is) distinctly Austrian. The barley used to make the wash is grown on the distillery owner's ten acres of land, and once the wash is distilled, the new make spirit is matured in Chardonnay and Trockenbeerenauslese casks sourced exclusively from Austrian vineyards and used by Austrian winemakers Alois Kracher and Heinz Velich. Just in case you are wondering how on Earth to pronounce Trockenbeerenauslese, it is TROCK-en-BEHR-en-OWS-layzeh. Quite a mouthful, but as Austrian-sounding as Schwarzenegger.

Reisetbauer's use of Austrian Chardonnay and Trockenbeerenauslese casks to mature their whisky is a breath of fresh air in an industry dominated by whisky aged in the bourbon casks, sherry casks, or port casks. Wine casks are certainly becoming increasingly popular for aging or finishing whisky, but the use of Trockenbeerenauslese casks by Reisetbauer is something particularly special. This is because Trockenbeerenauslese is a notoriously expensive dessert wine that is made from grapes that, once affected by a form of fungus known as "noble rot," are individually selected and handpicked one by one. Shriveled and raisin-like from the "noble rot," the grapes produce a wine with an intensely sweet and rich flavor.

REISETBAUER SINGLE MALT WHISKY 7 YEAR OLD 43%

Nose: Immediately floral notes appear, in particular potpourri and wilted rose petals, intermingling with chili dark hot chocolate and a foamy scented soap alongside a burning wax candle and undertones of vanilla. In typical Reisetbauer fashion, this whisky delivers such a unique bouquet that shifts its form as it rests in the glass. The floral and soapy notes soften as the whisky rests, and out

comes fabric, gym socks, and leather boxing mitts with sweet brandied orange segments dusted in cocoa and green peppercorns. Then a nuttiness develops, almost roasted chestnuts but not quite, as the chocolate theme continues but in the form of milk chocolate coated hazelnuts. The spritz of lime sits in the background, flickering gently but never really competing with the other aromas. With some more time, cherry ripe appears—coconut, dark chocolate and dried cherries—with notes of white wine that become more pronounced with each sniff.

Palate: Find chocolate, vanilla, honey, caramel, mars bar and mixed berries on the entry, and then coconut, hints of wood, and a quick shimmer of floral scented soap at mid-palate, which quickly fades into the finish. Also midway through, the berries become darker and slightly sour for a moment, but then a sweetness takes over. On the finish the whisky sweetens with syrupy and sappy sugars, cherry chocolate liqueur and ice cream sticks with a powdery note similar to vanilla and strawberry protein powder and nutmeg. That would make Arnie happy, no doubt! Consider it! Reisetbauer 7 year old struck me as a whisky with a nice balance that took me on an interesting roller coaster ride of flavors. It is less herbal than the Reisetbauer 12 year old, but an enjoyable whisky that showcases the unique way whisky can develop in Austrian wine casks to produce some delicious flavors—especially honey, floral, caramel, powdery, and berry notes. It may, as a result, have some flavors that whisky drinkers are not commonly used to...but that isn't a reason to snub this excellent Austrian whisky. Give it a go.

AC

REISETBAUER SINGLE MALT WHISKY 12 YEAR OLD 48%

The bouquet offers considerable depth and a rich herbal smokiness that immediately indicates that this whisky is very special and unique—the aroma of raspberries, cranberries, forest undergrowth, dry berry bushes, shiitake mushrooms, green olives, hazelnuts, water chestnuts, chocolate licorice bullets, pistachio baklava, and sweet vanillas sit over the most curious savory and sweet herbal notes that carry a whiff of astringent dryness. On the palate, the whisky is beautifully balanced with a tug of war breaking out between sweet and dry, no doubt the result of the Trockenbeer-enauslese casks, and then wisps of smoke drift over crumbling dried herbs and hard herbal candy, cranberries, red berry compote, hazelnuts, earthy snow pea shoots, anise, fennel, oyster sauce, Chinese mushrooms, and chocolate.

On the finish, the herbal notes remain with hints of cough syrup and drying prune notes at the top of the tongue.

Overall, the Reisetbauer 12 year old is an extraordinary whisky that is unmistakably Austrian. Being aged in Austrian Chardonnay and Trockenbeerenauslese casks, this whisky is infused with aromas and flavors that will not be easily found in the vast majority of other whiskies on the market. Get the flavor profile of Scotch, Irish, or even Japanese whisky out of your head. This is something very different, and yet intriguing, and downright delicious! Its deep rich herbal smokiness with fascinating umami undertones is certainly something to be experienced. I'm already salivating for more. Reisetbauer 12 year old is definitely a whisky to try before you die.

AC

WIESER "UUAHOUUA" PINOT NOIR CASK SINGLE MALT WHISKY 7 YEAR OLD 40%

The Wachau (an UNESCO World Heritage Site) is the beautiful valley of the Danube River between the cities of Melk and Krems, Austria, approximately 50 miles away from Vienna. *National Geographic* magazine listed it among the 110 best historic places around the world. Since Roman times, families have farmed stone terraced vineyards and orchards here. Grüner Veltliner, a white wine grape, and apricots are especially prized from this region.

Johanna and Markus Wieser are both descendants of long established wine-growing families. The Wiesers' apricot products, such as dried, sugar-coated, roasted, cooked as jam, processed into fruit nectars, apricot liqueur, and more, are well known throughout Austria.

But Markus and Johanna also wanted to expand the reach of the family farm, and have made bitters, aperitifs, gin, brandy, rum, and now whisky, which they branded as WIESky.

Markus began learning the craft of distilling in the late 1980s in his grandfather's distillery. By the 1990s, he was already playing and experimenting with whisky ideas. He saw no need to copy Scottish, American, Irish, or Japanese whisky. That made no sense to him. His idea was to re-interpret whiskies, but to create something that reflected the place where they were being made. One

of the results is Wieser "Uuahouua" Pinot Noir Cask Single Malt Whisky. The water for the whisky comes from their own bedrock wells. The whisky is stored in classic sherry and port casks, as well as red and Süßweinfässern barrels. This is a seven year old whisky aged in old Pinot Noir barrels. "Uuahouua" (pronounced Wachowa) means showers. Hints of cherry and Pinot Noir on the nose. "Fruity and velvety… Feminine wine tones paired with masculine Single Malt."

WEINGUT AICHINGER

AICHINGER WHEAT SINGLE MALT WHISKY 13 YEAR OLD 41%

A very unusual whisky, the 13 year old Aichinger whisky from Hartkirchen, Austria. What makes it unusual is its specific character as a Wheat Single Malt Whisky. While the classical single malt whiskies, as they are known from Scotland and Ireland, have been distilled from malted barley, the Aichinger 13 relies only on malted wheat. It is not so unusual to use wheat in the whisky production, but normally it is used in the making of so-called grain whiskies, which by no means are made from 100% malted wheat and thus play in a lower league. Compared to malted barley, wheat turns out to be considerably milder and softer, so that the cask character in this spirit is even more noticeable.

Also the maturation process of this whisky is interesting, since it was maturing in formerly wine-bearing barrique casks. The manufacturer Aichinger normally produces wine and is now keeping up with the times by producing whisky. However, the number of available bottles is still relatively low (13 years ago, today's whisky demand was certainly not anticipatable in the current magnitude) so that the Aichinger is no longer available anywhere. So you have to be a little bit lucky in order to get your hands on one of those bottles. Mine is already almost empty. There is also a "younger brother," the eight year old Aichinger Wheat Single Malt—but this one has also become quite rare.

The whisky comes at 41% alcohol and it is not artificially colored. However, it is chill-filtered, which apparently is intended to emphasize the soft notes of wheat. (This is also unusual, especially since there is still an extra word on this on the bottle. Many Scots try to hide the information of a chill filtration process and you won't find many confessions of this sort on Scotch Single Malt bottles)

Nose: strong and fruity notes from the wine casks but not in the style of a fruit brandy (or "Obstler," a German schnapps) like you can scent it in many continental whiskies, which are mostly made by distilleries that usually produce such fruit brandies. Vanilla and fine spices in the background. Relatively mild and soft, but with a full cargo of dark, fruity tones.

Palate: surprisingly pungent with spicy oak notes; once again vanilla and slight hints of chocolate. Again vinous fruit. Long and smooth.

SK

BELGIUM

BY CARLO DEVITO

Belgium, as most people already know, has a long and proud beer-brewing heritage. Belgian ales, especially Trappist ales, have been the gold standard in the beer world for centuries. From saisons to lambics, and so forth, the range has been deep and wide. These beers, which are highly sought after, can be drunk immediately, but many collectors instead prefer to cellar them. Belgium also has a long history of winemaking. There are five main winemaking regions marked with appellations d'origine contrôlées (AOCs), and Flemish sparkling wines have won generations of fans.

Jenever (colloquially known in English-speaking countries as Dutch gin) is the traditional spirit of the Netherlands and Belgium. A Juniper-infused spirit, this is the distilled progenitor from which gin evolved. It is produced by distilling malt wine. So there is a centuries-old distilling industry in Belgium that has absolutely embraced the whole notion of whisky-making. Only good things can happen when distilleries this experienced are unleashed on a new course. Belgian whisky is on the rise.

THE BELGIAN OWL DISTILLERY

BY MATT CHAMBERS & KAREN TAYLOR

The Belgian Owl is a single malt whisky that was the first to be produced in Belgium. The Belgian Owl distillery is located in the town of Grâce Hollogne, near the city of Liege, and was founded by Etienne Bouillon, who also owns a fruit liqueur distillery and business named Lambicool. The distillery was originally named Pure and the company was set up in 1997 by Bouillon and two partners, although the first spirit did not flow until October 2004. The name was later changed to The Belgian Owl Distillery—the name being chosen as the owl symbolizes wisdom.

The barley for the whisky-making is grown in the fields around Liege and the malting, mashing, and fermen-tation processes take part in an old converted farm on the city's outskirts. The fermented wash is then transferred to the distillery for its double distillation, before the new spirit is put in to first fill ex-bourbon casks and then matured. The single malt is matured for three years and then bottled in small batches at 46% ABV. The current annual production capacity is approximately 50,000 liters and the bottling program has five batches of single malt released each year. They also release new make spirit and part-matured spirit within their range. The Belgian Owl is currently only sold in Belgium, France, Germany, Holland, and Sweden, with the single malt selling for around €45-50 for a 50cl bottle.

THE BELGIAN OWL SINGLE MALT
3 YEAR OLD 46%

The color of this three year old Belgian Owl single malt whisky is a pale gold. The nose is delicate and subtle with some lovely fresh aromas coming through—think of crisp green pears, vanilla, honey, lemon zest, and more fresh fruit, this time reminiscent of greengages and unripe plums. These light, fresh aromas are backed up by increasingly distinct notes of malty cereal grains and dried grasses (imagine hay especially). On the palate, this whisky is tangy and very light to begin with. Here, the three main descriptors are distinct cereals, grassy, and fresh green fruits—these manifest themselves in notes of very malty/gristly barley, hay/straw, and green pear/greengage respectively. With time, the characteristics grow to include honey, vanilla, lemon zest, and some hot, tangy spiciness (think of chilli-like heat). This heat carries on into the finish, which is quite lively and zingy. The sweeter elements (honey and vanilla especially) appear, and then fade to leave some pleasant dryness.

This is a lovely, tangy, refreshing, and mouthwatering dram that would be perfect as an aperitif or on a hot day. The whisky shows plenty of very good characteristics, considering its young age, and stands up very well to its contemporaries from other new distilleries. It will certainly be interesting to see how the Belgian Owl whiskies taste in any future older releases and with further maturation. We thank our friend James Grant, who bought us back a small sample of The Belgian Owl single malt from a recent trip to Belgium.

MC & KT

HET ANKER BREWERY/
DE MOLENBERG DISTILLERY

BY RUBEN LUYTEN

Gouden Carolus is a highly respected beer from brewery Het Anker in Mechelen, Belgium. Besides a family brewing tradition spanning five generations, the family also distilled genever in a nearby village (actually almost in the backyard of my home).

This mill and later distillery, called De Molenberg, was renovated and in 2010, two pot stills were installed, custom made by Forsyths in Rothes. At that time it was the first pot still distillery in Belgium following Scottish traditions. Scotsmen Harry Cockburn (former manager of Bowmore) and Dr. James Swan (who helped to design

whiskies for Penderyn and Kavalan, among others) helped to define the processes.

I've had a quick chat with Charles Leclef, the owner of the brewery, and he stresses the fact that he wants to reach a wide audience of different experience levels, not just connoisseurs. Also he doesn't want to be bound by Scottish maturation traditions. For now, there are no plans for a range of a 5 year old, 10 year old, etc. New expressions are possible but long maturation is not a must.

GOUDEN CAROLUS SINGLE MALT WHISKY 46%

You may remember another Gouden Carolus single malt released in 2009. That was a totally different whisky, made in column stills at the Filliers genever distillery and matured in Jim Beam casks. A slightly quirky whisky.

The new one is produced in their own pot stills, matured in first-fill bourbon barrels with a finish in recharred (virgin) casks. Remember it's made from basically the triple beer mash, but without the hops and aromatics. It's just over three years old and bottled unchill-filtered and natural color in 50cl bottles.

Nose: Attractive nose, despite the obvious youth. Fruity notes (apricot jam and apples), moving to fruit gums and eventually also nice Guimauve / marshmallow notes. There's a slight Irishness to it. Quite some vanilla. Scented wax candles. Hints of fresh oak shavings as well. Slightly ahead of its age, good.

Palate: Full-flavored, very malty, still quite fruity, although there is also a slightly harsh grainy note (which may disappear with some extra years). Vanilla, soft ginger, and pepper. Medium-long, drying with the oak moving forward. Nutmeg and vanilla.

This new Gouden Carolus single malt is better than I expected. The obvious beer notes of the previous release are gone and replaced by classic malty notes and spiced fresh oak influence. Promising.

RL

CANADA

BY DAVIN DE KERGOMMEAUX

Canada has a long and, until recently, mostly unlucky history making single malt whisky. In the nineteenth century, Hiram Walker distillery and two Perth, Ontario, distilleries—John McLaren's and Spalding & Stewart—had some early success but ultimately could not compete with Canada's signature whisky: rye. So, when Bruce Jardine established Glenora, a Scottish-style malt distillery, in the kilted heart of Nova Scotia's Cape Breton Island, no one was surprised that he soon faced financial difficulties. Current owner Lauchie MacLean turned things around by promoting the Glenora Inn and Distillery as an upscale tourist destination. Twenty-five years on, their Glen Breton single malt sells well in Canada and abroad.

Two decades after Glenora began, and nearly 4,000 miles west in Campbell River, British Columbia, farmer Patrick Evans fired up two copper pot stills in Canada's second active Scottish-style distillery. He calls his distillery Shelter Point. Evan's 4 year old single malt is just mature enough now for bottling. Tourism also plays a significant role in Shelter Point's business.

The micro-distilling phenomenon that is transforming people's ideas of whisky in America has its counterpart in Canada too. The best known is Still Waters distillery in Concord, Ontario, on the northern fringe of Toronto. Forewarned by the fate of Canada's early malt whisky makers, Still Waters' initial focus on making Scotch-style single malt has broadened in recent years to keep pace with resurgent interest in rye whisky. In addition to malts, they now produce very respectable 100% rye and corn whiskies as well as single malt vodka.

Several dozen micro-distilleries have opened since Still Waters, and more than half a dozen of these produce malt whisky. The most successful is Pemberton distillery in British Columbia where Heriot-Watt-trained Tyler Schramm makes single malt whisky from British Colombia-grown organic barley. Organic and local are keywords in BC where at least half a dozen others are following Schramm's lead.

More than thirty micro-distilleries operate in Canada now, and that number increases regularly. Most, however, are focusing on vodka, gin, and fruit spirits that are not constrained by Canada's three-year aging whisky law, and so, can generate cash flow almost as soon as they are distilled.

BREWERS CASK SINGLE MALT WHISKY 46.1% (AGING, RELEASE DATE TBA)

In 2013, after ten years brewing craft beer, Central City began distilling spirits—gin, vodka, malt whisky, and rye. Although not legally whisky yet in December 2015 when I tasted barrel 17 (distilled October 2013), their Brewers Cask malt spirit showed its brewing heritage in a balanced range of malty and nutty flavors.

The waxy nose shows barley sugar and vague fruits. Creamy vanilla fudge and Werther's caramels precede spicy pepper on the palate. Very respectable young whisky that shows promise. If reviews were emoticons, this one would be a happy face.

DK

GLENORA INN & DISTILLERY

BY DAVIN DE KERGOMMEAUX

It is 25 years since Bruce Jardine began distilling Scottish-style single malt whisky in the distant hinterlands of Canada's most Scottish Cape Breton Island. This act of homage paid by their ex-patriate cousins did not amuse the Scotch Whisky Association, which sued to stop them.

Sadly, Jardine passed away before his distillery could launch its Glen Breton single malt, leaving new owner, Lauchie MacLean to bring Jardine's dream to fruition. Early bottlings of a 6 year old whisky were a bit rough. "We had bad advice in the beginning," distillery manager Donnie Campbell explains. Frigid Canadian winters in unheated warehouses slow the matu-ration process. The distillery eventually hit its stride with the release of a 10 year old version that has become its flagship. The oldest Glen Breton, a succulent 25 year old released in 2015, comes from those very first distillations. Another, finished in local icewine barrels, sports varying age statements.

According to Campbell, each batch differs, so people should not expect a rigidly uniform flavor profile. Watching a party of four hand-filtering newly disgorged spirit through coffee filters in a converted Quonset hut, you get the picture. Hand-crafted from start to finish.

GLEN BRETON RARE 10 YEAR OLD
SINGLE MALT WHISKY 40%

Cape Breton sits off the coast of Nova Scotia, a Scottish enclave in the most Scottish of Canadian provinces. The secrets for making malt whisky flow in their Scottish veins.

Although each batch of Glenora's flagship 10 year old is different, soft floral notes, grassy barley, and orchard fruit characterize them all. "Lupins and red apples," is how manager Donnie Campbell describes Glen Breton single malt. A mild soapiness found in some early releases has given way over the years to a pleasingly grassy, grain-forward malt whisky.

DK

Malt and Moose at
Canada's Glenora Distillery

BY KEITH ALLISON

They were an exceedingly fit, good-looking couple of border guards, and in typical Canadian fashion, terribly sorry about the wait. I suspected that crossing the border by car at Calais/Saint Stephen, laden with camping gear and the sundry accoutrements of a long road trip, would require a little extra time. I didn't anticipate still more time being added when an eighteen-years past record of an arrest complicated the process and necessitated a little extra attention being paid to my vehicle. Nor did I anticipate the discovery of contraband weaponry in my car in the form of a stun gun that had been abandoned and forgotten for years, sans power source, under one of the seats. It was a Christmas stocking stuffer from my mother, I explained, who had decided my outdoor hobbies put me at risk of being mauled by a bear.

As the customs agents mulled over my sad sack of a story, I had time to do work that probably should have already been done to plan this drive — as well as contemplate the alternatives should they turn me away at the border or haul me off to do whatever it is they do with hardened criminals. (What is it? Like, three weeks hard labor on a maple syrup farm?) Though I figured my case at the border would be better served by highlighting my interest in the natural wonders of Canada and the rich history of Nova Scotia, my end goal was actually what it usually is when I set out on a trip – whisky.

One of the most unique whiskies being made in Canada is distilled at the northern tip of Nova Scotia, in the tiny town of Mabou—Glenora Distillery. Only the whole of New Brunswick and Nova Scotia and the graces of a couple of suspicious border guards stood between me and a drive up the coast to the distillery. Founded in 1989 by local businessman Bruce Jardine, the goal at Glenora was to celebrate the close cultural ties between Scotland and "New Scotland," Nova Scotia. The distillery was even built in Inverness County. Jardine sought guidance from the distillers and managers at the Islay distillery of Bowmore and, armed with Scottish equipment and instruction, set out to make Canada's first single malt whisky.

Unfortunately, Jardine learned firsthand what many young distilleries have since learned: the overhead for making whisky—good, aged whisky—is massive, and it can be nearly a decade before you start to see any return on the investment. Glenora first brought on Nova Scotian and businessman Gary Widmeyer, and then later another local businessman, Lauchie MacLean, to keep the distillery operational. Complicating the financial issues was the wrath of Scotland's Scotch Whisky Association, the body that enforces international trade agreements and standards. The SWA took umbrage at Glenora's use of the word "glen" in their name, which the SWA considered to be Scottish property despite its widespread use. In the end, Glenora prevailed in an extended legal battle, and in 2000, Glen Breton Rare became North America's first single malt whisky. Sadly, Bruce Jardine was not there to see the culmination of the dream for which he fought so long and so hard. He passed away in 1999, leaving the distillery in the capable hands of Bob Scott.

When I learned about them while trying to decide on a summer road trip, my destination quickly solidified. Despite the special attention of border guards and my inadvertent new career as a weapons smuggler, we eventually made the long drive from New York City to the northernmost tip of Nova Scotia successfully, where on the outskirts of the majestic and awe-inspiring Cape Breton Highlands sits modest little Glenora.

It is an exceedingly "Canadian" experience, not just because an up-close encounter with a wandering moose is practically guaranteed. Arriving in mid-June, I found the distillery and its on-site inn scrambling to prepare for a sudden visit. Lesson learned — tourist season in northern Nova Scotia really doesn't start until July. After checking into a clean, non-descript room (the on-premises restaurant was not yet open for the season), I was given a tour of the distillery itself—a tour which consisted of a groundskeeper/distiller opening the door to the tiny stillhouse (which was not producing that day), then leaving me to my own devices, asking me to please close the door and lock up when I was finished. That included a tasting, self-serve and similarly lacking in a chaperone. That casual trust continued later in the night, when the last employee left for the evening and gave us a number to call in case we needed anything—leaving me alone with a distillery and an open warehouse full of quietly aging Canadian single malt whisky. I suppose they count heavily on honesty and, failing that, the difficulty of anyone stealing a 500 pound barrel of whisky.

While the distillery "tour" may be slightly lacking, the whisky itself is quite nice. Since launching their flagship single malt, Glenora has released several other products, including a cask strength version and an expression of their single malt finished in barrels previously used to age icewine. Glen Breton Rare, aged 10 years and at an ABV of 43% stands, perhaps not surprisingly, somewhere between the light, sweet character of more traditional Canadian whisky and the maltier, more substantial character of a Speyside Scotch. The nose is light, a bit floral, and dominated by oatmeal, honey, and cream. The taste boasts an initial attack of floral, grassy notes that slowly open to red fruit, crème brûlée, sour cherries and bread pudding. Through it all, it remains light, with a short, but pleasant finish. Early reviews complained of a soapy quality to the whisky, but that has since been tamed and eliminated, leaving a thoroughly enjoyable—if somewhat expensivev—dram.

In a way, the distillery's whisky can almost become secondary to the surroundings, the impetus that launches rather an amazing trip. Its location is an excellent launching point for an exploration of the wild Canadian north. Hikes through the Cape Breton Highlands National Park afford sweeping views of surrounding hills, valleys, and moors and the deep blue of the Gulf of St. Lawrence. A longer drive takes you down gravel roads to the isolated town of Meat Cove. Nearby amenities are minimal, but Glenora is there to offer a truly adventurous, remote notch in the belt of any whisky traveler. It may not be the most educational or immersive whisky experience, but one would be hard-pressed to find one more striking, remote, and memorable.

Just leave the stun guns at home.

SINGLE MALT WHISKY

Before Vancouver distiller Gordon Glanz began making whisky, he studied brewing and distilling at Edinburgh's Heriot-Watt University. He prefers barley grown locally, in Prince George, British Columbia, and then made into "pale malt" in the Okanagan Valley. After fermentation he distills his wort in pot stills.

At two years and two months, the spirit is alive with flavor and richly colored. Fruity esters, acetone (good), stewed prunes, and hints of grain characterize a surprisingly mature nose. On the palate, stewed fruit, sweet tobacco, hot but tempered pepper, and hints of vanilla fudge lead into a long spicy finish.

DK

LAIRD OF FINTRY LIMITED RELEASE
SINGLE MALT WHISKY 40%

Since 2007, Okanagan Distillery has contracted a local brewery to ferment enough British Columbia–grown barley for one barrel per year of whisky. When 210 bottles of their "Laird of Fintry" single malt were finally ready in 2013, unanticipated consumer enthusiasm for the whisky led them to boost annual production to 12 barrels.

Laird of Fintry's youthful vigor could use more rounding in wood. Still, its cooked orchard fruits, peppery spices, nutty grains, and rich oak caramels are a gustatory delight. Vanilla fudge, ripe fruits, and a slight oakiness linger into a medium finish.

DK

PEMBERTON DISTILLERY

BY DAVIN DE KERGOMMEAUX

About an hour north of Vancouver, in the Pemberton Valley, the Schramms distil a variety of spirits from organic potatoes, fruits, and malted barley. With glacial water from the nearby Coast Range Mountains, and traditional hands-on processing in shiny copper stills, their white spirits have won many awards, just as their single malts are beginning to as they reach maturity.

PEMBERTON VALLEY ORGANIC SINGLE MALT WHISKY 44%

What happens when a ski bum goes to school? If it's Tyler Schramm and the school is Heriot-Watt University in Edinburgh, you get world-class authentic potato vodka, and five years later, when it's ready, a promising single malt whisky made with local, organic barley.

The glowing golden hue of the 5 year old whisky reviewed here speaks of active barrel aging, while a slight haze indicates the whisky was not chill filtered. Linseed oil and a grassy waxiness on the nose precede sweetness, malt, and searing hot pepper on the palate. It's delicious now; it will be sensational in five more years.

DK

More on the Master
Distiller Tyler Schramm

"I was never really a whisky guy," Master Distiller Tyler Schramm told *Pique News-magazine,* as he poured a dram of lightly peated, 2012 Canadian single malt, single cask whisky from Pemberton Distillery. "But it only took one session with some teenage whisky lovers and I was in."

More than 200 people were wait-listed when Tyler and Pemberton announced they were going to be bottling a 2010 single malt whisky. According to the newspaper, the list accounted for two-thirds the barrel!

Pemberton Distillery is located in Pemberton, British Columbia, an area known as "Spud Valley," thanks to the region's highly touted potatoes. Tyler and Lorien Schramm established Pemberton Distillery in the fall of 2008, and began operations in June of 2009. Pemberton is known for focusing on sourcing locally grown ingredients. The idea is to create spirits with terroir. From mashing to fermentation, to distillation, all of Pemberton's spirits are completely produced on site. Pemberton Distillery is unique because its entire line is certified organic, one of the few distilleries to be able to claim that in the world.

"Whisky was always part of the plan. I knew with potatoes, we'd only have a season with them, and then we'd have a season where there was a gap," Tyler told *Food GPS* in an interview. "When I went over to Scotland, I was not that interested in whisky, especially single malts, and I guess one of the unique things about being in Scotland is the university I was at had a single malt whisky club that was run by the students and funded by the Student Association. Every Friday, they would get four bottles. There was an undergraduate program as well as the Master's program, and the undergraduates were in charge of the Single Malt Whisky Club, and a couple of them worked in some of the bigger whisky stores in Edinburgh, and they would buy four special bottles of whisky, and I decided to join. Pretty much the first Friday that I went, I fell in love with whisky. Early on, it became part of the plan to do a whisky as well as the vodka. They worked well with each other."

CD

SHELTER POINT DISTILLERY

SINGLE MALT WHISKY 46% (AGING, RELEASE DATE TBA)

Were it not for the gleaming copper stills and churning fermenters, this authentic Scottish-style distillery might remind you of an upscale hunting lodge with its leather chairs and comfortable lounge.

At four years, the whisky smells like a young bourbon-cask matured Speyside single malt. Still a bit harsh on the nose, it is mellow and creamy on the palate with soft spices, creamy barley, dry grain—like birdseed—and a soft citrus chocolate aura. There is more grain than wood on the nose and palate, a promise that, in time, it will blossom.

DK

STALK & BARREL
SINGLE MALT 62.3%

With indoor aging and careful selection of prime, first-fill bourbon barrels, Still Waters consistently produces 3 year old whiskies mature beyond their years. While Stalk & Barrel shows the eagerness of youth, its fruity, nutty flavors have mellowed splendidly in the barrel. Begin with sweet, poached pears, marzipan, juicy fruit gum, and apple pie. Add sweet ripe cherries, wet hay, wet clay, and earthy rye. Now sprinkle on grain dust, halva, cream of wheat, mellow hot white pepper, cinnamon, nutmeg, and ginger. Finally, bring a silky, buttery mouthfeel to a sweet, fruity medium finish. There you have craftsmanship: Still Waters.

DK

STILL WATERS DISTILLERY,
VAUGHAN, ONTARIO

When the first drops of Still Waters malt spirit flowed from their pot still in March 2009, Barry Stein and Barry Bernstein had revived two Ontario traditions. They became Ontario's first micro-distillers in over a century, and they rekindled the pioneering spirit that turned a vast wilderness into a thriving province.

The trails they blazed did not surmount the perpendicular escarpments, impenetrable forests, and raging rivers that disheartened so many of Ontario's early settlers. However, navigating the province's uncharted liquor regulations was a journey every bit as tortuous. Every Ontario micro-distiller who has followed owes them a debt of gratitude.

Still Waters Distillery makes single malt vodka and bulk gin. They keep the legers balanced. But Barry and Barry never take their eye off the ball. Their focus is whisky. They are long-time single malt fans and making great single malt whisky in Canada is their goal. They must feel considerable satisfaction then, knowing that just seven years after that first spirit flowed, Whisky Magazine named Still Waters one of the three top craft whisky producers in the world in their 2016 Icons of Whisky awards.

DK

URBAN DISTILLERY

BY DAVIN DE KERGOMMEAUX

URBAN DISTILLERIES

Kelowna is the capital of the Canada's Okanagan fruit and wine valley. There, the multi-award winning Urban Distillery has been turning local barley into single malt whisky in its German-made copper Holstein still since 2011. A wealth of fruit-based spirits round out the product line.

URBAN SINGLE MALT WHISKY 40%

After partially maturing his single malt spirit in barrels, Mike Urban bottles it, placing a small piece of a toasted oak barrel stave in each bottle. This changes the balance between flavors that come from the barrel breathing in oxygen and those derived from the wood itself. You remove the wood when the whisky suits your tastes, making each bottle, and possibly each drink, unique. Sipped right after bottling, Urban single malt is rich in grain flavors. As time goes by, the French oak asserts its woodiness and oak tannins. It's geeky fun that you can drink.

DK

BY DAVIN DE KERGOMMEAUX

What a treat to find micro-distillers willing to wait for their whisky to mature before releasing it. For Two Brewers Distillery of Whitehorse, in Canada's Yukon Territory, this meant waiting seven years. Their success as beer makers had taught Bob Baxter and Alan Hansen that quality doesn't happen in a hurry.

Expanding their brewery to include a distillery began in 2009 with a focus on making single malt. We all know what that is, right? Well, maybe not. These guys were brewers first and without a still to distract them, they learned a lot about creating flavor during fermentation. The result is spectacular. They begin with a range of different mashes made from a variety of malted grains and a range of roasting options. Barley malt? Yes. Chocolate malt? Yes. Rye malt? Yes, that too. They bring a whole collection of new options to making single malt whisky, then they blend their finished whiskies together to create wonderfully flavorful, multi-layered drams. These are offered in four ranges—classic, special finishes, peated, and innovative. Truly world-class whisky from North of 60.

TWO BREWERS YUKON SINGLE MALT RELEASE 1 (CLASSIC) 46%

Sweet, malty, fresh, and clean on the nose with all kinds of enticing flavor suggestions. Fruit salad, peaches and cream, and gentle caramels combine with honeycomb, spicy hints, and gentle oaky tannins on the finish. Excellent whisky.

DK

CZECH REPUBLIC

BY CARLO DEVITO

If the Czech Republic is known for anything, it is known as the home and place of origin of Pilsner beer. While the city of Pilsen has brewed beer since 1295, the golden lager of Pilsner Urquell was first brewed in 1840. Czech-styled Pilsner is considered one of the great game changers in the history of the art of brewing.

The Moravia region is known as the wine capital of the Czech Republic. Wineries (Vinarna) are famous for producing white wines such as Müller-Thurgau and Riesling, and reds such as Frankovka and Modry Portugal. During the cold season, Svarak, a hot wine like mulled wine, is also popular.

In the Czech Republic, there are three popular, traditional spirits: Becherovka, Fernet Stock, and Slivovitz. The first two are herbal-infused spirits, popular as much for their taste as for their purported medicinal or digestive use. Slivovitz is a plum-based and/or plum-infused strong spirit. The industry varies, producing versions from a lighter alcoholic base to a more potent one.

Distillers here are excited about the new opportunities whisky offers them and the public is curious to try these new products. There are high hopes here.

PRADLO DISTILLERY

BY GAVIN D. SMITH

Whisky distilleries have been springing up in some unlikely places during the past few years; from Sweden to Switzerland, and Tasmania to Thailand. But who knew that twenty-one years ago, the Communist old guard was distilling single malt in Czechoslovakia?

The whisky in question is called Hammerhead, and was made in 1989, just before the fall of the Berlin Wall, which changed Eastern Europe forever. It was produced in the Pradlo distillery in western Czechoslovakia, which had been making pot still spirits for many years before experimenting with making single malt whisky.

During the 1980s, the distillery was still a nationalized enterprise, and a decision was made to emulate the decadent capitalists of Scotland and create a high quality malt whisky. It is believed to be the only Bohemian single malt whisky in the world!

Hammerhead is available from Stock Spirits, who purchased the distillery without knowing that the whisky even existed. The company's Tony Roberts explained that, "With great effort Pradlo distillery was able to acquire and install a traditional cast iron hammer mill. Built in 1928, the mill was the same style and make as those found in most traditional Scottish distilleries at the time.

To create the whisky, the distillery selected only Czech barley and the crisp, clean water from the Bohemia region. The whisky was aged in unique oak casks made of 100 percent Czech oak wood, producing a single malt whisky unique to the world.

"In late 1989 the Wall fell and the whisky was forgotten, left to sleep in the cellars in its unique casks for twenty years. Although the whisky was maintained, it was only recently that the true quality of the whisky was rediscovered."

HAMMERHEAD SINGLE MALT WHISKY 21 YEAR OLD 1989 40.7%

Hammerhead offers an initially dry, roasted nut nose, with developing cream soda. Becoming more floral and perfumed with time, plus a note of furniture polish. More leather with the addition of water, and a hint of warm, rubber diving suits.

Very drinkable, with well-integrated spices, dried fruits and worn leather. Ultimately licorice and oak. Tobacco notes at the last, with the addition of water.

GS

RUDOLF JELINEK

BY CARLO DEVITO

Distilling has been a tradition in the town of Vizovice since the sixteenth century. The region was known especially for producing fruit brandies that have been known the world over, the most popular being Slivovitz (plum brandy). Rudolf Jelínek a.s. was founded in 1894. They produce vodka, fruit brandies, and other distilled spirits. It is the most popularly distributed and purchased brand in the Czech Republic. Their products can also be found around the world. They have been importing to the United States, for example, since the early 1930s. The company was nationalized in 1948, and then placed back into private hands by 1994. In 1994, R. Jekínek USA was established.

GOLD COCK 12 YEAR OLD SINGLE MALT WHISKY 43%

Gold Cock is the oldest brand of single malt whisky in the Czech Republic. Originally produced by Distillery Dolany, it is now produced by Rudolf Jelínek. They start with Moravian barley, malt it, peat it, and store the young whisky in Bohemian oak barrels for twelve years. There is also a three year old blended whisky and a twenty-two year old single malt whisky. It is the most popularly distributed single malt whisky in the Czech Republic.

Notes of fruit brandy and citrus on the nose and palate. A big puff of peat! Finishes dry and short.

CD

DENMARK

BY CARLO DEVITO

Denmark, like other Scandinavian countries, has a history of distilling that dates back to the fifteenth century. Aquavit is very closely associated with celebrating Christmas and Easter there. There has been a new boom of small craft distillers who have decided not only to make whisky in the past two decades, but also who have taken on the mantle of single malt. Several of these distilleries in fact only produce single malt. Spirits writers have been pleasantly assaulted with a whole host of small scale and micro-scale production of single malts aged in any number of ways, from traditional American oak to whisky, bourbon, and even older, used Scotch barrels, to wine and sherry barrels. Many are made using local grain. It is very much still a nascent industry, but the signs of solid, regionally-made stable single malts is very promising!

Brænderiet Limfjorden is a small little seaside distillery. Their location is somewhat magical, as they are situated on the western pier in Sillerslev harbor, where they are completely surrounded by the Limfjord. The tiny distillery is actually placed in the middle of the breakers! Primarily they distill single malt whisky, but they also produce rum, gin, brandy, and liqueurs made from local fruits and other ingredients, ølsnapse, schnapps, and bitters. They are of the opinion that their whisky acquires a unique character as a result of their barrels being stored there at the Limfjord. They feel that the humidity and fog from the sea are essential players in this process. For their whisky, these folks use organic barley to make their mash, which is processed at Thisted Brewery (which is more than 111 years old). Brænderiet Limfjorden Peated Single Malt is a small production single malt from this small but well regarded distillery.

COPENHAGEN DISTILLERY

BY THOMAS OHRBOM

Copenhagen Distillery is a tiny distillery setup in a beautiful and rustic house on the outskirts of Copenhagen. The facilities are actually from 1749, called Bryggergården ("the brewery house"), and initially housed a pottery and tile works. Later it became the location for one of the first breweries in Copenhagen. The brewery was closed down a long time ago, but with Copenhagen Distillery there is new life in the house.

Henrik Brinks is the owner and master distiller. This is very much a one-man show, and this one man has a clear philosophy and vision for his distillery: "Driven by a desire to discover, our mission is to create spirits imbued with new flavors and experiences. We expect every sip to pleasantly surprise and catch the breath of the taster, whether from unique flavor dynamics or lingering notes on the palate. If our spirits do not both surprise and delight, they don't go in the bottle."

It was very interesting to discuss this philosophy and what this meant in practice for Henrik, because it defines everything he does. For example, he has designed his own still, and worked with a local metal shop to have it built to his exact specifications. The still has flexibility in that he can switch out bits and pieces if he wants to play around and experiment. The still is tiny though and one production batch produces twenty-five liters of alcohol.

Another consequence of his philosophy is that he has opted to only focus on distilling and maturation. This means he is sourcing the wash from different partners—wash made to his specifications.

The whisky is casked at around 72% ABV, and matured in 30 liter casks. The casks are all virgin oak, mainly from Hungary but also from Macedonia. He revealed that he will probably move to 50 liter casks in the future.

The first whisky was not yet released in time for this publication,

and will be the start of a trilogy called First ("Første"), Next ("Neste") and Last ("Siste").

I tried a couple of his 'work in progress' whiskies, and I must say, I was very impressed. Henrik certainly is true to his philosophy. What was tasted was powerful and big on nose and palate. All his whisky is unpeated spirit, but he is experimenting with the casks to get a sort of peated character to some of the spirit. He is also doing a lot of experimenting of other kinds, but those were a bit hush-hush, so you will just have to wait and see what is revealed in the future.

All in all, very interesting, certainly a bit unconventional, but thoroughly fascinating.

BY THOMAS OHRBOM

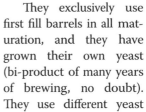

The Danish distillery Bryghuset Braunstein has been around for quite some time. For the first few years they were a brewery only, but as we entered the new millennium they started distilling whisky. Braunstein is owned and run by two brothers; Michael Dines Braunstein is the sales manager, and Claus Braunstein is the distillery manager. They have a total of eight employees, and the annual production is at around 60,000-75,000 liters of alcohol.

All their production is organic, and they would love to put out certified organic whisky. The problem is getting hold of enough certified organic oak barrels, therefore they do not label their whisky as organic.

Braunstein produces both peated and unpeated whisky. They source their peated malt from Port Ellen Maltings (60 ppm), and they say the phenol level in their peated whiskies is about 30 ppm on the bottle.

They exclusively use first fill barrels in all maturation, and they have grown their own yeast (bi-product of many years of brewing, no doubt). They use different yeast strains for the peated and the unpeated production.

The products are grouped in two series. The Library Collection typically includes two annual releases, one peated and one unpeated. Library whiskies are named YY:1 and YY:2 (YY = year of release). I've sampled the Braunstein 13:1 release, the unpeated expression released in 2013. The second series is called the Edition Series, and this is a single annual cask strength expression. The naming convention here is equally simplistic and straightforward. The Edition for 2013 was called E:5 (E:4 was released in 2012, etc.).

Braunstein whiskies are currently sold in Denmark, Sweden, and a few Asian markets in very limited numbers.

BRAUNSTEIN DANICA WHISKY DANSK 42%

Braunstein Distillery (Bryghuset Braunstein) launched their first-ever Travel Retail exclusive. The Braunstein Danica Whisky comes with no age statement, and is bottled at 42% ABV.

This product is produced in batches (of unknown size). This review is based on a bottle from Batch 2014-01. It was matured in a mix of bourbon and sherry casks.

Nose: The nose is well rounded, rich and soft. The bourbon sweetness comes through, and it is fruity and mild. I pick up a bit of milk chocolate as well. The sherry influence is hardly noticeable on the nose.

Palate: Now fruity, sugary and in general, rather sweet. Oranges mixed with a pinch of pepper and a vague hint of dark fruits. Oranges still, with more caramel added. Finally the sherry notes with the dark fruits are darker chocolate and more prominent.

A nice dram. Too bad it is only available on Travel Retail. Might have wanted it at a slightly higher ABV as well, but that is nitpicking.

TO

BRAUNSTEIN 14:1 9 YEAR OLD 46%

The Braunstein 14:1 was distilled in 2005, bottled on 2014-03-18. The whisky spent 7 years and 8 months in an Oloroso sherry cask, before receiving a little over a year to finish in a cognac cask. This is an unpeated whisky, as all the "1" releases in the Braunstein Library Collection are, whereas the "2" releases are peated.

Nose: Full, complex and rich. Leather, tobacco, chocolate, caramel, vanilla, and baked apples. I do pick up cognac notes here, sweet and slightly spiced caramel notes.

Palate: The sherry does shine

through more on the palate than it did on the nose. It is a bit dry. Lots of apples, and something that brings sushi to mind. Not at all sure what that could be, it certainly isn't anything fishy as such. Quite heavy and rich. Apples, oranges, and caramel. The finish is medium long, and quite pleasant.

A fine dram, if a bit different from previous releases I have tried from this distillery. The nose is really good.

TO

BRAUNSTEIN 14:2 46%

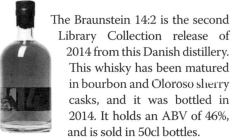

The Braunstein 14:2 is the second Library Collection release of 2014 from this Danish distillery. This whisky has been matured in bourbon and Oloroso sherry casks, and it was bottled in 2014. It holds an ABV of 46%, and is sold in 50cl bottles.

This is a medium peated whisky. The makeup of Braunstein 14:2 is peated spirit matured in bourbon casks and unpeated spirit matured in Oloroso sherry casks.

Nose: Peated, fruity and sweet. There

is a distinct note of berries on the nose, black currant, and cherries. The peatiness appears as notes of wood smoke.

Palate: Sugary and sweet. The berries are still quite prominent—mainly cherries. Mildly peaty now—more on the nose really. Dark fruits and a hint of chocolate. Sugary, soft and mild. A light peat base stays for a long while, on top of which I find mild fruitiness and chocolate notes.

A nice, sweet, dessert-like dram. Good stuff!

TO

BRAUNSTEIN CASK STRENGTH E6 61.4%

Braunstein Cask Edition no.6 was released on December 6, 2014. It was aged in a bourbon cask. This is a peated single malt, with a fruit-for-

ward appeal. Honey, vanilla, and toffee come through, as well as a dollop of peat.

TO

FARY LOCHAN DESTILLERI

BY STEFFEN BRAUNER

The wee Danish Distillery Fary Lochan is a very small distillery located in a small village called Farre. That's in central Jutland, not far from Billund (Legoland). There are two buildings; the small house is for storage and the slightly bigger one is the distillery with a small warehouse in the cellar.

It began in 2010 with the first seven casks. Owner/distiller Jens-Erik Jørgensen was supposed to use 50 liter casks but due to failed deliveries, he had to start filling "normal" 200 liter barrels. Once the quarter-casks were delivered, the plan was to empty some of the barrels into the quarter-casks, and also leave some in larger barrels for some longer time maturation. Now, as the batch size is smaller than 200 liters (around 60-70 liters) the barrels were filled step by step. Most of those barrels were partly filled. He was eager to fill some up as the official date of filling a cask would be when the last portion went in. But nosing two of these casks revealed the most intense butterscotch-fudge-toffee nose one could ever experience. He hadn't really found the reason for this. The whisky inside was between 0-4½ months old and the casks were filled to approximately 50-75% by now.

Here's another interesting thing. Jens-Erik Jørgensen said that when he received the casks, there would be quite a lot of charcoal bits inside. It looked like manufactured, charredm chipped wood. It wasn't just something that had fallen off the inside of the cask. His theory was that it was a little gift that could help the spirit mature. He removed it.

It was a very pleasant visit, with a nice guided tour by Jens-Erik, and also a chance to taste this new Danish whisky, which seemed semi-light compared to other new-makes I tried. I think these whiskies will age well. From the nose it seemed like it did unusually remarkable within a few months. Casks seemed to be good ex-bourbon casks.

MORE ABOUT FARY LOCHAN DANISH WHISKY

BY CHRIS HOBAN

When I started in the Scotch whisky experience, all those years ago, fresh faced, young, and cocky, I did my training about whisky, and suddenly, I thought I knew everything about booze. People would start saying I was a "whisky expert" (I hate this term). It's funny, because I think the more you learn and obsess about a topic (it's been over five years now I have been reading and writing about booze, pretty much every day), the more you realize you really don't know anything... If I was limited to Scotch, and the one hundred odd distilleries here (and growing), I think I would get more intimate knowledge of each distillery but lose any perspective of the business as a whole. That and Scotch does tend to follow quite a standard production process, with the odd tweak here or there. I am lucky enough that I occasionally get sent samples, which always excite me as I get to learn about something different, so it was great when the brilliant Steffen Brauner, sent me a sample of whisky from his homeland, Denmark. Here's a bit of background to Fary Lochan (if you want background on Steffen, take him for a pint).

Fary Lochan was founded by Jens-Erik Jørgensen. So far he has made around twenty-five casks a year from 2010 and onwards. Fary Lochan makes four different single-malt whiskies, named after the seasons:

Autumn: Smoked to 1.5ppm. Ex-bourbon matured, married in ex-sherry (I would call that a finish!)

Winter: Smoked to 13ppm. Ex-bourbon casks (he says he got some ex-Laphroaig casks as well)

Spring: Smoked to 7ppm. Ex-bourbon

Summer: Ex-bourbon. No smoke

Using the term smoke and not peat. The source is his own homemade smoked barley with nettles as "fuel." The undiluted homemade barley is 50ppm!

After his whisky has turned into real whisky that is at least three years old, he bottles a couple of casks a year. Most of his very small production is aimed to be older stuff but he plans to release a bottling every nine months.

FARY LOCHAN EFTERAR (AUTUMN) BATCH 1 48%

Batch 1 of Efterar, or "Autumn," was the original whisky release from Danish distillery Fary Lochan. Reportedly this was aged in quarter-casks (small barrels) for approximately three years, and then received a sherry cask finish for about five months. It was bottled at 48% ABV in 50cl bottles, and is now completely sold out.

All things considered, we hope there is a Batch 2 for Efterar, because it shows some promise. Fary Lochan bills itself as one of the smallest distilleries in Europe, and is basically a hobby project/garage business, turning out whisky in very small batches.

Like many of the best craft distilleries, Fary Lochan has made some interesting production choices, such as burning nettles to smoke their malt. Thus far the whiskies have been hit or miss, but the hits show enough to merit paying further attention, if you can get past the steep price tag, that is. In the glass, Efterar has a bronzed look, so you can tell it picked up some serious influence from the wood in a relatively short space of time. The nose struck me as being something like a whiskified Black Forest cake. Cherry and fruitcake spices mingled with a malty sweetness, a pinch of white pepper, and a tinge of pinesap. For such a young whisky, it certainly has a measure of complexity in the scent.

The flavor takes a turn into a cinnamon-based spiciness, with the sherry note once again appearing as a cherry-like flavor, with a modest ashy note coming on at the end. The palate has a good, solid body, although it isn't quite as lively as the nose. From there, the finish makes a simple and direct line to the end, packing quite a lot of warmth for the journey.

TO

FARY LOCHAN VINTER (WINTER) BATCH 1 54%

Danish distillery Fary Lochan releases its whiskies in small, three-digit batches named for the seasons, hence "Forar," or Spring, Batch 1. "Vinter" is a more obvious translation into English, and the Winter Batch 1 was a 663-bottle run of 54% ABV Danish whisky.

Perhaps the reason they named this winter has less to do with the seasons than with the degree to which the malt was smoked. Compared to Forar, Vinter has double the smoke content measured in parts per million (ppm), 15 to 7.

Yet despite that, it's a light whisky in the glass. The coloring is a light gold, and the nose isn't smoky at all. What it is a balanced scent, mixing malt and grass with honey and spices.

The smoke appears first in the palate, and gathers as the experience progresses. Smoke is the foundation upon which notes of sweet and spice sit, but so does a twinge of astringency that sits there like a chirping macaque in an Asian marketplace. An ashy aftertaste starts a finish that is as hot as it is warm, with the astringency and high alcohol content combining to make the liquid a little harsh going down.

My experience here is that this whisky shows the elements of a good foundation, but is too young and perhaps bottled at too high a proof (ABV). Winter, it seems, is not nearly as pleasant as Spring.

RT

MIKKELLER SPIRITS BOURBON CASK BLACK 43%

OK, OK, OK, so we are "cheating" a bit—again. So, technically this is not whisky, as it also contains hops. But there are still quite few Nordic whiskies, so we should be able to get away with bending the rules slightly, from time to time.

We must assume the Danish Mikkeller Brewery is well known to any beer drinkers out there. Not everyone is aware that Mikkeller also dabbles in the arts of distilling, not just whisky, but also rum, vodka, and gin.

Here's what Mikkeller themselves say about this product:

"The Mikkeller Spirits Black series is the sine qua non of Mikkeller Spirits. Here the connection between Mikkeller and Mikkeller Spirits is established. With our skilled collaborators of Braunstein Distillery we decided to distill one of our flagship beers: the Mikkeller Black. This 17.5% ABV imperial stout showed great potential for distilling. It was easy to decide that this was it; this is why we want to enter the micro-distilling world. A great beer turned into a great spirit."

Nose: Calvados and beer mixer, that's what strikes me at first. It is beer-like but at the same time very fruity, with predominantly apples in the mix. Malty. Very well rounded, but a bit odd. A slight alcohol sting, lots of apples, and also pears. It does appear quite young. There is no indication as to the age of this spirit, but it's doubtful if it is even three years old.

Palate: Sweet and smooth, with lots of fruits and pepper. The mouthfeel is rather thin. Pears and a distinctly perfume-y character. Short & sweet! Heh, take that as you like. Apples, simple syrup, and powdered sugar.

This was an odd one. Not exactly sure what to think. It wasn't bad though, just ... odd.

TO

MIKKELLER BREWERY

Mikkeller is without question the most famous phantom or gypsy brewer in the world. Why phantom? Or gypsy? Big clue: Because there is no Mikkeller Brewery! No physical such brewery exists. Two home brewers from Copenhagen, Denmark, Mikkel Borg Bjergsø, a high school teacher, and journalist Kristian Klarup Keller, founded the illusive microbrewery in 2006. Instead of buying all the equipment and investing in all the expensive infrastructure, they decided to make beers at, or with, other breweries (known as "collaborations"), and then put their label on it. They are known to make some of the most cutting edge beers in the world, and are considered the forefront of modern craft brewing. They love breaking rules and establishing new boundaries and combinations. Beer experts all over the world follow Mikkeller's exploits with a fanaticism usually reserved for Hollywood celebrities.

CD

"Hødalen" ravine was carved back during the glacial period. And that is where Anders Bilgram operates the micro-distillery Nordisk Brænderi, Northern Jutland. Bilgram, who owns and manages Nordisk, first gained experience as distiller through journeys and visits in Germany, Russia, and The Nordic countries. Anders delved furthered into the art distilling by spending more time in Southern Germany, under the tutelage of renowned distiller Herbert Rösch, who Anders acknowledges as his mentor.

Nordisk uses a handmade cobber still, and aroma column, invented by third generation manufacturer Bernd Muller, which was manufactured in Schwarzwald in Germany. Originally when Anders began production at the distillery, he used a combination of Nordic fruits, berries, and herbs to produce a unique line of brandies and schnapps. The distillery now produces those same brandies and schnapps, as well as vodka, and has been working to meet the market's demand for domestic gin, rum, and whisky.

The single malt whisky they produce is labeled "Thy."

THY WHISKY FAD NO. 1 'KRAEN KLIT' 3 YEAR OLD 60%

The man behind the distillery is Anders Bilgram. He produces gin, schnapps, and whisky. In 2013, he launched his first whisky, the "Special Edition No 1." We have not yet tried this whisky, but we have now tried the second released from Nordisk Brænderi, the Thy Whisky Fad No. 1.

Thy Whisky is the brand going forward, as the next release is also called Thy Whisky. "Fad" is Danish for cask, so this is Cask No. 1. The whisky is produced from two-row barley, grown at the Gyrup farm near the Thy National Park. The barley was floor-malted at Fuglebjerggaard Farm north of Copenhagen.

Thy Whisky Fad No. 1 is a single cask release, sold in 50cl bottles at $1250 (DKK). It was matured in a sherry cask, and the total outturn was 336 bottles.

Nose: Wow! What a perfectly lovely sherry nose! I am immediately blown away here. Very soft, very delicate—but also rich. Dried fruits, cinnamon, malt, and just a big dollop of Christmas, really. I also pick up notes of vanilla, toffee, and mint. Very nice!

Palate: Rich and full mouthfeel. Cinnamon, mild spices, and dried fruits. It feels a bit like a rich rum, really, and the hints of mint only strengthen that impression. Medium-long finish, quite warm. Caramel, dried fruits, and the mint is now more peppermint.

An impressive dram, I would say. Looking forward to try the Thy Whisky Fad No. 2A (bourbon with sherry finish) and Fad No. 2B (bourbon with bourbon finish—re-casked), and maybe we can manage to find a sample of the "Special Edition No. 1" somewhere...

TO

NYBORG DISTILLING ORBAEK BREWERY

BY CARLO DEVITO

Nyborg is a city in central Denmark, located on the island of Funen. The first mention of Nyborg was in 1193 of the Nyborg Castle, which still exists today. Nyborg was considered the capital of Denmark between 1183 and 1413, in the period when the Danehoffet, Denmark's legislative and judicial assembly, met there regularly. Christian II of Denmark, King of Denmark and Norway from 1513 to 1523, was born at Nyborg Castle. Now, it is a small town, with a beautiful harbor and surrounding area.

Nyborg Distilling is a small micro-distiller that is part of Ørbæk Brewery. Everything they make is organic, including their lines of organic gin, vodka, white rum, schnapps, coffee liqueur, and single malt whisky. Nyborg is a natural extension of the brewery. Nyborg produces its spirits distilled from the same mash and wort they use in all their brewery products at Ørbæk Brewery. They boast a patented column still that produces exceptionally pure, high-quality alcohol.

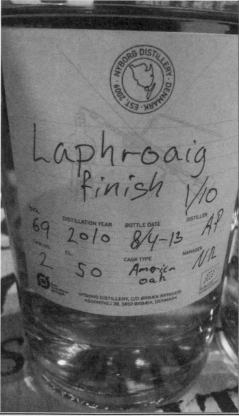

ISLE OF FIONIA —
CASK NO. 1 3 YEAR OLD 58%

This was the first whisky released from Nyborg Distillery in Denmark. They already have a further handful of releases to their name. This whisky is three years old. It was distilled in 2009, and bottled in 2012. It is organic and bottled at an ABV of 58%. It is a single cask release, with a total outturn of 362 50cl bottles. The Isle of Fionia – Cask No. 1 was matured in American white oak.

Nose: Vanilla, fudge, green apples, pears, oak, barley wine, mint, and peppermint. There is some alcohol here, giving more than just a hint of youthfulness.

Palate: Oh, boy! Fresh oak and cask strength, indeed! Very spicy, tons of vanilla, very creamy, and full mouthfeel. Mint and eucalyptus literally growing out of my ears. Hello! That was a wake-up call in a glass. Oily and warm. Medium-long finish. Tons of spiced honey and vanilla now. Quite herbal on the finish.

This certainly is a debut that packs a punch. It does feel a bit too young and immature yet, but it shows promise. Waiting for Cask No. 2 now!

TO

NYBORG DISTILLERY SHERRY FINISH ORBAEK 59%

Nose: Vanilla, just a hint of apples.

Palate: This has got apples like the bourbon-cask I tasted before this. I can't help thinking it has been pinpointed to my brain as I taste these two right after each other, because this is actually quite different. The texture and mouth-feel is different, this is a lot more full-bodied. I can't help think of cinnamoned apple pies. In a nutshell, this is apple, wood, and cinnamon. A bit fierce, but not something you would be surprised from as it's a 59% spirit. I quite like this. Looks like the distillery character of Nyborg is heavyweight apples. Medium, with the prickly wood spices lingering, apples, young spirit, and vanilla again in the end.

Again a hard one to rate as the apple character makes this very different from what I usually drink. But I like this and if I had some young stuff I wanted to bottle to make my whisky available for the public, this would be a good candidate.

SB

NYBORG DISTILLERY LAPHROAIG 3 YEAR OLD 69%

I assume this has been finished in a cask that previously held Laphroaig.

Nose: Apples, small casks' woodiness.

Palate: Quite woody and peaty and also a lot more full-bodied than the pure ex-bourbon. As with the other two samples I have the sense of a young, drinkable, and very appled whisky. Maybe Nyborg distillery is trying to target iPhone users? Well, I have a Galaxy so I am harder to impress! The wood impact on this one (and the sherry finish) can't help making me think it has been finished on smaller casks.

The peat, the apples, and the wood are well integrated. Again, a fine three year old expression, and as with the sherry finish, this is also something I could justify bottling.

The third sample is again apples for me, young spirit but this time it is very well balanced out by the wood and the peat. Long finish.

SB

BY CARLO DEVITO

Stauning Distillery is located on the west coast near the town of Stauning. The original intent at Stauning was to distill with the best Scottish tradition in mind. The founders wanted to create a smoky whisky in the best Islay-style. They use barley grown by local farmers, with the smell of the fresh sea air still on it. They also have their own malt house.

All their whiskies are labeled single malt. They make two kinds of single malt whisky: Traditional and peated. The traditional whisky is a barley-based, mild, unpeated whisky. There is no smoke in the traditional. The peated version has smoked malting barley with smoke produced by the peat excavated near the Klosterlund Museum. And then there is rye. This is a unique product. They produce rye whisky using malted rye, a rarity for sure.

STAUNING TRADITIONAL 1ST EDITION 3 YEAR OLD 63.3%

Stauning Traditional 1st Edition was a limited release of 728 bottles, bottled at a cask strength of 63.3% ABV. The whisky has been matured exclusively in first-fill ex-bourbon barrels from Maker's Mark. From what Stauning themselves say on their website, this was the second distilled whisky from the distillery, but the fifth bottling they released.

Nose: Sugary and rich. Lots of vanilla. Malty. Some licorice—the sweet kind. Mild fruity character. Hints of strawberries.

Palate: Way too raw for me! Big alcohol bite. Sort of minty and herbal. Pepper and licorice. Cough medicine. This does not really remind me of a whisky. Short finish. Warm. The burn stops, and there's more of the herbal sweetness. Not really balanced at all. This whisky was released too young for me. It certainly shows promise, and the nose is quite nice....

TO

STAUNING TRADITIONAL 2ND EDITION
4 YEAR OLD 55%

This is an unpeated whisky from Danish distillery Stauning. It was distilled in 2009 and bottled in March 2013. It is a limited release of 750 bottles.

Nose: Vanilla, powdered sugar, and strawberries. Solid base of soft oakiness, wet planks, and mild caramel.

Palate: Very soft mouthfeel. Still quite raw, but not as much as the 1st edition. Peppery, slightly malty. Turns chewy, almost gritty. Fun times. Spicy and oaky. Short finish. The spiciness is even more pronounced here—quite peppery.

Again, a dram that seems a bit immature, although a clear step up from the 1st edition. The early Stauning Peated was more to my liking, but then again peat can hide some of the youngish notes on a whisky, just like using a sherry cask. As such, this is a very naked and honest release. Cudos, Stauning.

TO

STAUNING TRADITIONAL 3RD EDITION
4 YEAR OLD 49%

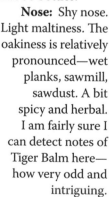

This whisky was distilled in 2009/2010, and bottled in 2014. It has been matured in 200 first-fill ex-bourbon casks. The outturn was limited to around 950 bottles.

Nose: Shy nose. Light maltiness. The oakiness is relatively pronounced—wet planks, sawmill, sawdust. A bit spicy and herbal. I am fairly sure I can detect notes of Tiger Balm here—how very odd and intriguing.

Palate: Soft and dry-ish mouthfeel. Very spicy—lots of pepper, chili and raw ginger. Chewy and rich. The spices are still very much present, but a bit mellowed out now. A deep sweetness comes sneaking in, rich caramel and honey, adding a needed extra dimension. Medium long and warm finish. It really does pick up very nicely towards the end.

Now we're talking. There is a very nice, and positive development through the three first expressions in this series from Stauning. This can only bode well for the future.

TO

STAUNING PEATED 1ST EDITION
3 YEAR OLD 62.8%

The Stauning Peated 1st Edition was distilled in 2009 and bottled in 2012. A total outturn of 715 bottles at 50cl each. The whisky was matured in first-fill ex-bourbon casks from Maker's Mark.

Stauning malts their own barley, and the peat used for the peated malt here is excavated by Klosterlund Museum.

There are still a few bottles to be had online, but they are getting quite pricey. You can for instance buy it from Denmark at the stiff price of $5,999(DKK) here.

Nose: Lots of peat and sweet licorice (candy licorice pipe, anyone?). Salt and oily. A fair bit of oak influence as well. Maybe they used small casks for this release?

Palate: Super smooth and almost silken mouthfeel. Then the chewy, rich and thick peppery, and ashen peatiness hits. It's rough and feisty, to say the least, but at the same time it is very charming! How very cool (and it is literally a bit cool as well, a minty touch). More minty now, still very peaty with a peppery edge. Vanilla and mild fruits coming through. I do not find any of the oakiness from the nose. Medium long, rich and full-bodied all the way. Honey mixed with ginger, ashes, licorice, and caramel at the end.

It is raw, it is rough, it is feisty, it is obviously a well-crafted whisky, although still too young, but also tons of fun!

TO

STAUNING PEATED 2ND EDITION 4 YEAR OLD 55%

This is the second peated release from Danish distillery Stauning. The Stauning Peated 2nd Edition was distilled in 2009, just like the 1st edition. This release was bottled a year later though, in 2013, making it four years old. The outturn this time was 750 bottles at 50cl each. Again the whisky was matured in first-fill ex-bourbon casks from Maker's Mark.

It bears repeating that Stauning malt their own barley, and the peat used is excavated by Klosterlund Museum. Quite an impressive and ambitious setup to do your own maltings.

The Stauning Peated 2nd Edition won the Best European Single Malt 12 Years and Under at the World Whiskies Awards in 2014.

Nose: Feels a bit fresher and more mature than the 1st Edition. More vanilla and sweetness from the cask coming through, tempering the peaty and vibrant spirit. Caramel, vanilla, and very rich and appealing chocolate-y wood smoke. It feels slightly maritime? A bit of salt and iodine.

Palate: Every bit as super smooth and silken as the 1st Edition. Again there's lots of chewy richness here. Peaty, fruity, and simple. Simple in a good way. OK? Okay. Medium to short finish. Warm, rich. A touch of the green towards the end. Slightly herbal.

So much more mature and well-balanced than the 1st Edition. It feels more whole now; there's more cohesion. Well done, Stauning! I must say it is fun working my way through these earlier releases. I hope you find it entertaining as well.

TO

TROLDEN DISTILLERY

BY JOHAN JOHANSEN

Trolden Distillery produces its single malt in the same address as Trolden Brewery, in Kolding, Denmark. They began distilling in 2011. They work with small, 350 liter, handcrafted pot-stills hoping to ensure a whisky with round mouthfeel. According to their process, 700 liters of so-called "wash" is roughly 60 liters of crude alcohol at 63% alcohol. From there, the liquid is aged in American oak barrels. All are brand new bourbon barrels from the United States, in sizes ranging from 8 to 50, 125, 190 and 225 liters. A large portion of the barrels are refurbished to Trolden's specifications at Speyside Cooperage in Scotland. All the whiskies are made using Danish barley, and are aged a minimum of three years by Danish law. They released their first whisky, eighty bottles, "Nimbus," on November 27, 2014. The second release was "Old No. 2." The next release for this small micro-distillery is scheduled for December 2017.

TROLDEN OLD NO. 2
SINGLE MALT WHISKY 45%

Question: What compels an individual of reasonably sound wit and intellect to set up a whisky production from scratch in a Danish seaside town of some 65,000 souls? Fortune? Fame? Recognition? Momentary loss of sanity? Since the beloved local brewery announced, some three years ago, the intent to craft a limited release Danish whisky in the town of Kolding, we've been trying to figure out just what compelled the local, reasonably suc-

cessful brewmaster turned master-distiller, Michael Svendsen, to choose to set up a whisky production in this lovely, sleepy little town.

It can't be the money. Nobody in their right mind sets up a whisky production to make a quick buck. Pretty sure whisky is about the most complicated and expensive spirit production you could choose to pick up. You need to not only find the perfect grain for the project, you also need to soak it just right till it nearly germinates, then dry it again, boil it, ferment it and distill it multiple times over, keeping only the best part of the distillate. Then you need to store it under perfect conditions in oak barrels for a minimum of three years, los-

ing large parts to evaporation during the period, before you can carefully blend it, dilute it and bottle it, hoping to make a buck off the fruits of your labor. The bottom line is, if you count the basic research needed and a bit of trial and error, you're looking at a period of at least four years before you can start making your money back. At what will probably be considered a pretty steep bottle price because you have nowhere near the volume of major distillers and need to price your product accordingly to win back your investment. Add to that a heavy taxation on alcohol in the Kingdom of Denmark and you'll end up with something that's an expensive niche product for a limited market at best. Pretty sure it's not the money.

Fame and recognition, then? Well, if those were your main drivers, you probably would have started off a little bigger and a little less humble than our local brewer and his limited initial run. Sadly, that leaves us with one of our initial theories: momentary loss of sanity? Ahem, well, I've been fortunate enough to hang out with master distiller Michael Svendsen on more than one occasion and he's definitely a delightfully twisted and humorous fellow—pretty sure he's not crazy—so what then is it that made him do it?

To find out, we went on down to the distillery, knocked on the door, picked up a half liter bottle of the recently released three year old Kolding Straight Whisky from Trolden Distillery—in an effort to not only support the local heroes that dare try new and exciting things, but also in an effort to find out once and for all:

What makes this man tick? And what the hell is this Danish whisky really all about?

Trolden Old No. 2 Kolding Straight Whisky 3 Year Old is rather an attractive bottle to look at, obviously hand-labeled and hand-numbered bearing the name "Old No. 2" in an apparent reference to a certain Tennessee Straight Whisky made by a certain Mr. Daniels. The marketing text on the bottle rather humorously tells the tale of a high rye-content whisky, already remarkably smooth from the day it was all but moonshine aged in "fancy" French oak barrels. What really steals the eye, though, upon first inspection is the content of the clear bottle: A golden brown almost light mahogany-like liquid, that looks a fair bit older and more developed than the 2012 birth certificate on the bottle indicates. Honestly, it looks a bit like products put out by less honest distillers who have a way of tainting their wares with caramel color to produce a golden glow of age and maturity. Pretty sure this is the real deal, though, and that no caramel was used in the making of this whisky.

How can you be certain? Well, I took the master distiller himself out for a few pints once in an effort to draw some secrets out of him. Failed horribly, of course, but I did manage to get him to confess to me late in the evening that he himself attributes both the surprisingly mature, dark color and the relatively quick development in flavors, aromas, and intensity to the use of small to very small barrels in the aging process.

And speaking of aromas, can we talk about aromas for a while? The first thing you notice when pouring this baby is a distinct hit of fruit. Initially identified it as red apple in the video tasting, but given some time and thought, it took on more of a pear-like note but still with hints of apple. Like your arch-typical Speyside whisky but with a bit more jazz. Given even more time in the glass and a few more sniffs, Trolden Old No. 2 also gave off fresh notes of lightly toasted wood and a faint smell of vanilla, another typical oak aging aroma. Underlying aromas included some fruity/bready rye notes, dark, dried fruits, and a whiff of alcohol that, at 45% ABV and after only three years in cask, was quite noticeable but not entirely unpleasant.

Given the first taste, first impressions on the tongue were surprisingly sweet and malty components, chased by and—honestly—incredible fruitiness with more immediate notes of apple and pear followed by a toffee/caramel-like sensation, more malt and a trace of oak. There was a burn, too, from the alcohol, which frankly—given the age of the product and the ABV—wasn't too surprising. It's not an entirely unpleasant one, though, and on a slightly cooler fall or winter day, it would probably be quite welcome and comforting. The flavors, by the way, were rather lingering as Trolden Old No. 2 has a somewhat thick and oily mouthfeel that basically covers the mouth and leaves the aftertaste swirling around the mouth for quite a while.

JJ

Vingården Lille Gadegård is a winery and distillery in Bornholm, Denmark. The winery was founded in 1995, and it is still owned and operated by Jesper Paulsen. Whisky production began in 2005, with the first single malt being released in 2009. They have released several expressions since then. They use a stainless steel still and double distillation, and age their whisky in their own wine casks for maturation.

LILLE GADEGÅRD BORNHOLMSK WHISKY NR. 2 51.5%

Lille Gadegård is a vineyard, but in 2005 they also started distilling malt whisky. The spirit is matured in French oak casks that have been used for maturing the vineyard's red wine first.

Nose: Relatively rough, with oaky notes and acetone. With water, burnt rubber takes over the nose and blocks any other aromas.

Palate: Tobacco, some acetone, oak, and burnt rubber. Raisins or other dried fruits on the finish. Hardly any development with water.

An example of ... "speed maturation," this is both too young (which the nose proclaims loudly) and at the same time the cask influence is

too heavy. I think the spirit in itself is pretty decent, but it's hard to tell, because it's not been given the chance to shine. The taste is better than the nose in this one, the tobacco saves it....

RSL

ENGLAND

BY CARLO DEVITO

English whisky? What?

"It's a fierce rivalry which goes back centuries. And the sometimes bitter relationship between Scotland and England has just got a little more tense. For the first time in one hundred years, a whisky made south of the border is about to go on sale," the British newspaper *The Daily Mail* announced in November 2009. The English Whisky Co. released its first single malt.

John Kaylor, chairman of the Perthshire branch of the Tartan Army, fan club of the Scottish international football team, told *The Daily Mail*: "It's flattering that the English want to copy us...No true Tartan Army member would ever wet their lips with English whisky."

The English Whisky Co. produced it from locally-grown barley near its St George's distillery in Norfolk. The first barrels were laid down in 2006.

England had produced single malt whisky in the past. But the last bottle of English single malt whisky was bottled around 1905, when the Lea Valley Distillery ceased production. There had been such names as Lea Valley Distillery, Bank Hall Distillery, Bristol Distillery and Vauxhall Distillery. All gone.

In 2006, farmer James Nelstrop founded The English Whisky Co., and released the first English single malt in more than one hundred years. Not to be out done, the St. Austell Brewery & Healey Cyder Farm released the first "Cornish" single malt whisky (7 Year Old) in more than 300 years in September 2011! And then in 2013, the London Distillery Company announced plans to produce the first single malt whisky made in London since Lea Valley Distillery closed its doors.

Today there are five distilleries in England making various kinds of single malts, and more on the way! Dashing good fun! Cheerio!

ADNAMS SOUTHWOLD

BY MATT CHAMBERS & KAREN TAYLOR

The No.1 Single Malt is the first single malt whisky to be released by the Copper House Distillery, which is located in the English town of Southwold in Suffolk, and owned by the well-known brewer Adnams. The distillery started production in November 2010 and has already released a range of other award-winning spirits, including gin and vodka. Master Distiller John McCarthy has hand-selected the casks for this initial whisky release, which have finally reached the minimum legal age of three years.

Adnams has been making beer there for over one hundred years and they produce a range of highly-awarded cask and bottled beers, plus they also own a chain of pubs, hotels, and wine shops. The Single Malt No.1 is made from 100% East Anglian barley and has been matured in new French oak casks. It is joined by a second release—the Triple Grain No. 2. This has been matured in new American oak casks and has been produced using East Anglian barley, wheat, and oats.

Both are released at 43% and are available online, the company's Cellar & Kitchen chain of stores, and selected specialist retailers at a cost of £43.99.

ADNAMS NO. 1 SINGLE MALT WHISKY 43%

The color is golden yellow and the nose is fresh, vibrant, and very woody. There are a mix of simple but expressive aromas fighting for attention—think of oak, honey, vanilla, coconut, and fresh pencil shavings. Underneath some bittersweet malty cereals and golden syrup, plus hints of butterscotch and cinnamon.

On the palate, this initially feels soft and creamy with some exaggerated honey and vanilla notes coming immediately to the fore. Then some creamed coconut and another note reminiscent of apricot jam begins to come through before BOOM, the taste buds are hit with a tsunami of oak and wood spices. These instantly dry out the palate to leave a tannic and slightly bitter edge. The oak is reminiscent of fresh wood shavings and the woody spice has a predominant cinnamon-like note to it, with hints of ginger and licorice underneath. As the woodiness subsides with time in the mouth, some malty cereals and dried grass notes appear.

The finish is long and very woody. It has a little chili-like heat to it, which is probably due to its youthful age. The woodiness is very oaky and the result is to dry the mouth out. The dried grass, bittersweet malt, and cinnamon add depth. Very little sweetness is detected, other than some background honey and caramel.

This No.1 Single Malt is interesting and some may find the increasing dry woodiness overpowering, but there is some sweetness there that attempts to balance it. The addition of water makes the whisky softer and creamier—the wood spices are knocked back and the vanilla, honey, and cereals are allowed to shine. We preferred it with water.

This product was released literally as soon as it hit the three year old minimum age limit, so it will be interesting to see how the spirit develops with extra maturation time or in different and larger casks. However, it is good to see another English whisky on the market and worth trying if you can.

MC & KT

COTSWOLDS SINGLE MALT ORGANIC ODESSEY (ANTICIPATED OCTOBER 2017)

Malt Organic Odessey will be the first-ever single malt whisky produced in the Cotswolds. The whisky will stored in select ex-bourbon and red wine barrels, which were first filled in 2014. They used 100% organic Cotswolds barley grown locally at Bradwell Grove Estate, a farm near by—only twenty miles away. Warminster Maltings floor-malted the barley that Cotswold milled, mashed, fermented, and distilled.

The English Whisky Co. is the first English whisky manufacturer to legally sell its products to the public in over one hundred years. They're creating some pretty amazing things, which is no surprise considering the top-notch talent they're working with.

CLASSIC SINGLE MALT ENGLISH WHISKY 46%

Its Classic Single Malt is a very basic single malt that is light and tasty but a little boring. Though that's not always a bad thing.

Sometimes you want boring and I honestly wouldn't mind having a bottle of this on hand for those nights where I want something that is light,

tastes good, and I don't have to think about while enjoying. Something that I can easily sit back and relax with while watching the latest episode of Bob's Burgers on Hulu.

Overall it's a very light and slightly fruity whisky that's easy to enjoy. Being non-chill filtered it retains that wonderful oily character that all single malts should have and I'm really glad I got to try it at the tasting Purple Valley hosted.

Color: Light yellow.

Nose: Starts out with a very light fruit, honey, and baklava that rolls into almonds, malt, citrus, and toasted grains.

Palate: The malt is very apparent with that same light fruit character from the nose moving alongside it. There is a touch of oak, some graham cracker, and citrus hanging out in the background. Oily and lazy like all good non-chill filtered whisky should be. A little dry, but balanced and very drinkable. A touch of oak and light orchard fruit with barley staying strong through a short finish.

JP

PEATED SINGLE MALT ENGLISH WHISKY 46%

When The English Whisky Co. was getting themselves set up and established, they enlisted the help of semi-retired Laphroaig distiller Iain Henderson, which is probably why their peated single malt turned out so damn good. There is an art to smoking the malt and blending the barrels to get the right mix of flavors while keeping a smoky backbone, which is something Iain surely knows a thing or two about.

If you're not a fan of big peaty monsters like Laphroaig, Lagavulin, Ardbeg and their kin, then you're in luck. This is a much more restrained and lighter peat that balances well with the light fruit and honey characteristics of the whisky that a heavier peating would completely obliterate. Like the Classic Single Malt, it's not chill filtered so it retains that smooth oily texture, and overall I love this whisky.

Color: Light yellow gold.

Nose: The smoky peat comes up first, but much lighter than most Islay whiskies. Underneath the smoke are some very wonderful notes of strawberry, burned corn, iodine, and anise, but strangely enough I didn't really pick up much malt.

Palate: There's that delightful smoky peat up first, but like the nose, it's a rather light peat. Next to the smoke are some notes of vanilla, honey, brine, light fruit, and of course, malt. Not quite as round and oily as the Classic Single Malt, but still smooth and well-balanced. The long finish has a nutty characteristic that is filled with peat and malt.

JP

CHAPTER 13 LIMITED EDITION RARE SINGLE MALT WHISKY 49%

I had the Chapter 14 before trying this one and felt it was a decent enough whisky. Not amazing but worth a sip to satisfy my curiosity about the first single malt whisky produced in England for 120 years.

This Norfolk distillery produced its first spirit back in December 2006 with the help of recently retired Laphroaig distiller Iain Henderson, and they managed to cask twenty-nine barrels of the new liquid. In August 2007, they opened to the public and the distilling reins were handed over to David Fitt, a brewer from Greene King.

Since then, it seems, they've been motoring along nicely using a bunch of casks and distillates to produce a variety of whiskies. Since this is only the second whisky I've tasted, I really don't know how good or bad the average spirit is. But by and large, the word on the street is positive.

I had heard good things about Chapter 13, a lightly-peated malt matured in Sassicaia casks (Sassicaia is a Bordeaux-style red wine) with an absolutely gorgeous label depicting a fire-breathing dragon.

What is even cooler is that, superstition be damned, the whisky was released in time for Halloween with 13 featured prominently. The ABV is 49% (4+9=13), it was launched on Friday the 13th (September), and priced at £66.60 (get it?). Nice little fun and games here.

The whisky inside is a vatting of casks 527, 528, 827, and 830, distilled in 2008 and bottled in 2013, and served at a strength of 49%.

Color: Young Sauternes.

Nose: Chocolate. Warm honey. Touch of smoke. Toffee pudding. Custard. Hint of cured meats, nice cured meats. Something bitter. But something sweet too. Like a marmalade glaze. Celery sticks. Nutmeg. Coffee beans. Sweet oak. Like a sandalwood but not really sandalwood. Berries. I like this nose. Really like it.

Palate: Great weight. Medium but silky mouthfeel. Quite peppery. Savory. Marmalade on burnt toast. Toffee apples. Oak. Cinnamon. Coffee. Vanilla. Quite a sharp barley. Not as good as the nose but quite nice. Very smooth. Cigar leaf. Coffee. Bitter chocolate. Quite drying.

The first nose on the whisky will

take your breath away. It's quite gorgeous. But as it sits and breathes, it loses its intensity a touch. Same on the palate and finish. Fresh out of the bottle when the spirit is wound up tight, all the flavors pack quite a punch. Let it breathe and it mellows out a touch. Is that a good or bad thing? I don't know. Still a mighty fine whisky.

TR

CHAPTER 14 UNPEATED SINGLE MALT WHISKY 46%

My first-ever English single malt. Didn't know what to expect. Didn't even know if there was a house style or a certain character that I should be looking out for.

Nothing.

Which is a good thing because I

like being pleasantly surprised. I go for big bold flavors, unusual flavor profiles, and insanely high strength whiskies. This one is just the opposite so it's quite unusual that I thought it was quite decent.

The English Whisky Co. is housed

in St George's Distillery in Roudham, Norfolk (Why Roudham? Clean water and barley they say. Fine.), and they've been producing some fine young 'uns of late. So I've read, to be honest. The sample is from a brand new bottle distilled in February 2009 and bottled in September 2014 (do the math) and is a blend of casks 206, 207, 208, and 209. It is matured in an ASB, which stands for American Standard Barrel (derived from the hogshead with the capacity rounded down to 200 liters).

Color: Sunlight.

Nose: Delicate. Vanilla. Freshly baked biscuits. Quite fruity. Demerara sugar. Marzipan. Almonds. Spun sugar. Lychees. Hard boiled sweets. Heather. This is a very delicate nose. Takes a while to open up. But then opens up nicely. Very sweet. It just manages to stay on the pleasant side of sweet by a hair. Quite a commendable balancing act.

Palate: Delicate still. Also sweet. Banana. Hint of lemon. Mild spices. Sugars. Vanilla. Touch of coffee. Oak. Has an almost gristy mouthfeel. The liquid feels super young. Almost like new make. In not entirely a bad way. Long. Dry. Touch of oak. Coffee. The finish is the best part. Lingers for a while. Even at 46% it felt quite underpowered. Overall quite balanced and the flavors work with each other.

This is quite a decent quality of spirit and oak. You can tell by the absence of any rough edges on the delivery and lack of off-notes on the nose. I feel the spirit is very young and needs a fair amount of time in a more influential oak cask to release even more. The flavors are just about making themselves felt.

TR

QUEEN'S DIAMOND JUBILEE COMMEMORATIVE WHISKY

To celebrate the UK's Royal long weekend, we decided to try a whisky that certainly marks the event: English Whisky Co.'s Diamond Jubilee Commemorative Bottling. This bottling is to commemorate the Diamond Jubilee of Queen Elizabeth II, which celebrated sixty years of her reign.

This small batch production whisky is produced from a combination of bourbon cask and red wine cask-matured whisky. It is bottled at 46% in a decanter style bottle as a limited edition, with 3,300 bottles produced and only 1,140 bottles available for sale in the UK.

St George's Distillery is operated by The English Whisky Co., which was founded in 2005 by Andrew and James Nelstrop. It was the first whisky distillery to be built and produce whisky in England for almost 200 years. The distillery is located in the heart of East Anglia, close to the town of Roudham in Norfolk (about two hours north east of London). The first spirit came off the stills in November 2006 and was overseen by legendary (and retired) whisky maker Iain Henderson, who had previously managed the famous Laphroaig distillery on the island of Islay, amongst others. The role of Distillery Manager now falls to David Fitt, an ex-brewer from Greene King, who was trained by Iain before he retired again.

St George's spirit is made, where possible, from locally grown Norfolk barley, and the entire process, from milling to bottling, occurs on-site. The distillery has already won many plaudits for its innovation and quality.

Color: This whisky is a vibrant golden hue that comes from the mixture of casks (no coloring is added), which is a shade described at a recent whisky tasting event as a "classic" whisky color.

Nose: On the nose, the first impression is sweet notes of butterscotch, golden syrup, and sultanas. This is not overpowering, as it is matched by fresh notes of green grass and tangy apples, with woody warming spiciness of cinnamon and nutmeg. With water the whisky shows more pronounced floral notes of rose and honeysuckle with green apple freshness, but certainly doesn't lose the sweetness or spiciness.

Palate: On the palate, the strength is noticeable and the whisky is less sugary sweet than expected, despite there being definite toffee and sultana characters. The red wine shows here in way of darker red apples and prunes along with plenty of warming spices and oily nuts such as almonds. The finish is short and dry with spiciness and mouthwatering tannins. There are lots of wood spices and a touch of red chili pepper. With water, the palate has extra creaminess but maintains sweet notes of toffee and apples. The spiciness is pushed to the back but remains on the finish. All in all we think that this whisky has extra desirable characters when tasted at the higher ABV strength so we are pleased that the decision was taken to bottle at 46% and allow drinkers to add to water to their own taste.

This commemorative bottling is a

whisky created to be collectable yet remarkably approachable. It is at a price, rarity, and strength that makes it a good purchase for the occasional whisky drinker who wants something to remember the event by that is more desirable than a collectable teapot. Having said that, we don't think that serious whisky collectors would be disappointed either. It is not overly complex but certainly offers fabulous value for money.

This is a remarkably affordable bottling to celebrate the Queen's Diamond Jubilee, especially when compared to many other less rare "limited" celebratory releases. While we expect that many people will be buying the bottle to collect we thoroughly suggest that you don't just leave it on the shelf but do give it a try.

MC & KT

FOUNDER'S PRIVATE CELLAR SASSICAIA CASK 61.1%

Sassicaia is arguably the first and the best of all the Italian "Super Tuscan" wines. It is produced by Tenuta San Guido, an Italian wine producer located in the DOC Bolgheri in Tuscany. The marchese Mario Incisa della Rocchetta, owner of Tenuta San Guido, planted Cabernet Sauvignon at his winery in 1944. The Cabernet Sauvingnon was his private reserve, until he finally decided to release the 1968 vintage commercially in 1971. Super Tuscans are not recognized by the Tuscan DOC. But the rest of the world clamors for their rich, deep hues, textures, and complexities. Sassicaia is among the most sought after of these.

The folks at The English Whisky Co. aged a single malt in a former Sassicaia barrel. This unique whisky is without a doubt a "unicorn single malt." Only 198 numbered bottles of this cask strength whisky were produced in 2015. Very rare!

CD

HICKS & HEALEY CORNISH WHISKEY CASK STRENGTH 61.3%

Hicks & Healey whiskey brings to life the almost forgotten English bio-diversity of apples with a powerful kick that would probably make Alan Shearer proud; whether that be the humble apple in different forms (raw, sliced, cooked) or many varieties of apple, it is evident that this whiskey is a fascinating glimpse into the complexity of Cornish apples and superb craftwork of the distillers at Healey's. This whiskey is a must try! You may not like it, but I am confident that you will be very impressed with the skill of the distiller and the unique character of this whiskey.

When I lived in England, my Australian taste for cold lager was slowly replaced by a love for apple cider and warm ale. I did not much like cider and ale at first, but the taste was slowly acquired and now my mouth salivates at the smell of a mahogany bar of an English pub.

Healey's is a Cornish cider farm and produces the Hicks & Healey whiskey, a whiskey made from Cornish barley and distilled twice in the smallest copper pot still in the country before being laid to rest for seven years in its oak casks alongside their reserve brandies and cider.

This is superbly crafted whiskey, and it is extremely enjoyable. This whiskey can easily be misunderstood, because it does not blindly replicate a particular flavor profile that is commonly associated with "whiskey." It brings something new to the table. Intelligently, Healey's have played to their strengths and produced a whiskey that oozes with the English taste of dry apple seed cider and notes of ale; certainly an acquired taste in my experience and while it is absolutely beautiful, there may be some who need some more visits to the pub to taste all the ciders on offer before they can fully appreciate it.

All I need now is a Sunday roast with a Yorkshire pudding...In fact, I can picture it now, washing it down with a dark bitter local ale and then once the munching is over, sitting back to the piercing cask strength apple rich glow of Hicks & Healey whiskey.

Nose: The fragrance of an apple core is first noticeable, as apple cider shines brightly. As though a green apple has been eaten to its core and browned slightly, there is some fresh sweetness that is accompanied by the apple seed and fragrance of an oxidized apple core. There is a plasticine note on the nose that accompanies the alcohol, which is smooth and soft despite this whisky being at 61.3%.

Palate: Incredibly sweet, it is lucky that I am a cider lover; the symphony of apples is incredible. Raw green apples develop with stewed

apple pie and the dry fizz of apple cider, as the oak gives a mild wood theme and a bitter English ale-like twist (there are many types of ales in England); a nice twist given that this whiskey is distilled from a mash that is like beer but without the hops. There is an initial surge of sweetness that is then counteracted by the most unique bitter-dry wave of wood, wood polish, and dryness.

The Healey's twenty-acre estate is scattered with about 3,000 trees, which include seven varies of native Cornish apples (such as the Katy used for desserts or the Ashton Bitter, which has, according to Healey's, a "sharp green twang"). What is fascinating is that England is home to thousands of apple varieties, and what you see in the supermarket is likely to be only two or maybe three of those. The bittersweet apple-themed dryness lingers. This is an example of a cider farm putting its casks to great use! Incredibly smooth for a whiskey at this strength, I love the uniqueness of the whiskey and its apple theme; beautiful work. Be warned, this may be shockingly sweet for some and not everyone's cup of tea. This whiskey is to be enjoyed with an open mind and an appreciation for creativity and difference.

AC

The Lake District, in North West England, is a scenic, mountainous region renowned for its lakes, forests and mountains (or fells). It was popularized by the Romantic era writings of William Wordsworth and the other Lake Poets. Now a national park, all the land in it, including Scafell Pike, the highest mountain in England, resides at 3,000 ft above sea level,. The park is also home to Wastwater and Windermere, the deepest and longest bodies of water in England.

The Lakes Distillery has a solid team guiding it. Paul Currie, who co-founded the famed Arran distillery, established The Lakes Distillery. And the production is managed by Alan Rutherford, council member of the Scotch Whisky Association, and one of the world's most famous whisky experts. The master distiller is Chris Anderson, from Scotland. The Lakes Distillery currently produces one of England's most decorated blended whiskies, The One—a well-balanced, slightly peaty whisky with a subtle, mouth-watering finish. Hopes are high for this new whisky, The Lakes Single Malt.

THE LAKES SINGLE MALT (ANTICIPATED 2018)

According to their notes, The Lakes Single Malt (scheduled for an early 2018 release) will be more like Highlands whisky, lightly peated. Even now, The Lakes Distillery is taking advance orders from the first one hundred casks through their Founders' Club.

FINLAND

BY CARLO DEVITO

How can you not love Finland? Its beautiful northern country-side, within the Arctic Circle, is home to Lapland, the mythical home of Santa Claus (and filled with reindeer). If that wasn't enough, it was Finland that brought us the sauna. And of course, it was the birthplace of Angry Birds.

But Finland has a long tradition of distilling. Grain spirits, such as neutral grain spirits, and vodka were at the forefront of the Finnish distilling industry. For example, Dr. Wilhelm Juslin established a distillery in 1888 at the glacial springs near the small village of Rajamäki, which is still in operation. It produces Finlandia Vodka, a brand invented by the state-owned monopoly Alko (now known as Altia) in 1970. Strom Vodka is, by comparison, a newcomer.

The most popular grain spirit is Koskenkorva Viina (also referred to as Koskenkorva, or Kossu), which is manufactured at the Koskenkorva distillery in Ilmajoki by Altia. There are other popular grain spirits brands on the market.

Whisky was manufactured in Finland at the Koskenkorva distillery from 1981 to 2000. It was Finland's most popular selling whisky. However, this was discontinued at the end of 2000. On November 8, 2001, Panimoravintola Beer Hunter's, a restaurant and brewery, began distilling operations with an aim toward making whisky.

Since then, other distilleries have starting making whisky, including Teerenpeli Distillery, Panimoravintola Koulu, Kyrö Distillery Company, and Helsinki Distillery. Not all make single malts yet, but there are many plans in the works. Finnish whisky has wowed many palates, and collected a string of awards and prizes. Experts around the world are curious to see what comes out next from this country sandwiched between Sweden and Russia.

Product:	Distilling date:
Helsingin Tislaamo Viljatisle	15.12.15
	Bottling date:
White Dog Straight Rye	17.12.15
	Batch/cask no:
Notes:	63/-
Viljaviina – Sädesbrännvin	ABV: 60,5 %
	Volume: 50 cl

THE HELSINKI DISTILLING COMPANY
HELSINKI — FINLAND

Product:	Distilling date:
Helsingin Tislaamo Viljatisle	12.10.14
	Bottling date:
White Dog Straight Rye 1YO	17.12.15
	Batch/cask no:
Notes:	RB3/46-47
Viljaviina – Sädesbrännvin	ABV: 60,5 %
	Volume: 50 cl

THE HELSINKI DISTILLING COMPANY
HELSINKI — FINLAND

Product:	Distilling date:
Helsingin Tislaamo Viljatisle	01.09.14
	Bottling date:
White Dog Single Malt 1YO	17.12.15
	Batch/cask no:
Notes:	5/13-21
Viljaviina – Sädesbrännvin	ABV: 58 %
	Volume: 50 cl

THE HELSINKI DISTILLING COMPANY
HELSINKI — FINLAND

WHITE DOG SINGLE MALT
1 YEAR OLD 58%

The upstart Helsinki Distilling Company has already made a name for itself with its stunning Helsinki Dry Gin. The Helsinki Distillery claims that it is the first distillery in Helsinki proper for more than one hundred years. Their goal is to make as high a quality product as possible. It's small, hand-crafted stuff, across a decent swath of products, done in small batches. And it's all locally sourced. They've made a big splash in a short time, and continue to turn heads. Their new single malt is eagerly anticipated.

PANIMORAVINTOLA BEER HUNTER'S BREWERY AND DISTILLERY

Viskin Ystävien Seura is Finnish for "Friends of Whisky Society," in English referred to as the Fellowship of Whisky, but mainly just VYS. Now this is a club that knows how to put on events. They have this series of utterly CRAZY tastings called "The Rare and Old"—the fourteenth of which was with whiskies distilled in the 1930s. The series is always sold out in advance, and this club, with some 700 members, really has a lot going on. To celebrate the club's second birthday, they had a private bottling of Old Buck, a Finnish micro-distillery from Pori.

OLD BUCK FINNISH WHISKY, BOTTLED FOR VISKIN YSTÄVIEN SEURA, 53.7%

Old Buck is distilled in the micro-distillery run by the Panimoravintola Beer Hunter's restaurant in Pori. The first distillation was done in 2001 and the first whisky was released in 2004 under the Old Buck label. I have, sadly, not tasted it. To honor VYS's second anniversary last year, a bottling of a single cask of Old Buck was made available. This is a peated four-year-old whisky matured in an ex-bourbon cask from Jack Daniel's. Unique and very interesting!

Bronze, tiny thin legs running very slowly.

Nose: There's peat in the background, not overly assertive, sweet lemon, orange, pickles in brine, smokiness drifts back in with notes of limoncello and honey. Water brings out malt and a wood fire, with orange peel and some floral notes.

Palate: Orange, peat and honey, with a sour/vinegar note creeping in with spices and sweet notes. The peat comes through with sour notes, wood smoke, some spice and a lingering sweetness. The spice notes remain on the tongue for a long time.

This is a very special whisky, both fun and complex. This was a great choice to bottle for the celebration of VYS's second birthday.

MB

SGOIL 3 YEAR OLD
SINGLE MALT WHISKY

In the spring of 2013, Panimoravintola Koulu in Turku offered a three year old single malt whisky named "Sgoil." Sgoil is Gaelic for "school." The malt is processed and brewed at Panimoravintola Koulu, but then distilled in Tuorla, Kaarina, as the brewery does not possess a still. The whisky was aged in old Jack Daniel's bourbon barrels. Only a small quantity was released, but another release is forthcoming.

Teerenpeli is the producer of the first commercially available Finnish single malt whisky. The distillery is located in the city of Lahti, where they started their whisky-making in 2002. Teerenpeli was established in 1995 as a beer brewery and it has five brewery restaurants in cities across Finland. Teerenpeli's barley, malting, and distilling water all come from local producers in the Lahti region.

TEERENPELI 8 YEAR OLD SINGLE MALT 43%

The 8 year old is matured in a mixture of 200-liter ex-bourbon (60%) and second-fill ex-sherry (40%) casks. I had a chance to taste it when attending a distillery tour at Teerenpeli's Taivaanranta Grill & Distillery in Lahti. Teerenpeli 8 year old was a positive surprise. Highland Park is Teerenpeli's main inspirer. The small pot stills are shaped like Highland Park's pots. Being it subconscious or not, in one's mind Teerenpeli 8 years felt a bit like Highland Park 12. Like a younger brother of HP12. Teerenpeli 8-year-old has less character and flavor but yet, the resemblance is there.

I think that Aki Kaurismäki is a great example, when trying to match Teerenpeli into the movie world. Kaurismäki and Teerenpeli both are Finnish pioneers in their own fields. *Drifting Clouds* is a nice movie by Kaurismäki on his way to better public awareness. In a way, Teerenpeli 8

year old is in the same caste. Lifting Teerenpeli to common knowledge in the whisky world. Giving a promise: "we know what we are doing and the best is yet to come."

Drifting Clouds is a story of a couple being hit by recession in Helsinki. About their ascetic life comes a nice story. Kinda like the story of Teerenpeli, even though their whisky production might not be that ascetic. But it is a lot smaller than the usual Scottish production.

The clouds don't drift, when it comes to the taste of Teerenpeli 8 year old. Keeping its balance nicely. Giving Teerenpeli distillery a better foot step in the whisky world, just like Aki's film did in the movie business.

JL

TEERENPELI 3 YEAR OLD 43%

This 3 year old single malt was their first release, sold solely in the restaurant. Teerenpeli is the first Finnish whisky producer for retail markets; their 8 year old single malt was first Finnish whisky for commercial use.

Tasted Teerenpeli 3YO in a whisky tasting in Teerenpeli's Taivaanranta Grill & Distillery. Not sure how it's been matured. For a whisky so young and from a young distillery, it is surprisingly good. It is rough and not as good as older single malts. But it doesn't lack too much character; the scents and the taste are just too short and edgy. Teerenpeli 3 year old is a bit like a very inexperienced boxer going into the first round swinging like crazy, and feeling exhausted already in the second round.

Roughness is good in my book, when it comes to whisky. The good ones usually have complexity or some smooth elements that balances the edges. Obviously Teerenpeli 3 year old didn't have those components but it had potential. Very fast and short hues of something good that can become great, when given time.

So for me Teerenpeli 3 year old is like Calamari Union, the second film by legendary Finnish moviemaker Aki Kaurismäki. Calamari Union is critically acclaimed but not one of my favorites by Aki. It has short elements of greatness that left me wanting for more of Kaurismäki's stuff. Just like Teerenpeli 3 year old made me excited about waiting for their older single malts.

Color: Amber.

Nose: Edgy liquor and malt. Sweet barley comes strongly with little hints of chocolate.

Palate: Sharply comes the sweet toffee and malted barley. Hints of cognac. Very short and peppery. Some character in a fast way. Good for its age but otherwise below average.

JL

TEERENPELI DISTILLER'S CHOICE KASKI 43%

The 8 year old Teerenpeli did very well with the 60-40 combination of bourbon and sherry casks. The expression was all you'd expect from a Finnish whisky, with a character all to its own, conjuring up forests, rain and wet earth.

You'd obviously expect that the Distiller's Choice, an expression wholly matured in sherry casks, to be that much better. You might also think you'd be facing a true sherry bomb. Alas, you'd be wrong on both counts. This expression is six to seven years old (as told to in a visit to the distillery). You might think that while being a definitely well-made whisky, it didn't have the depth of character the 8 year old had. Not sure if it's the 2nd fill casks or the age. One might wonder if there's a 100% bourbon cask matured expression out there. Judging from the 8 year old, such an expression has the potential to absolutely shine.

Deep bronze, thick and quick legs.

Nose: A layer of herbal and honey notes with some light lactic notes overlaid with a light layer of sherry with a rather wine-like nose that gets sweeter with time.

Palate: Zesty compote made from plums, nectarines and citrus, pinesap, brown sugar, pepper and cinnamon. The full mouthfeel creates some dryness on the inside of the cheeks. Some sweetness, hints of spice, and not much dryness left behind in this rather short Finnish finish. I do apologize for the corny pun, I just couldn't resist that one.

Had very high expectations coming to this expression from the 8 year old, which were unanswered by the whisky. Don't get us wrong, it's well-made and very drinkable. But on the one hand, it lost that incredible feel of Finland the 8 year old had, and on the other hand, it didn't deliver a true sherry bomb punch. Of the two Teerenpeli expressions tasted, the 8 year old is clearly the winner.

Eagerly awaiting to taste other expressions coming out of Lahti.

MB

FRANCE

BY CARLO DEVITO

O f course France has long had a reputation for alcoholic beverages. Its Bordeaux region produces the most high-prized wines in the world. Its other regions, such as Burgundy, Champagne, and others, have their dedicated legions of followers as well. The farmhouse ciders of France are also legendary, and have sparked their own army of imitators and devotees. And of course, Bière de Garde and France's own Trappist brewers have their admirers as well.

In the distilling world, France has long been a star with such brandy offerings as Armagnac, Calvados, and Cognac. These are highly collectible and world-renowned distillates. The aging of spirits in oak has long been a tradition here. However, one of the interesting things about France: They love Scotch! Huge Scotch drinking population! So it's no surprise that the industry would sooner or later blossom here, especially with the rich traditions, and national pride, so emblematic of France. Breton is the whiskey-producing region du jour. Some exciting people are doing really new and cool things in this country. Though the industry here right now is small, some of the whiskies coming out of this region are impressive. A good but small region to investigate!

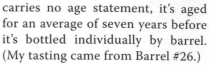

BRENNE FRENCH SINGLE MALT WHISKY

From Cognac, France, by way of an inspired collaboration between whisky importer and blogger Allison Patel and a third-generation cognac distiller, comes this unique single malt. Brenne French Single Malt is a new venture—Allison's first expression, Estate Cask, was released in late 2012—and, being French whisky (read: a rarity in the world of the Distiller's Art) suggests an air of adventure.

What Brenne French Single Malt Whisky shares with the single malt tradition is, of course, its malted barley base. What it shares with the world of craft distillers is an experimental boldness. What makes it unique among other whiskies is its distillation process, which is modeled on the cold fermentation technique common to cognac distillation. Brenne is distilled in a copper alembic twice before being aged in Limousin barrels. Its aging is finished in ex-cognac casks, which lends Brenne much of its distinct quality. Although Brenne carries no age statement, it's aged for an average of seven years before it's bottled individually by barrel. (My tasting came from Barrel #26.)

Brenne arrives in a bottle that shares the simple elegance of a classic wine. In the glass, it has the warm, light glimmer of dawn over a wheat field—think the airy, shimmering fields in Terrence Malik's *Days Of Heaven*, then imagine yourself about to enjoy a nice dram on the porch of the farmer's mansion.

I typically prefer spice to sweet, so my first sniff of Brenne worried me a bit. This single malt is heady with fruit, so much so that you'd be excused for wondering if Brenne really is whisky.

First impressions often breed unfair presumptions, however, and the variety of fruit and assorted delicacies that greet you out of the glass reward those who are patient and discerning—not unlike the music of the Austrian Modernist, Anton Webern.

A selection of market-fresh berries, Gala apples, dark chocolate, vanilla wafers, and banana-walnut muffin compose themselves like Webern's Bagatelles, and comparisons to Webern's precision continue from the first sip through a chromatic finish. A pinch of spice, redolent of malted barley, conducts singular notes of Lindt Orange Chocolate, red raspberries and whipped cream. A few pointillist dashes of clove in confectioner's sugar near the very end brings the work to a well-defined close.

A Rye drinker like me might pre-judge the underplayed spice the way a Classicist might criticize Webern's use of silence—which would be to misunderstand the whisky just as many have missed the point of Webern's technique. The flavors, like the notes of, say Webern's Variations for Piano, Op. 27, are so well balanced, so refined in their interplay, that the music they create finds fullness of form in what the composer has chosen to underplay.

SDP

BRENNE TEN 48%

Allison Patel first delivered cases of Brenne Estate Cask on her bicycle to a few restaurants in Greenwich Village in the fall of 2012. Since then, the rise of this Breton whisky has been nothing short of meteoric. Brenne received Whisky Magazine's Icons of Whisky "Highly Commended" for Whisky Brand Innovator of the Year, 2014. The same publication also awarded Allison "Highly Commended" for World Whisky Brand Ambassador of the Year, 2016.

In the fall of 2015, Brenne released 290 cases of their first 10 year old whisky. This very limited bottling is the blending of four casks, hand-picked by Patel, who selected them for their distinctive complexity. Each bottle is individually numbered. Brenne Ten got off to an impressive start. London's Wizards of Whisky named Brenne Ten the #2 World's Best Single Malt, in addition to awarding it a Gold Medal for Best European Single Malt.

Light amber in color, this whisky gives off luscious notes of dried fruits (apples and pears), as well as spice, vanilla, and orange zest. This is a smooth whisky on the palate, with the orange peel coming through as promised, accompanied by apple, pear, a rich spiciness, and hint of black tea and caramel. Honey, zest, and vanilla linger, on a smooth, dry finish. A delicious, luscious new limited whisky from the charming, and impressive, Ms. Patel.

Q&A WITH ALLISON PATEL: WHISKEY-MAKER, BLOGGER, AND TRADER

BY RICHARD THOMAS

Few people wear as many hats in the whisky business as Allison Patel. After starting the whisky import-export firm Local Infusions and becoming a whisky blogger, Patel made the leap into founding her own label, Brenne single malt. Offhand, I can think of half a dozen people who have filled two of those roles at different times, but no one who has managed all three.

In this first part of this interview with Mrs. Patel, we discuss the ins and outs of the whisky trade. Incidentally, if you're English or Scandinavian and can get the excellent bourbon coming from Texas distiller Balcones, you probably have Alison Patel to thank.

RT: You are the proprietor of Local Infusions, an import/export outfit; a whisky blogger; and a whisky-maker. Under which of these hats is it that you got your start in the whisky business?

AP: Well, I produce and I founded Brenne Whisky, but I am not the distiller, just to make that clear, just so that doesn't get misconstrued along the way.

I'm a little bit of an envoy I guess. I'd never worked in the industry before setting up my companies. It was a combination of passion and dreams and planning and the right time and opportunity that put the whole thing together for me.

RT: Looking at the product list for Local Infusions, if you were looking to the United States, the only import is Brenne. The rest are American micro-distilleries: Finger Lakes, Balcones, Kings County. As an expat in Europe, I'm wondering where is all this American whisky going?

AP: First of all, in the import-export world, it takes a long time to get your contracts set up and get your markets on board. In all honesty, once I started importing Brenne, it was agreed with the American craft whisky-makers for the most part that we would quietly stop work. I'd worked for two years building up the export portfolio and made contact with a lot of great potential buyers in other countries, a few deals were in the works, but as a sole entrepreneur, I didn't have the hours to manage it properly. I promised all the brands I worked with that I wanted to do right by everyone.

But Balcones we did launch in Norway, Sweden, and in London in the UK, and there were a couple of deals that were passed off to other companies, and that could do some things for Balcones.

RT: It sounds like the export side [of Local Infusions] is on the backburner for the time being. But you are importing your Brenne. Is there the possibility you'll import some other rare and hard-to-find whisky products into the United States?

AP: Absolutely, but I can't tell on those details.

But Brenne, I founded and I own that company, and that is my main focus now. Since […] my focus is the United States market and building the brand. I'm really just a passionate whisky geek, and the whole reason I started Local Infusions was because when I was traveling and going to these amazing distilleries and tasting some things and these whisky shows, and seeing the selections that were available in some of these countries that were not available in our country, in the U.S. a couple of years of waiting for those things, and clearly nothing was happening, so…

It was not my intention to have my own label, that was not the initial focus, but certain things happened and Brenne happened, and I was so blessed and so fortunate and so truly grateful that I've been able to do this. I've always been told that people starting out in business need to have a plan and need to have a focus, but I think that once you have that plan, the most important thing is to stay flexible. Until you get started, you never know how it is, and opportunities may come up that, for whatever reason, are better and more appropriate for you than what you [originally] set out to do.

RT: Before we even started, I could tell you've got your toes into a lot of different types of whisky. When you were working with those American micro-distilleries on export, what was it that you said to people in Europe about these crafty bourbons and ryes, when over here they drink mostly scotch and Irish?

AP: I love that. As much as we're all passionate about what's inside, you start with the bottle, because that is what people see. Principally, I wanted to work with distillers who were extremely honest about what they were doing, whether they were sourcing the thing or making it themselves. I didn't want any false or misleading advertising. Truth in what you were doing would trump a lot for me.

I have a soapbox just for that, because people paying attention to the craft American scene would ask me "are they really making that, or is it sourced whisky?" So that was number one.

Number two, perhaps people drink mostly malt over there, but perhaps that's because they don't have the selection we have here. I think there's a lot to be said for variety to being the spice of life.

RT: Speaking of Brenne, you've had it up and running in the States for several months. How's it doing?

AP: It's going so well! I'm so happy! Thank goodness it is going so well, and largely thanks to our blogger community. My God, what an amazing whisky-loving family that we've got.

RT: Brenne is a French single malt, and while most of the malt whisky-making activity in France is in Brittany, Brenne comes from Cognac, made by a third-generation cognac-maker. That seems to set Brenne apart from not just what is made in France, but anywhere else as well. What do you think your distiller being a cognac-maker brings to Brenne?

AP: That's a great question. Everything. I have learned that distillers are always playing with things, and I have been lucky enough to meet my distiller, and discover that he had been working on this whiskey. Well, I flew to Cognac the moment I heard about this. I was excited and apprehensive, but he's made this whiskey in the style of his cognac, every aspect of the way he looks at this whole whiskey thing is from a cognac perspective.

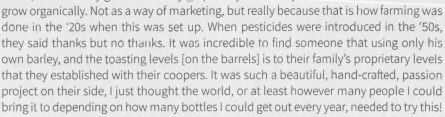

It's a farm distillery, his grandparents started it in the 1920s, and so every grain and every grape they distill they grow organically. Not as a way of marketing, but really because that is how farming was done in the '20s when this was set up. When pesticides were introduced in the '50s, they said thanks but no thanks. It was incredible to find someone that using only his own barley, and the toasting levels [on the barrels] is to their family's proprietary levels that they established with their coopers. It was such a beautiful, hand-crafted, passion project on their side, I just thought the world, or at least however many people I could bring it to depending on how many bottles I could get out every year, needed to try this!

A big part of the craft movement is getting to taste regional influences, and to me this whiskey screams that it is a whiskey from Cognac. I tell people all the time it tastes like a cognac and a single malt had a baby, even though there is no cognac spirit in it.

RT: That's what Scott Peters wrote when he reviewed it. Although Scott is principally our "Rye Guy," he loved that single malt meets cognac thing.

AP: That is so cool!

RT: Yeah, I think you really hit the ball there.

AP: I have to say that is truly the touching part about this whole thing. [...] You know, I did some market testing, but to produce something that is so different is a little scary. And Brenne is not different for the sake of being different, it's not a gimmick, I really believe in what I'm doing but I was of course very nervous and excited when I launched it. Something that surprised me from the start was that the really serious peat heads, or someone like Scott who is a rye-drinker, would tell me they don't typically drink other styles of whisky, but after tasting it would not only respect and understand [Brenne], but like it and admire it! It's really humbling.

RT: What is it about Brenne—your import—that would appeal to the typical American bourbon-lover?

AP: Brenne is definitely a malt with the most fruitful and dessert-like complexity… I hate to say sweet, because sweet can be so polarizing, but in a complex, dessert way, it's a sweeter whiskey compared to its Scotch brothers. It could be an interesting option for a bourbon drinker, because you're getting that malt kick in the finish, but you're also getting this interesting approach, and perhaps there are some nice parallels there between the two types of whisky.

RT: As a blogger, importer, and maker, what kind of qualities do you favor in your sipping whisky?

AP: I love something that takes me on a journey. Truthfully. I love something that evolves a little bit in the glass, while it opens up. I don't go for something that is one-dimensional. I want multi-dimensionality, and I want smooth transitions from one note to the next, and that's what I want.

RT: And how does that work out in terms of what your favorite tipples might be?

AP: In terms of mainstream and what's generally available, I love what David Stewart is doing at Balvenie. I get very excited about certain expressions that he releases, and I think they have beautiful, truly great whiskies.

Compass Box to me is another interesting one that I love exploring. Mackmyra, the Swedish, I like what they are doing and the avenues they are taking. And of course, they appeal to my entrepreneurial spirit, and my passion for craft, locally-focused whiskies.

Balcones, naturally. We've become really good friends, and it's nice to drink something made by a friend. That's a really special experience.

I also like to have things I can't get here, and that I pick up in my travels. I love the Japanese whiskies that you can't get here in the United States.

CELTIC WHISKY COMPAGNIE

A craft distillery founded in Côtes d'Armor on the northern coast of Brittany, France, the Celtic Whisky Compagnie is on the far end of "La Presqu'île Sauvage" (meaning "The Wild Peninsula"), directly facing the ocean. This spit of land is bounded by two coastal rivers—"Le Jaudy" and "Le Trieux." They offer many different expressions, most notably aging their whiskies in ex-Sauternes barrels. These small releases are usually difficult to come by outside of France.

CLONMEL IRISH SINGLE MALT WHISKY 5 YEAR OLD 40%

Around 1900, there were more than fifteen whisky distilleries in Clonmel, Ireland, the second largest number in that country after Dublin. Named after this town, Clonmel comes from the Gaelic Cluain Meala, which means "The Honey Meadow." This is a pot still Irish single malt. No chill filtration was used on this whisky. Clonmel claimed the Gold Medal at the Concours Mondial de Bruxelles 2002. Banana, apricot, honey, and caramel all come through on the nose and on the palate. Lovely spices show up late along with a slightly creamy, vanilla finish.

CD

CLONMEL IRISH PEATED
SINGLE MALT WHISKY 8 YEAR OLD 40%

This is a peated, light Irish pot still single malt whisky. They use no chilled filtration on this whisky either. The malt offers caramel, honey, dates, and apricot. The peat is light, not overpowering, and offers nice balance. Layers and layers of complexity, like a misty Breton morning. The peat is noticeable, but subtle. Those looking for a strong peat statement will be disappointed. Those looking for a suggestion, or a nice dose of it, will be happy. Dates, figs, honey, vanilla all come along for the finish, with hints of cocoa and other spices.

CD

The Glann ar Mor distillery is located in Breton, France. The name Glann ar Mor means "At the edge of the sea" in Breton. The light-house motif on their labels is the Héaux de Bréhat lighthouse in Breton. The Celtic Whisky Compagnie established Glann ar Mor in 1997. Their first bot-tling rolled off the line in December 1999. The current operation at Glann ar Mor went live in June 2005. Its first products came out in 2008 and 2009. The distillery's peated single malt is produced under the label Kor-nog, meaning "West Wind" in Breton.

KORNOG TAOUARC'H KENTAN 13 BC 46%

I suppose this baby wasn't distilled in 13 BC, when, according to Wikipe-dia, Drusus was governor of Gaul. It's peated.

Color: Straw.

Nose: The Taouarc'h with more lemons and grapefruits as well as a bigger briny side. More chiselled and a little fatter at the same time. Like this a lot.

Palate: A Sancerre from the best makers and at a higher strength. This is a style I enjoy a lot, very zesty, with an ultra-clean smokiness and bags of lemons and pink grapefruits (the sweeter ones). Yet it's relatively fat again, pretty thick in fact, always great news. Clean, focused, chiseled, perfect. No signs of youth as such; in a way there's an Amrut effect, mean-ing that it obviously matured quicker than under northern climates. Long, ultra-clean, lemony, peaty, salty...All good.

I don't know if this superb fatness comes from direct firing of the stills (live flames as they use at Glann ar Mor). That could well be!

SV

KORNOG 'SANT IVY 2015 PEATED SINGLE MALT 59.6%

What an easy name! It's a single cask this time, maybe not quite ex-Ivy League or is it?

Color: Straw.

Nose: Well, careful, this is a bit strong. It seems that it's a little more medicinal than the others but not sure. Water please... With water: a wee tad raw and barleyish, maybe, when compared with the previous one. A feeling of sake, maybe, but otherwise it's all perfect. Well I love good sake.

Palate: An ultra-lemony peat, this seems to be more or less the Taouarc'h

Kentan 13 BC (phew) at a higher strength, with more pepper too. Not too sure, this is no jet fuel but it's really strong. With water: the salt comes out, together with lemons and grapefruits.

All that is very peated, naturally. A little less oily and fat this time, but of course all that depends on the amount of water you're adding, on the kind of water, on the way you add it and on the waiting time (never taste whisky just after you've added water, always wait for a few minutes! Sipping is fine…). Long finish and just excellent. Don't I detect touches of pineapples again? That's youth!

Another obvious winner, it's just that the superb Taouarc'h Kentan 13 BC (yeah yeah) may have overshadowed it a tiny-wee bit.

SV

GLANN AR MOR 'TAOL ESA 2 GWECH 2013 46%

A vatting of three bourbon casks. Glann ar Mor is unpeated. Are Breton names nicer than Gaelic ones? Well, you decide, both are nicer than Alsatians anyway.

Color: White wine.

Nose: A combination of warm bread (baguette!), ginger, vanilla, tinned pineapples, wet earth, and sea air. It's very natural, whatever that means, fresh and young, absolutely not oak-doped like other young whiskies can be these days and still close to the barley, so to speak.

Palate: Yes! To be honest I did not find the nose extremely impressive—and it's maybe not a nosing whisky in the first place, especially since it's obviously quite young— but it really delivers on the palate. It does not feel youngish at all;

it's full, the barrels and the distillate blended together to almost-perfection and there's a big salinity. Remember, in wine salinity is the new mineral-ity. In whisky too? So it's very full, yet not quite oily, on sweet barley, salt (yeah), ripe pears (not pears from youth), salted butter caramel and, once again, tinned pineapples, or rather candied pineapples. Great balance but warning, this goes down

too well. A medium length finish, with clean, salty, fruity and fresh notes. Superb salty/lemony/melony aftertaste. I'm very fond of this palate. Great, great work, honestly.

SV

TAOUARC'H 48.5%

A visitor center exclusive. So this single bourbon cask was distilled at Glann ar Mor, where they also make a peated malt called Kornog, and it is peated, and yet it's not called Kornog, nor is it called Glann ar Mor. Ooh my poor head, I need some kind of remedy... Like this?...

Color: Pale gold.

Nose: Some kind of sweet brine. Maybe pickled fruits, or fig chutney? It's definitely coastal, only mildly smoky, with a barleyness that's still there in the background. In a way, it reminds me of a beer I was very fond of when I was twenty, Pilsen Urquell. Yes, I've almost dropped beer since then.

Palate: Shall I use the word 'salinity' again? It's one of the saltiest peaters I could taste—no peated Islay is as salty as this. But yet again, not many salted Islays mature near the sea anyway. Other than that, it's a moderately smoky whisky, the closest Scotch malt I could think of to that respect is Ardmore, but this Taouarc'h is more citrusy. Same level of fruitiness, though. Long finish, full, on "sweet peat" as we sometimes say (so not tarry, not ashy, not bonfire-y and not medicinal).

I think this is for whisky lovers who are wavering between sweetness and peatiness. It's got both and quality's high yet again.

SV

DOMAINE MAVELA

P & M PURE MALT WHISKY 42%

I've had a small glass of this, for me, unknown whisky, one night…It had a sweet smell. This time it was the NEAT glass.

This whisky reminded me of something. Can't place what…

The P & M Single Malt Whisky was distilled by Domaine Mavela, and comes from the island of Corsica. It is known for its taste, citrus, and oak.

P&M Single Malt whisky distinguishes itself by the softness of its fragrance, which is enhanced in part by the aging of the casks, made of the oak from the forests of Tronçais. The whisky is matured for three years in casks made of oak from the local forest, which lends it a depth of flavor.

When I'm writing forests, I think about high trees, colorful birds, wild bears, lots of bees and butterflies, just as colorful as the birds. Male birds are more colorful than the female kind … here it's the other way around. The female are from the colors. More than men … In history it was the other way… maybe in the future it will be like in the past! A world of colorful men. Colorful clothes, jewelry, some make-up for the finish!

This version of P & M is fruity with a taste that lingers in the mouth, and a beautiful amber color. This whisky is a rich complex and very imaginative whisky.

Color: Amber gold.
Nose: Citrus and oak.
Palate: Very fruity, long and pure.

If you're planning to taste this whisky, you need to have some more whisky experience! It's nice, but not for a whisky virgin!

FTS

VICOMTE SINGLE MALT WHISKY
8 YEAR OLD 40%

Vicomte is a rank of French nobility, originally a title bestowed by the King. This single malt whisky is made from 100% malted, organic, natural barley grown in the Charentes region of France. Charentes is a famous distilling region, known most famously for cognac. This 80 proof, single malt whisky is very much a product of terrior. Both the land and how it is made is all very French. This single malt is unique. It is hand-crafted and twice distilled in pot stills (copper alembic still). Unlike other small craft single malts, it is not aged in old bourbon barrels, nor old sherry casks from Spain. Instead, owing to its heritage, it is aged for eight years in French oak, Limousin barrels, which were former cognac barrels. So it speaks of its region. Honeycrisp apple, Bosc pear, Madagascar vanilla, ripe figs, brown sugar, and anise are prominent, with a whiff of smoke. Best straight with just a sprinkle of water.

CD

The whisky boom has been underway for several years now (two decades by some accountings), and with it has come both the opening of many new distilleries, as well as interest in whisky-makers in some out-of-the-way places. I think a common mistake among whisky fans is to assume that just because a whisky comes from a non-traditional place, it must come from a newcomer looking to cash in on the worldwide whisky boom.

While sometimes true, usually those distilleries in unexpected places have been there for decades, and have merely gone overlooked by the wider world. The Spanish distillery DYC is a case in point, as is the French distillery Warenghem, which has been around for over a century. If the idea of French whisky seems strange, just keep in mind that distillers like Warenghem are found in Brittany, long recognized as the last Celtic holdout of France. Separated from England and Ireland by but a small expanse of sea, the Bretons have a lot in common with their Celtic cousins further north, including a taste for good whisky.

ARMORIK CLASSIC WHISKY 46%

Armorik is the foundation of Warenghem's whisky line. This Breton single malt is married from whisky aged in ex-bourbon and ex-sherry casks, and is bottled at 46% without chill-filtration.

In the glass, Warenghem's Armorik has the honey gold coloring common to those whiskies among its Scotch cousins with good body and character. The nose is silky and rich, and predominately malty sweet, with a touch of cinnamon and a note of "meadow scent," what I like to call the place where woodiness meets thick, wet grass. It really is a delightful nose, full of character, and the sort of thing you'll want to sniff over and over again.

The flavor of Armorik shifts things around a bit. A fruity, plum-like sweetness overtakes the malty and woody aspects, which are still there but in the background. The dash of cinnamon is there too, but so is a new peppery bite. The latter gives good balance to what would otherwise be an overtly sweet palate. The finish is long, warm, and a little astringent from the wood, leaving a spicy afterglow in its wake.

Despite the mix of flavors and scents, Armorik is too bold, and too spicy in particular, to be subtle. Instead, it is a whisky with good balance

and robust character, and is therefore the sort of thing one can enjoy sipping on most any occasion. If you aren't devoted to peat smoke and want to try a single malt from a non-traditional region, Armorik should be on your short list.

RT

ARMORIK DOUBLE MATURATION 46%

Part of having a whisky tradition is having a region or regions where the bulk of whisky-making takes place. Britain might have English and Welsh whisky, but Scotland is where it's at. Whisky-making in the United States has spread to almost all of the 50 states in recent times, but Kentucky and Tennessee are still at the heart of American whiskey-making.

So it is with even within those whisky-making countries that are, in and of themselves, not a traditional whisky-making region, such as France. While whisky-making is spreading around France, with outfits like Brenne popping up in Cognac, the core of French whisky-making is Brittany. One of the oldest fixtures of modern Breton whisky-making is Warenghem, a family distillery that has been around for more than a century.

Warenghem's Armorik Double Maturation represents a new oak spin on their single malt. Primary maturation takes place in new Breton oak barrels made by a local cooper. I'm not sure if Breton oak is used in any other alcohol, and it certainly puts a thorough local emphasis on the whisky. It would be like Four Roses or Woodford Reserve saying, "our bourbon is aged in Eastern Kentucky oak" instead of American oak. After some years in the new oak, it is transferred to old sherry casks for finishing, and bottled without chill filtration at 46%.

In the glass, the whisky shows that new oak-aging off with a light copper coloring. The nose has a creamy, elegant sweetness to it, mixing citrus, apple, and pear, and caramel notes with just a tinge of pepper and musty wood.

The flavor was a bit of a let down after that sophisticated nose, but only just a bit. The taste is predominately that of leathery wood, with a dash of pepper and a certain malty character. It's not as complex as the nose, but if you like your whisky to run into old horse tackle closet territory, this is the thing for you. The finish brings on another surprise by rolling out on an ashy note, running lengthily into warmth and a smoky aftertaste.

RT

ARMORIK SHERRY FINISH 46%

Armorik uses the classic, traditional Scottish method to make its whisky, starting with 100% malty barley and using a double distillation process, attempting to produce a truly high-quality product made in Brittany, France. The whisky is then aged in bourbon barrels for some time to mature. The cellar master at Armorik then chooses specific barrels that are then transferred to former sherry casks (Spanish oloroso sherry barrels). The whisky stays in these barrels two to four months to finish. The normally-fruity Armorik is then enhanced by soft notes of dried fruit, prunes, and more exotic spices more closely associated with the characteristics of sherry. And that is exactly what happens. Honey and caramel on the nose. Prune, fig, apple, and pear come across. And a nice long nose of malt. Fig, apple, pear, honey, vanilla, and spice all come across. The honey/caramel and spice linger on the palate.

CD

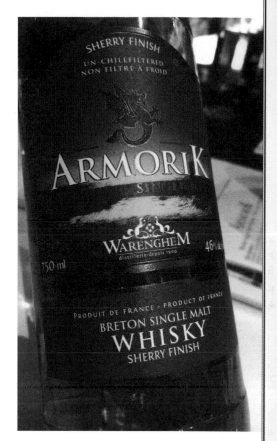

GERMANY

BY CARLO DEVITO

Historically, Germany was known for beer and fruit brandies. Indeed, many of the distillers in Germany creating whisky today have a connection to one or the other. Some have a connection to both. Many are family owned; some are even fourth-generation owned. Germans seemed to have developed a thirst for single malt whisky. Many of the distillers and breweries have made treks to Scotland to see how they do it there. One of the fun things to see in Germany is their desire not to emulate the great whiskies of the world, but rather, there is a movement afoot to create something that is very much an expression of the regions in which they are made. And one must also love their interest not in just finishing whiskies in the numerous casks of varying degrees but also their willingness to try German oak barrels. And I love that some of the barley is being smoked using local woods! Innovation is on the march in Germany. The goal is to make world-class whiskies, which some are achieving, but to make something unique of place is the higher expression that must be respected.

BY THOMAS OHRBOM

Ever heard of Meatloaf (the artist, not the food)? Ever seen the massive length of most of his song titles? Well, here is a single malt with Meatloaf-esque proportions on both distillery name and name of whisky.

The distillery is named Bayerwald-Bärwurzerei Spezialitäten-Brennerei Gerhard Liebl. My German is a bit rusty, to say the least, but let's try to decipher this. Bayerwald would be the Bavarian Forest. Bärwurzerei means they (also) produce Bärwurz, which, from what I can tell, is a sort of root schnapps. Spezialitäten-Brennerei is

specialty distillery, and finally Gerhard Liebl is the proprietor. In all fairness I have to add that they do seem to also go by the much simpler name Liebl Brennerei.

The company was established back in 1970, focusing on schnapps and similar products. In 1991, they built the first incarnation of the actual distillery. It was further expanded in 1999, 2001, and 2006. Then on February 8, 2006, they distilled the first drops of new make that would later become their first Bavarian single malt in 2009.

COILLMÓR EDITION VILLA KONTHOR
PORT CASK 46%

The whisky itself is called Coillmór—Edition Villa Konthor—Port Cask. Now this is a lot easier to remember. The brand is obviously Coillmór, and this single cask release was bottled exclusively for Villa Konthor in Limburg, and it has been matured in a Port Cask (cask #200). It was distilled in 2007.

Nose: Quite fresh with lots of port notes. Lots of spices and a fair bit of oak influence.

Palate: Sugar sweet, oaky, and a bit herbal. The port influence is quite obvious here as well. The sugary sweetness is taking over, dominating completely. Relatively short finish. Very cool to have tried this, and definitely want to try more, both from Liebl Brennerei and other similar German whisky distilleries.

TO

COILLMÓR 3 YEAR OLD AMERICAN OAK 43%

This whisky comes from Bavaria and was distilled in pot stills. *Coillmór* means *"large forest"* in Gaelic... Wait, Bavaria, Gaelic? Bah, who cares!

Color: Gold.

Nose: Very expressive, all on sour oak, vanilla, thick porridge, and spices. It's not unpleasant at all but we're extremely far from Scotch whisky here. Hints of pears and hops coming through the heavy oakiness after a while, the whole reminding me more and more of fleur de bière (distilled beer) like they make here in Alsace.

Palate: Rich and, to tell you the truth, more to my liking than on the nose, even if the flavors are in the

same vein, that is to say sweet and spicy. Chinese sweet and sour sauce, very ripe apples, pepper, nutmeg (a lot), cinnamon (a lot), Belgian beer (do you know Duvel?) and finally notes of gingerbread and speculoos (Belgian again). Rather long finish, balanced, rich, just as spicy and sweet. I think this works, even if it cannot be compared to Scotch whisky. Carefully and honestly made for sure.

SV

COILLMÓR SHERRY PEDRO XIMÉNEZ 6 YEAR OLD 46%

This Coillmór single malt whisky was made from Bavarian caramel and smoked malts that have been smoked over beech wood. Coillmór uses soft, local mountain waters from the Bavarian Forest, which they consider one of the best resources they have at their disposal. They feel it is responsible for the mildness of their single malt whiskies.

The distillery uses small pot stills, and the final whisky is twice distilled. In the early years the young whisky was

aged in American white oak barrels. The whisky was finished by spending two years in freshly emptied Sherry Pedro Ximénez barrels from the Bodega Tradicion of the Jerres region in Spain.

The finish should have a slightly sweeter tone than their normal product, which should make this whisky fairly accessible. Generally considered by experts to be one of the better drams on the European continent.

CD

DISTILLERIE BLAUE MAUS

Blaue Maus was originally founded at a family owned and run grocery and tobacco shop in Eggolsheim, Germany. It was there, in 1980, that Robert Fleishmann founded the Blaue Maus Distillery, making it the oldest whisky-dedicated distiller in Germany. He originally distilled brandy for the store to be sold alongside their other products. By 1983, he had distilled his first single malt, but it did not live up to Fleischmann's own personal standards. Robert did not sell his first finished bottle of whisky until 1996. In 2000 Robert retired, and the business is now run by his son Thomas and wife Petra.

BLAUE MAUS SINGLE MALT WHISKY 40%

Blaue Maus currently offers five different brands of whisky. Fleischmann's Blaue Maus Austrasians Single Cask Malt received a rating of 95.5 from famed whisky guru Jim Murray. A major accolade for sure. Other brands include Krottentaler, Spinnaker, Black Pirate and Green Dog.

DURR SCHWARZWALD BRENNEREI

When Nicolas and Sebastian Dürr fired up their first whiskey in 2002, they had no idea what would start out as a curiosity would end up becoming a passion. It became all too clear to them at an early stage that while they would use the greatest whiskies of Scotland and Ireland for inspiration, there was no need to make carbon copies of them. The idea was to make a whiskey expressive of the Black Forest region. Something that would show its terroir. The northern Black Forest around the Teinachtal is a harsh climate with soft water.

DOINICH DAAL BLACKFOREST SINGLE MALT WHISKEYS

Dürr produced two releases of their whiskey. Blackforest Single Malt Whiskey Batch No. 1 40% was released in the winter of 2012. It was a limited edition bottling of 200 bottles, all individually hand-numbered. The 100% malt whiskey was aged in bourbon and cognac barrels. Then it was finished in an apple apéritif barrel. Tasting notes include, "On the nose it unfolds with a complex sweetness... A slight touch of apple spreads and offers the palate a rich variety of flavors. Vanilla, cinnamon, fir, malt, and oak lead to a complex fruity finish."

In November of 2014, they released Doinich Daal Blackforest Single Malt Whiskey Batch No. 2 in two different editions. Batch No. 2 Malachit Edition 40% was another limited edition, this time with 1,200 individually hand-numbered bottles. The whiskey had been aged in bourbon and cognac barrels, and then again finished in apple apéritif barrels. The tasting notes read, "On the nose it unfolds fruity dry. A slight touch of apple spreads...Vanilla, striking fir, strong malt and soft mocha with some tobacco, lead to a complex fruity fin-

ish with a slight hazelnut." At the same time they released Batch No. 2 Azurit Edition 42.5% of which only ninety-nine individually numbered bottles were released. This whiskey was aged in wine and cognac barrels, and then finished in apple apéritif barrels. The tasting notes read, "On the nose it unfolds with a complex sweetness...A slight touch of apple spreads...Raisins, dates, caramel, cinnamon, striking fir, a hint of cognac, and deep oak open into a complex fruity finish."

Hammerschmiede Spirituosen is located in Zorge, in Lower Saxony, approximately fifty-three miles south of Braunschweig. The distillery was established in 1985 by Karl-Theodore Buchholz and his family in an old hammer mill. The old forge was built between 1250-1270 and is now mostly used as a barrel room. In the last quarter-century of the 1800s, it was home to a blacksmith and a foundry. Hammerschmiede Spirituosen is now one of the largest producers of single malt whisky in Germany and continental Europe, producing nearly 20,000 liters of malt spirit a year. They also make eaux de vie, liqueurs, and other fruit based spirits.

In the 1990s, son Alexander Buchholz joined the family firm with the idea of making regionally expressive whiskies. They released their first whisky in 2002. The Harz line of whiskies is the home of The Glen Els single malt whiskies, which were first released in 2005. The name Glen Els come from the water source—the River Elsbach. The Glen Els single malts are twice distilled in a pot still and are made from 100% barley grown in the Hercynian region. Some barley is lightly roasted, and some is wood smoked. One thing that distinguishes The Glen Els is the distiller's willingness to experiment with different woods and barrels. They have worked with marsala, cognac, sherry, Madeira, Malaga, Grand cru and port wine casks of various sizes, as well as with German oak quarter casks from Schwarzwald-Traubeneiche. The Glen Els line of single malt whiskies is well regarded and considered one of the better whisky distilleries on the continent. Two of their whiskies have earned Liquid Gold Awards in 2012 and 2013. The line is so popular that the distillery receives more than 20,000 visitors a year to boot! The Glen Els line has a number of releases and expressions; it is a mature and formidable quality whisky line.

THE GLEN ELS THE JOURNEY 43%

The Glen Els The Journey is among their most popular offerings in The Glen Els line. It starts with 100% pure barley grown in the Hercynian region. Alexander smokes 5% of the barley to give the whisky some texture without making it too over the top. He then ages the whisky in six different cask types, including former cream sherry barrels, tawny port, Madeira, marsala, Malaga and Grand cru Bordeaux, for a minimum of four years (this contains the 5% wood-smoked malt). This gives the whisky aroma, flavor, and complexity. The whisky is not chill-filtered. Tasting notes include fruitcake, raisins, vanilla, toffee, butter, bread, whiffs of sweet smoke. Finish is clean with caramel and a slight hint of smoke lingers. Hints of citrus/Mandarin close it out.

THE GLEN ELS THE ALRIK SERIES 52.3%

The Glen Els Alrik series is a line of whiskies that were extremely heavily smoked. They used wood smoked malt. Heavy, heavy smoke. For those who love a smoked whisky, this is the series. It was a huge success. Four versions of this whisky were released. They were packaged beautifully, in limited edition boxes. Alrik Edition 1912 First Try was released September 2012. It was aged in Pedro Ximénez (PX) sherry hogshead casks. Only 555 bottles were produced. Then Alrik Edition 1912 Early Bird 52% was released in 2013 with 1,111 bottles. Like the First Try expression, this whisky was matured in PX-sherry hogshead casks, but then finished in PX-sherry butts, giving it a little extra. The Alrik Edition 1912 Mid-Winter 52.3% was only available through the distillery. This limited edition (released in December 2013) saw the whisky mature in PX-sherry hogsheads for the primary storage but was finished in ex-Château D'Yquem Sauternes barrels. The last Alrik Edition 1912 Pearl Jubilee (available only at the distillery) was released in August of 2014. The whisky was aged in a PX-sherry hogshead, as had previous editions, but was finished by Alexander adding a quarter cask of honey wine to finish the whisky. The Alrik Edition 1913 was released in June 2014, and was made of whisky aged primarily in a marsala hogshead and then finished in a freshly used PX-sherry butt.

THE GLEN ELS EMBER EDITION 45.9%

The Ember Edition is meant to be a rustic, traditional, aromatic wood smoked single malt whisky. The barley is 60% un-smoked, 40% wood smoked using local Alder wood. Then the whisky is aged for four years in a combination of cream sherry, oloroso sherry, port, Malaga, marsala and Claret barrels. This whisky is sweetish with a nice smokiness, and lots of complexity. Raisins, figs, cocoa, caramel, cassis, and caramel all come across on the nose. Raisins, figs, and cassis come across first on the palate, with vanilla and spices bringing up the rear, all covered by a velvet fog of smoke.

BRENNEREI HOHLER

BY CARLO DEVITO

Established in 1895, by Johann Wilhelm Alberti, the Höhler Distillery produced quality fruit brandies and other liqueurs for many years. Karl Holger Höhler, who currently directs Höhler, is the fourth member in the family to guide the distillery. He took over in 1987. By 2000, Karl had installed a completely new distilling system. In 2001, he began making experimental batches of whisky using combinations of corn, wheat, and rye.

He aged these whiskies for three years before bottling and releasing them. These were limited editions and sold out quickly. Höhler produces a number of styles of whiskies, including rye, bourbon, Irish whiskey, and Scotch as their inspiration. The product line is called "Whesskey" as a combination of the words whisky and Hesse (the state in which the distillery is located). The single malt whisky is made from CaraAroma-Malt.

WHESSKEY HESSISCHER 44%

Right after the Limburg whisky fair, I convinced two of my friends to go on yet another distillery visit and we went looking for Brennerei Höhler, just a few kilometers south of Limburg. The distillery wasn't open at the time we finally located it, but we managed to get a wee look around by using sign language to a lady guarding the place.

Nose: Youth, Malt.

Palate: Very fruit brandy-like, some spicyness, doesn't taste a lot like whisky. Some sour, acidic not very pleasant notes. Shortish finish. It seems a bit more balanced on the texture, feels like a bit more heavy spirit.

SB

BADISCHE STAATSBRAUEREI ROTHAUS AG

The Rothaus State Brewery of Baden (Badische Staatsbrauerei Rothaus AG) is located right in the center of the Black Forest ("Schwarzwald"). The brewery was established in the same exact location where a Benedictine monastery had been built in 1791. They make all the beer for the Rothaus label. Rothaus delivers the mash to Kammer-Kirsch GmbH in Karlsruhe for distillation. Kammer-Kirsch was established in 1909. The distillery was used as a test site for the state of Baden. Originally they produced cherry brandy. Kammer-Kirsch was named Germany's Best Whisky Distillery in 2011 and 2012. Kammer-Kirsch double distills the brew from Rothaus. It is then stored in bourbon barrels. Sometimes the whiskies are "finished" in separate barrels for special bottlings. They release whiskies annually on March 16, which is Rothaus Master Brewer Max Sachs' birthday!

BLACK FOREST ROTHAUS EDITION 2013 PINOT NOIR FINISH 53.5%

The company from Karlsruhe, Germany is not only an importer of distillates. The core business has always been producing their own spirits. The Rothaus third special edition appeared in October 2013. The name? Black Forest Rothaus Edition 2013 Pinot Noir Wood Finish. A German whisky with so many Scottish parallels.

The facts for the preparation of the new Rothaus 2013 Pinot Noir Wood Finish sound like those of many Scottish distilleries. With this counter-trend, not all hide behind a fancy No Age Statement. The new Rothaus whisky matured first in ex-bourbon casks and then in 2011, obtained a "Finish" in Pinot Noir wine casks. The selected barrels came from Baden winery Franz Keller.

The Rothaus 2013 Pinot Noir Wood Finish is released at cask strength 53.5% and is not cold-filtered. As with all other whiskies, this means that there can be a slight turbidity at subsequent dilution with water.

This basic data for the preparation is clearly reminiscent of many production routes Scottish distilleries have used. Especially those like Glenmorangie, which likes to experiment with wine finish in their whisky.

PR

SCHLITZER DESTILLERIE

The Schlitzer Destillerie is located in Schlitz (Hesse) and has been making brandies and liqueurs since 1585. Over the years they also made wines and beers as well. Schlitzer Distillerie is the oldest distillery still in production in Germany. Under the Schitzerlander label, they make many whiskies, included unpeated and peated. The Glen Slitisa 14 Year Old Single Malt Wheat Whisky won third place at the trade fair InterWhisky in Frankfurt in 2013.

GLEN SLITISA 14 YEAR OLD 40%

Schlitzer considers this one of their finest achievements. And a small cadre of German whisky aficionados apparently agree. Glen Slitisa Single Malt Whisky is made from wheat grown right there in their region. The whisky in aged in oak barrels for fourteen years. Then they bottle it. This is a limited edition whisky. Tasting note: "Light-footed whisky with wonderful vanilla notes, very balanced."

SLITISIAN SOUR MASH 43%

According to Schlitzer, "new name but same content: *Glen Slitisa* becomes 'Slitisian Single Malt.'" The twice-distilled whisky is aged in used 200-liter barrels of American white oak. All the barrels are heavily toasted and stored. They age this whisky in the attic of the distillery, where the extremes of the weather push and pull the whiskies within. It ages whisky faster, and imparts bigger, bolder flavors. The whisky ages five years. Slitsian Single Malt Whisky Sour Mash has won several medals right off the bat, including international competitions. Notes include, "Deep golden. The nose: malty with beautiful strong vanilla tones, almost creamy...malty, fruity, rich vanilla, and caramel...."

SLYRS BAVARIAN
SINGLE MALT WHISKY 43%

Slyrs is a single malt whisky from Bavaria in Germany. It is aged for three years in American white oak and offers a conservative introduction into German whisky. The other whiskies in the Slyrs range offer some more interesting twists and turns, being matured in various wood types, but this Slyrs is a simple single malt matured in American oak in Bavaria—I can see a Fräulein bringing me a Steiner glass overflowing with foamy German lager right now... ah, the simple pleasures in life! This thought of mine may seem unconnected with whisky, but it just occurred to me that because whisky is basically made from distilling un-hopped beer then Germany has the potential to use its beer-brewing expertise to create a whisky that can be quite young and exhibit all the finer points of the barley, the malt, the yeast, and the wash.

On the nose, the smell of firm, husky cereal and mild vanilla wafts up with honey, soy bean yogurt, and malty notes interlaced with green apple, brown vinegar, and wet bird feed. On the palate, broiled chestnuts underpin a strange nuttiness that melds with apple and sultana as that sweetness then morphs into a slightly yeasty lager-type finish.

AC

A Visit to Slyrs–
The Bavarian Distillery

BY TOBIAS JOHNSSON

This summer I decided to make a short detour at the end of our family vacation. We drove from Innsbruck, Austria to Schliersee in the south of German Bavaria. We stayed at the cozy Gästehaus of Kögl in Neuhaus, the part of the town where Slyrs Distillery is located. From what I've heard, it's also easy to reach the distillery by train from Munich, which is only 31 miles northwest of Schliersee.

Slyrs' main goal is to create a Bavarian whisky in their own way, with their own crops etc. In my perspective, they do differ from many other distilleries in many ways, and I will primarily focus on those differences in the following description.

In 1999 Florian Stetter started Slyrs (which is the original name of Shliersee). The distillation was done in a facility where other spirits than whisky were made. In 2007 the Slyrs Distillery finally opened with brand new equipment. This is probably the main reason why many bloggers have noted a positive change in the quality and consistency of the whisky between the earlier batches compared to the later ones.

Schliersee is located at approximately half a mile above sea level, which makes it impossible to grow barley. To follow their own goal of making a Bavarian whisky, they buy malt from the town of Bamberg in the northern part of Bavaria. They only distill unpeated whisky simply because there are no peat bogs in the area, and it would ruin their tradition of making a Bavarian whisky by using peat from another area.

Here Slyrs differs again in many regards from other distilleries. They have three identical stills. The shapes are quite odd, but at the same time very beautiful to look at. The lyne arms are also very different, shaped like bows. The stills have a capacity of 1,500 liters each, and two of them are used as wash stills. The distilling time in the wash stills is six hours. Each still yields 350 liters of low wines at an ABV of 30%, which is quite high. The spirit still (which is locked in a glass room for tax reasons), runs for eight hours. The collected heart measures around 400-500 liters with an ABV of 70%. Another huge difference to other distilleries is that Slyrs throws the heads and tails away, they don't re-distill them.

The spirit is diluted all the way down to 55% before it's pumped into the casks. Slyrs only uses virgin American white oak barrels with a size of 225 liters. They mature the whisky for a minimum of three years. In the future, they will release their first 12 year old whisky (matured in second fill casks). The yield of the 12 year old will be extremely limited and it will probably sell out quickly.

The "standard" single malt has an ABV of 43%. Slyrs also produces a single cask version called Faßstärke (cask strength). Over the years Slyrs has also produced a number of different extra-matured whiskies.

They have a deep relationship with Bodegas Tradición in Jerez, Spain. They buy their Sherry casks from them, and they seem to hold an exceptional quality. For the best end result, Slyrs buys all casks (including the American white oak) fully assembled.

Their product range currently also include expressions finished in oloroso, amontillado, Sauternes and Pedro Ximénez (PX) casks respectively. The PX is extra-matured for less than a year, the other ones for more than a year. All of the bottlings are not chill-filtered and of natural color. To speed up the maturation in the casks, the doors to the warehouses are left open to permit as great temperature and humidity fluctuations as possible. Oh, and all the bottling is done by hand as well.

I then nosed and tasted all of the current releases of whiskies. All showed a consistent quality without any disturbing off-notes. The standard single malt is really good for a three year old whisky, not that complex in character though. The single cask showed more complexity, but it needed some water to settle down. Both of them are quite fruity.

All of the extra-matured ones were rounder and more exquisite, and thankfully there was hardly any sulfur notes. Complete tasting notes will follow after each bottle opening in the future. Considering many of the diversions from the golden standard of whisky production, it is fascinating to find their whiskies as good as they really are.

It was a fantastic experience to visit this super tidy distillery. I hoped that they would use some novel equipment and production tweaks, and I don't believe I could have experienced more novel ideas than at Slyrs, and still they have an end product that is whisky without question.

Every third week, the taxman comes to overlook the emptying of the heads and tails tanks. The spirit is watered down and emptied out into the common water drainage system, and the taxman deducts that alcohol off of the taxes that Slyrs has to pay. The quantity of this spirit is too low to sell for industrial use. The farmers in the vicinity are happy to collect the draff for their cattle.

Everything at the distillery follows the Bavarian tradition of construction. The building blends nicely into the surrounding scenery. Everything has been built with a high degree of finesse. The spacious tasting room overlooks the alps. A truly magic room to be sipping whisky in.

Sonnenscheiner Brennerie is located in Witten in the Ruhr region, and was established in 1875. It is a privately owned distillery, and has been in the family for four generations. Sonnenscheiner has 140 years of experience and tradition when it comes to distilling. They distill their single malt whisky from genuine Scottish malt.

SONNENSCHEINER 18 YEAR OLD 41%

This whisky is a vintage 1989 single malt whisky originally from distilled Scottish malt. The whisky is aged for more than seventeen years in American oak. It is then finished in former sherry barrels. Notes include, "a slightly peaty-fruity note, a fine vanilla and a delicate sweetness simultaneously."

ICELAND

BY CARLO DEVITO

If you grew up in Iceland, and you were drinking spirit beverages, you were probably drinking Brennivín. Clear and unsweetened, Brennivín is a schnapps. "Brennivín" means "burned wine" and is part of the same family as brandy. But in Iceland there's no fruit flavoring in the traditional Brennivín. In that way, it is more like aquavit or vodka. It's often made from potatoes, and might be flavored in some slight way. Traditional versions typically have caraway, but modern versions offer different infusions. Usually, one does a shot of Brennivín during Þorrablót (the mid-winter holidays). Whiskey is just catching on here. Everyone is curious to see where it goes.

FLÓKI ICELANDIC YOUNG MALT
1ST EDITION 47%

This is the very first 'almost whisky' from Iceland. Eimverk Distillery was established back in 2009, and here is their first product. The Flóki Icelandic Young Malt 1st Edition consists of eight single barrels released late 2014 and early 2015, all released as single casks. The ages of these barrels are one to two years, and they are all fresh 200 liter American oak barrels, medium+ toast and char level.

Floki Icelandic Young Malt is not a whiskey, and is not sold as a whiskey. It is a "young malt." The European whiskey regulations are exactly the same as the regulations for Scotch in this respect. You have to mature the spirit for a minimum of three years before you can call it whiskey. A slight difference is that for Scotch the maturation has to be in casks made from oak, whereas in Europe outside of Scotland the requirement is casks made from wood (this was the wording in the regulations for Scotch up until 1988).

We sent off a couple of questions to Halli Thorkelsson at Eimverk Distillery to learn more:

"Our young malt helps break in our new American oak barrels for the single malt. We found it hard to get a stable supply of quality, used oak so the young malt is on one hand a fresh and very young Icelandic Malt but also a part of our barrel cycle, breaking in controlled supplies of barrels for our single malt."

And here is a little hint at what we can expect from the distillery in the time to come:

"We will also be bottling Flóki Sheep Dung smoked young malt this year. Our first single malt bottling will be next summer."

Nose: Fresh cut grass, citrus, barley juice, and malt. A very fresh and young nose—but this is young in an upbeat and positive way. It feels very clean and vibrant on the nose. Given some time in the glass there is a distinct oakiness here—fresh sawdust with lemon juice sprinkled on. Fresh herbs and roots, tarragon, thyme, and licorice.

Palate: Full-bodied and dry mouthfeel. Pepper, oak, malt, and slightly bitter caramel. Pepper and honey. Dry, dark chocolate, then coffee and dark caramel with a slight burnt edge. Oaky spiciness and hints of ginger. Warm and of medium length. A positive first effort, I would say. I am very much looking forward to trying their first proper single malt, under the name Flóki First Impression. Look out for new whisky from Eimverk Distillery, good folks!

TO

SKOGAR ICELANDIC SINGLE MALT WHISKEY (FUTURE)

Skógar (pronounced /skou.ar/) is a small rustic village in a rural section of Iceland, with no more than 25 people. The town is located south of the Eyjafjallajökull glacier. The Skógá river is known for its waterfalls, especially the 60-foot Skógafoss, and for its hiking and old farm ruins.

Birgir Mar Sigurdsson went to Islay on the west coast of Scotland to try whiskey in the spring of 2010. He learned how they made whiskey and found the weather on that island wasn't much different than on his.

"So I thought 'why not make whiskey in Iceland?' And thusly the idea of an Icelandic-made whiskey was born." He wrote business plans in 2011, and by 2012, he was already branding his product.

"Good whiskey relies completely on pure and unspoiled nature," Birgir reasoned. Skogar single malt whiskey will eventually be produced in three releases: 10 Year Old, 15 Year Old, and 21 Year Old. This distillery is still in the planning stages.

CD

INDIA

BY DAVIN DE KERGOMMEAUX

The whisky world was gobsmacked in 2004 to learn that a distillery in India was quietly making world-class single malt whisky. That was the year that Ashok Chokalingam introduced Amrut, India's first single malt, to the UK. Early attempts to launch the whisky in Indian restaurants in Scotland had not been encouraging. It was a classic "Coals-to-Newcastle" scenario: "What self-respecting Scot would knowingly buy single malt whisky from India," reluctant restauranteurs asked him? So, Chokalingam went under cover. When he delighted drinkers at the Pot Still pub in Glasgow with an un-disclosed whisky he was pouring, then had them guess what it was, they declared it a fine example of 12 to 15 year-old Speyside single malt. Of course, it was Amrut, straight from the Bangalore-based distillery. Amrut and Chokalingam, its indefatigable champion, led the Indian malt invasion.

Now along comes the second wave, Paul John distillery in Goa on the west coast. Needless to say, they need no subterfuge to entice people to taste their whisky and are drawing rave reviews just as Amrut did.

Compared with the rest of India, Bangalore and Goa have relatively temperate climates, but whisky still ages quickly in the Indian heat. After four, five, six years, it is ready for bottling, and most importantly, just as flavorful and well-balanced as the long-aged Scotch whisky it emulates.

India is the world's largest consumer of whisky and has many distilleries. Until recently, though, most have focused on making IMFL—Indian-Made Foreign Liquor—for the local market. For now, only Amrut and Paul John are known to make single malts, and these can be difficult to find in India. Given their global success, let's hope many others will follow.

AMRUT DISTILLERIES

Since 1948, Amrut distillery in Bangalore, India has distilled brandy from local "Bangalore Blue" grapes. Early in the twenty-first century, they turned their hand to single malt whisky, gaining global recognition in 2008 via the Malt Maniacs' annual blind tasting competition.

AMRUT PORTONOVA BATCH #6, 62.1%

At Amrut distillery in Bangalore, India, everything is done by hand. Even the spent grains are loaded into trucks one shovelful at a time. Portonova is matured in bourbon barrels "until it is ready," then finished in port pipes to yield a very fruity whisky that surprisingly, shows little port. Rather, dried dark fruits reminiscent of prunes and figs bathe in wonderfully pleasing aromas of burley tobacco, and doeskin leather. Tempered white pepper and slightly tannic barrel notes complement exotic spices and sweet honey.

DK

AMRUT SINGLE CASK PEATED BARLEY PORTPIPE FINISH 59%

Distilled from peated Scottish barley and unpeated barley from Rajasthan, this robust dram was matured in bourbon barrels, and then finished in port pipes. Bluntly, this tastes like a well-crafted single malt Scotch.

Spearmint, bushels of fruit, and hints of milk chocolate balance delicately in a rich peat smoke. Bracing spices turn sweet when a recommended dash of water is added.

DK

AMRUT FUSION 50%

Close your eyes. Think of a distillery that stops mid-afternoon for its staff to take tea. Warm breezes riffling through the coconut palms out front carry a fragrance that is at once floral and laden with grain. Now, open your eyes and if you're lucky, you're at Amrut distillery in Bangalore.

A complex blend of tropical Indian fruit and heathery Scottish peat smoke in the finest tradition of single malt whisky. Caramels, maple syrup, and a dash of vanilla balanced by apple pie with chocolate ice cream, and muted peppers that segue into a long, smoky finish.

DK

AMRUT PEATED 46%

The exotic aromas of India are nowhere more exhilarating than in bustling Bangalore, home of Amrut Distilleries. A bank of cement fermenters dwarf three handmade, pyramidal copper pot stills. The whisky they produce is fascinating too, in being so eminently quaffable.

A ritual dance of fruit and smoke, around milk chocolate, maple syrup, and an odd sandalwood spiciness. That smoke could be from peat but equally from firewood. Vaguely tannic barrel notes provide a structure for peaches, red currants, and brisk citrus zest to inhabit. Finishes in a smoky, fruit punch.

DK

CLASSIC SELECT CASK 55.2%

Vanilla fudge with a smattering of savory Asian spices and Texas barbeque sauce. Its grassiness coupled with strong dried grain notes are so like a young Scotch whisky, though the granular licorice-like mouthfeel is its own. Rich, burley tobacco notes and fresh, clean oak add complexity though the overall impression is of youth—like drinking young, well-made Scotch.

DK

BRILLIANCE 46%

Juicy, grassy whisky with the punky softness of moist, freshly harvested grain. Sweet, creamy toffees dissolve into an earthy licorice-like mouthfeel. A fairly complex synthesis of grassy and grainy notes is offset by gunpowder, blistering hot spices, ripe apples, and sweet/bitter kumquats. Becomes more complex and interesting as it sits in the glass.

DK

EDITED 46%

A carefully choreographed dance of peat smoke and cereal notes entwined. Malted barley with echoes of hot piri-piri sauce. The palate is peppery hot and spicy, balanced with a sweet fruitiness and a creamy rich mouth-feel. Hints of oak tannins in the finish add complexity that typifies age. Like some of the Amruts, you have to look at the label to be sure it's not Scotch.

DK

PEATED SELECT CASK 55.5%

Strongly peated in the style of classic medicinal Islays, while retaining its own personality. The peat overwhelms in a bonfire that consumes what other flavors might be present. Though not complex, it amply rewards the avid peat lover. The feel of black licorice in the finish adds interest. Like all Paul John whiskies, it improves after the bottle has been open a few weeks.

DK

IRELAND

SINGLE POT STILL VS. SINGLE MALT IRISH WHISKEY

BY AMANDA SCHUSTER

If you've been tasting Irish whiskies lately you might have come across the term "Single Pot Still" on the label, and had a few questions. Is it the same as single malt (a term which basically means that all the liquid in the bottle was made from a single type of malted grain, at the same distillery), as with Scotch and other world whiskies? What is a pot still, anyway? Why does its singularity matter?

To answer the first question, it's almost like a single malt. Same basic concept—the whiskey is produced at a single distillery from a single grain. But what distinguishes single pot over single malt is that single malt is only made from malted barley and produced all around the world, whereas single pot is only legally produced in Ireland and made with both malted and "green," a.k.a. unmalted, barley. The reason for this is the unmalted barley adds a unique character to the whiskey, and makes it more, well, barley-ish. When you taste them, you might have noticed a distinctive spiciness, more of a weighty, grainy texture and funky cereal flavor that isn't as present in a Scotch, or even other types of Irish whiskies. It has more depth.

The reason this mashbill method came about, by the way, harkens back to a time in the 1800s when Irish distillers were paying up the swan's neck (more on that below) on malt taxes. As a work around with the excise agents, they began cutting their malted barley with green barley so they could turn more of a profit. Lucky for them it actually had a pleasant effect on the whiskey when done right.

Another difference is that unlike most single malts, with the exception of precious few such as Auchentoshan Scotch, single pot still is always triple distilled.

· Which brings us to the still itself. If you think about it, referring to the type of still used for this specific category is kind of bizarre considering that a lot of the world's finer whisk(e)ys (and rum, tequila, and other distillates) are made in a version of a pot still, which is the copper one with the rounded base and collared, bent neck, or "swan's neck." The other kind, the column still—a.k.a. continuous still, Coffey still, or patent still—is usually made of steel and is the kind used to make most of the world's clear beverages such as vodka and dry gin, as well as grain whiskey used for blends. So basically, if you want your spirit to have some inherent flavor and complexity to it, you make it in a pot still.

To make matters even more confusing, up until 2011, the whiskies were labeled as "Pure Pot Still." If you see these on a label, you know you have a "vintage" bottle.

At present, there are only a couple of brands out there making Single Pot Still Whiskey for commercial purposes. The category became less popular in the twentieth century when Scotch began to dominate the marketplace, not to mention complications from the Irish Civil War of Independence and the American Prohibition. But with the resurgence of classic drinking habits in the 2000s, it's finding a new fan base with whiskey aficionados and various history-minded booze nerd enthusiasts. Hopefully we start to see more on the way.

SINGLE POT STILL TO TRY:

• Redbreast 12 Year Old Cask Strength—the full flavored proof version of this fine aged whiskey.

• Green Spot and Yellow Spot—new to the American market in just the past couple of years (the Yellow Spot only started importing!), these whiskies get their flavor from both bourbon and sherry cask aging. The richly flavored non age statement Green Spot is aged seven to ten years while smooth, sweet, and mellow Yellow Spot is aged twelve years and gets an additional finish from Malaga wine casks.

• Powers John Lane—Don't shoot! This SPS version of the popular blended whiskey is named for the now shuttered distillery where Powers was first produced. It's meant to be sipped.

SINGLE MALT IRISH WHISKEY TO TRY:

• The Irishman 12 Year Old—This bronze medal winner of the 2014 NY International Spirits Competition is mostly smooth, honeyed, and satisfying.

• Tullamore D.E.W. 10 Year Old—Aged in four different types of casks—bourbon, sherry, port, and madeira—this criminally overlooked whiskey is beautifully complex.

• Knappogue Castle 14 Year Old—Aged in both bourbon and sherry woods, this delicate whiskey is light in texture, but heavy on substance.

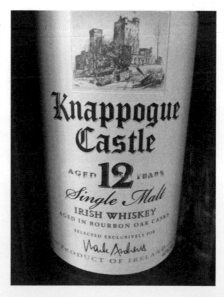

BROGANS LEGACY 10 YEAR OLD 40 %

P.G. Brogan & Company Limited is the manufacturer of the famous Irish Cream Liqueur. This single malt whiskey is triple distilled, and aged ten years in a combination of American bourbon barrels and Spanish sherry casks. Patrick Brogan hand-selects the casks used for this bottling. The whiskey was stilled in 1996, and bottled in 2006.

CD

THE OLD BUSHMILLS DISTILLERY CO.

BY MATT CHAMBERS & KAREN TAYLOR

Bushmills has legally distilled in the area dating all the way back to 1608, though not at the current distillery. The distillery is named after the town of Bushmills in which it is located and lies close to the northern County Antrim coast in Northern Ireland, just two miles from the famous Giant's Causeway. Global drinks company Diageo was once the owner (now it's Jose Cuervo). Now sales are growing rapidly following a sustained promotional campaign. The distillery is once again running at full capacity (approximately three million liters per year) to meet current demand. In addition to being the oldest licensed distillery in Ireland and the world, Bushmills also has the longest continually used logo. In 1784, the pot still logo was introduced in order to celebrate the formal registering of the distillery and this is still in use today, over 200 years later!

BUSHMILLS 21 YEAR OLD 40%

Bushmills' whiskies are all triple distilled in the traditional Irish way and the core range is a mixture of single malts and blends—the 10 year old and 16 year old are single malts, with the Original and Black Bush being blends. These are occasionally joined by special limited releases, such as this 21 year old. The 21 year old is an annual bottling, which was first released in 2001, and the 2010 release was limited to just 6,000 bottles. About a third was allocated to the US market, with the remainder shared between France, Ireland, the UK and the rest of Europe.

This 2010 release has spent its first nineteen years maturing in a combination of ex-bourbon and ex-sherry casks, before being transferred for the last two years into ex-Madeira casks. It is positioned at the top of the Bushmills range, both in price (rec-

ommended price is £120) and age. We were delighted to be invited to the UK launch, held at the Waxy O'Connor's pub in central London, where the Bushmills Master Blender Helen Mulholland opened bottle number 0001 of the 6,000 for the assembled crowd to taste.

This 21 year old 2010 release is bottled at 40% and the color is golden amber. The nose is fresh and fruity, with plenty of dried fruits immediately present (think of raisins, sultanas, and apricot). These are backed up by distinct malty cereal notes,

some toffee and caramel aromas, and then something nutty (imagine toasted almonds) and some baking spices (especially cinnamon and nutmeg). On the palate, this whiskey feels incredibly soft and pleasantly coats the inside of your mouth. There are notes of distinct, almost sugary, sweetness (think of toffee and caramel again) and plenty of malted cereals, reminiscent of a robust biscuit like an oatcake. Then come some of the other characteristics from the nose— the dried fruits (especially raisins), toasted almonds, and baking/woody spices. The overall combination of notes reminded us of Christmas pudding or rich fruitcake. A hint of dark chocolate develops right at the end. The finish is again initially sweet with that chocolate note coming through more prominently, before becoming incredibly spicy and drier—think of those woody baking spices again (cinnamon and nutmeg), plus a hint of clove.

What's the verdict?

This Bushmills offers a lovely dram of whiskey that gives a good mix of sweetness and spices. The aromas on the nose and flavors that come through on the palate are particularly good, with an interesting and excellent complexity. The finish is not quite to the same standard but still enjoyable, although it may be too spicy for some. Overall, this version of the 21 year old is a deliciously rich and pleasant whiskey that is well worth trying, if you get the chance.

MC & KT

BUSHMILLS 10 YEAR OLD 40%

There is something spectacular going on at Bushmills, because their whiskey is among the most well balanced I have tasted. There is almost perfect harmony of flavors as the silky smooth whiskey releases a complex character that involves the tastes of sweet, bitter, sour, salty, and savory dancing on the palate in almost perfect synchronization. This whiskey is in my "top whisky" list.

I was thinking of something Irish to write about, so naturally my imagination developed an image of a line of Irish people kicking away a riverdance! Wanting to avoid comparing an Irish whiskey to a riverdance, I am going to liken this whiskey to Roy Keane. Yes, Roy Keane. The sensational Irish footballer whose silky smooth skills and magic in midfield helped Manchester United to many victories. This whiskey is magical, silky smooth, and exceptional. Superb!

Nose: Beautiful and malty, this whiskey has the sweet fizz of an apple and pear cider ordered from the mahogany bar at an old Irish pub. It has notes of bitter oak that

balance against sweet fruit, such as apple, lemon, and orange. Floral notes develop as the sweet perfume of flowers mingles with grass and fresh rainfall. So complex, yet so smooth and vibrant!

Taste: An initial dry burst of Chardonnay floods in, carrying spice and pepper with the tang of green mango and lime, and that apple cider develops into a bitter-sweet pear cider with fizz and life. Bitter wood also merges with that sweet pear and apple as savory saltiness, such as soy sauce, spills on the palate with herbaceous notes. Brilliant balance! Boasting a fabulous finish, this whiskey glows on the tongue softly and recedes gracefully.

AC

OLD BUSHMILLS DISTILLERY

BY MIC LOWTHER

The Old Bushmills Distillery was officially registered as a distillery in 1784 by Hugh Anderson, but earlier history traces it back to an operation "in the hands of smugglers" in 1743, and even further back to a license to distill granted in 1608 to landowner Thomas Phillips by King James I.

Throughout its 400+ years, Bushmills has endured closures and production interruptions due to fires, wars, US Prohibition, bootlegger competition, and changes brought by a succession of new owners. Purchased in 2005 by Diageo, and in 2014 by Jose Cuervo, production is now being significantly increased.

- Malted barley dried with hot air is ground to coarse flour and mixed with hot water.
- Yeast is added to trigger fermentation to about 8% alcohol.
- The "wash" is boiled and triple-distilled in copper pot stills with tall slender necks.
- Aging ensues in used American oak barrels, Spanish sherry casks, and even port or Madeira barrels.
- Different casks of whiskey are blended to achieve each product's expected taste.
- Bottles are filled and labeled for distribution throughout the world.

Traditional products are Bushmills Original, Black Bush, and Bushmills 10, 16, and 21 year old single malts. Bushmills 1608 was created for the 400th anniversary and made only in 2008. A 12 year single malt is available only at the distillery, and Bushmills Irish Honey, which tastes like Bushmills Original with a note of honey, has recently been added.

The distillery is located in the small town of Bushmills in County Antrim on the northern coast of Ireland. The area has many tourist attractions and facilities for visitors of all motivations.

Those who come to sightsee will find ancient castle ruins to tour, a selection of windswept golf courses, and continuously spectacular views along the entire Antrim coast. The Giant's Causeway is an area of hexagonal black basalt columns formed 60 million years ago from the slow cooling of volcanic lava. Legend tells that Irish giant Finn McCool ripped away cliff faces and hurled them into the ocean to make stepping-stones across the North Channel to Scotland. The town of Bushmills itself has ample inns, hotels, and restaurants staffed with friendly local people to make your stay pleasant and memorable.

The distillery is a short walk from town. There are tours each day mid-morning to mid-afternoon, and you are welcome to take them hour after hour and day after day until servers in the tasting room know your name and have your drink ready, served with their compliments in an official Old Bushmills Distillery tasting glass. If such is the purpose of your visit, it is best to keep a taxi on retainer.

KNAPPOGUE CASTLE 12 YEAR OLD 40%

This is an interesting and fun whiskey with much to offer, but that fun comes at a cost, and that cost is paid in fruit. It's flavorful and easy to drink, but sooner than you would think the fruit goes from soft and simple to completely overwhelming the palate. By the second glass it's a bit difficult to taste anything other than the peach and banana notes. Which is a shame because it starts out so nice and crisp. I rarely give advice on how to drink a whiskey, because how someone decides to down a dram is their own business, but unless you want a banana peach explosion in your mouth, I'd highly recommend just keeping this one neat. Water just seems to make the banana and peach even more explosive.

One interesting thing about this whiskey is that it's most likely been distilled by Bushmills. Traditionally the Knappogue Castle is distilled by either Cooley or Bushmills and this one happens to have been triple distilled. Traditionally, Bushmills distills three times where as Cooley typically only distills twice. It's entirely possible, but not very likely, that Cooley triple distilled this one, but if we're playing the detective gam, it's far more likely that it was created by Bushmills. Which technically makes this the sweetest Bushmills I've ever had. Knappogue (and Clontarf) are all made at Cooley.

Enough semantics and on to the whiskey.

Color: Golden Honey

Nose: Right off the bat are some green apples, honeysuckle, and a touch of lemon rind. The malt and spice are definitely in there, and as you might expect, some hints of vanilla and caramel. Though something you might not expect is how strong the scent of peaches and banana cream pie come though. To be honest, it's a bit overwhelming.

Palate: This is one of the fruitiest whiskeys I've had in a long time. The same green apple from the nose comes through in full force right away and is

followed by some red berries, grapes, and tropical fruit. There are also some really surprising notes of salt water taffy, mint, caramel, vanilla, and bourbon spice, and if that's where it stopped that would have been fantastic; however, there are some peach and banana gremlins in this glass. The sweet peach and banana notes border on overwhelming, and like mogwais from hell, they become even bolder and gnarlier when water is added. Particularly the banana. Big peach and banana hang around for a really long time, but as they fade the malt and just a hint of bourbon spice shows up before it fades completely. The heavy peach and banana throw it a bit off balance for me. Though a nice medium body and an incredibly smooth and satiny texture at least make for a nice drinking experience. It's a decent enough single malt , but lacks some of the complexity of its Scottish counterparts that hover around the same price range. It also suffers a bit from a balance issue with the orchard, peach and banana notes weighing so heavy on the nose, palate, and finish.

JP

KNAPPOGUE CASTLE 16 YEAR OLD TWIN WOOD 40%

Knappogue Castle has two expressions in the Twin Wood line: a 14 year old and a 16 year old. Both are no-peat, triple distilled malt whiskeys in the Irish style, aged in both bourbon and sherry barrels, but there are some differences beyond the extra two years in the aging statement. The 14 Year Old is a marriage of bourbon-aged and sherry-aged whiskeys, each coming from 14-plus year old sources.

The 16 Year Old Knappogue, on the other hand, spent fourteen years in ex-bourbon barrels before being transferred to ex-sherry casks for another couple of years of aging. In this respect, it's technically more of a sherry finish (albeit a deep one) than a double wood. The whiskey was distilled back in November 1995, when the US government closed in a budget showdown and Yitzhak Rabin was assassinated, and was bottled at 40% in December 2012 in a run of 4,500 bottles.

Color: In the glass, the Knappogue Castle Twin Wood is a deep amber-gold with a touch of reddish-brown, giving a dark depth to its appearance. Compared side by side, it's markedly different from the pale yellow of the other whiskeys from Knappogue Castle thanks to its sherry stint.

Nose: On the nose, Knappogue Castle Twin Wood offers a complex set of aromas. There's a deep chocolaty sweetness paired with a lighter fruity sweetness, a strong dose of grainy malt, and spice.

Palate: Take a sip and notice a soft, velvety mouthfeel and a smooth, varied profile offering first sherry, spice, and pepper, as well as wood, and a subtle fruit and nutty undertone. The finish begins with a somewhat hot combination of pepper and wood, which gives way to spice, malt, and vanilla. The warmness stays with you long after your sip, providing the ongoing satisfaction of a whiskey well enjoyed, particularly sampled as it was in the midst of another round of Washington, D.C.'s ongoing winter turmoil and record low temperatures. On ice, more of the sweetness of Knappogue Castle Twin Wood comes out, with mellow tones of vanilla and fruit with a malty nuttiness in the background. Knappogue Castle Twin Wood is very easygoing. It's a well-made Irish whiskey that shows its age in its depth and complexity of flavor as well as its smooth character. A well-honed historical harkening from Knappogue Castle.

JE

CLONTARF 1014 IRISH SINGLE MALT 40%

I'm sure there are stories that'll explain "why 1014?" Clontarf was largely available in France a few years back. They had some smart—yet ugly—three-bottle packs that used to fit together. Yup, some liqueur makers have them as well.

Color: Straw.

Nose: Light, undemanding, marshmallowy, easy, not repulsive. But very light.

Palate: Light, yet oily, grassy fruity... It's very boring whisky, but it's flawless. I even enjoy these touches of sappy herbs, with "ideas" of fir liqueur. Now, it's light, but less so than most Scottish blends. In fact, I find it pretty good (would you please make up your mind, S.?). Not that short finish, with a pleasant oiliness. I had feared this would be a disaster, and it was not.

SV

Cooley Distillery is owned by Beam Suntory. It was established in 1987 by John Teeling on the Cooley Peninsula in County Louth, Ireland. For more than two decades they were the lone independent operating Irish whiskey maker in Ireland. They produce a number of labels, including: Connemara, Cooley, Gre-

Connemara,

PEATED SINGLE MALT
IRISH WHISKEY

enore, Kilbeggan, Tyrconnell and small bottlings (single casks, etc., AD Rattray, Cadenhead, and Adelphi). Their revenue, as of 2010, was approximately €15.9 million. Jim Beam bought the distillery in January 2012, and Beam was in turn bought by Suntory in 2014.

CONNEMARA 12 YEAR OLD PEATED 40%

Connemara is the only peated Irish whiskey that is in regular production and has a peaty/smoky level that is about half of the strength of famous Islay Scotch whiskies such as Ardbeg, Lagavulin, and Laphroaig. Other Irish smoky whiskies are occasionally released but are extremely rare.

Connemara is produced at the Cooley distillery, which is located on the County Louth coast roughly halfway between Belfast and Dublin.

Cooley was founded in 1987 by John Teeling and his idea was to resurrect some of Ireland's oldest whiskey recipes and traditions that had become extinct. He converted an old vodka distillery and Cooley has since won over 100 awards worldwide. At the end of 2011, the distillery and company were taken over by drinks giant Beam Global. The first expression of the modern Connemara was launched in 1996—this 12 year old is actually the oldest version of Connemara released to date.

Connemara, which is named after the original site of the Connemara distillery on the west coast of Ireland near Galway, and its old traditional recipe had disappeared into history before being resurrected by John Teeling. To produce this expression of Connemara, some of their oldest premium casks were used. There are just 7,000 bottles available, although it is planned for the 12 year old to become a regular annual release. This version has been bottled at 40% ABV and should cost around £60-65 from specialist liquor retailers.

The color is a pale golden yellow and the nose has a delicious freshness to it. There are a number of aromas that help to give it this freshness and these include green pear and apple, honey, vanilla and a hint of lemon zest. Backing this up are deeper notes of malty cereals and mossy, earthy peat—this peat is not as obvious or vibrant as in younger versions of Connemara, but instead softly drifts around your nostrils.

On the palate, this feels soft and creamy, almost a little bit oily in texture. There are prominent notes of vanilla and honey, which are backed up by malted barley and a hint of yeast—this combination is reminiscent of bread dough. The fresh green fruitiness from the nose is still there but has taken a bit of a step back, while the zesty lemon has come more to the fore and has a lemon meringue pie feeling. The earthy peat smoke is never far away and makes you think of damp moss. It comes across a touch more feisty than on the nose and it

has a mild chili-like heat and spice to it. The combination is sublime and very moreish.

The finish has a decent length, although it is the peat smoke and tingling heat that last longer than anything else. The sweet vanilla, honey and malty notes, plus the zesty lemon fade quite quickly and leave a slightly dry feeling in the mouth.

This is a good effort from Connemara and shows an increased depth, complexity, and class from its very good younger siblings. Also, the smokiness is less prominent and more integrated than in other expressions. The only slight disappointment is the lack of depth in the finish and this stops it from being a great whiskey in our opinion. Having said that, it is lovely, easy to drink, and very enjoyable.

MC & KT

CONNEMARA 8 YEAR OLD 59.2%

A peated Cooley from when some bottlings started to become pretty impressive... Cask #K01/101196

Color: White wine.

Nose: It's not the peat that's impressive; it's rather the fruits, around white peaches, then all this lapsang souchong. The strength is rather impressive too, so... With water: gets much more medicinal. Bandages, all that. Antiseptic. Got much drier.

Palate: It's got this slightly burnt side that wasn't absent from several

young Connemaras as far as I can remember, some candy sugar, burnt herbs, sugar coated fruits... A little strange so far. With water: much more to my liking. Raw sweet peat, and much less burnt herbs. It remains a little barnyardy, though. Long, very smoky, peppery, citrusy. More "Islay," whatever that means. Needs water, then swims very well. A bit rough, though.

Oh Limburg, maybe we could try one that was bottled for some Limburgian entity, and that was distilled around when that Connemara was bottled... And why not?

SV

CONNEMARA TURF MÓR 58.2%

This Cooley malt is the peatiest of their peated brand: Connemara Turf Mór. Here's the Turf Mór (Gaelic for "Big Peat") description per the Liquid Irish blog:

"...a few years ago Cooley had trouble sourcing its usual amount of 20ppm peated malt from Scotland (malt made in Ireland is not peated). To keep the stills going, they bought a higher 58ppm malt and mixed it with the unpeated variety to moderate the intensity.

As an experiment, however, they distilled some of the highly peated malt on its own and that is what has appeared today as Connemara Turf Mór."

Liquid Irish's source of this information appears to be Brian Quinn, the Kilbeggan Distillery (also owned by Beam) manager, so I'll go with that tale.

My palate does not take to Cooley's malt at all. So the thought of strong peating and wine finishes on their malt actually does give me some hope going in, hoping that "the Cooley thing" is covered up by other elements. I found the regular Connemara Cask Strength to be very hot, woody, smoky, and well, that's it. I was hoping this Small Batch edition of Connemara would bring about a better, more interesting experience.

Neat: The color is amber. The nose's strongest scent is that of new sneakers. It permeates everything else. Alongside there are rye-like spices, cinnamon rock candy, damp moss, black licorice, fresh apricots, and unripened peaches. And lots of hot ethyl. On the palate, I find a note that's like burnt hay meets brown sugar syrup. The sneakers and moss show up here, along with something green (like live grains and grass), and "the Cooley thing" (a.k.a. vanilla-coated stale sugary breakfast cereal dunked in white vinegar). It finishes sweetly. Lots of vanilla beans as well as the Cooley thing. The peat becomes very Lagavulin-ish with time. The smoke isn't as heavy as I'd expected but it lasts the longest.

With Water: "Black licorice farts and a lot of them" (as per my notes) on the nose and "floral perfume trying to cover it up." Balsamic vinegar reduction, a little turpentine, sugar cookies, and clementines. Oh, and dog hair. The palate flattens and blands out. Bitter peat, generic vanilla, and a slight tang. But then it finishes very sweetly. There's a little malt mixing with peat ashes. Then a weird vinegar tang that gets sourer after time.

My final note from this tasting: "WTF is going on with this whiskey?"

With water, the nose gets very odd and inconsistent, burping up clashing odors every few seconds. The hydrated palate goes nowhere, but then the finish picks back up in its oddities. The neat nose is a weirdo too, but easier to take and occasionally matches the palate. It's quite hot while neat, but with the water it's just strange. This could be a symptom of its youth.

There are definitely many characteristics pouring forth from this whiskey, and I can imagine it seemed kind of fun when the Cooley folks nosed the cask. But the total package is totally off kilter. I don't know why they were in such a rush to release a barely legal whiskey. A few more years in a good cask wouldn't have hurt. This could have been fun as an 8 year old, so I hope they held onto a few casks of the big peatin'.

I do think it's more interesting than the regular Cask Strength, but have my doubts that it makes for a better drinking experience. It makes me think that Connemara has many miles to go before it can compete with its Beam brethren, Laphroaig, and Ardmore.

MK

CONNEMARA 1992/2008 SINGLE CASK 46%

Color: Straw.

Nose: Ah, the "famous" slightly buttery peatiness! It's very dry, especially after the Bushmills and Greenore, very grassy, rather sooty and, indeed, rather buttery as well. Reminds me of some butter mixed with seaweed that's very popular in French cuisine these days (Monsieur Jean-Yves Bordier's butters). Also fumes (a little). Globally austere—pleasantly so.

Palate: This works quite well. Cooley's relatively "naked" fruitiness (gooseberries, pears and such) needs time to mingle with the peat in my experience (unless you make it all up with heavy bourbon or sherry) but that's starting to happen here, at sixteen years of age. Cider apples, soft pepper, seaweed again, peppermint, grapefruits... It's all pretty good, if not brilliant. No water needed here. Long, smokier and grassier finish. Rather nice aftertaste on kumquats and pepper.

Fairly good stuff, one of these Connemaras that is approaching the peated Ileachs in my opinion, although this has more "young" fruits. Having said that, some 1992s at cask

strength have been up there with the 'begs, 'vulins and 'phroaigs.

SV

TYRCONNELL 10 YEAR OLD MADEIRA CASK SINGLE MALT WHISKEY 46%

Neat: The color is a very orange-tinted gold. It's possible this is its natural color, gaining hues from the wine cask. The nose begins with strawberry preserves, warm nectarines, orange marmalade, and peach schnapps. Warmed dessert wine and sugar cane show up next. In the far background rumbles the Cooley

malt. The perfumed palate holds flower kiss candy, blackberry and boysenberry jam, and lychee. Vanilla and milk chocolate notes develop with some time. It's a combo of sweet and tart along with a buzz of heat. The blackberry and boysenberry jams stick around for the extensive finish. Orange Tang and Pixie Stix cover the tongue. The milk chocolate registers with more subtlety. An odd fruit tone shows up sometimes, maybe bitter or underripe fruit?

With Water: Stinky cheese jumps into the nose first. Then some milder cheeses, along with the afore-mentioned fruit preserves. After that eases off, it's much similar to the neat nose, but mellower. Maybe some orange rind and tart lemons. The jams kick back in on the palate, followed by vague citrus and vanilla pudding notes. It's very creamy with that Cooley thing keeping its distance. Intense sugary sweetness on the finish.

This still holds its charms as a dessert drink. But is it whiskey? Technically, yes, but the malt only makes brief cameos. Due to my feelings about the malt's quality, I wasn't terribly disappointed it remained evasive. On the other hand, it is intensely sweet like a flavored whiskey rather than a finished one. Thus in a blind tasting, one might guess it's a liqueur.

While it doesn't feel, smell, or taste like whiskey (to me), I do still like it, especially the jam and fruit notes. I would recommend this whiskey to someone who isn't big on single malts but does have a sweet tooth, as the sugar is very aggressive. Some of us just can't take the sweeties as much as we used to.

MK

TYRCONNELL 10 YEAR OLD PORT CASK 46%

Color: Salmon-y—at Cooley's they wrote "antique copper."

Nose: Certainly more marked by the wine at first nosing but, most curiously, less demonstrative than the Madeira. More on blackcurrant buds, apple juice, leaves, then spices such as very soft white pepper. Hints of new leather and again that farmyard after the rain. Rather inoffensive and not as talkative as the Madeira but maybe a little more elegant.

Palate: Much closer to the Madeira now. Not creamy but very rich again, sweet, fruity and candied, reminding me of tawny Port indeed. We have strawberry jam (all sorts of jams actually, including cherry), then cake, then it switches to malt and candy sugar, caramelized cornflakes, honey... I'm sorry but I like this, too! Especially the finish is perfectly balanced, richer again, long, coating, sweet... Maybe a tad decadent. Just like the Madeira, it's not complex whiskey but it's dangerously drinkable, even if you're a hardcore Scotchfreak.

SV

CADENHEAD 12 YEAR OLD 1992/2004 60%

One of those first indie Connemaras...Imagine the surprise at the time. 224 bottles.

Color: Straw.

Nose: Indeed, imagine the surprise. A massive smoky and partly medicinal hit, unknown in Ireland at the time, with plenty of burnt herbs and then some leather and rubber and sour cream and Riesling. Phew! With water: wet dogs (apologies, dogs), kilny smells, raw wool (yes it's wooly), sourdough... All this is perfect.

Palate: In-cre-di-ble. Extreme peat and lemon, a bit in the style of a blended malt that would have involved 80% of Supernova-style Ard-beg and 20% of the most citrusy Rose-bank. Does that give you a proper idea of the stuff? With water: gets a tad bit-ter and too grassy, careful with water. Very long finish, perfect, zesty peat, ridden with phenolic…stuff, and lem-ons and salt and oysters.

A shame that they seem to have broken the mold.

SV

LIMERICK SELECTION 23 YEAR OLD 1991/2015 'SLANEY MALT' CASK #8585 59%

As a previous Limerick/Slaney by Adelphi has been utterly superb, I gave this one a try. 134 bottles.

Color: Dark gold, almost amber.

Nose: Passion fruit and mango cake, liquid caramel, herbs, teas, tobaccos… And myriads of other tiny

aromas. With water: menthol, euca-lyptus, camphor… just what the doc-tor ordered.

Palate: Extraordinary. Herbal fruits and fruity herbs every-where. Plus just the right amount of tobacco-ish herbalness. Walnuts. Bit-ter oranges. Salt. Not an easy-easy chappo when undiluted, but boy, it delivers. With water: uses the velvet glove this time, with papayas, guavas, vanilla, and honey. Plus, once again, many tinier flavors. Quite a long fin-ish, with an impressive freshness. Always a little tobacco.

No quibbles, this is one of the great-est Irish out there. What a session!

SV

LIMERICK SELECTION 23 YEAR OLD 1991/2015 'SLANEY MALT' CASK #8265 58.1%

The label states 'Slaney Malt.' 202 bottles.

Color: Gold.

Nose: More fruity than fruits. Or one of the fruitiest malts ever. Guavas, papayas, bananas, mangos and all that. But not only that, there's a fair amount of sweet and soft tea that support that extravagant fruitiness, and it never becomes cloying or simply "too much." I don't know if that rings a bell to you, but in Switzerland, they have some sweets named "Sugus" that smells just like this. Well, you need at least twenty unwrapped Sugus to match this. Ah, childhood memories... With water: meadow flowers, nectar, and tinned fruits. All of them.

Palate: Extreme fruits, but with elegance. Would make a Lochside 1966, a Clynelish 1972, or a Benriach 1976 taste bitter and grassy in comparison. Well, quite. More citrusy than on the nose, with mainly tangerines and pink grapefruits. Oh, and Sugus. And you don't even notice that it sings at 58%, which may be a little dangerous. With water: less dangerous—and just as great. Rather long finish, very fresh, very fruity. Spring in Provence.

very cool. It's absolutely fab to be able to taste both the thesis and the antithesis from the very same distillery. Great work Adelphi and Cadenhead.

SV

ON THE TRAIL OF IRISH WHISKEY

BY GAVIN D. SMITH

Scotland has its Speyside Malt Whisky Trail, Kentucky has its Bourbon Trail and now the Irish have joined in with their very own Ireland Whiskey Trail.

This is a comprehensive guide to Irish whiskey in all its guises and embraces the working distilleries and whiskey museums of Ireland, along with the best whiskey pubs, bars, and shops in the country. Additionally, the website provides a comprehensive guide to Irish whiskey and the "lost" distilleries of Ireland.

The Ireland Whiskey Trail is the brainchild of Heidi Donelon, arguably Ireland's best-known independent whiskey expert. For many years, Heidi has conducted tastings, seminars, master classes, and shows throughout Ireland and Europe. This interaction with consumers of every nationality, coupled with numerous visits to Scotland, led her to the realization that Ireland, despite its rich whiskey heritage, did not have a whiskey tourism "product" that captured everything that is best about whiskey in Ireland. Eighteen months of research by Heidi have led to the Ireland Whiskey Trail website.

Ireland's active distilleries and whiskey museums are the perfect place to learn about the history and heritage of whiskey, as well as the skills of distilling, maturing, and blending; however, Ireland is as famous for its many pubs as it is for its native whiskey, and no Irish Whiskey Trail would have been complete without including the best whiskey pubs and bars in the country.

This particular "whiskey journey" took Heidi Donelon to some fascinating corners of Ireland, and in the process she unearthed many interesting and unusual pubs, full of history, character, characters, and great whiskies.

Every pub and bar selected for inclusion on the Trail is unique, and has been chosen because it offers either an excellent range of Irish whiskies or because it has a historical link to one of Ireland's old whiskey distilleries. Some pubs are small, rural establishments, off the normal tourist tracks, while others are better known and stand as popular landmarks within their localities.

The Ireland Whiskey Trail also includes a range of the best hotels and golf clubs in Ireland, not to mention the country's finest retail whiskey stockists, so that visitors can be sure to take home a bottle or two for further experimentation.

Heritage often plays an important part in visitors' enjoyment of Ireland, and it is notable that in 1886, when Alfred Barnard was researching his now classic book, *The Whisky Distilleries of the United Kingdom,* he visited no fewer than 28 distilleries while in Ireland. At that time, whiskey was one of the country's largest exports.

In preparation for the Trail, Heidi Donelon recreated Barnard's journey, researching in detail these old—and often forgotten—distilleries, with the aim of unearthing intriguing aspects of their history and seeing for herself what tangible remains are to be found today.

Along the way, she unearthed some fascinating material, including the story of the owner of Bishop's Water distillery in Cork, who is probably the only legal distiller ever to have been shot by an exciseman, and the fact that the long-lost Phoenix Park distillery in Dublin played an important role in the early life and subsequent writings of James Joyce. She even discovered what is thought to be the last known bottle of Cassidy's whiskey. Her research now provides the most comprehensive internet guide to Ireland's old distilleries, and it can be found in the Whiskey Heritage section of The Ireland Whiskey Trail website.

The Trail has been backed by Irish Distillers, the Cooley Distillery and Tullamore D.E.W owners C&C, as well as the various participating outlets. By supporting the initiative, the featured distilleries and pubs have found a way to help fight back against the recession, and early indications are that the venture is already proving a success. Despite a recent town road bypass, and an overall decline in the number of tourists visiting Ireland, Locke's Kilbeggan distillery has enjoyed significant growth in visitor numbers. And the work goes on. Heidi Donelon plans to expand the Whiskey Trail, researching the old distilleries and best Irish whiskey pubs of Northern Ireland.

GLENDALOUGH DISTILLERS

In 2011, by five friends from Wicklow and Dublin founded The Glendalough (Glen of Two Lakes) Distillery in an attempt to revive craft distilling in Ireland. Throughout the eighteenth and nineteenth centuries, Ireland was home to over 200 legal—and many more illegal—distilleries. Nowadays, only a handful of them are left. The distillery is looking to produce innovative spirits like whiskey and gin.

GLENDALOUGH 7 YEAR OLD 46%

As the distillery was only founded recently, the spirit for their 7 Year Old Single Malt was produced at the Cooley Distillery. The 7 Year Old was double distilled and matured in first-fill ex-bourbon casks. It was cut with

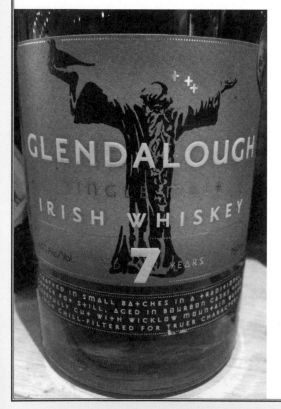

local Wicklow spring water. No chill-filtration took place.

Color: Golden.

Nose: My first impressions are new oak and nail polish remover. Fortunately, I also find barley, grass, hay, orchard fruit (pear), nuts, custard, citrus peel, honey, milk, pineapple jam, mineral notes, cinnamon and mint. The alcohol is not fully integrated. It's a relatively simple nose, but not quite as clean as its triple-distilled brothers and sisters. But that's okay with me, as I must admit I'm not a huge fan of triple distillation as it tends to take out too many aromas and flavors.

Palate: Young and edgy with varnished oak, alcohol, bitter tea, grapefruit, lemon, malt, grass, pear, peach, pepper, cloves, and cinnamon. Short finish, slightly bitter, hot and spicy with alcohol, varnished oak, lemon, grapefruit, pear, peach, honey, malt, pineapple jam, pepper, nutmeg, and cloves. I added a couple of drops of water, and on the nose, the alcohol retreats. I get more pear, apple, pineapple, vanilla, and barley. The nose certainly benefits from a little water. Palate and finish become too thin though for a whiskey. The nose is okay... but on the palate and in the finish, this single malt is young, edgy and too much hot alcohol, varnish and spices that don't give sufficient space to the fruit.

JVE

GLENDALOUGH 13 YEAR OLD 46%

This 13 Year Old, green label edition of brand new independent distiller Glendalough features St Kevin of Glendalough, who founded an abbot alongside the area's lakes. This single malt is aged in first-fill bourbon casks and using Wicklow water, it is cut to 46%. Glendalough originally scheduled this whiskey to be released as an industry standard 12 Year Old. However, when Irish rugby great Brian O'Driscoll (who wore lucky #13 on his jersey) became a shareholder in the company, it was decided to age the whiskey an extra year in his honor. A recent release, it won three gold medals in 2015, including two (Best Irish Whiskey and Best Single Malt) at the San Francisco World Spirits Competition 2015, as well as at the Irish Whiskey Awards 2015.

Nose: Caramel and butterscotch mingle with dried apples and figs, with hints of vanilla and spice. Also a hint of citrus on the end.

Palate: All the same flavors come across the palate. A nice citrus touch here again as well. A smooth finish. Not a big, overpowering whiskey.

CD

Hyde Whiskey, located in rugged West Cork, is handcrafted in small, limited edition batches. Hyde is named for the inaugural appointment of Ireland's very first president, Douglas Hyde, and the establishment of the Irish Free State in 1922.

HYDE 10 YEAR OLD NO. 1 PRESIDENT'S CASK SHERRY CASK FINISH 46%

Hyde 10 Year Old No. 1 President's Cask is a single malt Irish whiskey by Hibernia Distillers, who are planning to make their own whiskey in five years or so, but until then are sourcing their products from up-and-running distilleries—a familiar business model by other new Irish whiskey companies, like Teeling or Walsh Whiskey. This limited edition of 5,000 bottles takes its name from the first President of Ireland (1938-45), Douglas Hyde. The malt whiskey is from Cooley distillery and it's been matured in Kentucky ex-bourbon barrels before getting a six month finish in first-fill Oloroso sherry casks. Bottled without chill filtration and double distilled.

A whiskey that gets its name after the first Irish President elected after the ratification of the first Irish Constitution, and also a whiskey, which happens to have some nice barley notes in it, has to be referenced with *The Wind That Shakes The Barley*, a movie about Irish war for independence. Following the War of Independence, after the foundation of the Irish Free State, Douglas Hyde (who also had a major influence in protecting the Irish language) was elected into Irish Parliament. Over ten years after that, he became the president.

Hyde 10 Year Old Single Malt has history and pride in the name. And this Skibereen, West Cork-based Irish whiskey company can be proud of their new product. Even though the malt comes from another distillery. Well-sourced and matured Irish single malt whiskey.

Color: Deep amber

Nose: Quite mellow, yet good. Smooth sherry notes with apricot and hints of licorice. Barley and oak are present as well. Promising start.

Palate: Malty and warm, hints of warming spices. Dry oak along with dried fruits and a bitter floral feel. Needs a few drops of water and some air to get better. After that, the malt gets sweeter and nice fruit and sherry notes rise from the back. Like orange marmalade with wee smoke buried very, very deep. Long and dry finish. Dryness goes away a bit when water is added. Licorice and pepper, along with warming spices make a nice aftertaste. Sherry and oak are present as well. Quite nice dram when you really get to know it. Arrange time (and water) for this whiskey. I found that the nose was actually better without water, but the taste got lot better with few drops. So my tip would be: first, lots of sniffing, then some water dripping. Enjoy it with patience.

JL

HYDE 10 YEAR OLD NO. 2 PRESIDENT'S CASK RUM CASK FINISH 46%

This 100% malted Irish barley whiskey was distilled in a traditional copper pot still. This single malt is double matured: It is first aged in flame-charred, first-fill 200-liter American white oak bourbon barrels. The whiskey is later finished in vintage Caribbean dark rum casks for an additional nine months. These are charred 200-liter Caribbean rum casks, made from American white oak, which originally helddark rum for about two to four years. It is non-chill filtered.

Nose: Vanilla, honey, dark-fudge, and butterscotch along with figs and dates and ripe apple.

Palate: Figs, apples, and dates come across with butterscotch and toffee, spicy ginger, bitter orange marmalade, vanilla, and butter. Lovely!

CD

Ryans' Beggars Bush has been a popular pub since 1803. The Ryan family bottled their own Ryan's Malt that they made at The Dublin Whiskey Distillery, until 1946 when the distillery's doors were shuttered. The Ryan family decided to revive their Jack Ryan's Malt to celebrate an important anniversary.

JACK RYAN BEGGARS BUSH 12 YEAR OLD 46%

On the bottle's label is a 1913 image of the exterior of the landmark public house, along with the original lamppost, which still stands today at 115 Haddington Road, Dublin. Jack Ryan and his handwritten signature also appear on the label. The whiskey was aged for 12 years in ex-bourbon barrels hand-selected by the family themselves. Only 1,450 bottles were produced; 250 bottles of the limited edition Cask Strength Single Malt were also made, signed and numbered by Eunan Ryan. The whiskey was named "Best Irish Single Malt Whiskey" at the Irish Whiskey Awards in 2014.

CD

THE QUIET MAN 8 YEAR OLD 40%

I believed initially The Quiet Man whiskies were named after one of my most favorite John Wayne films, *The Quiet Man*, with Maureen O'Hara. That is a connection I believe many Americans will make, however the storyline clearly shows the name of this Irish whiskey has nothing to do with the movie. Ciaran Mulgrew (managing director and co-owner of Niche Drinks) developed The Quiet Man to honor his father, John Mulgrew.

Whereas the basic Quiet Man is a blended Irish Whiskey, this is the 8 year old single malt version. Just like its blended counterpart, it is bottled at 80 proof. This single malt also had a similar appearance to its cousin: eye-catching gold, with thin to medium legs.

This one is a subtle whiskey experience, but not quite as much as The Quiet Man blend. You will find the nose to be a crisp floral fragrance, but the oak is more apparent in this version. In addition, finishing this whiskey in bourbon casks adds the traditional vanilla notes as well. I would encourage you to take some additional time catching the subtle aromas. They are very pleasant, but simply require more time.

This drinks like a bigger whiskey, in spite of its 80 proof. Almost all of the action is at the back of the mouth until the long finish eventually (slowly!) migrates all the way to the front. You will find hints of honey, vanilla, and spicy oak. However, it's all in a context of a very, very smooth experience. This is a very good whiskey, not only for newbies, but also for experienced whiskey drinkers. It can be experienced at multiple levels of enjoyment.

FJR

SHANAHANS SINGLE MALT WHISKEY 40%

Shanahan's on the Green, on St. Stephen Street, Dublin, Ireland, is perhaps one of that city's best-known eateries. The bottling was done exclusively for their restaurant and extremely hard to get hold of! The restaurant's famed room, The Oval Office, features JFK's personal rocking chair from Air Force 1, as well as other signed documents from famous political figures, including Abraham Lincoln. This Irish single malt was distilled at the Cooley distillery in County Louth. A smooth, fruit forward, light-bodied Irish whiskey.

CD

BY ANGELO CAPUANO

Once upon a time Ireland was the world's leading producer of whiskey (which the Irish spell with an "e"). Then hard times hit. England closed its doors to Irish whiskey after the Irish won their independence in the Irish War of Independence, which lasted from 1919 to 1921. The United States era of Prohibition from 1920 to 1933 meant that even Americans could no longer legally buy Irish whiskey, and so within the space of about a decade, Irish whiskey lost its two most important export markets. The Scots were also nipping at the heels of many Irish distilleries by making whisky that many around the globe found quite palatable—the more approachable blended whisky, made from softer grain whisky using the Coffey still. This still allowed a whisky maker to produce lots of whisky very quickly, but it was an invention shunned by the Irish who preferred to stick with pot stills to make whiskey.

Brands such as Johnnie Walker soon dominated the globe, and soon after Prohibition ended and the Americans were allowed to drink again (assuming, of course, the law-abiding masses abstained to begin with!), Scotland was the world's leading source of whisky that could meet the demand of the newly awakened American market. That whisky even became known as "Scotch." Even James Bond developed a fondness for it, and Irish whiskey was very much in the shadows of Scotch. Until now. Brands of Irish whiskey such as Jameson and Bushmills have however gained considerable global market share in what appears to be a rebirth of Irish whiskey appreciation, and this whiskey renaissance also brings to light of some the lesser-known distilleries that ply their trade on the Emerald Isle. Once such distillery is Teeling.

TEELING SINGLE MALT
IRISH WHISKEY 46%

Even as Teeling opened its distillery in 2014, taking their first step in transiting from bottler to full-on, all in-house distiller, the company continued to expand their line of Irish whiskeys. They recently added one more to the collection in the form of the Teeling Single Malt.

Teeling has a trio of other Irish single malts out, all super premium expressions aged 21 years, 26 years and 30 years. With even the 21 Year Old running for north of $200 a bottle, these are the sorts of whiskies most of us would buy or receive only

on special occasions, and then dole out sparingly thereafter.

The new Teeling Single Malt, on the other hand, is a regular premium whiskey intended to occupy that niche of finer, but still regular, drinking. It's a no aging statement whiskey, drawing on stock up to 23 years old and aged in five different types of wood—Sherry, Port, Madeira, Cabernet Sauvignon and White Burgundy—for its one distillery blend. This five wood approach is a new one for Irish whiskey, and the resulting whiskey was bottled at 46%.

In the glass, the Teeling Single Malt has a bright yellow coloring. I'm revealing the old, ex-comic book geek in me by saying the color in the vein of Sinestro's power ring kind of yellow, a real four-color yellow territory. That makes it a marvel to look at in decent lighting.

The nose is a crisp with green apples, and has the overall character of an odd fruit salad. There are those apples, plus melon, ripe figs, and a mild citrus note. Add in a little toffee and a touch of musty, old wood, and you have it, making it a complex nose, but not one that is hard to come to grips with.

The flavor concentrates on just two fruits: dried figs and tart lemon. The wood goes from musty to dry, and the seasoning picks up with vanilla, cloves and a hotter blend of cookie spice. The finish dry and toasty, with a just slightly spicy afterglow.

Came away from the Teeling Single Malt thinking it would make a nice general-purpose sipper, especially with its look and scent. However, I suspect its real place might be as an aperitif whiskey, and the next time I get the chance I am going to try it in exactly that role.

RT

TEELING 21 YEAR OLD SILVER RESERVE 46%

Teeling produces a number of expressions, but this review is for the Teeling 21 Year Old. This particular whiskey was matured in bourbon barrels and then finished in Sauternes barrels for 12 months.

On the nose, mild perfumed soap combines with apricot jam, butter menthol cough drops, caramel, honey, oregano and rosemary herb bread, anise seed and sweet ethanol often found in a cleanly distilled white rum. There is an underlying woodiness about this whiskey, which sits beneath the sugars and occasionally prickles the nostrils with the smell of newly varnished furniture and the whiff of warm leather infused

with incense, as lemon-scented soap and floral notes develop with intensifying buttery notes and candied peaches. On the palate, this whiskey is initially sweet and fruity as it rests on the tongue, releasing toffee apple and cooked apricot as it swirls around the palate. The wood then snaps at the taste buds as the whiskey is swallowed, and the sugars are suddenly lost to a wave of drying wood and bitter floral notes—similar to potpourri—and green olives with lemon and shades of honey. The finish offers lingering hints of honey with yellow peach and notes of brine with olive pips and dried petals.

Overall, Teeling 21 Year Old is an elegant Irish whiskey that offers undertones of sweetness that do their best to reign in the woody twang that rages at mid-palate, but it turns out that the oak is simply too big and bold to be tamed—strangely, that is precisely what seems to make this whiskey work so well. Teeling 21 Year Old is an interesting whiskey that I found enjoyable, but it did not leave me yearning for more. Be warned, there was a distinctive woody/bitter floral note that some may find odd and others may either love, hate, or feel indifferent towards. It is best to try this one at a bar before buying a bottle.

AC

TEELING 26 YEAR OLD GOLD RESERVE 46%

Building on 2013's release of their 21 Year Old Silver Reserve single malt, Teeling Whiskey Company upped the ante by releasing a pair of even older Irish single malts this year, including the 26 Year Old Gold Reserve. That age would be make this a novel enough Irish whiskey, but the choice of wood for the whiskey's marriage makes it doubly so.

Distilled in 1987, the same year the Teeling-founded Cooley Distillery opened, this whiskey was double distilled (not triple) and aged in ex-bourbon barrels. After the barrels were dumped and the whiskey married, it was transferred into old white burgundy barrels to finish. While plenty of whiskey-makers are experimenting with using wine casks for finishing, the norm is red and not white wine, so that is a particularly interesting twist and the first time white burgundy wood has ever been used in the Irish whiskey industry. As one might expect for a 26 Year Old, the production run was small (1,000 bottles), and bottled at the customary mark of 46% abv.

In the glass, the Teeling 26 Year Old has a solid gold coloring. It's that simple, the same coloring as a gold bar.

The nose is delightfully aromatic, with the white grape scent carrying out of the snifter and across the room. It's a rich, nutty nose, and with that white grape and green apple current,

it's clear the white burgundy wood has made a hefty imprint on the scent.

The flavor is not quite so dominated by the white wine side of the whiskey, showing an appropriate shift in balance. It's a little woody and a little grassy, but the main notes are golden raisins until a dash of spiciness rises to the surface. The finish is moderately spicy and fruity, warm, and pleasantly long.

More than interesting enough to make for a fine sipper, but also sweet in the way that would make it an outstanding dessert single malt, this is a stand-out Irish whiskey.

RT

Interview with Jack Teeling

BY KURT MAITLAND

KM: First off, let's talk about how you got into the business.

JT: Cooley gave me my start in Irish whiskey and instilled my own passion for the industry. From my ten years with them, I received a well-rounded experience as I worked myself up from a commercial role to Sales & Marketing Director to eventually Managing Director. This gave me both a very good understanding of the commercial side of the operation and the distilling side, in particular reinforcing the importance of product but also how it is presented. I have tried to apply these learnings to the new venture to avoid many of the mistakes we made and to build on what worked during our Cooley days.

KM: What do you feel the new Teeling whiskey will bring to the current Irish whiskey landscape?

JT: The Irish whiskey industry is dominated by multinationals but it's currently lacking the breadth and choice that most other whiskey categories can offer. Our goal is to be the leading independent Irish whiskey company, in particular taking the lead in driving choice and selection of unique handcrafted small batch expressions.

KM: What do you think are the main/best characteristics of your whiskies?

JT: That they are different and also highly drinkable like any good Irish whiskey should be.

KM: Who do you want to appeal to with this release and what is your thinking about future releases from Teeling?

JT: With our Teeling Small Batch Irish whiskey, we were trying to produce the most flavorsome, interesting blended Irish whiskey we could. We learned a lot from different maturation projects we had been involved in and applied this to the Blended Irish whiskey segment. We used the guys in the Irish Whiskey Society in Dublin as a sounding board on many different expressions but the one that shone like a star from these tastings was our higher proof non-chill filtered rum-married blend and our Small Batch was born. The unique marrying and bottling process used in the Small Batch allows us to retain the smooth taste profile people enjoy from Irish whiskey but layer on top delicate and more flavorsome, dry raisin, Moorish rum notes to complement this. We think this appeals to people who are looking to discover a more interesting expression of Irish whiskey and hopefully will lead them to discover future releases of Teeling whiskey as we have plenty more unique expressions to come.

KM: What's your vision for the growth of Teeling? Do you just want to focus on your core three spirits, or do you want to add even smaller specialty batches to your release schedule?

JT: Our goal is to eventually have a portfolio of Teeling bottlings that will give people a very different and unique ladder of expressions of Irish whiskey to discover. We are currently examining the possibility of doing a range of Single Cask/Barrel bottlings to showcase a few other projects we are currently working on, but once we are back in production, our aim is to really push the boat out in terms of innovation. We are very excited to be able to revive long-forgotten old mash bills that would have been commonly used during the last golden era of Irish whiskey in the ninteenth century when Dublin was at its epicenter.

KM: What does it mean to you, personally, to be the first new distillery in Dublin in over 125 years?

JT: To able to go right back to where our family first got involved in the industry back in 1782 and at the same time revive the distilling industry in Dublin means the world to me. The last Dublin pot still ran cold back in 1976 when all production was consolidated into Cork, and since then the history and stories around centuries of distilling in Dublin started to slip away. We are very proud and honored, as born and bred Dubs, to be able to revive the Teeling family involvement in Irish whiskey and to forge a new future for distilling in Dublin.

TULLAMORE D.E.W. 10 YEAR OLD 40%

Even before Grant's bought Tullamore D.E.W. in 2010, the brand was already experimenting with new expressions, as was the case when they released the Tullamore D.E.W. 10 Year Old Single Malt in 2009. This single malt was reportedly double distilled at Cooley, instead of being triple distilled at New Midleton, as is the case for the standard Tullamore D.E.W. whiskey.

Another feature separating the Tullamore D.E.W. 10 Year Old Single Malt from the pack is that the whiskey blends malts aged in old bourbon, port, Madeira and sherry casks. Tullamore's 10, 14, and 18 year old whiskeys are the only whiskeys in Ireland (or well, anywhere) that bring together whiskey from four different types of used barrels. Bottled at 40% in Tullamore D.E.W.'s traditional, Victorian-style squared bottle, this whiskey has a substantially different flavor profile from anything I've seen, not just out of Tullamore D.E.W., but Ireland as a whole.

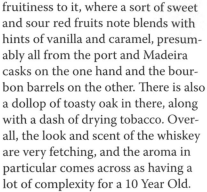

In the glass, the 10 Year Old Single Malt has the look of a deep golden honey, a far cry from the typical paleness of young and middle-aged Irish whiskies. The nose has a certain lush sweetness and fruitiness to it, where a sort of sweet and sour red fruits note blends with hints of vanilla and caramel, presumably all from the port and Madeira casks on the one hand and the bourbon barrels on the other. There is also a dollop of toasty oak in there, along with a dash of drying tobacco. Overall, the look and scent of the whiskey are very fetching, and the aroma in particular comes across as having a lot of complexity for a 10 Year Old.

On the palate, the Tullamore D.E.W. 10 Year Old Single Malt brings over all the notes of the nose in bold, but not overpowering fashion. There is a bit of pepperiness there, but that is the only surprise. Everything about this whiskey is quite mild, but there is no chasing for the wine, bourbon, and malt flavors. Everything is right there and easily found, both balanced and somewhat sophisticated. In keeping with Tullamore D.E.W., the whiskey is more sweet than anything else. The finish winds down from that new spicy note, into a long and mild warmth.

The blend behind this Irish single malt gives it a character that one just would not expect from a Hibernian 10 Year Old, making it noticeably superior to its peers, such as Bushmills 10 Year Old. It is really stand-out stuff in its class, and in keeping with Tullamore's core style, it emphasizes sweet flavors over toffee, smoke, and wood.

RT

THE IRISHMAN SINGLE MALT WHISKEY 40%

Matured for more than a decade. 1,000 cases.

Color: Pale gold.

Nose: This is much straighter than the Tullamore (*tout l'amour*, say my compatriots), starting much more on pear and pineapple drops, but it gets then a tad spirity and oddly woody. Cold tea, then hints of incense, tinned litchis and maybe a little crushed fresh coriander. Whiffs of wet iron. An unusual nose, not unpleasant at all despite a growing meatiness that's a tad offbeat.

Palate: A tad weird in the attack, slightly weak. Gets then much closer to the Tullamore—almost similar in fact. Pear drops and vanilla, hints of Parma violets. Short-ish finish, on peppered pears. I like this one... complex on the nose.

SV

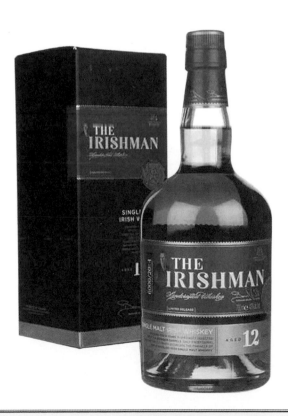

WEST CORK 10 YEAR OLD 40%

West Cork Distillers was established by three very good friends in the small fishing village of Union Hall in West Cork, Ireland. West Cork Distillers is an independent distiller that has been producing handcrafted spirits since 2007. This specific whiskey was not made at West Cork, but it was finished and bottled there. West Cork produces a non-chill filtered whiskey matured in first-fill bourbon barrels. Smooth, soft, approachable, light. Lots of honey, apricot, figs, and spice, with a hint of vanilla. Easy finish. Good for those who like a light whiskey.

Nose: Big green apple dominate aroma, with hints of vanilla, toffee, molasses, and cereal.

Palate: Doesn't offer as much fruit upfront as the nose promises, but nice. Good solid dose of malt, caramel, and vanilla all come through. A nice clean finish. Some spices linger. Vanilla and caramel stick around. A hint of the tropical? Cocoa? Improves with a little air, and with water green apple gets even bigger, as do caramel and vanilla. Lovely.

CD

THE POGUES SINGLE MALT WHISKEY

BY CARLO DEVITO

The Pogues, whose Celtic punk rock in the 80s took the world by storm, and who are known for their hit "Fairytale in New York," have an Irish whiskey (made with single malt whiskey) that is produced by West Cork Distillers (one of only two remaining independently owned and operated distilleries in Ireland). The Pogues Irish Whiskey is a unique blend of 50% 10 year single malt Irish whiskey aged in sherry casks and 50% 5 to 7 year Irish grain whiskey aged in bourbon oak casks.

"It's been brilliant working with the team at West Cork Distillers in creating a whiskey that we all think reflects our spirit and energy, and that we all enjoy the taste of," stated Shane MacGowan alongside fellow Pogues band members Jem Finer, Andrew Ranken, Spider Stacy, James Fearnley, Terry Woods, and Darryl Hunt. "It's wonderful to add a product bearing our name to the ranks of great Irish whiskeys, and we think it will stand the test of time."

Officially, it's not a single malt—but we couldn't resist!

ITALY

BY CARLO DEVITO

Italy became famous for making wine before the Roman Empire, dating back to the Etruscans and early Greek settlers. Today, some of the most famous wine-producing regions in the world are located in Italy. Italy accounts for nearly one-third of all total wine production globally. Regions such as Piemonte, Fruili-Venezia Fiulia, Veneto, Umbria, Toscana, Aosta, and many, many more are coveted by wine collectors around the world.

The country has had a centuries-old reputation of making "grappa," a pomace-based brandy that is clear and is made in oak-aged reserves. In the last half-century, one woman, Giannola Nonino, and her distillery, Nonino, in Percoto, Italy has completely changed the way grappa has been perceived. Her family's operation has been making fine spirits since 1897. They took grappa and turned it from a rustic product to a refined work of Italian art. Others have followed.

Italy has even made vodka. But Italy and PUNI Distillery are relative newcomers to the whisky game.

PUNI DISTILLERY

BY RICHARD THOMAS

One aspect of the global craft-distilling trend is that many countries that have never made whisky before are now doing it, and since most of them are most familiar with Scotch, that is the model they follow. Hence Italy's PUNI Distillery, which released its first batches of three-year-old whisky last year.

Since three years is the statutory minimum for Scotch whisky and Irish whiskey, and although most were pleased and curious about the notion of an Italian distillery, the minimal aging raised a degree of skepticism from some of the more observant world whisky fans in Europe.

Yet there are ways to make a pleasant sipper out of a young whisky.

For example, when I caught up with Kavalan's Taiwanese whiskies about a year after the initial buzz, what I discovered was that a big chunk of the people who wrote about them missed how, to a large extent, Kavalan made good use of the tropical Taiwanese climate coupled with a heavy finish to offset the youngish whisky at the base.

Clever use of wood is part of the whisky-maker's craft, and I don't find anything wrong with that. Nor, in fact, do the legions of fans devoted to Laphroaig's Quarter Cask. The results might not be subtle, but they can make for a very enjoyable whisky, and that is what PUNI accomplished with their Alba single malt.

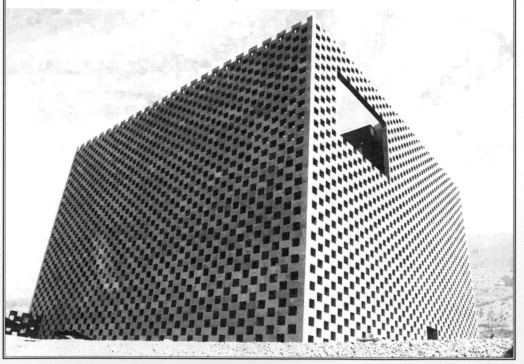

PUNI ALBA SINGLE MALT 43%

The Puni Alba I tried was from Batch 2, bottled at 43%. What the distillery did with this single malt was conduct their primary aging in Sicilian marsala wine casks, then put a finish on the whisky using second-fill bourbon barrels already used to make whisky in Islay. Those Islay barrels held their single malt for between ten and twenty-four years.

On the one end, the maturation is in wood soaked with a heavily spiced wine; on the other, wood endowed with the peat and sea spray of Islay. The result takes the juvenile malt whisky base I encountered in PUNI's Nova and layers it with a very enjoyable palette of flavors.

The appearance in the glass was a cloudy gold, the cloudy part no doubt due to the fact that PUNI doesn't chill-filter its whisky and I keep my stores in an unheated room. The nose, equal parts fruity and grainy, wasn't encouraging, but the whisky started looking up with my first sip.

The silky texture of the liquid glides over the palate, delivering a well-balanced blend of dark fruit and cookie spices on the one hand, with smoky creosote on the other. Not subtle, but definitely enjoyable. The finish winds down with a nice warm trail.

RT

JAPAN

BY STEFAN VAN EYCKEN

Even though whisky-making in Japan is slowly approaching its 100th anniversary, the presence of single malts on the Japanese whisky scene is a much more recent phenomenon.

Yamazaki, the first malt whisky distillery in Japan, started production in 1923 but it took parent-company Suntory more than sixty years to launch its first single malt whisky. The company credits Keizo Saji, the second son of Suntory founder Shinjiro Torii, with the "bold decision to introduce single malts into the market" in 1984. The truth of the matter is a much smaller whisky producer—Sanraku Ocean—had already taken that "bold" step eight years before The Yamazaki Single Malt was launched.

In July 1976, Sanraku Ocean released their Karuizawa Single Malt whisky. They used the highest quality malt maturing in the warehouses and had a special hand-blown crystal decanter designed for it. Because good malt stocks were very limited, the company could only produce 10,000 bottles of Karuizawa Single Malt per year, and they never actually promoted the brand, seeing as they didn't want to create more demand than they could possibly satisfy. This partly explains why Karuizawa has been written out of the history of single malt whisky in Japan. The current Emperor of Japan, then-Crown Prince, was given a bottle of this while on holiday in Karuizawa with his wife in 1978. Apparently, he liked it so much that he had some more bottles ordered. Today, that would be a marketing department's wet dream, but at Sanraku Ocean they were in no position to make a big deal of all this.

Nikka entered the single malt market around the same time as Suntory in 1984, when they released their Hokkaido Single Malt 12 Year Old. Only 10,000 bottles of that initial Hokkaido single malt were released, so the appeal of single malt whisky was really quite limited at the time, even though whisky consumption in general (i.e. blends) was at an all-time high in the early 80s. In 1989, Nikka released a new 12 year old single malt produced at and named after their other distillery, Miyagikyo, and for the sake of consistency, renamed the Hokkaido Single Malt after the actual distillery on Hokkaido—Yoichi.

Over at Suntory, the marketing department was keen to launch a second single malt—from their other distillery, Hakushu—as soon as the distillery was twelve years old (1985). However, the blenders felt they didn't have the requisite stocks to create a quality product, so that plan was shelved until 1994.

Single malt whiskies were mostly "vanity projects" for the big companies, meant to flesh out the upper-end of their portfolios and wow the critics with the quality of their products. Their actual bread-and-butter was—and still is—in the blended whisky category. When stocks are running low, as they are now because demand has picked up again after a 25-year decline in domestic whisky consumption, the first part of the portfolio to suffer are the single malts, which are either discontinued en bloc (as Nikka did, replacing the entire line-up with two new non-age statement expressions) or on strict allocation (as Suntory is doing, by drip-feeding the market while they build up sufficient reserves again).

The smaller whisky producers in Japan (Chichibu, Mars Shinshu and half a dozen new distilleries being set up at the time of writing) are very much focused on the single malt category and, in a way, the stock shortage the big boys are struggling with is giving them an advantage in that niche category. They're not cutting corners, however, and the quality of their malts is of the highest level. When the big boys have enough malt in the warehouses to intensify their efforts in the single malt field again, there should be a plethora of stellar Japanese single malts on the shelves of liquor stores, at home and abroad. Everyone's got their sights set on the 2020 Tokyo Olympics, so at least in the field of whisky, Japan won't have anything to worry about.

THE YAMAZAKI SINGLE MALT WHISKY

THE YAMAZAKI 12 YEAR OLD 43%

This is a classic. It's the longest-selling and by far most popular single malt in Japan. The recipe for this is incredibly complex but it's a whisky that doesn't wear its complexity on its sleeve. It's very lush on the nose, which makes it instantly recognizable among Japanese single malts: sweet fruitiness (peaches and assorted tropical fruits), zesty notes (candied orange peel), Danish pastries and pre-cious oils. It's very dynamic on the palate, with a progression from cereal notes via vanilla and fruit to woody and sour notes (goya, grapefruit peel). The finish is dominated by citrus notes initially, but these give way to sweeter elements (crème brulée, cotton candy) with a bit of clove and nutmeg as it fades out. If you see old bottles of this, don't hesitate and pick them up. The difference between what you get now and what it was in 1984 is as striking as the difference between Macallan 18 now and Macallan 18s from the 70s. Nuff said.

SVE

THE YAMAZAKI 25 YEAR OLD 43%

Here's one Japanese whisky you can pick out in a dark room any day of the week, even if you've only tried it once. Only ex-sherry, Spanish oak is used for this expression. Sun-tory is a bit obsessive when it comes to their ex-sherry casks—not just any old cask will do. They've invested in forests in the north of Spain where they handpick trees for their sherry casks, which are then seasoned to their specifications before being shipped over to Japan. It must be worth the trouble. In any case, this is a small miracle in a glass. On the nose, you get raisin juice, figs, thick strawberry jam, black plum stew, stewed peaches, mulled wine, cocoa, borscht (with loads of Worcester sauce and soy sauce), and jamon iberico. There are also hints of toasted macadamia nuts, old leather-bound books, and bit of tarragon. What a fantastic nose: super lush yet superbly

balanced. On the palate, it delivers truckloads of dried fruits, blueberry jam, blood sausages with cherry sauce, Seville oranges, dark chocolate with a bit of chili pepper, almond butter, cinnamon, and clove as well as some slight tannins (sometimes less slight, depending on the batch). The finish is extremely long and mouth coating, with a bit more wood coming through but nothing beyond the pale. An iconic Japanese single malt—try it once and then you too can pick it out in a dark room any day of the week.

SVE

THE HAKUSHU 18 YEAR OLD 43%

Hakushu 18 was launched in 2006, a time when whisky sales in Japan were abysmal. It was one of those single malts that you saw everywhere, but not many people were actually buying or drinking it. Now that stocks are tight everywhere in Japan and limited releases sell out in a matter of seconds, more and more people are discovering this high-end "standard" expression...but there's not as much to go around as there used to be. Same old story. Anyway, on the nose, you get a beautiful assemblage of honeydew melon, roasted apple pie, nutmeg, pepper, antique furniture, and a hint of smoke. On the palate, you get digestive biscuits, toffee, honey-baked apples, sweet-and-sour sauce, and smoked nuts. The finish combines overripe stone fruits and subtle wood smoke in a beautiful, gentle fade-out.

SVE

Silky smoothness and spreading aroma, the gift from Mt.Fuji

JAPANESE WHISKIES,
TRANSLATED FROM THE SCOTTISH

BY ROBERT SIMONSON

[After] decades as an also-ran in the American whisky market, Japanese whisky is on the ascent. Last year, Suntory's sales in the United States rose 44%, according to the company, which found it difficult to keep up with demand. So it increased prices of the Yamazaki 12 and 18 year olds by 10% last year and this year. "We like the consumer to recognize Japanese whisky as very high end," said Yoshihiro Morita, Suntory's executive manager for American sales and marketing.

Japanese whisky has been produced commercially since the 1920s, when the Yamazaki distillery was built. Compared with Scotch, Irish whiskey, and bourbon, it is still the new kid on the block.

But now that those other categories have been thoroughly rediscovered by Americans over the last thirty years, it's Japan's turn. The embrace has been nudged along by the fact that you can finally buy Japanese whisky here.

Suntory quietly introduced the Yamazaki 12 year old in 1990, and that was the only option until 2005, when the 18 year old arrived. By 2010, the United States had its first Japanese blended whisky, Suntory's Hibiki. And [then], the Hakushu 12 year old made its debut. The company's domination of the American market [was then] challenged when its archrival, Nikka, [released] in the Single Malt Yoichi 15 year old and Taketsuru Pure Malt 12 year old.

"Up until two years ago, if one in twenty customers had tasted Japanese whisky, we were lucky," said Flavien Desoblin, owner of Brandy Library, the TriBeCa spirits emporium. "Now, out of twenty, a good five know that it exists and they've had it. That's quite a lot for the land of bourbon."

Sales have grown enough that Suntory has seen fit to draft two brand ambassadors in the United States, first the New York mixologist Gardner Dunn and then the San Francisco bartender Neyah White. At the time of his hiring two years ago, Mr. White was no great devotee of Japanese whisky. "I respected it, but I wasn't swinging that flag around too heavily," he said. "I was a little dismissive of it, to be honest. The world of whisky was so big."

For much of the twentieth century, Japanese distillers were perceived as little more than Scotch makers manqué. Masataka Taketsuru, Suntory's first master distiller and Nikka's founder, studied his art in Scotland and chose distillery sites that resembled its terrain and climate. Producers even spelled whisky the Scottish way, without the "e." While there's no denying that Japanese whiskies taste more like Scotch than, say, bourbon, connoisseurs now focus more on what sets them apart.

"The founder of Suntory wanted to create an authentic Japanese whisky that appealed to the delicate palate of the Japanese: subtle, refined, yet complex," said Mike Miyamoto, who was Suntory's master distiller for ten years. "To make such a subtle taste, you need a lot of whiskies to blend. If you have one or two colors, how good a picture are you going to make?"

But finding all those blending elements is not easy. Unlike Scotch makers, who swap liquid back and forth to build their blended whiskies, the Japanese distillers do not trade. Instead, they create countless in-house variations, using various yeasts, variations of barley and peat levels.

They send the distillates through an array of stills of different shapes and sizes, then age them in a wide variety of barrels: virgin American oak, used American barrels from various suppliers, former sherry butts and wine barrels. Adding a distinctive native flavor to some of the whiskies are barrels of expensive Japanese oak (called mizunara), which is thought to lend aromas of incense, and used plum-liqueur barrels.

With all those treatments on hand, distillers can let their passion for blending run wild. And there lies another difference. In Scotland, the single malts are the fair-haired tots, while the blends are the moneymaking, sometimes uninspired workhorses. The Japanese take their single malts seriously, too, but their blends never take a back seat.

"The Japanese blend for completely different reasons," Mr. White said. "Blending for them is not an efficiency thing. They make all these different whiskies so they can pull them all in, in a way that will perform well in a Japanese drink, which is almost always a sort of highball."

Hibiki, which is composed of more than twenty different whiskies, "shows best when you water it down," Mr. White said. "It's subtle and complex at the same time. It's hard to define."

Mr. Desoblin had no trouble defining the appeal. "Japanese whiskies are very much the fine-wine-drinker's take on whisky," he said. "There is more attention paid to the body and the texture in Japan than in many other countries. They are looking for that delicate, suave, mouth-coating feel, but never really aggressive. They seem to be powerful, but it's all silky."

Because of the high price points, aside from the Yamazaki 12 year old, the Suntory products are not often used in cocktails. In fact, when Suntory's chief blender, Shinji Fukuyo, first heard about Mr. Schuman's Shogun's Grip, he was not happy. He thought it a desecration of his masterpiece. So Mr. Dunn took him to Ryu to sample the offending drink. "After a moment," Mr. Schuman said, "he gave a nod of approval."

WHITE OAK AKASHI NAS 46%

Eigashima was the first Japanese whisky "producer," legally speaking, since it got its license to "make" whisky in 1919. "Making whisky" meant something different in those days. In 1984 they set up a new, proper malt distillery but they only make whisky for a few months a year and have very little mature stock. They make a bit and sell a bit. It would be better to make a lot and sell a bit, but that costs money and their focus lies elsewhere (shochu, nihonshu).

The house malt, Akashi, doesn't carry an age-statement, but it's clearly very young—under 5 years old. It's very barley-forward, spirit-driven with first-fill bourbon casks delivering toffee and vanilla, and refill-sherry casks supplying some soft fruit notes. Well-made and very reasonably priced, it's designed to work in as many different contexts as possible—neat, on the rocks, with soda—and it does, just don't expect the world!

SVE

MARS MALTAGE "SATSUMA" 15 YEAR OLD

The Hombo headquarters are in Kagoshima and for a very short period (1978-1984), while they were looking for a better site, whisky was produced there. Satsuma being the old name for the western part of present-day Kagoshima, they adopted that name for the few releases exclusively containing whisky produced during that period. If you see a bottle, pick it up. It literally is liquid history, as Hombo itself no longer has any stocks from that period. The 15 Year Old shows that they knew very well what they were doing back then. On the nose, you get hints of barley shochu, apple peel, under-ripe peaches, pineapple lumps, and old magazines. The palate is lush, again fruit-forward with a bit of nougat and crème brulée thrown in. The finish is medium-long, featuring milk-chocolate-and-salt-caramel mousse and café latte. A glorious flash from the past.

SVE

MARS "KOMAGATAKE" 3 YEAR OLD SHERRY & AMERICAN WHITE OAK 57%

Mars has had a very rocky whisky-making history, full of false starts, early stops, more gutters than strikes, but not because they were doing anything wrong, really. They just always happened to be doing the right thing at the wrong time. After a nineteen-year hiatus, they fired up the stills again. This was in 2011. Three years later, they released The Revival, and then soon after this vatting of malt matured in ex-sherry and American white oak casks. It bears its youth on its sleeve, that's for sure, but it's refreshing in this day and age when finding an age statement—let alone a proud 3 year old—on a bottle of whisky is a bit like finding a pot of gold at the end of the rainbow. On the nose, you get white chocolate, rhubarb jam, and apple compote with lots of lemon. On the palate, it's a slightly perplexing mix of stewed fruits, goya, and grapefruit peel, with white pepper and herbal bitters on the finish. This is for whisky drinkers who like a bit of wrestling... with the liquid in the glass, that is!

SVE

KIRIN WHISKY

FUJISANROKU 18 YEAR OLD 43%

Kirin, the owners of Fuji Gotemba distillery, used to have two different 18 year old single malts from the same distillery in their portfolio, one being twice as expensive as the other. One was called "Fuji Gotemba 18," the other "Fujsanroku 18." Obviously, there was confusion all round. A few years ago, they ditched the cheaper one, and kept the latter. But then, in early 2015, they released a small batch 17 Year Old. Someone clearly needs to sit down with the Kirin folk and give them a 101 in age-statement branding. In any case, the Fujisanroku 18 (literally "at the foot of Mount Fuji") has carved out a nice little niche for

itself—not as high-profile as the Yamazaki 18 or Hakushu 18, but more reasonably-priced than those two, and with the 15 to 20 year old single malt offerings from Nikka gone, this is basically the only high-age Japanese whisky you can buy without either breaking the bank or having to take a sabbatical. It's very smooth with a textbook balance of cereal notes (and nuts), gentle fruit (apple, pineapple, a bit of citrus), wood, and a very subtle smoke accent. It's meant to be middle-of-the-road, but it's really good middle-of-the-road.

SVE

NIKKA WHISKY

YOICHI NAS 2015 45%

When Nikka replaced their entire Yoichi range with a new singular no-age-statement expression, you could hear jaws dropping all over Japan and soon after in other markets as well. This new NAS expression is actually closer to the old 10 year old than the old NAS in terms of composition. You get a lovely barley sweetness, pencil shavings, over-ripe orchard fruits, and soft smoke on the nose; oak and soft peat lead the dance on the palate with some candied orange peel thrown in; the finish is earthy and vegetal, with some tea on the side. Not as bold as some die-hard Yoichi fans of the first hour like their favorite tipple, but it may be instrumental in attracting new fans until such time as Nikka has built up sufficiently mature stock to bring age-statement expressions back.

SVE

YOICHI 1988/2013 SINGLE CASK 62%

This—brace yourself is a heavily peated Yoichi that has spent a quarter of a century in virgin oak (a butt, to be precise). It doesn't sound like this would work, but it does and how! On the nose, you get pencil shavings, new plank, annin dofu and furniture polish—that's the virgin oak speaking—as well as "farm smells" (reminiscent of some Port Charlotte single casks), smoked nuts, and a bit of fruit (apple butter barbecue sauce). The combination of new oak, heavy peat and that typically 'dirty' (in a good sense of the word) Yoichi character works a treat. On the palate, you get sour cherries, smoked duck, marzipan, rhubarb jam, milk chocolate, smoked nuts again, and the last of a summer campfire. Time has integrated the peat beautifully: it's not as frontal as you'd expect from a heavily peated malt. The finish is long and lingering with the peat smoke more pronounced and a slight hint of orange peel. A little miracle of nature— "extremes that were made to meet," Aldous Huxley would say.

SVE

MIYAGIKYO SINGLE MALT NAS 45%

In September 2015, Nikka shocked the whisky community at home and abroad by discontinuing their entire range of single malts and replacing them with a single no-age-statement expression for each of their distilleries, not to be confused with the NAS expression that used to be the entry malt for each of those. This will be the order of the day until the maturing stock laid down (or not laid down, to be more precise) a decade ago catches up with demand. This new Miyagikyo offers apples and pears on the nose with grassy and light floral elements in the background; dried fruits, vanilla, and anise on the palate, with a tiny bit of bitterness (grapefruit peel, grape skin), nuts, and some milk chocolate on the finish. A beautiful daily dram.

SVE

MIYAGIKYO 1996/2014 SINGLE CASK #66535 62%

It looks like it will be a while before we will be able to pick up the occasional Miyagikyo single cask again. This is the last one Nikka let go before they decided they'd freeze their single cask program for the time being. On the nose, it is an explosion of fruit (apricot jam, pear drops, green apples, grape skin) but with lots of intriguing secondary notes floating by, too: pumpkin pie (with a good dose of nutmeg), smoked dried pineapple, maraschino cherries, honey doughnuts, and a little bit of bacon in the background. The peat is very light and subtle—on the nose, it adds something reminiscent of clothes the day after a barbeque, or a campfire doused with water. On the palate, it has the same fruits at its center but surrounded by sour (kabosu, shikwasa jam) and bitter (grapefruit peel, walnut skin) elements. It evokes crêpes Suzette but it's also markedly spicy (chili peppers, sansho) and everything comes wrapped in a lovely thin blanket of peat. What a delight and what a way to say goodbye to the good old days...

SVE

Masataka Taketsuru

BY STEFAN VAN EYCKEN

The name doesn't exactly roll off the tongue and until very recently most people in Japan wouldn't have had a clue who Masataka Taketsuru was. Now, however, if you ask a few random people on the street about "Massan," nine out of ten will be able to tell you all about the founding father of Japanese whisky, his trials and tribulations, his personal quirks and even his love life. How did that happen?

"Morning Drama" (or "Asadora" in Japanese) is a serialized TV series produced by Japan's national broadcaster, NHK, which airs when most people have breakfast in 15-minute installments over the course of half a year. The series are immensely popular and watching the episodes is a little daily ritual for many people in Japan. From September 2014 to March 2015, Taketsuru—lightly fictionalized, of course— was the focus of the morning drama, and the rest is history as they say. Now, even people who've never been near a glass of whisky—let alone Japanese whisky!— know exactly who Taketsuru was.

Born into a sake-brewing family in Hiroshima in 1894, Taketsuru studied chemistry and brewing at university, the idea being he would contribute to the family business. History had something else in mind for him, though. He discovered whisky and other so-called "Western liquor" and entered the Settsu Shuzo company in Osaka in view of pursuing his interests in whisky-making. The company sent him to Scotland in 1918 where he enrolled at the University of Glasgow, studying chemistry, and apprenticed at various distilleries around the country, most notably Longmorn and Hazelburn. He also studied grain whisky manufacturing and the art of blending. It's clear that whisky wasn't the only sort of chemistry he was interested in, as he

returned to Japan in 1920 with a Scots lass, Jessie Roberta ("Rita") Cowan, whom he had married earlier that year.

Shortly after his return to Japan, Settsu started struggling financially and the whisky project was abandoned. After a short stint as a high school chemistry teacher, Taketsuru found a new employer interested in making whisky in Japan, Kotobukiya Ltd. (Suntory). He coordinated the building of Yamazaki distillery and was distillery manager for a while. Ten years later, when his contract was up, he left Kotobukiya and set up his own company. He clearly didn't waste any time: He left Kotobukiya in March 1934, had set up Dai-Nippon Kaju (the "Great Japan Juice Co. Ltd.") by July, and had built his own distillery by October of the same year. Try doing that now!

Whisky in Japan, in those days, was whatever producers wanted it to be and "authentic whisky" (as in, following Scottish practice) was few and far between. Taketsuru knew very well what the real deal was, but convincing people in Japan was a different story. His struggles were intense enough to fill a soap opera with—in fact, that's what they did in the morning drama "Massan" (Rita's nickname for her husband). In those day, blending whisky in Japan mostly meant adding neutral spirit to a small percentage of malt whisky, and sometimes even just flavoring neutral spirit. Taketsuru knew this was just cutting corners and imported two Coffey stills from Scotland (in 1963 and 1966, respectively) to make proper grain whisky. Keen to have access to malt whisky of a different character, he set up a second distillery near Sendai in 1969.

By the time of his death in 1979, Nikka Whisky Distilling Co. was the second-largest producer of whisky in Japan. Soon after, whisky fell out of favor with the Japanese drinking populace, as they switched to lighter white spirits. But two decades later, the rest of the world started taking notice. In 2001, a Yoichi single cask won Whisky Magazine's "Best of the Best" award, the first time a non-Scottish whisky had won the top prize. In 2007, the premium blended malt carrying Taketsuru's name (21 year old) was crowned "Best Blended Malt in the World." Step into any convenience store in Japan now, head on over the canned drinks section and you'll see Massan and Rita looking at you from canned whisky highballs. They finally made it…even at home, which is the hardest place to make it when you're from Japan.

KARUIZAWA VINTAGE 1968/2010 SINGLE CASK #6955 61.1%

At the time this was released, this could have been yours for a few hundred dollars; now, you'd have to sell an arm and a leg. This is one of those Karuizawas that's in the pantheon of whisky and it won't get kicked out any time soon. What an experience... On the nose, you get cola cubes and then a whole kitchen pantry: chutneys, preserves, fresh fruit as well (mangoes, overripe pineapple, honeydew melon), prosciutto, rillettes, pretzels, old rye whiskey... there is no end to the marvels waiting to be discovered here. On the palate, it is the most amazingly smooth cross-fade from sweet (jams, sweets of all kinds, baked goods...) to sour (freshly squeezed citrus fruits from all corners of the world) with various tertiary notes floating by (any mention of these would be hopelessly partial anyway, so we won't even go there). The finish integrates the two dimensions (the sweet and the sour) whilst adding precious oils, aspects of old wood and a touch of spice. The stuff that dreams are made of...

SVE

KARUIZAWA 1981/2013 SINGLE CASK #3555 60.6%

Extreme and definitely not for the vegetarians among us. This is a sherry monster! The color itself is unlike anything I've seen before...deep kakhi brown. The nose is intense, up there with the most extreme Karuizawas out there: earthy (a forest in fall) with old chapel notes, stewed prunes, blueberry jam, barbecued spareribs, balsamic glaze, smoked horsemeat, oven roasted burdock, mimolette cheese and much more... On the palate, you get more grilled meat, mole sauce, smoked duck and figs, Seville orange marmalade, duck à l' orange (I know, more duck!), smoked macadamia nuts, and sudachi (a small, green Japanese citrus fruit that's a signature note of old Karuizawas). Towards the end, a sharp bitterness emerges, leading into the finish, where it merges with dark chocolate mousse, smoked bacon, and dates. A showstopper of a whisky... you need hours to recover from this.

SVE

ICHIRO'S MALT CARD SERIES THE COLOR JOKER 57.7%

In 2005, a year after rescuing the few hundred remaining casks from his grandfather's bankrupt Hanyu distillery, Ichiro Akuto started releasing the best of the best as part of a "Card Series." Each release featuring a playing card, it quickly became a completist's worst nightmare. The first few years it was relatively under the radar, but towards the end, getting hold of a new release was like trying to find a four-leaf clover. Ichiro completed the series with two Jokers, a monochrome single cask one and a color one, which was a vatting including all vintages and cask finishes from the series, an

omnibus release as it were. Even the latter, with 3,690 bottles, was anything but easy to find in stores! On the nose, it's got all the characteristics of vintage Hanyu, lush and hyper-fragrant, that is. The initial impressions are sandalwood, furniture polish, oregano, thyme, and incense. Then, you get fruit-flavored marshmallows, candied apples,

marzipan, maraschino cherries, but also some gentle savory notes (iberico ham, barbecue ribs with cranberry sauce, chicken liver paté) and a hint of saffron. The attack on the palate is all spice and citrus: Seville orange marmalade again, dark chocolate with chili peppers, and some raspberry sorbet thrown in for good measure. Then, you get grapefruit peel, yuzu candy, cereal notes (oat bran), hints of crème caramel, and a touch of fennel. The finish is medium-long and quite dry, on dried mango, aniseed, tamarind and Orangina. A beautiful adieu to Ichiro's iconic card series.

SVE

CHICHIBU 2011/2015 BEER BARREL SINGLE CASK #3303 FOR LA MAISON DU WHISKY 59.7%

This is quite an extraordinary single cask bottling and it's probably the best 3 year old whisky you'll taste in a very long time. They don't like to waste materials at Chichibu distillery, so after lending their barrels to local craft brewers, they get them sent back and refill them with whisky. This is from one of those itinerant barrels, used to age an imperial stout before being refilled. The nose on this is unlike any other whisky you've ever had: tons of manuka honey and baklava, assorted pastries (apricot Danish, almond-and-marzipan roulade), yuanxiao, grapefruit jelly, bergamot tea, and a tiny hint of duck-a-l'orange. A sweet tooth's wet dream...On the palate, there's still plenty of sweetness, but there's a light savory dimension that is most welcome: steamed endives, pear ginger chutney, cider-glazed turnips and apples with a bit of sage ...The mouthfeel is incredibly creamy, suggestive of crème d'anjou, white chocolate mousse, and oatmeal. Citrus (candied grapefruit peel, Seville oranges, sudachi) takes over the palate after a few seconds and leads the dance all the way through the long finish with a touch of rosewater in the afterglow.

SVE

CHICHIBU THE PEATED 2015 CASK STRENGTH 62.5%

Bottled at a whopping 62.5%, this is not for the faint-of-heart. It's very peat-forward but the smoke is supported by honeydew melon with prosciutto, grilled apple pie, crema catalana, and a myriad of other treats. On the palate, you get all of that with a bit of citrus and spice. It's a great swimmer, too, so have some water handy to find the sweet spot that suits your palate. Like the earlier peated Chichibu releases, this is made using barley imported from the U.K. However, preparations are under way at the distillery to distill some batches using local barley, some of it smoked with local peat, in the near future. Stay tuned!

SVE

Ichiro Akuto

BY STEFAN VAN EYCKEN

If you had asked a random whisky aficionado about "Ichiro" ten years ago, chances are you were talking about baseball. Now, that's clearly no longer the case but back then, Ichiro Akuto was an unknown quantity. He had worked as a sales rep for Suntory for a couple of years after graduating from university but was called back to help out with the family business. Established in 1625, the company was built on sake brewing, but expanded its operations in 1941 to shochu, rum, whisky, and other types of liquor. In 1983, at the height of whisky consumption in Japan, a proper whisky distillery (Hanyu) was set up… Who could have imagined decades of sharply declining interest in whisky and an economic recession lay ahead? When his father called him back to the family business, the ship was clearly sinking.

In 2004, the company was sold but the new owner had no interest whatsoever in the whisky branch. Sake and shochu was quick business, but whisky was seen as yesterday's drink and a waste of time and space. The 400 barrels of maturing whisky were earmarked to be reprocessed into shochu…unless Ichiro could find the money to buy them and a warehouse to move them to. Against all odds, he managed to do both. In the months and years following this courageous—some would have said reckless—act, Ichiro was spotted at bars around the country with increasing frequency, trying to interest bartenders in the saved Hanyu stock a cask, a case, or even just one bottle at a time. It was during one of these visits, that the idea for the "Card Series" was born. Struck by how difficult it was to remember whiskies, Ichiro and a designer friend of his thought it would help if bottles stood out visually in a way that anyone could relate to, like playing cards in a deck. People could just ask for an Ace of Spades or a Two of Hearts, and if they liked it enough to want to drink it again later or buy a bottle that would be all they needed to remember.

The rest, as they say, is history. His first Card was the King of Diamonds, released in 2005; the last release the two Jokers (2014). In those ten years, many things changed on the Japanese whisky scene. If the first dozen releases were on the shelves of liquor stores around the country for years, trying to get hold of the last couple of Cards was akin to looking for a four-leaf clover. If Cards released in the noughties [2000-2009] were bought primarily for drinking, those released after 2010 were being treated more and more like collector's items (with all that this entails: fetishized, unopened, sold on…). By the time the series came to an end, bottles were going for twenty, thirty times their original price on the auction circuit. In 2015, two complete collections were sold, each for the price of an average house in Japan.

Realizing early on that the Hanyu stock would soon be depleted, Ichiro started dreaming about setting up his own distillery. He traveled to distilleries in Scotland and asked distiller friends at home to teach him the ropes. In part because of the money coming in from the sales of the rescued Hanyu stock, he succeeded in setting up the first new whisky distillery in Japan in more than thirty years. In 2008, the first spirit flowed off the stills at Chichibu distillery. At the time of writing, Chichibu releases are so eagerly anticipated that it makes the Pappy-craze in the U.S. look like a walk in the park by comparison. Releases sell out within seconds and change hands on the secondary market for ten times the retail price and more—all the more mind-blowing since we're talking about 4 year old, 5 year old whisky here…

Ichiro has surrounded himself with a young team at Chichibu distillery, because he knows that the future lasts a long time. His ambition is to be around long enough to be able to savor a 30-year-old Chichibu and to then hand over the reins to the next generation. Many up-and-coming distillers, from Japan as well as further afield, now travel to Chichibu to learn from Ichiro. From zero to hero in a little over ten years… and we're still in the first Act.

THE NETHERLANDS

BY CARLO DEVITO

Formerly known in older times as Holland, the Netherlands has a strong, rich history of distilling. Most famously, the Netherlands produces Genever (sometimes referred to as Dutch gin). It was also called genièvre, jenever, peket, or in old times as Holland gin or Geneva gin. Historically, genever is based from malt wine that was twice distilled. Because the resulting spirit was still considered not very palatable, it was re-distilled, this time being infused with Juniper berries and other flavors to soften the palate, improve the nose, and boost its alleged medicinal benefits. Genever remains popular in the Netherlands, Belgium, France, and Germany.

Dutch whisky remains a very small percentage of the distilling output of the Netherlands. However, Zuidam and Us Heit have forged a new identity for Dutch single malt and are key players in that country,

SINGLE MALT WHISKY

FRYSK HYNDER

Golden Spirit of Frisia

✱

FRISIAN SINGLE MALT WHISKY IS DIS-
TILLED IN THE FINEST CELTIC TRADITION
IN BOLSWARD, ONE OF THE ELEVEN
TOWNS IN THE LOWLANDS OF FRISIA.
MATURED IN WOODEN CASKS, THIS
UNCHILLED, UNFILTERED AND UNBLENDED
FRISIAN WHISKY IS SUFFUSED WITH
UNIQUE AROMATIC FLAVOURS.

PRODUCT OF FRISIA

US HION DISTILLERY FRISIA
SNEKERSTRAAT 43
8701 EC BOLSWARD
THE NETHERLANDS

MALT TYPE	Barle
MASHMAN	Acu
DISTILLING DATE	01 12 0
STILLMAN	
CASK TYPE	Redwine
CASK NUMBER	51
BOTTLING DATE	26 0 0
BOTTLE NUMBER	434
ALC % / VOL	40
CONTENT ML	700

US HEIT DISTILLERY

BY CARLO DEVITO

Us Heit Distillery makes a variety of whiskies in Frisia, a coastal region near the North Sea. Frisian is the main language here, spoken by local people of Germanic descent, who speak this rare language very closely related to English. Us Heir Distillery calls their whiskies, "Golden Spirit of Frisia." It is owned by Aart and Marianne van der Linde.

Us Heit Distillery is perhaps now best known for their Frysk Hynder Single Malt. Aart van der Linde, formerly known only as a brewer, is the head distiller here. He makes the beer for the whisky himself at the De Friese Brouwerij. He uses 100% malt, which is malted in his own malt house. They use the pot still process. Linde emulates the Scots, only distilling twice, and then stores the new whisky in oak barrels from France, Portugal, and Spain, being barrels that have been used for wine, cognac, or sherry. The whiskies are aged anywhere from three to five years.

FRYSK HYNDER SINGLE MALT 3 YEAR OLD 40%

Aart van der Linde fires up this whisky after making the beer himself. The whisky is aged between three and four years. Aart and Marianne only produce small bottlings. Linde stores the new whisky for three years in used casks such as red wine barrels, Sherry barrels, Port, and cognac barrels. They also age a portion in red wine barrels.

Notes have included a nose with forward fruit, and cocoa. There is a malty note on the palate, along with cherries and malt. The nose comes across as older than the whisky, but this whisky finishes nicely. Despite being only three years old, it tastes older.

FRYSK HYNDER SINGLE MALT CASK STRENGTH 55%

Frysk Hynder makes a cask strength whisky. It is aged in a combination of red wine barrels, sherry casks, port and cognac barrels. It is aged for five years. The casks are filled at 65% alcohol, and the final draw down is at 55%. The alcohol content varies per barrel.

The nose presents exotic spices, car-amel, wood, and hints of honey. Notes of toast and wood. The honey comes across on the palate, as well as the spices. Dried apricots, honey, raisins, and more spice also come across, with a hint of vanilla. The flavor lingers for a while, with a slight, slight hint of sweetness.

"The Zuidam Distillery was founded in 1974 by Fred van Zuidam and his wife Helene and is currently run by their sons Patrick and Gilbert," wrote whiskey writer Jan van den Ende. "Patrick manages the distillery and production, and Gilbert looks after the customers. Their distillery has a total production capacity of 280,000 liters of pure alcohol per year," added Thomas Ohrbom.

Zuidam Distillery "is located in Baarle-Nassau on the Dutch-Belgian border and is the only distillery in the Netherlands that ferments, distills, ages and bottles at its own premises. Next to Malt Whiskies, Zuidam also produces Rye Whisky, Gin, Rum, Genever and Liqueurs. The name Millstone derives from the Windmills that are used by Zuidam to mill the Malted Barley," continued van den Ende.

MILLSTONE 8 YEAR OLD
FRENCH OAK 40%

Zuidam Distillers, a leading Dutch liquor producer, currently has gin, five kinds of genever, coffee liqueur, chocolate liqueur, cinnamon liqueur, vanilla liqueur, amaretto, rye, and…single malt whisky in the EU/UK marketplace.

Let's go backwards with this whisky.

Zuidam ages their whiskies in a warm warehouse, which actually doubles the maturation/aging/alcohol-loss rate. Sort of like India (of all places), but a little less extreme. That's why they've done 5-year and 8-year releases, as opposed to 10- to 16-years.

This whisky matures for six years in former Jack Daniel's barrels, then another two years in new French oak casks. Rarely will a producer reveal whose former barrels they're using, so that's a fun maturation fact to know. The good news is that there's not a hint of Jack in this whisky.

According to the distiller's site, they ferment small batches of distillate at low temperatures for a long period of time inside large, wide pot stills. This gives the pre-maturation spirit ("new make") soft and fruity characteristics.

But before they can ferment anything, they need some barley grist. And how do they mill the barley? Via windmills!

I was somewhere around Baarle-Nassau on the edge of the tulip fields when the whisky began to take hold.

On to the Dutch whisky!

NEAT

Color: Solid Gold.

Nose: Very fragrant and floral at first nosing. Sweet oak. Very similar to The Glenlivet French Oak. Sugary pencils.

Palate: Candy! Brown sugar. Vanilla. Maraschino cherries. Fresh orange juice, maybe? Mild and dessert-y. Medium length. Tiramisu and vanilla.

WITH WATER (about 32% ABV)

Nose: Wood. Raisins. More oak character. Sulfur (which is weird because there were no sherry casks).

Palate: The water makes it much fruitier. Sweet fruit juices. Almost sherryish (which is weird because there were no sherry casks). Still decent. Sweet. Gets a touch bitter and sour at the close.

Maybe it's because expectations were set low for this one, but we liked

this one a bit. It would even stand up well against The Glenlivet 15-year French Oak. It's uncomplicated, but it works as a dessert malt. Probably a little better without water.

It probably wouldn't hurt if the whisky was released at a higher ABV (43% or 46%) to give it more oomph and strength. But as it stands, it's a good starter whisky. We wish good things for Zuidam because they clearly know how to make a whisky.

MK

MILLSTONE 10 YEAR OLD
FRENCH OAK 40%

The Millstone 10 year old tasted here was actually distilled in 1999, matured in French oak casks, and was bottled in 2013. That's 14.5 years! The ABV of 40% is lower than the 43% Zuidam is using today. The 200ml bottle hails from Cask #351.

Color: Dark golden.

Nose: Sweet with new oak, varnish, butterscotch, vanilla, orange marmalade, light honey, nutshells, dried apricot, pencil shavings, toffee, light spices, and light floral tones. It's okay but not overly exciting.

Palate: Malt, toffee, brown sugar, vanilla, oak, light honey, light menthol, orange, light varnish, salted butter, nutmeg, pepper, and cinnamon. Middle-long, fruity, spicy, and bittersweet with oak, vanilla, orange peel, buttered toast, nutmeg, pepper, cinnamon, licorice, menthol, varnish, and a little salt.

Added a bit of water, and on the nose you get more vanilla and floral, soapy tones. A little more fruit in the finish as well. You can experiment with a few drops at a time.

Neat was good. Although there's nothing specifically wrong, the French Oak is not our favorite Millstone. It's not a subtle whisky, and the oak and oak spices are quite present. Prefer the 12 year Sherry Cask anytime. The Sherry Cask is similar to Sherried Speyside Whisky while the French Oak has all the main characteristics of a European mainland whisky with oak, vanilla, and spices as the main drivers. Looking forward trying the 1999 Special #1 PX Cask who has just been nominated Best European Single Malt Whisky in the thirteen to twenty Years category. Well done Millstone! It looks like Zuidam Spirit and ex-sherry casks were made for each other. Cheers!

JVE

MILLSTONE 2001 12 YEAR OLD
SHERRY CASK 46%

The Millstone 2001 12 Year Old Sherry Cask is produced by Zuidam Distillers, of Baarle-Nassau in the Netherlands. The production is not limited to only single malt whisky, as they also produce rye whisky, genever, rum, gin, and liqueur. They started producing whisky in 1998, and released their first single malt in 2007, a Millstone 5 year old.

The Millstone 2001 12 year old Sherry Cask was distilled in 2001, matured in Oloroso sherry casks, and bottled in 2014. The diligent reader will immediately spot that this 12 year old whisky is actually 13 years old. That cannot be all bad?

Nose: Very soft and delicate sherry nose. Very fruity, with apples dominating. It has a soft spiciness as well. Very nice.

Taste: Dried fruits, pepper, and oaky spiciness. The mouthfeel is rich and soft. Dark caramel, rich and sweet sherry. I also get honey and coffee, then maple syrup and dark chocolate.

This is a very well balanced and fully integrated whisky. It is a solid product, through and through. Color me impressed! I will certainly try more products from Zuidam Distillers.

TO

NEW ZEALAND

BY CARLO DEVITO

Scottish settlers in Otago first started distilling whisky back in the 1830s. The industry started to swoon for the first time in 1870s as the New Zealand government's heavy regulations began to destabilize the industry. New Zealand whisky enthusiasts did not have anything to cheer about until the 1950s, when a new boom started. That culminated in 1974 when a distillery, Willowbank, was established in Dunedin. It had the distinction of being the southernmost distillery on the planet. When Willowbank was bought by Seagram's, and sales skyrocketed, the skies in New Zealand seemed incredibly blue. By the 1980s, the Lammerlaw line of single malts was very popular.

But the good times soon ended. Willowbank, the country's last distillery, closed in 1997 after the distillery changed hands. The whisky was placed in storage and the doors shuttered. The whisky remained untouched until 2010.

Various independent bottlings have been released since, with many going on to claim accolades and awards at international judgings.

BY ANGELO CAPUANO

The New Zealand Whisky Collection is producing some fine whiskies, including the South Island Single Malt 21 Year Old, the 1989 and 1988 bottlings (remember, these latter ones are single cask expressions so different bottles may taste different). The NZ Whisky Co. range is vast, including a number of older whiskies, which were distilled in New Zealand in the late 1980s and early 1990s. This means that, with so many expressions, some may pale in comparison to other whiskies in the range.

NZ WHISKY CO. 1988 CASK STRENGTH 25 YEAR OLD 52.8%

NZ Whisky Co. has acquired casks of whisky that have been distilled on the South Island of New Zealand at the Willowbank Distillery in Dunedin, and each cask provides its own unique story of New Zealand whisky. This particular expression was distilled in 1988 and sat maturing for twennty-five long years, until it was bottled at cask strength as a single cask offering. This means that this whisky is not cut down with water, which ensures that

the pure snowmelt originally used to make this whisky remains untainted—after all, this snowmelt from the Southern Alps of New Zealand has been filtered through the Great Moss Swamp and it would be a real shame to mix it with another water source. Great thinking NZ Whisky Co.!

Nose: This whisky is dense in the glass, and its aromas are forcefully blunt rather than piercing. It is very complex, which is evidence of its long maturation in a high-quality oak cask. Almost immediately the aromas of freshly polished leather rise up, interlaced with sweet stone fruit (nectarine, yellow plums) and dark berries. The tartness of the fruit balances the sweetness, as a creaminess develops with white chocolate drops and mixed fried fruit. As the whisky rests, the white chocolate develops into thick chocolate milkshake and, would you believe, cherry coke...and that cherry cola intensifies and then more closely resembles Dr Pepper.

Chocolate-coated licorice then develops with mud cake layered with cinnamon, whipped cream, dried apricots, and crushed walnuts and hazelnuts. Within all that complexity also chimes a dewy and grassy, pristine and wet forest-like note with gentle shades of oak...this is never ending, and each nosing brings something different.

Palate: Big sharp oak surges of oak and cocoa are mellowed by creamy vanilla, white chocolate, and caramel. The sweet caramel lingers on the palate with fudge cake and the bitter buzz of cocoa acts as a counterbalance to the sweetness—a sweetness that changes form on the palate, from white chocolate and honey-coated hazelnuts to ripe berries with maple syrup and crushed nuts and then to apricot jam. The oak keeps the sweetness in line, whipping it into line when it risks taking over. The apricot jam lingers with shavings of orange peel and nuances of subtle vanilla soften the oak, which leaves a medium-dry finish and the gentle shine of menthol—this is beautiful!

This whisky explodes on the palate with oak notes that are softened by white chocolate, caramel and vanilla as sweet and tart apricot jam, berries, syrup, and crushed nuts lead to an oak-driven and medium-dry finish of vanilla, apricot jam, and orange peel. Highly complex and uncut, which provides for a thoroughly enjoyable whisky that can be explored for hours.

AC

NZ WHISKY CO. 1989 CASK STRENGTH 22 YEAR OLD 51.4%

Sensationally smooth and boasting a beautiful balance, this is very drinkable whisky with a beautiful freshness and earthiness. While it is drinkable, the whisky needs (and deserves!) lots of attention to be unpacked properly.

Nose: Gusts of freshness swirl in the glass with the beautiful aroma of dried barley as notes of vanilla and dark chocolate raisin cake topped with a wedge of lime add some sweetness and citrus tang to an otherwise earthy character. The oak does not dominate, and instead plays its moderating role while lovely spice in the form of cloves and nutmeg buzz with energy. As the whisky rests, the chocolate raisin cake becomes more noticeable with some roasted marshmallow and shavings of orange peel.

Palate: A powerful surge of lime and lemon zest cuts through the oak as waves of dark chocolate and vanilla bean mellow the fierce onslaught of spice. This is seriously beautiful whisky, an old New Zealand whisky rescued by the NZ Whisky Co. and bottled at a great time in its maturation. A strong bitterness lingers on the base of the tongue, almost like a recently consumed honey-coated block of dark chocolate.

AC

NZ WHISKY CO. SOUTH ISLAND SINGLE MALT 21 YEAR OLD 1990 40%

The New Zealand Whisky Collection is in an enviable position, because it very wisely purchased some old barrels of whisky produced by a New Zealand whisky operation that ceased decades ago. It all started with the Willowbank Distillery, which was opened in 1974 and taken over by the Canadian company Seagram's in the 1980s and then Foster's, who closed the company in 1997. The New Zealand Whisky Co. website reads:

"The New Zealand whisky company purchased the last 600 barrels of mainly Lammerlaw malt and the whisky has been maturing in the towering seaside bondstore in Oamaru's famous heritage precinct ever since."

Now that was a great investment! The New Zealand Whisky Co. South Island 21 Year Old was distilled in 1990, and placed in an American oak ex-bourbon barrel that sat idly and risked being lost through indecision. It was rescued just in time by the NZ Whisky Co., which bottled it and stopped the onslaught of oak and wood.

This whisky is now included in my "Top Whisky" list. It is a unique whisky with a peculiar character, but that peculiarity is what makes it a beautiful whisky with "individuality!" It is bottled at 40% ABV, but packs a nice strong New Zealand rugby tackle!

This whisky has a peculiar character that is quite unique. This is not a bad thing, because while it is very oak-dominated, the phenolic flavors in the whisky are pleasant and do not cut the tongue with a sharp gust of bitterness. Instead, that strange but enjoyable oak smacks against the palate bluntly, releasing a denseness and mustiness that somehow also shines with some sweetness. The character on the nose does not seamlessly move onto the palate, but despite this perceived mismatch, it is lovely!

Nose: This whisky was strange, pure and simple. This is not bad, but it had a peculiar smell that I could not quite put my finger on. Then it hit me—old library books! The leather bound variety, almost like walking

along law reports from the 1880s. It is a dusty library and the smell of aged paper mingles with the leather and carpet. Then, suddenly, youthfulness and color fills the glass as sweet blackberry and mint fuse with the spritz of lime as dense orange cake and aniseed are held together with that lovely old wood. Moving on from the library, I can smell the tobacco-stained cigar box that was common in Melbourne bars before the anti-smoking laws, and a childhood memory of chocolate bullets (chocolate-coated licorice). Now, this may sound strange, but the waft of wet wool also presents itself. This is strange because all my tastings are done blind and I almost fell off my char when I realized I could smell wool in a New Zealand whisky! Well, there you have it, there is wool on the nose; but not any wool, a thick lambswool.

Palate: Obviously, I do not eat library books or wool so I could not detect any of these flavors on the palate. Some mint notes here and earthiness there, vanilla and blackberry too. Again, that peculiar flavor was present. "What is that?" I wondered while tasting this whisky. It was hard to identify, but it was very much like the dry bursts of fructose from sour grapes combined with sweet licorice and some sprinklings of dry basil with hay. It was weird but very nice! Thoroughly enjoyable. The finish is powerful and this whisky ends with a bang! Though it fizzles a bit towards the end, it is still a high-quality finish.

AC

THOMSON DISTILLING

Matt and Rachel Thomson have released three different whiskies from the Thomson Distillery in Auckland. In an attempt to help revive the New Zealand distilling industry, the Thomsons have installed a hand-beaten copper pot still at Hallertau Brewery, just north of Auckland. Experimenting with numerous materials, they recently produced a new whisky first—a 100% New Zealand malted barley, smoked with local manuka wood. The resulting texture gives this whisky a manuka-accented smokiness uniquely expressive of the region. They have also experimented with other ingredients in an effort to push the envelope of whisky-making. In the meantime, they are producing some product that is being taken very seriously.

THOMSON 21 YEAR OLD 46%

One example of a superb New Zealand whisky is the Thomson 21 Year Old, though frustratingly that sharp painful jab of oak unsettles the experience. Bursts of blackberry and blackcurrant work with notes of licorice to rescue this whisky from the over-influence of sharp cutting bitter oak, as notes of vanilla and sea salt develop to create a whisky that is very complex and enjoyable. This whisky seemed to be on the brink of no return, but it appears to have been rescued from the barrel just in time. Even still, that oak influence is there.

The Thomson 21 Year Old is a limited edition New Zealand whisky, so if you enjoy in a whisky the sharp bitterness of oak against sweet licorice and blackberry all carried by a salty sea breeze then you better hurry! It is a single cask release from the Thomson Distillery.

I blind tasted a group of nine whiskies four times, and this group included the Thomson 21 Year Old which was certainly a standout whisky. Its nose is superb, though its taste is less impressive. I gave its nose a high rating but its taste dragged it

the glass, its nose develops with hints of blackcurrant and raisins as a mild licorice and marshmallow weave in and out of a salty sea breeze and milk chocolate. This whisky has such a beautiful and complex nose, as nutmeg adds a buzzing spiciness.

Palate: Spicy bursts of dry oak strike the palate, and just when I think the oak has hijacked yet another promising nose, in comes that spark of blackberry and blackcurrant. Heavy on the oak, this whisky would have scored higher if its fruity character was a little brighter and moderated more the bitter dry oak. Though it does dominate at the start, bursts of sweetness weigh against it to provide a character that is somewhat balanced. The milk chocolate develops into dark chocolate as the licorice gains in intensity. All the while, the gentle sea breeze gently blows, bringing with it a saltiness and notes of dried seaweed. The problem is that the oak almost cuts the palate sharply, and an additional (fifth) blind tasting made it clear that this was probably not going to go away. The finish on this whisky is moderate, though its flavors do radiate from the tongue mildly for a long while.

AC

down. That sharp cutting oak...such a pity.

Nose: Gusts of fresh pine and blackberry twirl around the dense spicy oak, as helpings of vanilla add creaminess to an otherwise bouquet of dried fruit. As the whisky rests in

THOMSON 18 YEAR OLD 46%

The Thomson 18 Year Old has an impeccable nose, busting with blackcurrant and spicy oak. It has quite a presence in the glass, and it is not hard to take delight in it. Then, on the palate, the character of this whisky is also very enjoyable, with bitter oak merging with some hints of spice and dense berry fruits. It is all very lovely, until the most peculiar flavor begins to shine through, almost like soapsuds, cutting the back of the tongue—

overly spicy at this stage. It is an experience I did not much enjoy, but as I have said, this occurred towards the end of the tastings. Also, this is a single cask offering, so the character of the whisky might be a reflection of the cask.

I blind tasted this whisky several times, and again alongside whiskies of a similar style and strength. Because of its peculiar finish that whips the tongue in a way I do not much like, I like this whisky, but do not think about having another dram.

AC

NORWAY

BY CARLO DEVITO

Norway's distilling history goes back centuries, like the rest of Scandinavia, to the Middle Ages. Norway has a long tradition of distilling many kinds of akvavit, as well as vodka, gin, and other eaux de vie. Akvavit, akevitt, or aquavit, is derived from Latin aqua vitae, meaning the "water of life." It has been suggested that the word "whisky" is derived from a similar Goidelic phrase *uisge beatha*. It is traditional to toast with akvavit on Norwegian Constitution Day (May 17).

Whisky however is a new endeavor for Norway, and really still very much in its infancy. But there is a strong desire to make both traditional Scotch-styled single malts, as well as a small cache of those who want to break all the rules. A lot more to come from Norway!

ARCUS

BY THOMAS OHRBOM

Arcus AS is Norway's largest wholesaler of wine and liquor. It was created when it was demerged from the state-owned wine and liquor retailer Vinmonopolet on January 1, 1996. The split was a result of an EFTA ruling and the outcome was to keep retail operations in Vinmonopolet, while the import, export, production, and storage operations were transferred to Arcus.

Vinmonopolet ("The wine monopoly") was established as a private company under state control on November 30, 1922. The company was created as a consequence of the laws in place during the Norwegian prohibition period. The name reflected the fact that at the time wine was the only "strong alcohol" that was allowed to be sold in Norway. Over the years, Vinmonopolet (and later Arcus) have been heavily involved in spirits production, especially the flavored spirit akevitt ("aquavit"). They are also well-known for the blended scotch, Upper Ten.

GJOLEID SVENNEPROVEN CASK 9305
3 YEAR OLD 47%

In 2010, Arcus started an internal project to look into whisky production. This is the first result of that ongoing project. This is one of the two first releases from spirits giant Arcus in Norway.

The Gjoleid Svenneprøven Cask 9305 was matured in an American oak Oloroso sherry butt. It was distilled in early 2010, and bottled in late 2013—the age is given as 3.5 years on the bottle. The total outturn was 1,221 50cl bottles. Arcus experimented with different mashbills (recipes), and for these two first releases they used a mix of pale barley, pale wheat, and beech wood-smoked barley. The name "svenneprøven" can be translated as "practical exam" in a craft.

Nose: My immediate association here is nuts! Not that the whisky is nuts in anyway; it is a sound product. It has a distinct nutty character on the nose, specifically almonds and dry peanut shells. I also pick up almond pudding, some fruits, and mild spices. There is a hint of rubber here—think bicycle wheel repair kit.

Palate: Creamy and oily. Again pronounced nuttiness—almonds. There's fruits here—definitely some sherry influence. Full-bodied and robust. More of the same really, but not for long. It has a rather short finish. A hint of caramel is added.

This is a promising product, but it is as yet far too young. Releasing a 3.5 years old sherry butt-matured whisky is bold, I would say. We love the fact that they put it out there for us "whisky nerds" to try. We will definitely keep an eye out for further releases from Arcus.

TO

GJOLEID SVENNEPROVEN CASK 9359
3 YEAR OLD 47%

This is the companion release to the Gjoleid sherry cask-matured whisky. Again this is a single cask release. Gjoleid Svenneprøven Cask 9359 has been matured in a first-fill American oak bourbon cask. It was distilled in early 2010 and bottled in the autumn of 2013. The total outturn was 448 50cl bottles.

Arcus, the producer, has used different types of malt in the mashbill here, just as with the other Gjoleid release. They have used pale barley, pale wheat, and beech wood-smoked barley. A rather long fermentation time of ten days has been used in the production.

The label on the bottle gives the age at 3.5 years old, but I will stick with the more traditional 3 year old in our categorization of the whisky.

Nose: Rich and quite malty. Mild licorice—which increases over time. The nose does get sweeter and sweeter in the glass. You also pick up some berries, especially black currant.

Palate: Smooth and dryish. Vanilla and red berries dominate upfront. Dry and very short finish, showing the young age. One finds some ginger and ginger soda which adds an extra element to the vanilla sweetness.

Again a promising dram, but I preferred the sherry-matured Gjoleid. One supposes this is due to the sherry cask masking more of the youngish character of this whisky. Give it a few more years and we will have a great whisky.

TO

DET NORSKE BRENNERI (FORMERLY AGDER BRENNERI)

This company was previously called Agder Brenneri, and was the distillery that launched the first ever Norwegian single malt back in 2012. But they since have had a change in ownership. According to Scandinavian whisky writer Thomas Ohrbom, "The duo that pull the strings now are Stig Bareksten and Odd Johan Nelvik. These ambitious guys want to build a Norwegian whisky legacy. Having launched the first Norwegian single malt is a great start, but it takes more, and they know it."

The duo announced that they would launch their new super premium single malt, Eiktyrne; that Audny (the first Norwegian whisky) would be continued with a new design and new bottle; and that they would increase their current holdings from 12,000 liters to approximately 20,000 liters. They also told Ohrbom that they had used almost exclusively sherry casks up to that point, but they would start using more virgin oak going forward. They also plan on experimenting more with smaller casks. Det Norske Brenneri said that they plan to release one to two whiskies per year going forward.

AGDER AUDNY SERIES 1 SINGLE CASK 3 YEAR OLD 46%

Agder Brenneri released the first ever Norwegian single malt whisky just before Christmas of 2012. This was a historic moment. It was high time that Norway had a whisky distillery selling single malt. The Swedes and Danes have quite a lead on Norway, so Norway needs to do some serious catching up!

Agder Brenneri was established back in 1951, and mainly produced apple juice, cider, and apple wine. In 2005, they managed to break the 80-year-old Norwegian state monopoly on spirit production. One can only imagine the battle against the authorities to achieve this was a long and hard one.

They started producing spirits on November 5, 2005, and whisky production started in 2009. In addition to whisky, they produced and sold aquavit and various fruit-based spirits. The whisky production is very limited.

Agder Audny Series 1 has been matured in a single ex-sherry butt (cask #39). The outturn was 1,750 bottles at 35cl.

Nose: It all starts off quite promising. I like the nose on this whisky.

There's a pleasant sweetness with mild spices. The sherry influence from the cask is certainly noticeable. After a few minutes in the glass you start picking up a few more aromas; it was a bit timid at first. Now you find leather, malt, some oakiness, Bran Flakes and other cereals, with a few bits of dried fruit sprinkled on top. There is also the slightest hint of smoke here. It's good!

Palate: Warm, sherried, and quite sweet. Banana and banana cake (minus the cream filling). Lacking in complexity, and the alcohol is a bit too prominent. You can definitely tell this is a young whisky. A few more elements do enter the scene here; mild caramel, sugar, and some fruits. The finish is slightly metallic; it brings to mind well-chewed wooden pencils—the type we used to have in elementary school. The finish is rather quick, again showing the young age.

This was a good first attempt at releasing a Norwegian single malt whisky. Hopefully we would see a more mature, slightly older whisky next. It was good to have Norway on the world whisky map, finally!

TO

AGDER AUDNY SERIES 2 SINGLE CASK 3 YEAR OLD 46%

This was the second release of the first Norwegian single malt whisky. This whisky was released by Agder Brenneri, but since then the dis-

tillery has changed its name to Det Norske Brenneri.

Audny Series 2 Single Cask was distilled in 2009 and bottled in 2012. It was matured for the full length in a first-fill sherry butt (cask #36). The outturn was 1,750 bottles at 35cl each.

Nose: Chocolate, dried fruits, apples, and licorice. Round and pleasant. I did find the nose on Series 1 to be slightly better, but it is a very close call.

Palate: Full and sweet. Caramel, licorice, white pepper, apples, and some dried fruits. A notch up from Series 1. This feels slightly more mature. Pepper and caramel. Not much more really. It is clearly a young whisky, and the finish is relatively short.

A young whisky that shows promise, much like Series 1 really. Strongly recommend you try this distillery's other whisky, Eiktyrne, which is a much more mature and balanced product.

TO

AGDER AUDNY SERIES 3 SINGLE CASK 4 YEAR OLD 46%

The third release in the Audny series from Norwegian Distillery Det Norske Brenneri (formerly Agder Brenneri). The Audny Series 3 Single Cask is a four year old, sherry-matured whisky. It is released in a limited run of 1,000 50cl bottles.

Nose: Milk chocolate, banana, citrus, apples, red berries, and a bit of oak. It does have a slight sting of alcohol, letting us know this is still a quite young whisky. Given some time in the glass you can detect mild sherry notes, cardamom, and malt.

Palate: Peppery attack. A bit aggressive, as they also say on the back label on the bottle. The mouthfeel is rich, and slightly oily. White pepper morphing into black pepper faster than you can say pepper-morphing-whisky. There is more than just pepper here, of course; it is fruity with apples and pears. Vanilla, mild caramel, honey, and canned pears. The finish is warm-ish and relatively short. It has a metallic and woody touch right at the end.

A decent dram, but was hoping for a bit more really. This was not the step up from Series 1 and 2 that one was expecting. It is also nowhere near as good as their Eiktyrne, a whisky that has had a finish in small blood tub casks (40 liters). The right way to go for Det Norske Brenneri is to use more small casks in the mix, while their whisky is still so young.

TO

EIKTYRNE 3 YEAR OLD 46%

Eiktyrne was released in the autumn of 2015. This whisky was matured for three years in a first-fill Oloroso sherry butt, before receiving a six-month finish in an Oloroso sherry blood tub (40 liters). The taste we had was from one of the blood tubs, which yielded eighty-three bottles, but the full release in September 2015 was about 1,000 bottles at 50cl.

The name Eiktyrne is from "Eikþyrnir" (Old Norse meaning "oak-thorny"), which is a stag that stands upon Valhalla in Norse mythology. In the ancient text Grímnismál, the following can be found:

Eikthyrnir the hart is called,
that stands o'er Odin's hall,
and bits from Lærad's branches;
from his horns fall
drops into Hvergelmir,
whence all waters rise:

Síd and Víd,
Soekin and Eikin,

Svöl and Gunntro,
Fiörm and Fimbulthul,
Rin and Rennandi,
Gipul and Göpul,
Gömul and Geirvimul:
they round the gods' dwellings wind.
Thyn and Vin,
Thöll and Höll,
Grad and Gunnthorin.

Nose: Soft and delicate sherry nose. There is a soft rubbery note at first, but it is mild and does crawl into hiding after a few minutes in the glass. What is a lot more noticeable is a lovely mix of spices: cinnamon, cardamom, white pepper, and nutmeg. Accompanying the spices you also find malt, nuts, oranges, and hints of oak. Leaving it in the glass for a while opens it up further. It is quite rich and full. Well integrated, and it feels mature despite its young age.

Palate: Full bodied and sweet. The sherry influence is immediate here, as it was on the nose. Rather peppery on the delivery. Digging a bit deeper, you pick up on something floral, with a hint of vegetables. The sweetness is a mix of dried fruits, fresh apples, and sugar. Full and rich on the finish as well. Medium long and warm. Cinnamon, white pepper, dark chocolate, caramel, nutshells, and oak. It becomes dry towards the end, but at the same time it is mouthwatering.

It is young, but it has a fun "attitude" that you find charming. It is the best Norwegian whisky so far. Bring on the next!

TO

AASS & EGGE 3 YEAR
OLD NORSK SINGLE MALT 40%

Let's start with a confession. This is not really a whisky. It is a single malt, but it is not purely made from barley, yeast, and water. It contains hops. In fact, this is an eau de vie de bière. Two old and distinguished Norwegian producers are behind this creation, which was launched in 2012. The oldest active brewery in Norway, Aass Bryggeri—established in 1834—made a batch of beer for this project. The beer made the base for the spirit distilled by Egge Gård, a farmyard producer with roots back to 1702. Egge Gård today makes a lot of cider and apple-based products.

This product was launched in 2012, with a limited run of 3,000 bottles. It has been matured in oak barrels and sherry casks—no further specification is given.

So, if you can forgive us for reviewing a non-whisky, we can get on with it…

Nose: Sweet and malty nose. It is surprisingly rich. Mentholatum, camphor, apples, and oak. Straight off, it reminds me a bit of Mackmyra Ægirs Bior, the lovely beer cask-finished creation from Mackmyra, although this Norwegian effort does not quite reach the same levels on the nose. In fact, give it more time, and detect some alcohol and a faint trace of gasoline fumes. Still quite nice!

Palate: Apples, a bit like a young Calvados. Caramel, white pepper, soft oak, and some alcohol. Medium to short finish. Sugary, dry, and slightly metallic. It still remains a little raw, and there's some alcohol here as well.

A decent effort. It's always fun to come across unusual products like this. I think this should have been left in the casks for another year or two, and then been bottled at 46%. Maybe next batch?

TO

POLAND

BY CARLO DEVITO

Poland has a rich tradition of producing and drinking fine alcoholic beverages. Piwo (or beer) is one of the most popular drinks in Poland. Popular brands such as Żywiec, Tyskie, Zubr, Lech, Okocim, Warka, and others dominate the market for quality beer in this country. Some of the smaller breweries are producing collectible brews.

Nalewki are regional Polish liqueurs. They are usually 40% ABV and are eaux de vie, either named for their place of origin, the fruit that they are made from, or the flavor they are infused with. Most are aged for at least a period. In some families, nalewki recipes were handed down from generation to generation, and rarely shared outside of families or clans.

Of course wódka (or vodka) distilling has its origins squarely placed in the history of Poland. It is the national spirit of Poland. In Poland, vodka is made mainly from grain, potatoes, or sugar beets. Poland is seen in Europe as part of the Vodka Belt, which includes Russia, the Ukraine, Finland, Lithuania, Latvia, Estonia, and Sweden.

Balsam Pomorski, Belvedere, and Chopin are the most internationally known brands from this country, which easily supports another dozen-and-a-half brands or so in its market. With this rich tradition behind it of spirits and beer and brandies, people are eager to see the whiskies that will emerge from this country.

KOZUBA & SONS DISTILLING

PROLOGUE SINGLE MALT WHISKY 43%

The times when whisky was associated exclusively with Scotland or Ireland are slowly going to an end. Now, whisky is produced in many countries. Starting with Japan, where it comes from hailed by Jim Murray's the best single malt of 2015—Yamazaki Sherry Cask 2013, by France, Germany, Norway, Sweden, Finland and many, many others.

As Mikolaj Rej said, "Poles are not geese and have their own language" (to oppose Latin in written language), and now we have received the first Polish Single Malt Whisky—Prologue. The liquor comes from Kozuba & Sons from Jabłonka near Nidzica in Masuria. The company was founded in 2005, and began with tinctures, and then flavored vodka, vodka, and now we have a single malt whisky.

It is worth noting that the owner's effort to provide good quality liquors was awarded in 2008 by winning gold and silver medals in a competition organized by the Beverage Testing Institute in Chicago. Another gold medal came in 2012 for the Starkus, vodka matured in oak barrels.

Let's go to the single malt. Prologue was matured three years in fresh (new, nothing has been matured in it) casks from American white oak. This three year period is the official minimum for single malt whisky. Bottled at 43% ABV. The producer gives us the mash bill: 40% Pale Ale, 40% birch smoked, and 20% caramelized. The whole series was created from four barrels, which produced 1,400 bottles. My bottle is No. 207. We don't have an information about the coloring and chill filtration on the bottle. I was told by the distillery representative that these processes were not used. In fact, I probably haven't tried whisky matured only in fresh barrels before. If this occurred, there is usually an additional aging (Glenfiddich

Rich Oak or Jura Boutique Barrels). And I have Bunnahabhain Darach Ur, where we can find a fresh wood too, but I do not know if they used 100% of it to create a whisky.

Color: Gold.

Nose: Sweet, vanilla, caramel, slightly soapy, and immediately pungent, peppery, in a moment like perfumed, and further ginger – so much to start with; after deeper and longer sniffing I have apple and peach, traces of herbs, then the feel of wet earth, young again, with a sort of dry straw.

Palate: Strongly warms, and even burns on the tongue, with ginger, bitterness, with a touch of sweet; after major attempts I have a brush of dark chocolate and maybe also a timidly emerging grapefruit; evidently I feel the youth here. The finish was medium length, dry with elements of ginger and bitterness.

In my opinion, it would do well to give more power here, I have a little hunger—maybe a place for water would appear and we would be able to watch how whisky is changing. I added a little of water only for an experiment; the smell mellowed, but also the taste definitely watered down and became orange (like a soft orange drink). Then I added more water, but the whisky didn't cloud, so I don't know how it was un-chillfiltered.

Smell and taste are appropriate to the age and, of course, reveal the elements of youth. I'm curious how this whisky is going to taste in an older age, although further maturation in fresh barrels may deepen the ginger and bitterness, but we'll see. As for the debut, I have to congratulate, which of course I do. I am glad that I was able to taste the first Polish single malt whisky. I am waiting for the next editions. I wish the distillery a lot of success and keep my fingers crossed for further development.

LK

SCOTLAND

BY CARLO DEVITO

Okay, let's start with the obvious. There is single malt whiskey and there is single malt Scotch. Single Malt Scotch is made only in Scotland. It can't be made anywhere else. It is to the whisky world as what Bordeaux or Napa are to the wine world. Single Malt Whiskey are whiskies that are made around the world and are produced adhering to many of the tenants of the making of single malt Scotch but not solely so.

Now, to pretend to write an introduction to Single Malt Scotch is a fool's errand in such a short pace. Whole books have been devoted to the subject. A quick, flashcard-like refresher is more in keeping here.

Distilled spirits made from barley in Scotland date as far back as the late 1400s. The Exchequer Rolls of 1494 mention, "Eight bolls of malt to Friar John Cor, by order of the King, wherewith to make *aqua vitae.*"

Through the ages, various Scottish governments have attempted to tax whisky. Some was made legally, and others not. Finally, in 1823 Parliament established a commercial distillation act that made producing legal spirits much more profitable. The first commercial license was requested and received in 1824 by George Smith, who founded Glenlivet Distillery. Others followed.

By the next decade, a new method, making commercial distilling much more viable, was introduced. Aeneas Coffey fine-tuned a concept first put forth by Robert Stein, creating a continuously operating still, which was much more efficient than the traditional pot still. Since then, arguments over which produces the spirit with the better flavor have spurred many a considerable bar fight.

Two things helped make single malt Scotch the coveted drink it is today. Firstly, it was Prohibition in America. Before Prohibition, there were thousands of small family-run distilleries making numerous potables, including whiskies such as bourbon, rye, and blended whiskey. But their stocks or aged goods were wiped out by Prohibition. When the law was finally appealed, there was little to no aged whiskey in America. The Canadian and Scotch distillers were happy to fill the void. Single malt Scotch began a real foothold.

During World War II, many Americans stationed in the UK had their first taste of Single Malt Scotch, and a burgeoning market was born. But Americans were only discovering what the French already knew. Today, the French drink more single malt Scotch per capita than any other country in the world. This, and other factors, helped catapult Single Malt Scotch to an iconic level.

The approved regions where Scotch is officially produced have become legendary. The business boasts a huge, high-end, high-quality product, commands relatively high prices, has exacting standards, and is a booming tourist industry!

Today, according to the Scotch Whisky Association, "The Scotch Whisky industry adds just over £5bn of value to the UK economy, continues to support around 40,000 jobs, and supports salaries of over £1.4bn to UK workers. In its direct impact, the Scotch Whisky industry...employs 10,800 workers. Over 7,000 workers in the Scotch Whisky industry are employed in rural communities."

The selection of whiskies that follow is not meant to be an all-encompassing representation of the state of single malt Scotch in Scotland. There are several classics that may be missing in the reader's opinion. Typically aged expressions or traditionally made products have not been listed, unless those methods happen to represent more current trends within the industry. The intention of this selection of Single malt Scotch is only to show whiskies that are being produced as the result of finishings, peatings, etc., that are more in keeping with new-world ideas and methods mentioned throughout the rest of this book. Several of these ideas, like double- and triple-wood finishing actually started in Scotland.

This selection represents that spirit. It is an exciting time in the single malt Scotch industry, and new, inventive expressions are finding their way to market every day. This is a salute to those adventurous distillers.

ABERLOUR A'BUNADH BATCH 45
CASK STRENGTH 60.2%

Aberlour A'Bunadh ("The Origin" in Gaelic) is a whisky that whips the senses—sight, smell, and taste—with a piercing vibrancy that engulfs the palate with flames of dry sherry and spice as the burning embers leave a complex array of fruitcake and dark chocolate layered with helpings of orchard fruit and berries. With water the magic softens, as ripe red berries mingle with dark chocolate to leave a creamy chocolate milk finish that coats the tongue.

Nose (Neat): Piercing dry oak and sherry cuts through dense prune and raisin-packed Christmas cake layered with vanilla bean whipped cream and topped with shavings of dark chocolate, sprinkles of cocoa powder, and mint leaves. The smell of freshly brewed filter coffee is in the distance, with some notes of dried cranberry. With water: The piercing oak and sherry mellows, as the pulsating diversity of orchard fruits—blood plum, ripe apricot, and yellow peaches—wafts up with sprinklings of nutmeg, cinnamon, and rose petals. The cocoa also softens into milk chocolate while strawberries and cream deliver a more subdued aroma of sweet sherry spilled over a bed of lush green. The sweetness develops in the glass, as the fresh very ripe strawberries develop into jam, as shimmers of sugary sweetness weave in and out of soft oak and an orange chocolate sponge cake.

Palate (Neat): The dry surge of oak and sherry is met with a crisp bite of alcohol that has been clearly distilled with utmost love and care. Dry fruitcake loaded with raisins and dried cranberries is layered with pure cocoa, orange peel, and burnt toffee as energetic gusts of cinnamon and anise seed bring spiciness. With water: Soft pulses of sweet sherry and red berries—fresh strawberry, cranberry, and raspberry—hit the tongue in waves. It is replaced with mild bitter dark chocolate that leaves a coating of creaminess, and a lingering milk chocolate consumed to the bottom as the chocolate powder brings bitter-dry sweetness. The dry oak and sherry is a constant theme, which on this finish develops into the bitter-dry burst of red grapefruit that leaves the palate salivating for more! On the finish is the bite of a homemade tiramisu; the snap of good alcohol (hence the "homemade" emphasis), the cocoa, and the creamy sweet coffee-laden center. With water, the bright burst of red grapefruit and dark chocolate only develops moderately with some dry oak, as the character softens to milk chocolate with dashes of preserved strawberry and jam.

AC

ABERLOUR 16 YEAR OLD DOUBLE CASK 43%

Aberlour has taken 16 year old whisky and finished it in a combination of first-fill oak Bourbon casks and the finest Sherry butts. This expression is alive with rich, fruity notes, highlighted by a lovely spiciness, and finishes with just a touch of sweet.

Color: Golden amber.

Nose: Raisins, dates, and figs, some floral, complemented by a nice nuttiness.

Palate: Raisins, dates, figs, and plum all come across. A nice spicy oak also lingers. Beautiful long finish with figs, honey, and a touch of spice.

CD

ABERLOUR
ESTD 1879
HIGHLAND SINGLE MALT SCOTCH WHISKY
DOUBLE CASK MATURED
16 YEARS OLD
DISTILLED & BOTTLED IN SCOTLAND
ABERLOUR DISTILLERY COMPANY LIMITED

Innovation and Experimentation in Whisky: A Chat with Dr. Bill Lumsden

BY STEFAN VAN EYCKEN

In the fall of 2015, Dr. Bill Lumsden did a whirlwind mini-tour of Japan. Stefan Van Eycken caught him at the end of a busy day at the MHD headquarters in Tokyo and started by asking him what the first whisky was he remembered having…

Dr. Bill Lumsden (DBL): The first whisky I tried was Glenmorangie 10yo in 1984. I had tried blended Scotch in my youth, which was illegal of course because I was a teenager at the time, but the first proper whisky I had was a Glenmorangie at a party in Edinburgh, and that turned me on to the world of single malt Scotch. So there's a sense of destiny that I'm now doing what I'm doing.

SVE: How did you end up in the whisky industry? Was that a serendipitous thing or were you intent on working in the whisky industry?

DBL: I wouldn't say it was serendipitous because it was basically as a result of becoming a malt whisky lover and studying for my PhD at Heriot-Watt University. That kind of led me into the whisky industry. But it was because I was a lover of malt that I wanted to work in the whisky industry, and happily it has sort of worked out for me.

SVE: People tend to see innovation in whisky as the province of the so-called "new world distilleries," but there is a great deal of experimentation and innovation going on in Scotland. You have been at the forefront of this for two decades. Let's start by focusing on your work in the field of maturation. In your experience, are there finishes that don't really work well with whisky in general? Or can any sort of finish be made to work given the right circumstances?

DBL: I would say no, and there are some utterly appalling examples out there of things that have completely dominated over the house character of the whisky. There's ones where people have finished for clearly a few weeks and a few months so why bother with that? And there's other things—other spirits, other barrels—which, in my opinion, kind of fight against the flavor of the Scotch. So it's certainly not the case that you can make everything work.

SVE: Vice versa, are there cask types that lend themselves more to finishes, rather than full maturations?

DBL: I think the fortified wines lend themselves to finishing and personally I think that full maturation in a sherry butt, for example, in most cases will ruin the whisky. But, you know, I may be expressing a bit of personal preference here. Also, if you're using French wine oak barriques, a full maturation will generally be a disaster because there's far too much tannins in French oak. I know some people have done it, but in my opinion, they've churned out products that I wouldn't drink!

SVE: With Ardbeg, the experimentation in terms of maturation is not focused on finishes at all, so what shape does experimentation take there?

DBL: What we tend to do is: fully mature the spirit and then blend it with classic Ardbeg from bourbon barrels. Finishing just doesn't work so well with a whisky of that style, in my view.

SVE: Word on the street is that there is a cask shortage and wood isn't what it used to be (in terms of quality)? What are your thoughts on those two rumors?

DBL: I agree with both points. There is a cask shortage. We [at Glenmorangie and Ardbeg] don't have a cask shortage because we've got long-term relations with our main suppliers. But you know, if someone wanted to go out today and buy an extra 50,000 bourbon barrels, they would just get laughed at. There is not a chance they would get them. I think that will ease over the next few years as more bourbon barrels are getting emptied again, but certainly I am watching very carefully what's happening out there and I know some distilleries have actually scaled back production because they couldn't get wood to fill into.

And in terms of barrels not being what they used to be, I think there's definitely something in there. I'm hearing stories—and you know, they might be anecdotal—that it's taking barely eight weeks from the tree first being cut to it first being filled with spirit in some parts of the US. You know, that will have an impact on American whiskey, and then it will have a knock-on impact on Scotch whisky. But again, in the Glenmorangie company, we've got a program to combat against that for our designer casks, which are not being made into barrels until the wood is at least two years old, after it's been cut.

SVE: People tend to focus on wood as the prime area of experimentation, but that doesn't mean you don't focus on other aspects of the whisky making process, for instance, the barley... We'd like to start by asking you about Signet. Can you give us some insight into what inspired that expression and the specifics of the way in which you went about creating it?

DBL: The inspiration for that—believe or not!—was born out of a dissatisfaction with coffee, in the first instance, because I was always intrigued by the fact that if you go into a coffee place or if you boil coffee up yourself, the beguiling aroma is absolutely fantastic and I found that the taste seldom lived up to that. So I was always a little bit disappointed. So it led to me, in my student days, mucking about, trying different types of roast, trying different types of beans and the one that I really, really liked—and still do, to this day—is Jamaica Blue Mountain with a medium roast. And it was that roasting process, coupled with my new-found love of malt whisky—a merging together of the two—that made me think: gosh, wouldn't that be fun, instead of drying it over a peat fire (to use a technical term) to 'roast the f*ck out of it'. And then, I thought, practically that will be difficult, so I then used my knowledge of craft beer and my love of craft beer and thought: ah, stouts and porters… high-roast chocolate malt! It's there! So then, I started making secret batches of Glenmorangie spirit using the high-roast chocolate malt and then, took it from there. So that's where the original inspiration came from, but it took a long time to finalize a recipe that I was happy with, because the whisky from the high-roast chocolate malt on its own was just brutal, frankly. So that's the reason why it is this horribly complicated assemblage of about seven or eight Glenmorangies.

SVE: How often do you put Signet together, and how difficult is it to maintain consistency across batches?

DBL: In terms of the recipe, it gets put together once or twice a year and it is very difficult. And you know, it is not a consistent product, I will admit that. There's just so many things going on there, how could it be?

SVE: Turning to a more recent example of experimentation with barley, let's talk about Tusail a bit. For that, you used a different variety of barley…

DBL: That came about from my early days as Glenmorangie Distillery Manager. I had a very good relationship with one of my malt suppliers, Pauls Malt and a gentleman called Iain McLean. And Iain and I always talked about trying something different so I tried some parcels of winter barley, just to see if there was any difference, but I didn't do 100% winter barley. It was like a 50-50 blend with spring barley, or 75 spring/25 winter, and I felt there was possibly a difference there, but couldn't quite put my finger on it. So I thought: right, once and for all, I'm going to do this experiment properly. So that's when I had Maris Otter grown for me and had it floor-malted, and the end results I was delighted with. You know, it's not a black-and-white difference if you compare it to Glenmorangie Original. I'm always wanting to try things like that and see what happens.

Then, there's yeast, generally a neglected area of experimentation.

I have been working on many experiments with yeast over the past few years but it might well be another few years before I am ready to release the results of that. All I'll say is: I found some really exciting things out and I've got one project in particular which I am just tickled pink with. I called it "Project Godisgoode" because "Godisgoode" is what the Ancient Egyptians called yeast. Well, they didn't know it was yeast that turned cereal juice into alcohol so they said 'God-is-good'. Obviously, I'm being a little bit evasive; I like to keep my powder dry.

SVE: Since it's in the nature of an experiment that the outcome cannot be foreseen, can you give an example of an experiment that didn't work out?

DBL: To be honest, my success rate is very, very high in these things. The one that spectacularly did not work, I would not be allowed to release anyway (the SWA [Scotch Whisky Association] made that very plain to me)… all I can say is: Brazilian cherry wood is not a good type of wood to use for whisky barrels.

SVE: Most expressions of Ardbeg and Glenmorangie that you have developed don't carry an age statement. Some people make a big deal of that. What would you say to those who are suspicious of whiskies that don't carry an age statement?

DBL: It's going to be an ongoing fierce debate and it sometimes makes me a little bit annoyed to see somebody mouthing off saying "that's obviously 3 or 4yo whisky in there." None of my NAS whiskies have ever been that young apart from ones I've deliberately done that with… By that I mean, Ardbeg Very Young which was 6 or 7 years old and the Ardbeg Oogling, which was 4 years old but the 'Oogling' was just a joke, really. It wasn't serious. But what I would say to people is: it's not about the age as far as I'm concerned. There are more important factors in giving taste to whisky and any of the NAS products I have put out always have to be of a high standard before I would allow them to carry the brand name. But you know, you're always going to get doubting Thomases criticizing that.

SVE: Let's talk about Perpetuum a bit, which was released in May 2015 to mark the 200th anniversary of the distillery.

DBL: For Perpetuum, rather than doing what I wanted to do myself in terms of an experiment or create a different taste profile, it was all about the 200th anniversary, so I thought: I could do something boring, like vat 200 casks together—and marketing actually suggested that at once stage, to which I said "get the f*ck out of my office—it's my job to decide this." So I thought, over the last 200 years, lots of things have happened to Ardbeg Distillery and over our 10 years, I've tried lots of things. I just happened to have a habit of holding back a few barrels of most of the things I've done. So I thought, why don't I just try and create a whisky where it has a little bit of everything in there. So that's the idea behind that.

SVE: What do you think are the challenges lying ahead for the brands that you're responsible for?

DBL: The challenges I see ahead for Glenmorangie and Ardbeg are that there is an almost insatiable demand and appetite for new products, and you know, there's only so many things you can do. That's always a bit of a challenge. Keeping up with demand will be a challenge. For example, if India finally did dramatically reduce their importation tariffs, the Scotch whisky industry doesn't produce enough whisky to satisfy India alone! And, you know, we wouldn't just suddenly start selling everything to India, but I am just saying that demand may well go up. Once the Latin American countries get a taste for single malt Scotch whisky, that'll put pressure on it, as well.

SINGLE MALT SCOTCH REGIONS:

Highland Single Malts

Island Single Malts (a sub-section of the Highland region)

Speyside Single Malts

Islay Single Malts

Lowland Single Malts

Campbeltown Single Malts

—Scotch Whisky Regulations 2009

ARDBEG

BY MATT CHAMBERS

The Ardbeg distillery is located on the southeastern coast of the famous Scottish whisky-producing island of Islay. It was founded in 1815 by John MacDougall, although records show a distillery operating on the site as far back as 1794. Its recent history was slightly checkered—there was no production between 1982 and 1987, or for the majority of 1996 and 1997—until Moet Hennessey (LVMH), the current owners, took over in 1997. The distillery is small with a capacity of just one million liters per year. The range of single malts from Ardbeg has built up a cult following amongst whisky drinkers across the world.

ARDBEG SUPERNOVA COMMITTEE RELEASE 2014 EDITION 55%

This whisky is the third edition of the Supernova bottling from the cult Islay distillery of Ardbeg. It is released to coincide with the return of a very special sample of Ardbeg. A sample was sent into space and orbited earth on the International Space Station before landing back on earth. The idea was to analyze it against a sample from the same distillation that had been matured in a warehouse at the Ardbeg distillery to determine if weightlessness and zero gravity have any effect on the maturity process.

The Supernova series is labeled as being Ardbeg's peatiest ever malt. The Supernova 2014 is bottled at the cask strength of 55% ABV and has again been made by Dr. Bill Lumsden, Ardbeg's Director of Distilling & Whisky Creation. It is available now at any Ardbeg Embassy or via the Moet Hennessy Selection website.

The color is pale lemon yellow, and the aroma of feisty peat smoke imme-diately catches in the nostrils. This has a hot, peppery, and sooty edge to it. With time, other aromas begin to shine through—malty cereals, burnt oat cookies, golden syrup, and icing sugar plus hints of lemon zest and something floral that is difficult to pinpoint.

On the palate there is an instant mix of profound sweetness and intense, savory smokiness. The sweetness is reminiscent of golden syrup and icing sugar, while the smoke has a distinct sooty, ashy, coal-like quality. This later becomes slightly hotter and more earthy/mossy. Rather than battling against each other, the two elements complement each other well. In similar fashion to the nose, a malty cereal barley note battles its way through the intensity, as does increasing zesty lemon. There are also hints of buttery shortbread, red chilli, white chocolate, and a pinch of saltiness.

The finish is very long and intense. The sweeter elements fade quickly and leave the smoke and peatiness to smolder away for what seems like ages. It becomes increasing dry, ashy, and acrid with the spicy chili-like heat slowly fading.

This is a BIG and intense whisky. Not really for the faint hearted or beginner. But what did we expect? When Ardbeg, which produces some of the smokiest whiskies anyway, say that something is their peatiest ever then you know what you are going to get.

However, this whisky is a bit cleverer than just being mega-peaty. It has much more going on and the delicious sweeter elements balance the expressive, hot smoke very well. This is a whisky very much for the fans of very smoky malts and Ardbeg in particular, and should be celebrated as such. If you like both of these things—hurry up and grab a bottle before it sells out...

MC

ARDBEG GALILEO 12 YEAR OLD 49%

Ardbeg Distillery announced the release of Ardbeg Galileo, a limited edition 12 year old single malt whisky, as a special celebration of its "world first" space maturation experiment, which had previously been announced at the Edinburgh International Science Festival in April 2012.

Ardbeg Galileo is a special vatting of different styles of Ardbeg laid down in 1999, all married together. According to Ardbeg, "The heart of this limited edition Ardbeg is spirit matured in ex-Marsala wine casks from Sicily that is combined with hallmark Ardbeg matured in first and second fill ex-Bourbon casks. The ex-Marsala casks add fruity aromas and textures to Ardbeg's famed peaty, smoky house style. Bottled at 49% and non-chill filtered...."

Ardbeg named the whisky after the famed astronomer Galileo, who is considered the father of modern astronomy. In late 2011, Ardbeg began working with Houston, Texas-based space research company NanoRacks LLC, in a two-year experiment to test micro-organic compounds drawn from the distillery's production on Islay, and see what affects it would experience far up in space on the International Space Station.

Vials were launched by a Soyuz rocket from Baikonur, Kazakhstan. The concept was to see if a zero gravity environment would affect the flavor profile of the maturing whisky. Only a few thousand cases were made available upon release.

Nose: Smoke, peat, soot, campfire, tar, whiffs of honey and apricot, and a touch of vanilla.

Palate: Fruits come across first. Lemon. Green apple. Touch of pineapple and honey. Some nuttiness. Malt. Earth-dried flowers. Smokey, weedy, with hints of sweetness, and a creamy finish.

CD

ARDBEG CORRYVRECKAN 57.1%

Corryvreckan is named for the famous whirlpool located north of Islay. In the Corryvreckan Channel, very strong Atlantic currents and unusual underwater topography produce an intense tidal force. The Corryvreckan is numbered as the world's third largest whirlpool. The British Admiralty's guide calls it "very violent and dangerous" and recommends that "no vessel should then attempt this passage without local knowledge." As Ardbeg said, their whisky, like the whirlpool it's named for, is not

for the faint-hearted! That said it is an extreme whisky. High alcohol, aged in French oak wine casks.

Nose: Powerful. Intense. Tar. Campfire. Seaweed. Menthol. Treacle. Cocoa. Prune. Raisin. Dark cherry. Vanilla.

Palate: Seaweed and peat and black pepper and tar all come across. With undercurrents of prune, blueberry, and cherry that melt into smoked seaweed and espresso coffee bean. A swirl of tar, black pepper, and black coffee combine with blueberry and cherry, with a big dollop of black pepper. A nice woodiness also comes through. Very big and very handsome!

CD

ARDBEG AURIVERDES 49.9%

Ardbeg Auriverdes, meaning "gold-greens," ticks a few boxes for my most beloved Islay distillery. It served as their annual Limited Edition release, launched on Ardbeg Day, but it also points us in a not-so-subtle way to the fact that 2014's biggest sporting event, Football World Cup, was happening in the far-away land of Brazil. As you all know, football is religion over there and the national team, commonly referred to as the Canarinhos, is also sometimes called, you guessed it, the Auriverdes. Two different references to the colors of their kit. A tad unimaginative of course but what do you expect from the world of a sport played with a round ball?

Ardbeg's nod to the World Cup doesn't end here. The Ardbeg Day was graced by the launch of the first ever Peat Football Tournament, culminating in the Ardbeg Swamp Football World Cup, played in Argyll in Scotland.

You may love the creative ideas or you may loathe them. I understand if you think the football thing is a bit obvious and heavy-handed. But personally I think it's all very Ardbeg and if there was ever one brand that was going to pull a World Cup theme off, it was going to be them, right? And ultimately it's good to see LVMH stick to their guns in creating what's probably the most quirky and fun single malt brand in the world at the moment. Despite some minor points I raised in the past, I love everything they do and I'm the biggest sucker for their NAS Limited Edition releases in the world.

And that's not because of their

super-clever brand work, the visual aspect of their projects that is an absolute treat every time, the people, the place, the heritage, or the legend of it all.

I love them because of the liquid. Doh!

Nose: Sharp, cold smoke. Burned rye bread toast. Smoked mackerel, crème brûlée, spun sugar.

Palate: Smoke, aye, but also rich coffee and praline overtones. Bitterness well in check and doesn't behave like 50%-er. Warming and, finally, quite tannic. Milk chocolate and vanilla with a spoonful of crushed charcoal.

This really takes me back to my favorite Ardbeg—the Renaissance. It has that clean-cut elegance and balance to it. Make no mistake, this is not the most intense Ardbeg out there and if you're in the peaty game just to get repeatedly punched in the mouth, this is not it. This is, as strange as it may sound when talking about the Green Monster, subtle. Behind smoky biceps there beats a heart of all things good and gentle.

The point of interest here is of course the specially toasted cask heads. My understanding is that each cask was fitted with two different ones; the press release mentions one imparting mocha character and the

other geared more toward vanilla— presumably, and logically, this is achieved by two different toasting levels.

It has Dr. Bill Lumsden written all over it, right? Again, it's refreshing and encouraging to see a major player in the premium category not shy away from experiments and, perhaps most importantly, talk about them and turn them into a commercial success. And while I personally think the price is a bit high and they would make me a much happier bunny if they shaved a tenner off it, if faced with the choice of spending £80 on 70cl or truly tasty, interesting whisky, I choose to help the innovator, not the bore. And that's all there is to it. The liquid will put a smile on your face, that much I can promise, but whether you want a bottle or not is, as always, up to you.

TW

ARDBEG ARDBOG 52.1%

Do you remember when you were young and there wasn't a day of the year that really came close to the magical feeling of Christmas? That feeling you have when you lie awake in bed waiting for a fat man in a ridiculous

suit to enter your house and leave presents under a plastic tree? That, my friends, is the stuff most children's dreams are made of!

Then comes the day you learn the truth and you never really recapture that feeling again and life ticks on. Now I, personally, find that a little bit saddening.

That's why I really understand the people who excitedly strike the days off their calendar counting down to that one day of the year they have been waiting for. For some it's Mother's Day. For others it's St. Patrick's Day. But for some of the people who are reading this, well, for a great number of them, it might be Ardbeg Day. Or should I say Ardbog day?

Ardbog! The newest release from the audacious Ardbeg distillery. What's it all about? Well, I was lucky enough to partake in an online tasting with Ardbeg Committee Chairman Mickey Heads and these are the key facts;

- It is matured in a mixture of manzanilla sherry and American white oak casks.

- It is the grand old age of ten years old.

- It is cask strength at 52.1% ABV (yes, the angels really took their liberties with this one).

I asked Mickey just how much manzanilla was used compared to American white oak and he didn't specify but assured us that it was truly the heart of the whisky. It seems they've kept the tradition of not finishing the whisky but vatting different wholly matured casks together.

It's all very well and good knowing what it's about but how is it? Let's just see…

Nose: Right off the bat, it's reminding me of a great plate of antipasti. There's cured meat as well as good, salty olives and their distinctive brine, and bread that's been soaked in olive oil. Left in the glass a little bit it opens up to a sweet, unbaked dough aroma.

Palate: A huge, salty wave is what grabs me first and really defines the start of this whisky before changing into the sweet meats that were present on the nose. Strangely for an Ardbeg the smoke doesn't really sneak through until the end and even then it's evenly balanced and warming.

I really like it but I think it's going to split people into three camps. The first who adore it, the second who say it isn't as good as the Galileo, and the third who are tired of the marketing side of Ardbeg who will make their minds up before trying the whisky. Personally, I feel it's time that Ardbeg added something to the core range that we could enjoy all year round. On the other hand, though, it is nice that Christmas only comes but once a year…

JT

ARDMORE 12 YEAR OLD
PORT WOOD FINISH 46%

"A smoky Highland whisky… what?" or a phrase to that effect is usually exclaimed when I first introduce people to fairly under-the-radar Ardmore distillery. Up to now, there has been only one expression in the core range, Ardmore Legacy, which goes some way to explaining why a substantial number of people have not encountered it before. However, Legacy has now been joined by a rather exciting addition, Ardmore Port Wood Finish. After spending 12 years in ex-bourbon barrels, it is then finished in half port pipes before being bottled.

Nose: Sweet and juicy: new leather, fig, treacle, cinnamon, manuka honey, cocoa beans, apple wood, and aromatic smoke.

Palate: A plummy sweetness, sultana cake, singed heather and lavender are balanced by toasted marshmal-

low and creamy vanilla. Dry wood smoke permeates all. A lingering rich sweetness, possibly fudge, combines with wood smoke and some dark chocolate. A rather rewarding dram, with a pleasing rich fruitiness and pronounced, but not overwhelming, smoky notes. Definitely something I'd recommend to those who enjoy things like Talisker Port Ruighe and other port-finished peated whiskies. A solid expansion of Ardmore's portfolio.

TW

BY ANGELO CAPUANO

Auchentoshan is a distillery located in close proximity to Scotland's largest city, Glasgow. The distillery's claim to fame is its practice of distilling its whisky three times, which, while the norm in Ireland, is unusual in Scotland where most whisky is distilled only two times. Auchentoshan therefore take a page from their Irish cousins and produce a whisky with more concentrated and cleaner ethanol, which matures into a light and fruity whisky often described as a "breakfast dram" due its smoothness.

AUCHENTOSHAN HEARTWOOD 43%

Auchentoshan Heartwood is triple-distilled whisky that has been matured in bourbon casks and Oloroso sherry casks and then bottled for Travel Retail in large 1 liter bottles at 43% ABV.

The nose presents with nutty overtones of almond, walnut, and unsalted pistachio that combine with herbal mint/menthol cough drops and the drying woody aroma of oloroso, cherries, chocolate, dried fruit and fresh herbs sitting on a newly made wooden table. On the palate the whisky is balanced and very smooth, immediately releasing drying Oloroso sherry with an almond and cashew nuttiness, pistachio shells, dark dried fruits such as raisin and prune, soft licorice, honey, dark chocolate, and the flicker of picante spice with cinnamon sugar that fades at mid-palate into a herbal glow of mild eucalyptus and mint hot chocolate. The finish curiously sweetens as undertones of oloroso remain dry, offering cherries, alcohol-soaked raisins, creamy vanilla, dusted cocoa, and dry wood.

Overall, Auchentoshan Heartwood is a smooth and light whisky that offers a fusion of dark dried fruit, dry oloroso with powerful wood notes, nuttiness, and a herbal glow. With booming Oloroso sherry notes and a

constant nutty hymn, this whisky is delectable with a block of creamy goat cheese or some Buffalo mozzarella—absolutely perfect while star gazing, watching a movie, or puffing on a mild cigar. Talk about *la bella vita!*

AC

AUCHENTOSHAN VIRGIN OAK 46%

Virgin Oak is all the rage for Morrison Bowmore at the moment. Since the turn of the millennium, Auchentoshan has been putting batches of whisky aside to wholly mature in North American virgin oak casks. Nothing had been in the casks before. No sherry, no bourbon, and no fancy-pants wines. Pure whisky on oak, unadulterated by the touch of another alcoholic footprint. In theory this means the wood imparts a whole heap of flavor on the whisky, so most distilleries choose to finish in virgin oak casks for a few months, rather than solely mature for the whole maturation. The thought behind the Auchentoshan Virgin Oak release is best explained by Brand Ambassador Gordon Dundas:

"Auchentoshan is one of the few distilleries to produce a virgin oak single malt. The lightness of the triple-distilled spirit makes it perfectly suited to absorbing the unique qualities of the charred virgin oak casks. The result is a lowland whisky that is subtle as well as complex in nature."

The triple distillation process at Auchentoshan does mean that the final distillate from still No. 3 is one of the strongest in the industry—an amazingly high 80–82.6% ABV (according to their website). Does the lightness of the spirit mean that it provides an excellent base to absorb the flavors of the virgin oak? Or will the Auchentoshan Virgin Oak be overpowered by the strength of flavor from the naked wood? I really hope it is the former! Personally, I have high hopes. The Auchentoshan Virgin Oak is bottled at 46% ABV, which is a little more punchy than the standard releases, and, from experience, I really like strong Auchentoshan (e.g., the awesome Auchentoshan Valinch).

Nose: Straight away I get the typical banana custard note that I loved about the Auchentoshan Valinch and a big whack of vanilla. It becomes richer and spicier with hot toffee apples and cinnamon. Opens up with pineapple chunks and quite a strong citric note.

Palate: A big flavored vanilla Angel Delight with a tin of fruit cocktail poured over the top. The pineapple from the nose is prominent, alongside kiwi, orange, and spiced apple. The cinnamon is back with hints of ginger and nutmeg. Fruity and vibrant on the palate. A little bit of lime, salt and prickly pear skins comes at the finish. Sweet, light and lasting. That prickly pear and lime adding a bit of a kick to the finish.

This is a great offering from Auchentoshan. A nice vibrant whisky, which is packed with a variety of light and spiced fruit notes. Leaves the palate tingling and happy. There is enough there to justify paying the full whack for this bottle, especially if you are a fan of these big, vibrant, fruity whiskies. Personally, I think I prefer the slightly cheaper Valinch, but I would still deem the Auchentoshan Virgin Oak experiment as a definite success.

GG

AUCHENTOSHAN THREE WOOD 43%

Auchentoshan Three Wood is an aggressive, forward-thinking experiment in single malt oaking (especially because of the unique types of casks). It has been matured in three different cask types: American bourbon barrels, Spanish Oloroso sherry barrels, and Pedro Ximenez sherry casks. This creates an incredibly rich, multi-layered whisky with astonishing flavors. Three Wood needs to be savored!

Color: Honey.

Nose: Brown sugar, caramel, toffee, blackberry, blueberry, plum, and raisin. Spicy notes as well.

Palate: Plum and fig and raisin all come tumbling out of the glass, with overtones of butterscotch and caramel, and raisins and a lovely spiciness. Toffee and nuts and oak linger a long, long time.

CD

BALBLAIR VINTAGE 1983 46%

Balblair re-launched The Gathering Place, their online community and discussion forum for all things Balblairy. I was asked to jot down a few vaguely coherent thoughts for them to celebrate the revamp and to review one of their upcoming new releases, the 1983 vintage. My mumblings have appeared on the Balblair website but you can also see them below. Many thanks to the guys at Balblair for asking me to write a piece for them; it's always a pleasure... particularly when a sample of 30 year old makes its way into Tiger's den...

1983. That seems like quite a while ago, particularly for those of us smug enough who can say we weren't even around then. Since then we've seen the invention of the compact disc, the birth of the internet, the release of Nelson Mandela from prison, the fall of the Berlin Wall, the cloning of Dolly the sheep, the election of the first black US president and much,

much more besides. What's my point here? The passage of time.

Thirty years ago, the whisky industry was in dire straits, with one newspaper running the infamous headline "Scotch on the rocks." Distillery closures were an almost monthly occurrence and warehouses were crammed full of maturing whisky, the so-called "whisky loch." How times have changed. Fast-forward to 2013 and the industry couldn't be in a healthier state. New distilleries are opening, sales are increasing year on year, demand has never been higher, and whisky is once again the drink to be seen with.

1983 also saw the filling of some very special ex-bourbon casks, casks that would lie sleeping for the next thirty years oblivious to the changing world outside. From the big shoulder pads and neon-colored leg warmers of the 80s, to the playsuits and skinny jeans of the current day, these casks have been quietly resting, biding their time. These casks have been patiently holding maturing Balblair spirit, and their work has now been deemed complete.

Nose: Initial notes of fresh flowers, banana fritters, ripe pears, and crystallized pineapple. Underneath there's rum truffles, toffee pennies, macerated cherries, and sandalwood, all covered with a dusting of cocoa powder.

Palate: A burst of fresh fruitiness

to begin: green apples, lemon sherbet, vanilla slices, and spiced pear. Then the richness surges to the fore with cinnamon, rich toffee, butterscotch, manuka honey, and the woodiness of freshly chopped logs. Long and lingering with dry oak and tingling wood spices.

This is a magnificent whisky, with layers of vibrant energy tempered by years of wisdom and experience. Light, fruity notes are complemented with rich toffee, honey, and cinnamon notes. The wood is there too, but it's not overpowering. The bottling of these casks has been timed right, timed when the spirit is at its peak, timed to perfection.

TW

THE BALVENIE DISTILLERY

BY CARLO DEVITO

The Balvenie distillery is located in the Speyside region, in Dufftown, Banffshire, Scotland, and is owned by William Grant & Sons, the world's largest whisky maker and distributor. This distillery was first an estate home. It is the birthplace of the legendary distiller William Grant, who was born there on December 19, 1839. Originally apprenticed as a shoemaker, he later became a bookkeeper at Mortlach distillery 1866. Twenty years later, Grant quit Mortlach, bought a field near Balvenie Castle, and by the fall of 1886 the foundation stone for this distillery had been laid. Grant himself remained active in the company until his death in 1923 at the age of 83.

Balvenie produces whisky in a traditional style by using locally grown barley and preparing it on its own malting floor. Balvenie is one of only six distilleries with its own malting floor in all of Scotland.

THE BALVENIE 14 YEAR OLD CARIBBEAN CASK 43%

This is a forward-thinking master at work! To create a new finish, Malt Master David Stewart filled American oak casks with a blend of his choice of West Indian rums. After he calculated the barrels had soaked up the character of the rum, he drained the rum and filled the casks with 14 year old Balvenie single malt whisky to finish this unique elixir.

The resulting single malt is a whisky brimming with honey and toffee and fig, with a warm taste sensation that lasts an incredibly long time.

Nose: Honey, toffee, and fig all come across along with nuts, spices, and vanilla.

Palate: Sweet oat notes, fresh fig, toffee, and honey dominate with a lingering vanilla overtone. A creamy, soft whisky with honey, cream and vanilla lingering for a very long time.

CD

THE BALVENIE 12 YEAR OLD DOUBLEWOOD 40%

Famed Master Distiller David Stewart created Balvenie DoubleWood, which was a distilling breakthrough and milestone all in one. He was the first to take older single malt Scotch and plan consecutive maturation in two different types of cask, a process often referred to today as "cask finishing."

The technique he established is what drives The Balvenie Double-Wood. First they start with the distillery's famed The Balvenie 12 Year Old single malt Scotch, a classic in its own right. The whisky is matured first in American oak barrels and then transferred to European oak sherry casks. The goal is that this two stage process adds richness and flavor that changes the essential character of the original 12 Year Old. The American oak imparts sweet vanilla notes and spice, while the sherry casks add rich spicy flavors and depth. There is no question that the DoubleWood is distinctly different from its original cousin, which much bigger vanilla notes, whiffs of green apple, and pear, honey, and toffee.

Nose: Green apple, pear, honey, nuts, and vanilla.

Palate: Dried apples and pears, fig, spice, toasted nuts, spice coated with toffee and caramel and vanilla. Vanilla, nuts, honey, and spice all linger a long time.

CD

THE BALVENIE PORTWOOD 21 YEAR OLD 47.6%

This extraordinary whisky is a combination of rare whisky and extreme wood. It is a marriage of Balvenie that has been aged 21 years and has been finished in port casks (also called "pipes"). It is non chill filtered and bottled at a higher strength of 47.6%.

Nose: Ripe apples, pears, raisins, figs, and nuts dominate.

Palate: Apples, pears, raisins, and figs dominate, with hints of honey, spice, and vanilla. Spices, nuts and vanilla linger and linger.

CD

SIR DAVID STEWART

BY CARLO DEVITO

David Stewart has been—for more than half a century—one of the most forward thinking master distillers in Scotland and the world. While the Malt Master of William Grant & Sons, he invented several of the techniques and styles that craft distillers have emulated around Scotland and around the world. In the meantime, he has created some of the most memorable and popular single malt Scotches in the world!

David was born in Ayr, Scotland in 1945. He began as an apprentice at the age of 17, in 1962, at William Grant & Sons. Single malt Scotch had not yet been exported to the United States. Glenfiddich was the first single malt Scotch sold outside of Scotland a year after David entered the business.

By 1974, after 16 years of toiling at the independent distiller, David was elevated to Malt Master of William Grant & Sons. His drive toward excellence and his longevity made him the longest-serving malt master of any distiller in the industry.

During his historic career at William Grant & Sons, David developed a long list of award-winning single malts and blends, including the Balvenie, Glenfiddich, Grant's brands, as well as working on the launch of Monkey Shoulder. His whiskies helped the independent William Grant & Sons become Distiller of the Year an unheard of five times by the International Spirits Challenge (ISC), four times by the International Wine and Spirit Competition (IWSC), and for the first time by the World Whiskies Awards in 2011.

What makes David truly unique is his breakthrough developments in maturing whisky and cask finishing. In the 1980s, David invented the technique we refer to today as "finishing." He took older whisky, and aged it for a short period in a different kind of cask—ale, port, sherry, and eventually even rum casks. The Balvenie Double-Wood 12 Year Old is the classic result of this method. It has since become a standard industry technique, now emulated around the world.

Another of David's inventions was to introduce the Solera method to whisky-making. The resulting whisky was Glenfiddich Solera Reserve 15 Year Old, which at the time of its initial release was the first and only single malt to use the innovative Solera maturation process borrowed from the sherry and port industries.

After a decade of working closely with apprentice Brian Kinsman, David officially handed over the role of Glenfiddich Malt Master and Grant's Master Blender in 2009. He remains Malt Master at The Balvenie Distillery in Dufftown.

In 2012, David celebrated 50 years at the distillery, Scotland's longest serving Malt Master. To commemorate the day, the company released a limited bottling of The Balvenie Fifty Cask #4567. The whisky, distilled in 1963, was matured in a European oak sherry hogshead cask (a rarity in whisky-making today). Only 88 bottles were made available. By his own estimation, David had nosed more than 400,000 casks of whisky in the course of his career.

Commenting on The Balvenie Fifty, he said: "Cask 4576 and I have shared the last five decades together at The Distillery and it's a great delight to discover how after half a century this unique cask has turned out a truly special single malt."

Over the years, the accolades came. He was recognized with various industry awards including the Grand Prix of Gastronomy (by the British Academy of Gastronomes) and garnered lifetime achievement awards from the International Wine & Spirit Competition and *Malt Advocate* magazine. He was named an Icon of Whisky and a Master of the Quaich.

The ultimate recognition came in 2016, when David was awarded an Most Excellent Order of the British Empire (MBE) for services to the Scotch whisky industry. MBE is the "order of chivalry of British constitutional monarchy," rewarding contributions to the arts and sciences, work with charitable and welfare organizations, and public service outside the Civil Service. It was established in 1917 by King George V. A recipient is named knight if male, or dame if female. When he was knighted, David had been in the industry 53 years!

Stewart told the press, at the time, "I am truly honored to receive this award. When I started my career as a whisky stocks clerk in 1962 I didn't expect to become a malt master so when I first found out about the MBE it came as a massive shock. The hardest part has been keeping it quiet even from my own family. It's a privilege working in this industry so to be rewarded and recognised in this manner is very humbling."

Stella David, CEO of William Grant & Sons, said: "David's innovative approach and total dedication to his craft, coupled with his modest, unassuming manner have made him one of the best loved and respected craftsmen in the business. The company is absolutely delighted for David, and this honor is testament to the fact that David is one of the greatest master blenders of a generation. Not that he would ever admit it himself."

David lives outside Glasgow with this wife Ellen and has three children (Heather, Colin, and Alan) and two grandchildren (Rory and Lily). He's an avid Ayr United football fan and also finds time to indulge in curling and an occasional round of golf.

Compass Box: Blends, but WOW!

BY CARLO DEVITO

Now, if you are an aficionado you will immediately balk! Compass Box produces blends! Yes, this is true. And of course, we should have barred the door there. But so many of our contributors balked that Compass Box was not included, we decided to include them. Why?

Firstly, some of their blends, included here, are made from blends of single malt Scotch. Secondly, their finishing of whiskies is so far out ahead of many producers, it almost seems like we need to find a way to get them past the whole "single malt thing." Thirdly, we included them because so many in the single malt world are keeping an eye on this impressive little house. They are producing high-quality, cutting-edge whiskies.

Compass Box Oak Cross is a blend of three single malts from three different producers and is aged in French oak and in a variety of American oak casks. Their Enlightenment is a blend of Highland single malt Scotch. Their Orangerie begins with a soft, sweet blend of Highland single malt and single grain whisky from Fife, aged with orange zest and spices. The Peat Monster is a super blend of peated single malt whiskies from different regions of Scotland. The Spice Tree is their most controversial whisky.

"In some circles, it is whispered that The Spice Tree is the whisk(e)y the larger scotch industry doesn't want you to have. Micro-distillery Compass Box first launched The Spice Tree in 2005, but were forced to discontinue production by the Scotch Whisky Association (SWA) under threat of legal action. The SWA objected to the use of French oak inner staves in the casks," wrote Richard Thomas.

Compass Box then reintroduced the whisky with unmatched cheek. For the relaunch of The Spice Tree, Compass Box had a unique custom, hybrid barrel created featuring French oak heads and American oak bodies. The barrels ranged from standard barrels, to vanilla toast, to infrared toast, and finally to mocha toast.

"In the glass, The Spice Tree has a golden look to it, like a lighter honey. No surprises on the nose for a scotch named "The Spice Tree," because it smells like an open spice box. The whisky has a strong scent, packed with cookie spices like oaky vanilla, nutmeg, cinnamon, and peppery ginger. On the palate, the Spice Tree delivers a rich, sweet flavor. The cookie spices remain standing out in front, supported by a woody tinge. The peppery spiciness of the whisky came to me as only just a hint at first, but grew into a more noticeable presence right up to the finish. The finish is big, warm, and has a bit of a spicy kick to it. This is a complex, full-bodied scotch," concluded Thomas. The rest of the new single malt whisky world agrees with him.

BENRIACH 15 YEAR OLD
TAWNY PORT FINISH 46%

BenRiach has a simply enormous line of whiskies, embracing ages out to 40 years, peated and unpeated Scotches, and virtually every sort of finishing barrel imaginable. Nestled right in the middle of that range is their 15 Year Old Tawny Port Finish. Primary maturation was carried out in American bourbon barrels, with the finishing done in tawny port hogsheads. Bottled at 46% ABV, this unfiltered Scotch was part of a 2006 limited release of only 2,040 bottles.

In the glass, the BenRiach 15 Year Old Tawny Port had a bright orange, copper-amber coloring. The nose was rich but subdued. The creamy sweetness of seasoned orange zest and wine red fruits are there, with a minor note of apple cider tartness. Backing all that up is the scent of musty oak. The aroma is too unbalanced to be called complex, since the creamy sweet side half-smothers everything else, and it takes a good bit of swishing to bring out the best in it, but even so it's pleasant to sniff at.

The flavor switches things around a bit and brings the Scotch into better balance. The musty oak is now up front, supported by dashes of pepper and a dollop of fruit syrup. The fun-damental character of the 15 Year Old Tawny Port remains, so it remains a mellow whisky, despite the peppery bite. The finish spins out of the spicy bite, rolling out into a long, lingering warmth. BenRiach scored a Silver at the 2008 International Wine and Spirits Competition with this whisky.

RT

BOWMORE MIZUNARA CASK FINISH 53.9%

ESTᵈ 1779
BOWMORE®
ISLAY
SINGLE MALT
SCOTCH WHISKY

#EastMeetsWest—that hashtag was how I was first introduced to Bowmore Mizunara Cask Finish. A teasing Japanese Himitsu Bako puzzle box arrived on my desk, with a note to share a photo of the box on Instagram or Twitter using #EastMeetsWest in order to receive instructions on how to open it. Cue a frantic search for my phone, which was somewhere on my cluttered desk, me stubbing my toe on my desk chair, many, many swear words, and eventually a rather heavily filtered photo of the box.

Now, without wishing to sound like an utter smug bastard, I know how these boxes work. With a bit of pushing, pulling, and sheer bloody-mindedness I popped the box open, and boy was the whisky as impressive as the marketing stunt. This bottling is limited to 2,000 bottles and will retail at £750 when it's available on allocation. Pretty damn pricey for an NAS bottling, despite considering its uniqueness of being finished for at least three years in Japanese mizunara oak and being bottled at cask strength. Apparently all the whisky is 1990 distillations meaning it's between 15 and 25 years old (why avoid an age statement then?). Still hugely on the high side for me, but here goes…

Nose: Lavender honey, heather, and toasted rosemary notes give this whisky a herbaceous start. Then candied pineapple, singed orange peel, ripe bananas, and dried apricot. A creaminess comes through, possible vanilla fudge, before sandalwood and some dark chocolate emerge. Eventually soft smoke and rock pools can be found. Beautiful.

Palate: A real salty, briny tingle to start. Possible even a hint of wasabi prickle. Then lime zest, white grapes, and peaches emerge. Given a few seconds this whisky really changes on the palate, with cinnamon, clove, soft smoke, leather, and matchsticks becoming dominant. Long, with leather, wood tannins, rich spices, and mild peat.

Impressive. Very impressive. But I simply cannot ignore the astronomical asking price. Yes it's cask strength, yes it's finished in mizunara oak, and yes, it's f'ing tasty, but I fail to see how a 15-25 year old whisky can be valued at £750 a pop. It may well turn out to be the new Devil's Casks—that rather sexy Bowmore fetched several-fold its asking price at online auctions as soon as the bottles sold out. I fear the Mizunara Cask Finish will become a collector's/investor's wet dream as no doubt it'll be worth at least £1,500 once the 2,000 bottles are snapped up. This is a real shame, as the liquid is simply too good to sit on a shelf and be admired. It's f'ing delicious and, after all, whisky is made for drinking, not looking at.

TW

BRUICHLADDICH

BY ANGELO CAPUANO

Bruichladdich is a distillery located on the island of Isay in Scotland, where hundreds of years ago the island natives learned the art of distilling from Irish monks. Over the next hundred years demand for whisky gradually expanded, and to service this demand Bruichladdich was founded in 1881. It closed in 1994, and aging stocks of whisky were left to do what they do best—absorb phenolic compounds from the oak. The distillery was subsequently purchased by private investors and re-opened in 2001. Jim McEwan was signed on as Master Distiller and the team has been keeping a lot of people very happy ever since. This history therefore explains how the distillery, having re-opened in 2001, can offer whisky that was distilled in 1990.

BRUICHLADDICH OCTOMORE 7.4 VIRGIN OAK 61.2%

The self-proclaimed "progressive Hebridean distillers," Bruichladdich, have released a new addition to their super peaty Octomore range, and this time it's a '.4'. Previously, we've seen .1 (ex-bourbon casks maturations), .2 (ex-wine cask maturation), and .3 (made from local barley) releases and so the first .4 release steps into the generally unchartered territory, in terms of Scotch whisky maturation anyway, of virgin oak maturation. Octomore 7.4 isn't entirely matured in virgin oak, however, with only 25% of this whisky being solely matured in these casks, sourced from the Allier region of France, for seven years. The other 75% initially spent three

unstoppable force meeting the immovable object about it: 167ppm worth of peaty power coming up against a mighty virgin oak influence. Seconds out, round seven-point-four...12,000 bottles.

Nose: The B&Q shed department! Creozote, wood chips, sawdust, and charred logs. Then smoked bacon, clove, honey-glazed ham, and black peppercorns. Finally, BBQ embers, black tea, cigar, and cocoa beans.

Palate: A huge spicy hit of smoke—dry peat, cinnamon, bark, pencil, cracked dry leather, smoked paprika, and a chili tingle. Then dark treacle, burnt marshmallow, dark chocolate orange, sticky dates, and charred steak. Long, with dry peat smoke, smoky bacon crisps and lingering wood spice.

A very impressive whisky. The heavily peated spirit is obvious from the moment the bottle is opened, but the virgin oak has sweetened this whisky right up and given it a rather delicious dimension. However, the price tag is a bit on the outrageous side for a 7 year old whisky, and it's a tipping point for me. Although it's quite complex for its age, and undoubtedly a full-flavored whisky, for me it's not worth parting with 150 quid for.

TW

years in first-fill ex-bourbon casks, before being dumped into the French virgin oak casks for two years before being shifted back again into first-fill ex-bourbon casks for two years. Still with me? Good.

The first thing that struck me about this maturation regime was the two-year stint in virgin oak casks in the middle of a seven-year maturation, and why the whisky wasn't just finished in these casks after spending five years in the ex-bourbon casks. Seems a bit of a strange one to me, but I'm sure head distiller Adam Hannett has his reasons. Either way, this whisky has something of the

BRUICHLADDICH ISLAY BARLEY ROCKSIDE FARM 50%

Reflecting on the importance of barley to whisky-making, it comes as no surprise that Bruichladdich—those self-proclaimed progressive Hebridean distillers—push the boundaries of the whisky world by creating a whisky made from barley that has been grown on the isle of Islay in Scotland. They aptly call this creation Bruichladdich Islay Barley. The barley used for this whisky was grown for Bruichladdich by Mark and Rohaise French in the Minister's field at Rockside Farm.

Emblazoned on the whisky's bottle are the words "we believe terroir matters." Bruichladdich, standing on the shoulders of wine- and brandy-making giants in France, have decided to employ this theory of terroir to whisky-making. This means that the barley grown in Islay is likely, once it is used to make a wash that is distilled, to give whisky a different flavor to barley that is grown in the mainland of Scotland (or elsewhere, for that matter).

We have been very fortunate to be able to taste Bruichladdich "new make," with tasting notes available. This includes Bruichladdich "new make" made from Islay barley, bere barley, and organic barley. The Islay barley was quite earthy and full flavored with oils and heavy congeners weighing down the ethanol. It had earthy, herbal, and peppery flavors with a foundation of vanilla, caramel, honey, chocolate, saltiness, and nuttiness.

Bruichladdich put this "new make" into oak barrels, which over time give the "new make" a golden straw color, infuse it with oak flavors and alter some of the compounds in it. Bruichladdich Islay barley is unpeated, presumably to ensure that the flavor of the barley is not lost to the peat, and bottled at a generous 50% alcohol by volume.

Color: Often in Cognac circles the way a brandy looks is part of its aesthetic pleasure—its color, the way it catches the light and clings to the glass. The color of Bruichladdich Islay Barley is a light golden wheat color, but the way it hugs the glass—leaving thin legs that slope down as the oily film fades—is particularly impressive.

Nose: The bouquet is immediately quite sweet and sumptuous, with nutty Argan oil, banana, raisin, porridge, honey, whipped cream, pineapple, banana and raisin bread with crushed nuts and soft vanillas. A mild earthiness sits beneath that lovely aroma, with soft hints of pepper, mixed olives, anchovies, and the backbone of the "new make" untouched by the oak—chocolate nut oils, and shades of golden and dark honey.

Palate: On the palate find vanillas and a soft creaminess, through which shines pepper, spice, mild anchovy, and earthiness. There is something

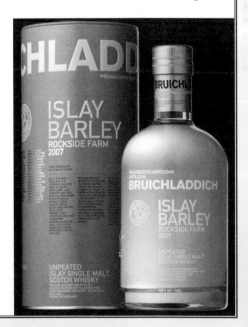

salty and earthy about this whisky, like a lick of rock salt and a sip of a platinum tequila. The finish offers lingering flavors of honey, chocolate, nuts, and a mild salt/saline. That saline is interlaced with rock and minerality, like tasting a sodium rich natural sparkling water.

Bottom line: Buy it. Bruichladdich Islay Barley is a fascinating malt that offers a very earthy, mineral, and salty character that can only be explained by the Islay barley. This malt showcases the Islay barley without letting the wood get in the way, and it is a delicious incarnation of Islay's saltiness, earthiness, and minerality in a bottle. The French have known for centuries that the soil that feeds grapes gives brandy made from those grapes important flavors and character. Glad to see the Scots have finally caught on, with a conscious attempt at bottling a piece of Scotland... literally.

AC

BRUICHLADDICH
BLACK ART 4 1990 49.2%

Black Art 4 is the fourth release of Bruichladdich's popular "Black Art," which is comprised of whisky from a selection of casks that are kept a closely guarded secret. The only information released about this mysterious whisky is that it was distilled in 1990, aged for 23 years during which American and French oak casks are used, and bottled at 49.2% alcohol volume. All other information appears to be suppressed, just like the recipe for the Big Mac sauce, the Colonel's herbs and spices, or what on Earth my girlfriend wants for Valentine's day!

Bruichladdich states that "Black Art is Master Distiller Jim McEwan's personal voyage into the heart of Bruichladdich" and that he worked "with the very finest American and French oak to explore that most esoteric relationship between spirit and wood." That relationship between spirit and wood is probably the most important aspect of whisky-making, because the oak either imparts flavor compounds into the spirit or alters those existing compounds. New make spirit is not as interesting as an aged whisky, because it needs to draw out flavor and have its own flavors altered by being aged in the wood and exposed to oxygen. The Black Art 4, in my opinion, is a great example of the complex aromas and flavors that oak can impart into a whisky beyond the usual suspects—sherry, bourbon, vanilla…WOOD!

Black Art 4 offers some very fascinating twists and turns and very complex flavors that are not overly oak-dominated. This explains Jim's quest to seek balance between spirit and wood. What I love about Black Art 4 is that despite its age of 23 years, the barley still shines within subtle nuances of wood-driven character and on the palate the complex sweetness morphs without warning into a smoky haze of salt and bristling Asian spices—a very interesting and unique twist! I think the team at Bruichladdich have done a superb job.

Nose: Burnt citrus peel (orange and lime in particular) accompany buttery barley and bitter hazelnut, which develops more sweetness and into Nutella, dark chocolate cherry, ripe and toasted coconut with deep vanilla notes softening the bite of drying polished mahogany. There is a wine theme in this bouquet, quite dry with oak-driven sugars providing balance. Water softens the burnt citrus peel into orange cake and seems to release more lemon and dill aromas.

Palate: This whisky has a great mouth-coating texture, and it coats every crevice of the palate. It is powerful, assertive, bold, and sweet. Almond nougat develops first with licorice, glazed cherries, and chocolate, but then the sweetness gradually recedes at mid-palate into a smoky haze of fresh salt and oriental spices. This is where it gets really interesting. The haze of salt and oriental spices then resembles a sizzling sweet and sour hot plate with chilies. The smoke, which began to develop on the palate, is now more noticeable. The finish therefore offers mild smoke and spice with salt and a moderating sweetness of an apricot danish with cinnamon.

Complex, interesting, innovative, salt notes within sweetness—a real charmer.

AC

PORT CHARLOTTE THE PEAT PROJECT 46%

This sharp whisky offers complex layers of sweetness pummeled by dense coastal peat. Yummy!

As the name suggests, this beauty is peated and proud of it, boasting that it is part of "the peat project." "The peat project" combines whiskies of different vintages that are basically peated Bruichladdich, the classic of which is not peated despite being from Islay. The result is a garden on fire, with floral notes burning in the smoky haze that is the coastal peat— beautiful.

Nose: Let us return to our walks with Henry, our King Charles Cavalier, along the beach. The lush green meadows are dotted with flowers as the sweet, fresh, floral fragrance meets the gentle sea breeze that adds the salty earthiness of the beach. The Laddie Classic reminded me of those walks, the smell of the flowers and the beach. The Port Charlotte adds some burning peat to that, almost like a smoldering campfire beside the beach that is nearing its end as the embers burn the dry grass that are used to fuel the flames.

Palate: This is beautifully complex whisky, with a sharp peat explosion that is accompanied with coastal notes of saltiness and earthiness, though not too earthy and almost like a gentle spray of sea water while sitting on an old wooden pier. The peat offers a powerful bitter start that is dense and cigar-like, but this bitterness is counteracted by sweet fruity notes of sliced green apple and preserved strawberries. This whisky is vibrant, energetic and youthful. The peat glows on the palate as its bitter vegetal character remains on the tongue for a long while, moderated by the sweetness that is at the heart of the Bruichladdich distilling. Smooth peat magic without noticeably large ripples.

AC

What You Need to Know
About Bruichladdich:
Interview with an Executive
BY ANGELO CAPUANO

AC: Do you think that your products are distinctive? If so, what makes them distinctive from other Scotch and Islay whiskies on the market?

I would suggest that Bruichladdich is distinctive in a number of different ways. We make a very wide range of whiskies. These are presented under three different brand names: unpeated Bruichladdich, heavily peated Port Charlotte, and the super-heavily peated Octomore. We have a history of celebrating the extremely diverse range of styles possible within the single malt genre rather than homogenizing.

We do not make whisky for blending. Everything we do goes into single malts.

We have developed a style of presentation, which is considered to be quite radical with our aqua-colored bottles and minimalist, modernist styling. Our aim is to make the most thought-provoking whiskies possible.

AC: From what I have read, Jim McEwan (Bruichladdich's Master Distiller), worked at Bowmore since he was 15! Does Jim remember the first whisky he bottled as a distiller? How did it turn out?

Jim was apprenticed as a cooper at Bowmore from the age of 15, steadily developing his skills in all different areas of the business. This included invaluable experience at the Roseburn Bonding Co. in Glasgow's Bridgeton as a trainee Blender and his subsequent promotion to manager of The Tannochside Bonding Co. in January 1978, a large blending facility owned by Bowmore. Jim has a great admiration for Bowmore whiskies.

The first new spirit Jim distilled was at Bowmore in 1968. His first blend was one that was designed for South Africa in c.1978. It is called Three Ships and the brand is still available, although Jim does not know whether the style remains the same.

Jim still has a bottle of Three Ships in his house—and recalls it as being a good quality Speyside-style blend of comprising around 75% grain and 25% malts. He describes it as medium bodied with a fair amount of age to it.

AC: Bruichladdich regards itself as "progressive Hebridean distillers." Why is there a need to be "progressive?" What progress are you trying to make?

This is a précis of our company philosophy…. It has been published before in various forms, but I cannot really improve on it…

We are proudly non-conformist. We believe the whisky industry has been stifled by industrialization and self-interest—huge organizations have developed that require a stable status quo to ensure that their industrial processes can run to maximum efficiency, producing the maximum "product" with the minimum input and variation, all to the lowest unit price.

We reject this. We believe that whisky should have character; an authenticity derived from where it is distilled and the philosophies of those who distil it—a sense of place, of terroir that speaks of the land, of the raw ingredients from which it was made.

We believe in variety. We believe the world needs an antidote to homogeneity and blandness.

Our raw ingredients are paramount. We use 100% Scottish barley—we believe it's called "Scotch" for a reason. We are the major distiller of organic barley in Scotland and have been instrumental in support for organic farming in the single malt category. In 2010, we released the first single malt whisky to be made purely from Islay Barley, probably the first in the island's history.

We believe our spirit should speak of where it comes from and where it is matured—Bruichladdich is the only major distiller to distil, mature, and bottle all its whisky on Islay.

We passionately believe in terroir—in authenticity, place, and provenance, in ultimate traceability. We seek to produce the most natural, thought-provoking, intellectually stimulating, and enjoyable spirit possible. Obsessive? Probably—but if all you want is a whisky, the world is awash with the stuff.

AC: What do you think of age statements?

We do not reject age statements, but feel they have made the industry a bit lazy. A 10 year old must be better than a five, but not as good as a fifteen, etc. etc. This is not necessarily the case. We accept that age is important—but we don't believe that it is necessarily as important as the quality of ingredients or the cask or the method of distillation. Age is just one of the myriad variables that are brought into play when creating a whisky, and it is not necessarily a reliable indicator of quality. Leaving whisky in old, tired wood will result in old, tired whisky.

AC: Bruichladdich make it clear that 100% of the barley you use is from Scotland. Why is it important to use barley from Scotland and Islay?

Essentially, we are fascinated by the qualities and variety imparted by provenance. We start with the premise that Scotch whisky should be made from Scottish ingredients. We believe it is called Scotch for a reason. As a reasonable analogy, we would also suggest that a product calling itself "Australian wine" ought to be made from grapes grown in Australia.

There are also good technical reasons as to why Scottish barley is particularly appropriate for distilling, relating to the growing season and soil types.

And then we have set out to explore the variety possible under the Scottish barley umbrella. We are fascinated by the qualitative differences extant between barley crops from different places. The analogy with wine is strong here. Wine has developed a hierarchical classification based on perceived quality that has developed over centuries. The exploration of terroir in wine can be extremely complex and challenging to appreciate.

We are not there yet—we have only been doing this for twelve years and that is nowhere near long enough but it is a fascinating journey. We are excited by our demonstrating that different barley varieties produce demonstrably different new make spirit. And also by the demonstrable fact that the same barley varieties, planted in different places, also produce subtle variations. Exactly as you would expect with fine wines.

We are a long way from being able to quantify these differences, or grade them, but we have literally set out on a journey of discovery, and an absolutely fascinating portfolio is emerging.

AC: Bruichladdich offers organic Scotch whisky that is made from organic barley. What exactly is meant by "organic whisky"? Do you think that organic whisky offers anything different in terms of aroma, taste, and finish?

In the UK, organic certification is regulated by government, the Department for Environment, Food and Rural Affairs (DEFRA), and our suppliers and farmers have to meet the criteria set. As do we.

Does whisky made from organically grown barley taste different from that distilled from conventionally grown barley? Yes, but we have never conducted a properly controlled experiment to test the hypothesis. Our central belief is that barley varies from place to place, so we would need to grow barley conventionally alongside an organic crop (on the same farm in exactly similar terroir) and treat it in the same way. We have never done that, and are unlikely to do so. It is very easy to demonstrate the difference between our organic spirit and conventional spirit, but we do not know what causes those differences. Is it the farm, or the way the grain is grown? Or the climate?

We are also interested in the ethical/environmental implications of organic farming, and do what we can to support the principles it enshrines.

AC: How do you select your oak casks? How do you prepare them before maturing whisky?

All our warehouses sit on or above the shores of Lochindaal—the sea loch that defines the westerly Rhinns of Islay. The effect of this Islay-maritime environment on our suite of casks is very significant. To Bruichladdich, this is fundamental and non-negotiable. We will not mature our casks of whisky anywhere else.

Combining extensive wine experience, hands-on barrel coopering, and decades of whisky knowledge, we have a unique understanding of the complex interaction of wood, air, and spirit— and we continue to explore it keenly.

We are intrigued by the effects of oak from America and Europe's greatest forests on the flavor of Bruichladdich malt; over the years American white oak (*Quercus alba*) imparts lush, vanillin flavors, whereas the influence of French oak (*Quercus robur, Quercus petraea*) is more subtle and fine.

The finest oak is a raw material just as important as barley or spring water. We are uncompromising in our choice of cask; we can work with the best, so we do. The proportion of ex-American bourbon casks to casks from other sources that we use varies over time, although we always use a significant majority of bourbon, again from a wide range of sources. We are privileged to have relationships with some of Europe's greatest wine-makers and their estates; from Rioja and Jerez in Spain, to Bordeaux, the Languedoc, the Loire and Alsace in France, to the Neusiedler See in Austria, we have access to the finest oak casks that have previously contained the world's greatest wines. The complexity and subtlety of the effect these casks have on maturing whisky are fascinating, and for us when our single malt is put into cask this is the start of a journey of discovery, not a final resting place.

No two casks of spirit are the same or mature at the same rate or in the same way. So it is essential that we are here, on the ground, watching our maturing malt with a hawk's eye. Not only is that required for quality, but also every now and then the whisky gods surprise us and give us something rare, capricious, and unexpected—the difference between artisanal craft and commercial production.

The maintenance of cask quality involves continual monitoring, tasting, and the ruthless rejection of casks that are not performing as expected. The best indicator of this is the huge piles of reject casks that build up!

AC: Is there a flavor profile that you aim to achieve when malting, mashing, fermenting, distilling, and maturing?

Yes, very much so, but it is impossible to write down. It is very carefully and constantly monitored by all the stillmen and by our master distiller Jim McEwan, distillery manager Allan Logan, and his assistant Adam Hannett.

AC: Why did you offer an unpeated whisky from Islay? Do you think maturing this whisky on Islay allows it to develop a different character from whiskies that have matured elsewhere in Scotland?

I believe that Bruichladdich was designed and built in 1881 by the Harvey Brothers to produce unpeated spirit. The best evidence for this is contained within one of the most well-respected whisky books ever written, Alfred Barnard's *The Whisky Distilleries of the UK,* which specifically describes the malt drying process of every distillery on Islay. He says that every distillery uses peat—but does not mention peat at Bruichladdich.

AC: Why do you think people choose to buy Bruichladdich?

Because they are interested, inspired, curious, and like to be challenged.

AC: What three words do you want people to associate with Bruichladdich?

Progressive, Terroir, Challenging

AC: What is a typical day like at Bruichladdich?

Not long enough. Extremely varied. Interesting. Stimulating. Challenging. Spectacular. Beautiful.

AC: Do you have a favorite whisky?

Black Art 4

An Evening with Master Distiller Jim McEwan of Bruichladdich

BY ANGELO CAPUANO

More than one hundred people gathered within the walls of the iconic Kelvin Club in Melbourne, Australia to meet a man who has been involved in the production of whisky for half a century. That man, ladies and gentleman, was Jim McEwan. The vast majority of people may utter the words "Jim who?", but anyone who enjoys a dram or two (or who knows what "dram" means) will know that the name "Jim McEwan" belongs to a man who is perhaps the world's most famous whisky distiller. Starting his career at the Bowmore distillery at the age of 15, Jim went on to learn the craft of cooperage (making or assembling barrels) before becoming the Master Distiller at the Bruichladdich distillery in Scotland, where he now plies his trade. His career in whisky has spanned half a century, and while at Bruichladdich he has gained a reputation for producing whisky that is innovative, exciting, and that tastes darn good!

Before this appearance, Jim embarked on a much anticipated national tour of major Australian cities where he has conducted a tasting of whiskies from Bruichladdich, and the scene for his visit to Melbourne was the Kelvin Club.

On arrival at the Kelvin Club guests were greeted with gin and tonic, made with Bruichladdich's The Botanist Islay Dry Gin—a gin made using classic aromatics that tend to be used for gin, such as orris root, cassia bark, and coriander seed, and 22 other botanicals hand-picked on the isle of Islay in Scotland (where Bruichladdich is located). As the bottles of gin were slowly emptied, a progression of people began to eagerly make their way to the upstairs room where Jim would be conducting the whisky tasting. The room was large, and energy filled the air as people looked around for anyone who even remotely resembled Jim. It soon became clear that Jim is not a man to enter a room unnoticed, and to the bellowing sound of bagpipes Jim entered the room marching proudly behind a bagpiper dressed in a traditional Scottish kilt. He had arrived, and the room fell silent. "Hello," he said happily. "Hello!" he repeated. With a gesture of his hands, not dissimilar to the one made by an old friend who wants a hug and not a handshake, the crowd realized its mistake and finally responded "Hello Jim!" That set the tone for what was a hilarious evening. It was not the formidable legend Master Distiller McEwan up there, ready to teach everyone about whisky. It was Jim, ready to share half a dozen drams with us and talk whisky.

One of the first points Jim made was that the color of a whisky is meaningless, because caramel (the oft-called "E150") may be added to whisky and therefore its color is not a reliable indicator of its age or the type of casks that were used to mature the whisky. This was demonstrated by Jim pouring cola into a glass of whisky, which darkened it, and with this altered color he sarcastically observed whether the whisky—now dark in color—was matured in Fino sherry casks for a number of years. This was a good point made by Jim, but it was also a confusing point given that Bruichladdich doesn't add caramel coloring to their whisky. The color of Bruichladdich whisky therefore is a clue as to what casks were used to mature the whisky, though admittedly Jim is correct that a whisky's color reveals nothing about its age.

The tasting featured whiskies in the Bruichladdich range—the Laddie Classic, Islay Barley 2006, Black Art v3, Port Charlotte Scottish Barley, and Octomore 6.1. All whiskies were impressive and thoroughly enjoyable, and my picks of the evening would be the Islay Barley 2006 and Black Art v3 (curiously both of which are—despite Islay being the heartland of peat—made without peat) and the Octomore 6.1 which, despite having a terrifying 300ppm as the world's most heavily peated whisky, is surprisingly well balanced and complex.

With wobbly knees from all the whisky and a measure of gin, we were made to stand with one foot on the table and one foot on our chairs while yelling out a Scottish toast, which lasted several minutes (and almost saw me fall face first into some leftover Octomore—yes please!). The evening then ended, and the mood soon deflated. Everybody had to go home, but I get the feeling no one really wanted to—there was still plenty of whisky, and Jim's jokes and humor left us all in a state of constant laughter (it was either Jim, or the whisky).

Overall, Jim's visit was a fun-filled journey through the Bruichladdich range that was filled with laughter, jokes, and some whisky education in between. If you see Jim, tell him Gunta is at the door—he'll know what I mean!

Note: Jim McEwan retired in July 2015 after 52 years in the business. But his presence still looms large.

BY RICHARD THOMAS

GlenDronach is a Speyside distillery, located near the town of Huntly and owned by BenRiach. It is one of the older distilleries in Scotland, having been founded by James Allardice in 1826. It passed through a number of hands in the 19th and early 20th centuries, including Charles Grant's (of the famed Grants family) in the 1920s, and was one of the last distilleries in Scotland to use coal fires to heat the stills. In modern times, the distillery was owned by Teachers between the 1960s and 2000, when the distillery was shut down. It flickered between being open and being mothballed (the coal burners were replaced with steam units in 2005, forcing one such closure) until BenRiach bought it, putting it back into regular operation again in 2008.

Today, GlenDronach has three basic lines of single malt scotch. The main line consists of scotches ranging from 12 to 33 years of age, and the distillery also has a line of limited edition, single cask whisky.

GLENDRONACH TAWNY PORT FINISH 15 YEAR OLD 46%

Launched in 2011, the GlenDronach Tawny Port Finish 15 Year Old comes from the distillery's Wood Finish line, which also includes moscatel, Sauternes, and virgin oak finished whiskies.

The GlenDronach Port Finish spends at least fifteen years aging in old sherry casks made from European oak, and then finished for a spell in ex-tawny port barrels. This is an old style Scotch, so it's not chill-filtered and has no additives, and it is bottled at 46% ABV.

In the glass, this port finish has a gold-amber coloring, but with a tinge

of pink to it, something I thought gave the liquid a lighter, clearer appearance when viewed from certain angles. The nose has a certain dried fruits florality at its core, like a basket of basket plums and raisins with some rose petals thrown in for decoration. There is a little bitter graininess in there, as well as a little musty wood and a little peaty smoke.

The flavor follows from that scent, but with a few surprises. It's a little wine-sweet, a little peaty and ashy, and a little woody, but there is also a note of ginger and cinnamon spice in there. The finish starts on the smoky, ashy flavor and winds down at a fairly quick pace with a moderate amount of warmth, ending with a chili-spice glaze covering the insides of your mouth.

This Scotch has exactly the wine, wood, and Scotch flavors that one might to expect from a middle-aged Speyside single malt finished in tawny casks, a highly specialized and narrow category to say the least. Good port-finished whisky is a rare bird; it doesn't come cheap, and it has aspects that make the price tag worth it.

RT

GLEN GARIOCH VIRGIN OAK 48%

For a long time now, it's been rather fashionable to stick new spirit into an interesting type of cask to mature, or to finish a whisky in a cask not normally used. Whether it's sherry butts, port pipes, rum casks, white wine casks, red wine casks, ale casks, or irn bru casks made of ivory from a highland unicorn, finishing is quite the thing. Well, that last one might not be strictly true, but you get my point. A more recent trend is to stick whisky into virgin oak casks to mature. The casks are brand spanking new, untouched by alcohol, and have not yet had their maturation cherry popped, so to speak. Some distilleries have been known to finish their whisky in virgin oak for just a few months, mainly because the wood imparts such strong flavors into the whisky that a full maturation may swamp the natural character of the spirit and ruin the end product. However, Glen Garioch released a limited edition fully-virgin-oak-matured whisky with only 120 cases of the stuff being made available to the UK market. Rachel Barrie, master blender at Morrison Bowmore, says, "Glen Garioch's intense flavor means it holds up well in a new fill cask, allowing the liquid to be fully matured in virgin oak and not just finished in the barrel." A bold statement, but has it worked?

Nose: Pine trees, toffee popcorn, Danish pastries, heaps of vanilla, honey and sugary porridge. There's a green apple note in there too. Very sweet and inviting.

Palate: Chocolate éclair sweets, toffee, honey, buttery caramel, and gingersnap biscuits swiftly give way to a hit of sweet oak, cinnamon, cloves, and all sorts of wood spices. Creamy vanilla with a touch of chocolate and lingering wood spices.

Big and full of flavor—lots of sweet notes and spicy notes to chew on. Good balance and enough depth of flavor to justify shelling out seventy quid on a bottle. Bottling at 48% ABV also perhaps gives this whisky a bit more verve than if it was bottled at 40% ABV. A really good dram.

TW

GLEN GARIOCH 1999
SHERRY CASK MATURED 56.3%

This is a small batch release of Glen Garioch 1999 that was bottled in 2013. Their Highlands-styled single malt was not just finished in Oloroso sherry casks, but it has matured in those casks since 1999. A truly unique product. Lots of toffee, caramel, cocoa, hints of maple, and a nice dose of spice and vanilla. A full-bodied and intensely sherried single malt.

Nose: Toffee, caramel, candied cherries and dried apples, honey, nuts, maple, vanilla.

Palate: Very nice mouthfeel on this very rich single malt. Toffee, dark chocolate, maple syrup, and spices such as nutmeg and ginger come through as promised, along with hints of orange zest, dates, raisins, and a hint of licorice.

CD

GLENGLASSAUGH EVOLUTION 50%

When Glenglassaugh restarted operations in late 2008, it was only the latest turn in the distillery's long history of ups and downs. The distillery opened in 1875, only to be shuttered in 1908. Some say it was opened again in the 1930s, but the evidence for that is reportedly all oral hearsay at this time. Glenglassaugh's next certain run was between 1960 and 1986. Like many Scottish distilleries, it was closed during the mid-1980s recession, and when it wasn't reopened in the 1990s it seemed set to stay that way.

With a history like that, having a single malt dubbed "Evolution" seems not only natural but also positively called for. Glenglassaugh Evolution (50% ABV) comes from a single variety of oak cask styles, ex-George Dickel Tennessee Whiskey first-fill barrels. From that, Evolution is aptly named not just from the distillery's history but also for its agility in blending a harmonious profile of whisky and oak.

The overarching impression of Evolution is that it is a bottle of renewed vigor. With the first drops in a Glencairn glass, one could already surmise that this whisky pours more with the attitude of a champagne than a Scotch; its unadulterated golden and delicate pallor celebrates its natural color and non-chill filtered origins. It exudes a youthful representation of its flavor to follow.

Upon first introduction, a prominent oak invites the nose to a creamy molasses and butterscotch. A pleasant hug of a green grape rubbed with nutmeg delicately graces the scent, leading one toward the palate. Immediately, a thin and energetic fluid dances to the lips with no viscosity, knocking with exuberance on the lips with instant vanilla, caramel, ginger, and spice. When the taste reaches center mass on the tongue, its energy instantly dissipates in a simple sweetness not represented by any honeys or syrups. Instead, it is cloaked in a tropical, domineering spiciness throughout.

It's like a creative bartender crafting homemade simple syrup in an old-fashioned ginger root beer with nothing but powdered sugar and playfulness. That said, the spice is a guest who overstays his welcome, sitting on the tongue long before the fluid vacates, and even sits outside on the lips, hanging out on the porch. A contingent of the wood and spice slides down the throat with the same enthusiasm as the prior contingent of ginger fire but leaves a large wake of astringency with a plastic boot. The finish dissipates extremely long in the same tone, vanishing completely at the end, and one might be convinced to go back to the nose and palate, even if the eccentric finish must follow after.

Evolution definitely demands attention with

its energetic profile, quite aptly named with an enthusiastic nod to the bourbon. That said, too much publicity in the spiciness and forceful finish tells only half the story, as if we are simply in the process of evolution, not yet fully specied in the form of an exquisite whisky.

DKC

GLENGLASSAUGH TORFA 50%

Whisky can be an unpredictable business, a fact that has closed the doors many distilleries and good whiskies from every distilling region in the world. The good news is that sometimes they get a second chance. That's what happened when whisky veteran Billy Walker revived the defunct Glenglassaugh Distillery in 2008, a comeback that eventually found its way into the hands of the BenRiach Whisky Company in 2013. Located on the Sandend Bay overlooking the Speyside's section of the North Sea, it reminisces on its history at home while exuding a nouveau riche attitude in America through importer Anchor Distilling Company.

Anchor Distilling's media release described this expression as "brooding and edgy," but I had a slightly different interpretation of the overall character of this whisky. The peated nature of my dram explains the name "Torfa," which refers to the Old Norse word for peat. That said, while it was a consistent backdrop to this whisky, in no way did it dominate the palate, and the entire character of the expression can be better described as a regal and stoically masculine, not very complex, but domineering in its execution. Here's why.

The color of my dram as presented in a Glencairn glass, neat, was a pleasant sandy yellow, mute in its pallor with a slight tint of green. Upon the slightly closed nose, a peaty tone laced together a briny fragrance, which held the scent together. The very first indication prickles the nose a bit with its cooling sensation like a sea-facing breeze, expressing the attitude of the whisky, but that reminder of a slightly stronger 50% ABV quickly falls away to a salty warmth embracing a shy molasses.

The simple nose is backed up by an extremely memorable palate. Unlike the nose, the brine becomes the steady (but not overpowering) backdrop as a viscous sweet coated my tongue and throat on the way down. This Persian-honey encapsulated a noble peat, dramatically sweet and saccharin. As the drink slides with no great hurry down the palate, it slightly saps the tongue of moisture with the heavy pull of nectar. The finish is heated, spicy on the tip of the tongue, hiding a shy pear at the very end. Every aspect of the palate is extremely assertive, including the finish, but it does not linger and simply vanishes with its smoky calling card for next time.

DKC

THE GLENLIVET XXV 43%

The XXV is a batch-produced whisky finished in individually selected ex-sherry butts.

The Oloroso-soaked oak imparts a nutty spiciness and enriches the flavor of the expression.

Each cask is individually monitored in the finishing process to ensure only the subtlest sherry tones are added to this intense, silky, and elegant whisky with intense and opulent character.

Color: Rich amber with ripe gold hues.

Nose: Dark chocolate with scents of dried sultanas.

Palate: Silky, sweet and caressing with cinnamon notes. Incredibly long, rich and balanced.

THE GLENLIVET NÀDURRA OLOROSO BATCH OL0614 60.7%

The Glenlivet Nàdurra line of single malt whisky is usually bottled at natural cask strength. The whisky is usually aged in bourbon casks. This special expression was aged in first-fill Oloroso sherry casks from the Jerez region of Spain.

Nose: Dried apples, dried figs, and dates come through. Dark chocolate with several whiffs of licorice, spices, and vanilla.

Palate: Blood orange marmalade, dates, and dark chocolate dominate with hints of spices. There is a hint of sea salt and licorice toward the end. Dry cocoa lingers, spices. Dark honey. Smooth finish.

GLENMORANGIE DISTILLERY

BY CARLO DEVITO

The Glenmorangie distillery is located in the Highlands region, in Tain, Ross-shire, Scotland. Glenmorangie possesses the tallest stills in Scotland. The earliest record of alcohol production at Morangie Farm is dated 1703, now the home of Glenmorangie Distillery. In the 1730s, a brewery was built on the site that shared the farm's water source, the Tarlogie Spring. A former distillery manager, William Matheson, acquired the farm in 1843 and converted the Morangie brewery to a distillery, equipped with two second-hand gin stills. He later renamed the distillery Glenmorangie. The Macdonald family bought the distillery in 1918.

The Macdonald family retained ownership for several generations, building the brand up, and eventually, in 2004, the company was sold to the high end French conglomerate Moët Hennessy Louis Vuitton (MHLV) for around £300 million.

With the change of ownership came a change in direction. The wood finish whiskies were given new names such as The Quinta Ruban, Nectar D'Or, and Lasanta. Glenmorangie has been the bestselling single malt in Scotland almost continuously since 1983. It manufactures approximately 10 million bottles per year. Glenmorangie has a 6% share of the single malt world market.

GLENMORANGIE NECTAR D'OR 46%

The Glenmorangie Nectar D'Or is matured in bourbon casks, and then finished in Sauternes barriques to help infuse the whisky with some flavors from that particular style of wine. Sauternes is a sweet French wine made from sémillon, sauvignon blanc, and muscadelle grapes affected by Botrytis cinerea (otherwise known as "noble rot"), which makes the grapes raisined and therefore concentrates the flavor. This particular whisky therefore has the foundation of vanilla, coconut, and raisin from the ex-bourbon American oak, but with overtones of sweet white wine that produce a nutty almond-like twist with hints of peach, orange zest, and dashes of spice.

Nose: Creamy barley is interlaced with crushed biscuit, shavings of orange zest, and crushed cinnamon with sharp whips of spice loaf softened by raisin-filled bread and butter pudding.

Palate: The soft barley emerges with buttery hot cross buns, waves of chocolate orange, wood vanilla and sweet winy notes, which emit Riesling with peach and almond overtones. The wood and sweet wine begin to

dominate at mid-palate with more spice and accompany an increasingly tannic and bitter finish. The chocolate darkens, balancing against the sweet wine notes as the wood remains dominant with hints of honeycomb, coconut, menthol, peppery papaya, and a resurgence of the cinnamon.

This is an interesting whisky because it has quite a strong Sauternes influence, which is counterbalanced by the bitter wood notes that gradually intensify toward the finish—powerful flavors that may possibly be amplified as a result of the signature Glenmorangie light style which quietly sit beneath the storm of character from the oak. It is therefore nicely balanced and certainly recommended for wine drinkers! The whisky itself is certainly more dominant on the nose, but on the palate, the wood and wine influence dominate at mid-palate and into the finish.

AC

GLENMORANGIE LASANTA 46%

Lasanta is Gaelic for warmth and passion. This complex single malt whisky has a complicated background. The whisky is first matured for ten years in American white oak ex-bourbon casks. The liquid is then transferred into Oloroso and PX Sherry casks from Jerez, Spain for another two years!

Nose: Honeycomb and caramel toffee come through as promised. Dark chocolate and raisin are also there, as well as hints of red grape varieties.

Palate: Hints of orange, mature ripe figs, honey, malt, as well as maple and toffee. Spices at the end devolve into a creamy finish that stays with you for a long, long time. Bitter orange marmalade, cocoa, and other spices and vanilla make it all worthwhile.

CD

GLENMORANGIE QUINTA RUBAN 46%

Glenmorangie Quinta Ruban spends ten years maturing in American white oak casks before being transferred into handpicked ruby port barrels (pipes) from the wine estates of Portugal. Non chill-filtered.

Nose: Tangerines and Seville oranges come through as promised as well ripe fig, dark chocolate, oak and walnut, pepper, nutmeg, and vanilla.

Palate: Seville oranges, figs, dark chocolate, caramel, and dark honey all come through. Dark honey, dark chocolate, and oranges linger for a while. Smooth.

CD

HIGHLAND PARK
DARK ORIGINS 46.8%

Dark Origins was inspired by Highland Park's infamous founder Magnus Eunson. This is a monster single malt. This 12 year old whisky is amped up by a huge dose of twice as many first-fill sherry casks than in their classic Highland Park 12 Year Old. This results in a darker whisky with lots of flavor.

Color: Mahogany.

Nose: Lots of spice. Big whiffs of dates, dark cherries, baked apple, nuts, spices, and a big shot of peat.

Palate: Dark cherries and dates come through along with dark chocolate and lots of spice, all complemented by a nice shot of farmyard campfire. Dark chocolate, figs, and smoke linger a long time.

CD

ARRAN PORT CASK FINISH 50%

NEAT

The color is a little purple or red apple skins mixed in with the malty gold. I find toasty, slightly nutty malt in the nose up front. Then grape juice and blackberry syrup sneaks up next. Some Chambord, ripe plums, and orange pixie stix. Then there's some toffee and a hint of apple juice. Behind all of this is a bit of an alcohol nip from the young spirit. The palate is not port heavy (which is a good thing for my palate). More grape skins than juice here. Rich caramel. Brown sugar syrup. Seawater, milk chocolate, and a moderate sweet level. It can be a little hot. It finishes with the caramel; I actually wrote "caramel" twice in my notes, so I guess there was a lot of it. Hints of the salty seawater, toffee, and milk chocolate. A sweet orange candy note. And plenty of spirity bite.

WITH A FEW DROPS OF WATER

The port reveals itself more in the nose with the water added. Some berries. Now there's some blueberry syrup mixed in with the blackberry. Orange peel. "Tiny grapes," not sure what I meant, but there it is. The malt is still quite present though, swimming amongst the port notes. More port in the palate too, reading as sour berries. There's a nice bitterness too. And again, the malt hangs on. The finish brightens up. Milk chocolate, salted caramels, sweet grapes, and sour grapes.

Without a doubt this feels young due to all of that alcohol heat. It doesn't take much water to calm the whisky down. But I'd love to see what it would be like with a couple more years in bourbon barrels. At 10-12 years old, this Arran Port Finish could be mighty.

MK

ARRAN SAUTERNES CASK FINISH 50%

NEAT

Its color is a dark gold. The nose is full of very rich toffees and caramels. Honey on baked peaches, roasted almonds, creme brûlée, and the current corn syrup version of Frosted Flakes. It actually reminds one of a wheated bourbon. It smells like it's going to be a sweetie. Indeed, the palate is sweeter than that of the Port finish. Honey and caramel mostly, along with some dark berries. The heat is

present but less so than in the Port. The berry note in the palate turns into jam in the finish, like boysenberry and grape jams (yeah, perhaps a little unusual for Sauternes). The sticky sweet fermented grapes and honey that follow are more Sauternes-like. Again, the heat.

WITH A FEW DROPS OF WATER

The nose is slightly plummy, but mostly it's fresh peaches and apricots. It's lightly floral, maybe a flowery honey. Perhaps a little sulfur too, but quietly, like a mild seasoning. The palate is almost all caramel sauce on vanilla ice cream. Now it reminds me of a hypersweet Speysider. Sweetness continues on into the finish with moments of sour and salt.

Like other Sauternes-finished whiskies I've tried, this is a dessert malt. While Glenmorangie's Nectar D'Or could be considered "richer," the Arran Sauternes Finish is actually less syrupy and less winey. As a result, it actually feels better arranged and more casual. But it's still quite sweet.

MK

MACHRIE MOOR 46%

At 20ppm, this is the peated Arran. Located on the west coast of the Isle of Arran is the famous Machrie Moor for which this whisky is named. It is home to Bronze Age stone circles and giant standing stones that tower over the barren, sprawling terrain. The most famous of the stone circles is known as Fingal's Cauldron Seat, where sits a stone with a carved hole. The legendary Scottish warrior Fingal was said to have tethered his favorite dog Bran to this stone. Machrie is also home to a well-known peat bog. This is aged in ex-Bourbon barrels.

Color: Honey and wheat.

Nose: Peaty. Smokey. Hints of fruit like pineapple. A hint of coconut comes through as promised. Apricot and touch of honey and vanilla.

Palate: Green apple and lemon cut across first. But the smoke and peat string it along until nuts, and honey and vanilla finish it. On the finish, honey, nuts, smoke, and vanilla all linger nicely.

CD

The Kilchoman distillery (pronounced Kil-ho-man) is a whisky distillery near the town of Kilchoman, on the western side of Islay, an island of the Inner Hebrides. It is the most westerly distillery in Scotland. It began production 2005 (they are the first new distillery in the region in more than 124 years). This is a farm-to-glass distillery. They use barley grown on site at Rockside Farm and malt at the distillery. Kilchoman is one of only six Scottish distilleries still doing traditional floor-maltings in Scotland.

KILCHOMAN SHERRY CASK RELEASE 45%

You know, on the day in the build-up to trying this dram, I felt rotten. Proper rotten. My brain felt like it was coming out of my ears. My stomach grumbled like some sort of injured bear. No idea why I felt like this. Maybe too much partying over the last few weeks. Whatever the reason, I was not a happy chappy. Then I got given a sample of this. A dram sorts out many things, and I actually did feel much better after tasting it (screw pain relievers!). This dram encouraged some musings on my part, which I will share just now (sharing is caring after all).

It is really bacon-y, oily, and a little fruity. And that got me to wondering. Where does this bacon/meatiness come from? I notice it all the time with Bruichladdich's Port Charlotte bottlings (which are my favorite Bruichladdichs). Almost like a BBQ sauce. Sweet, smokey and rich in combination. Is it where they cut the spirit? Is it the nature of young peaty spirit? Do many distilleries that use peat show this at a young age, which then disappears as it gets older?

This got me thinking about young peaty whiskies. The ones I have tried

have generally been very good, in comparison to young non-peated spirit. Is it just that the peat covers imperfections? Is young peated whisky just really good? Is young peated whisky better than its older counterparts? I haven't had enough tasting experience to say, so I would be very interested to hear from folks who have tried young Lagavulins, young Laphroaigs and young Bowmores. Get in touch!

CH

KILCHOMAN LOCH GORM 2015 46%

Kilchoman released a new range called Loch Gorm, named for the peaty loch at the end of the Kilchoman drive. Loch Gorm is the only fully ex-sherry cask matured release from Kilchoman. Loch Gorm periodically re-releases more mature versions of each bottling differentiated by distillation and bottling years printed on the label.

The first release of Loch Gorm was matured for more than five years in Oloroso sherry butts. The 2015 expression saw whisky that was five years old finished in Oloroso sherry hogsheads for six weeks to give added depth of color and character. It was a limited release of 10,000 bottles worldwide.

Master of Malt Anthony Wills said at the time of the release, "Previous sherry matured Kilchomans have been very popular with our customers and I'm sure this… shows wonderful balance between the peat smoke and spicy rich flavors typical of sherry cask maturation."

Nose: Blueberries, black berries, currants, figs, dates, cloves, campfire, bog.

Palate: Ripe dates, dark raspberry, dark cherries, ash, spices, peat in a campfire. Sweet dates and dark cherries accompanied by campfire.

CD

MADEIRA CASK MATURED 50%

Released in late 2015, the Madeira Cask Matured is the first bottling of such an expression. In 2010 approximately 20 Port, Madeira, and Sauterne casks were filled with new whisky. Rather than the industry norm of finishing the whisky in wine casks for just a few months, the whisky matured for the whole time in the same casks.

Nose: Dates, figs, dark cherries, spices, vanilla, and a nice nuttiness with a healthy dose of campfire.

Palate: Dark cherries, dark chocolate, nutty, a hint of sweetness and salt to offset healthy shot of smoky peat. Smoke dominates, but the final finish is sweet with firm fruit and rich flavors.

CD

LAGAVULIN DISTILLERY

LAGAVULIN DISTILLER'S EDITION
1995/2015 43%

Lagavulin Distillery is one of the oldest distilleries in Scotland and is located near Lagavulin Bay on the island of Islay. In 1816, John Johnson founded the first legal distillery on the site. Less than a year later Archibald Campbell opened a second distillery. The two were eventually purchased by Alexander Graham acquired both distilleries and eventually united them under the Lagavulin name. Lagavulin single malts are known for their intense smokiness. The peated barley used to create Lagavulin Single Malt has up to twenty times more exposure to peat smoke than typical Scotches.

Nose: Earl Grey tea, wood, and peaty smoke dominate. Hints of vanilla and sweetness fight their way through.

Palate: Earl Grey comes through as promised. Caramel and dark fruits also come forward. Salty notes and big peaty smoke dominate. Salted caramel comes through at the end and mellows out the smoke. Very complex. Lots of layers.

CD

LAPHROAIG DISTILLERY

LAPHROAIG TRIPLE WOOD 48%

Laphroaig distillery is an Islay distillery at the head of Loch Laphroaig on the south coast of the Isle of Islay. They have been distilling for more than 200 years, as Donald and Alexander Johnston founded the Laphroaig distillery in 1815.

The non-chill filtered whisky in Laphroaig Triple Wood has experienced a triple maturation in three types of cask. The first maturation is in American oak, ex-bourbon barrels. The liquid, after the first aging period, is then transferred into small nineteenth century-style quarter casks for a second maturation. The final maturation or finishing is in large Oloroso sherry casks.

NEAT
Color: Gold.

Nose: Dates, raisins, and apricots all come through as promised, along with honey, nuts, and a big dollop of smoky peat.

Palate: Smoky peat belies push across the palate, but soon fruits like plum, fig, dates, nuts, and vanilla start to come forth. The sherry begins to show beautifully. A balanced whisky with smoky peat that dissolves into sweet smooth caramel and cream.

WATER
Palate: A sprinkle of water brings out the peat in this dram. Some citrus notes come through. All the other flavors are then muted, but the ashy, campfire of peat refuses to fade. The peat is bigger, smokier, and there is a tang to the dram but the creamy finish remains.

GORDON & MACPHAIL PRIVATE COLLECTION SAUTERNES WOOD FINISH
45%

This bottling is an example of, for me, what is great about independent bottlers like Gordon & Macphail. If they decide to take a cask that they own of Wick's finest maritime malt, and finish it in Sauternes casks, then they can just go ahead and do it. Independent bottlers can experiment with different casks and just sell them as one-offs. They provide a bit of intrigue and variety.

Now even though I was told this bottling was awesome by my friend, I was a bit apprehensive. My lovely Pulteney finished in casks that can be a bit hit or miss for whisky. Let's see what it's like:

Nose: Buttery, apricot, melon, raisins, and rum raisin. With a bit more time in the glass; blackcurrant, white chocolate, maltesers, Crunchy Nut, and honeycomb. I spent so long nosing it, my mate was already on his second glass. It's a really nice, balanced nose.

Palate: Apricot, and a spicy, charred oak spiciness on first taste. Followed by lime, lemon, gooseberry, grapefruit. The finish has white grape, kiwi, and more of a blackcurrant fruit syrup thing going on.

A lovely dram. If you can't get hold of it, buy another weird independent bottling. Maybe even on auction.

CH

OLD PULTENEY NAVIGATOR 46%

Old Pulteney entered a yacht in the Clipper Round the World Race. The distillery's decision to sponsor a yacht in the Clipper Race was rooted in the whisky's strong maritime heritage and long-standing involvement with sailing. However, there was a certain, very special cargo on board: the first case of a brand-new limited edition of Old Pulteney Navigator. The whisky was aged in ex-bourbon barrels and old sherry casks.

Color: Golden honey.

Nose: Dried apples, orange zest, honey with hints of cocoa and vanilla. Nice spice.

Palate: Honey, oranges, and apples all come through. Kind of like a bitter orange marmalade. A nice spiciness comes through with a little blast of sea salt to keep the sweet from overpowering the flavor. Fantastic: Briny quality saves this from being a lollipop. Very nicely balanced. A smooth, languid finish. Lovely.

PORT ELLEN ELEMENTS OF ISLAY PE5 57.9%

Port Ellen closed in 1983, and since then its whisky has been highly sought after as it becomes rarer with the passage of time. Located on the Isle of Islay, Port Ellen is known for producing whisky with a distinctive smoky peat flavor that is characteristic of whisky from the island.

The Elements of Islay Pe5 is part of the "Elements of Islay" range, which offers bottlings of whisky from Islay distilleries each of which have their own periodic table like name. "Pe" is for Port Ellen, and Pe5 signifies that this is the fifth release. Fitting, because whisky is very much influenced by the phenolic compounds and chemistry of oak as it interacts with the new spirit and the previous contents of the cask (sherry, bourbon, etc.).

Elements of Islay Pe5 is taken from whisky that has been aged in ex-sherry casks, and the interaction between the sweet sherry and peat has the potential to be quite magical. The magic does not happen automatically though, because it all depends on how the oak and sherry impart their character into the whisky and this is different for every cask. This is why I think some luck is also needed, though the skill of the distillers, quality of the casks, and environment in which the casks are placed are also very important.

In relation to this bottling of Port Ellen, everything seems to have fallen into place including the chemistry between the oak, sherry, peat, and spirit.

Within the smoldering embers burning brightly with peat and the earthy saltiness of the sea sits an "X-factor"; the way the sparks of sherry sweetness interact with the dense peat and oak is almost magical. It releases wonderfully complex shades of peat, sweetness, and oak-themed character that, when working together, are an almost perfect symphony.

Nose: Powerful in the glass, this work of art radiates strong peat without piercing the nostrils as sweet sherry shines like a lighthouse in a smoky storm. The oak plays a perfect role in moderating the peat and sherry, and zesty, citrus bitterness wafts up to complete the balancing act. Sweet fig, raisin, and prune then shimmer as a gust of sea breeze brings sea salt and the earthiness of the beach. After ten or so minutes, the character in this whisky becomes more complex. The sherry sweetness develops a distinct candy/lolly aroma, as glazed cherries and candied apple weave around dark chocolate and fudge; much like a dense dark Black Forest mousse cake. Then the smell of cigars is noticeable as a trip down memory lane reveals a

childhood favorite raspberry confectionery. This whisky is powerful and elegant, assertive and explosive with a heavenly balance. On a final nosing of this whisky, the character continued to develop as the fudge has notes of mint and peppermint.

Palate: On the palate a powerful explosion of peat comes with brilliant force. The peat is varied, with notes of dry grass developing into lush green and mossy earthiness. The wonderful sweetness then glows brightly, bringing the earthiness and sea salt of the beach with cigar ash and smoky dry wood. That sweetness is spectacu-lar, with particularly dense sherry radiating with the theme of red confectionery identified on the nose. The character on the nose moved to the palate seamlessly, though the surge of peat was more dominant as it delivered burnt wood and shades of vegetation. Heavenly and seemingly endless, the linger of sweet sherry beams through the shades of peat as gusts of soft berries and a sea breeze gently linger on the base of the tongue. Toward the end the magic act then bursts into a plume of dry woody smoke and gradually fades.

AC

TALISKER STORM 45.8%

New whisky from Talisker! Strength upped, mixture of younger and older whisky, interesting use of oaks (de-char/re-char). It's exciting stuff.

The instant fear, when hearing that Talisker Storm was coming out, was that it was going to replace the 10. Now while I admit, I am not the biggest fan of the 10, I know some diehard Talisker fans who would rampage (or at least complain loudly), if the 10 was to disappear. Fear not, Talisker 10 Year Old is not disappearing. It is just being joined by Storm (a Talisker with a bit more guts).

Seeing these releases reminded me of what I said about Macallan Gold. If you are going to release new, non-age-statement whisky, make it interesting and challenging. Up the strength, use different casks, come at it from an angle. I think it's great news that Talisker is releasing new drams to keep their audience interested. With this younger, smokier, gutsier feel, Storm reminds me of the 8 Year Old they used to bottle and I am definitely looking forward to the next new edition.

I have already suggested that I like the Talisker Storm, but how much do I like it?

Nose: Nice notes of berries, ginger, vanilla, and pear, all clustered around the smoke. A nice, simple clean smoke, that isn't overpowered at 45.8%.

Palate: Salty and a nice level of peat. Not too hot. Nice burst of beach bonfire, peppery notes, and seafood notes. Tiny notes of dark chocolate and charcoal.

It's got guts, but it is still easy drinking. I like it more than the 10, as I think the 10 can be too peppery for me at times. The flavors in this Talisker are more appealing to me.

I was lucky enough to taste Talisker Storm with oysters. I had never had an oyster before. Quite an experience. Like being hit in the face with a bucket of salty water (in a good way), with a rich, whisky finish. Oysters bring the richness out in the whisky. It was an excellent first experience with oysters and I thought it really worked. I would recommend it.

CH

TAMDHU DISTILLERY

TAMDHU 10 YEAR OLD 40%

Tamdhu was established in 1897 and it produced whisky for about 113 years, and then it ceased production and fell silent. Ian Macleod distillers then acquired the distillery and picked up the baton in 2012, and it has decided to re-introduce Tamdhu into the market with the release of the Tamdhu 10 Year Old.

On the nose, caramel and vanilla chocolate fudge sit beneath honey, plump sultanas, honey nut crunch, sliced green apples, golden honey, and dried autumn leaves, as jelly beans (red, green, black, and white in particular) cut through the underlying malt with hints of anise, mint leaves and freshly waterproofed suede and treated new leather—it reminds me very much of a red leather handbag full of jelly beans, with notes of sugary anise, red berry, coconut, pear, and mint accompanied by a "new car smell." On the palate, the whisky is immediately sweet, with brown pear nectar developing with dark chocolate, cherries and toasted coconut, cinnamon, dried paw paw and honey drizzled over toasted muesli as a drying vegetal and nutty bite is softened by layers of caramel and toffee apple. The finish presents with sugar dusted lemon rind and tropical fruit in syrup, as the sherry wood lingers on the tip of the tongue with notes of golden honey and toffee.

Overall, Tamdu 10 Year Old is a delicious sherry matured malt whisky that I have found far too easy to drink. It might take some seriously strict self-discipline to stop at one dram, especially where this whisky is paired with a 70% cocoa dark chocolate. On its own Tamdhu 10 Year Old is a delicious malt, but when paired with 70% cocoa dark chocolate the sherry wood influence in the whisky really comes to life on the palate. Lucky I went for an extra-long swim before, because without much thought I've just gleefully wolfed down half a block of Lindt dark chocolate and four drams of Tamdhu 10 Year Old. This is the life.

AC

TOMATIN DISTILLERY

In 1897 at the height of the Victorian whisky boom, John MacDougall, John MacLeish and Alexander Allan, and a few other investors, opened a distillery, naming it The Tomatin Spey District Distillery Ltd. It was located on a site that was rumored to have been distilling spirits for many years, some rumors placing illicit production as far back as the 1400s. The name "Tomatin" translates roughly to "Hill of the

TOMATIN
EST? 1897
SINGLE MALT
HIGHLAND SCOTCH WHISKY

Juniper Bush." Illegal distillers often used to burn juniper bushes to mask the other smells that were the byproduct of the process to remain secret. "The Old Laird's House," which remains on the property, was a popular stopping point for cattlemen driving livestock from the north of Scotland to the city markets. It was believed that they stopped here to fill their jugs and flasks with the illicit distilled product.

TOMATIN 14 YEAR OLD PORT WOOD FINISH 46%

Somewhat ashamedly, I spent a week in Portugal and did not have a single drop of port. Fail. I had plenty of beer (Superbock and Sagres), tried many non-fortified wines (red, white, and

the unbelievably drinkable Vinho Verde), and even drank the morello cherry brandy Ginjinha from a tasty chocolate shot glass. Yet, not a smidgen of port. Not much of a drinks writer, eh? Oh well, at least I had some Tomatin samples waiting at home and they just happen to be the new 14 year old Tomatin Port Wood Finish and the Tomatin 1988 which is vatted from a combination of ex-Bourbon and ex-port casks. Basically the same thing as drinking port in Lisbon, yeah?

These two Tomatin releases are both part of the new Tomatin core range. They join the Legacy, the 12 year old, the Oloroso 18 year old and their new lightly peated Cù Bòcan (in my mind it sounds like Hadouken! of Street Fighter fame... probably wrong). Ex-Port cask finish whiskies are usually awesome and, as I am sure you have heard me say before, I normally love them. Hence why my port-less trip to Portugal is such a failure. But hey-ho! I now have the Tomatin Ex-Port bros. to keep me company, and here is what I thought of Tomatin 14 Year old Port Wood Finish 46%:

Nose: Not a great start. A little hint of paint at first but moves into an over-sweet artificial butterscotch. Does start to soften up though and the sweetness becomes more like a rich honey with dried apricots. Develops into baked cheesecake and some livelier red berry notes.

Palate: Again it has a strange start, a little metallic, and quite astringent. However, some syrupy fruits start to come through. Mango and peach in syrup at first and then some yogurt-coated apricot. A very enjoyable, chewy, dried mango note is predominant with a nice vanilla sponge background. That lovely, chewy mango note lingers and complements the vanilla notes, which have grown very well. Persevere with this, a slow start but a lovely end.

The Tomatin 14 Year Old Port Wood Cask is not that impressive at the start but grows into a good whisky. It also grows into an interesting whisky. Well-balanced, nice fruits, good vanilla but for me it is just making up for the initial unpleasant notes. Not a bad price in my opinion but I would recommend trying a dram in a bar first before buying a bottle.

GG

TOMATIN 1988 VINTAGE 46%

Nose: Much better straight from the start. Plenty of lovely stewed fruits. Soft berries, hot jam doughnuts, and some fresh ground pepper. Hints of stewed orange and peppermint.

Palate: Smooth and sweet with a gamey tinge to start. The sweetness pushes through with a buttery Caramac note, popping candy, and vanilla sponge. Then comes the red berries (very jammy) and some fresh plum. The mint is there again and fits in with the ever-present oak and pepper side notes. Great intensity, slightly spicy and peppery. Lots of depth.

Very interesting addition to the Tomatin core range. The Tomatin 1988 Vintage is an excellent whisky. A

good £50 cheaper than the old 30 year old (also very good), which I believe it has replaced, and so it is pretty decent value. If you want a great whisky, and you can afford it, I definitely recommend trying it! With these ex-Port styled additions, the Tomatin core range is shaping up to be a pretty strong team.

GG

CÙ BÒCAN 1989 53.2%

When I was but a growing child, anything even remotely within the world of the supernatural used to turn me into a jabbering, quivering wreck.

Every single time my parents turned off the bedroom light, in the hope I'd drift off into the soft embrace of a candy-coated dreamland, I would pull my covers over my neck and keep watch for the possible (and in my mind probable) onslaught of witches, vampires and goblins that had spent all the daylight hours in waiting.

You may think I'm being overly dramatic but I had more cause to be terrified than most nippers as I grew up on a street named Witchwood Crescent. Witchwood! As in a wood that is teeming full of witches.

Just think about that. It's a terrifying idea as a child. The town planner that named the street must have known something that other people didn't or was just plain despicable. I mean, if you wanted to give a kid nightmares that bad, you may as well have just have the Child Catcher from Chitty Chitty Bang Bang as the caretaker of the local primary school.

I spent my nights imagining the terrible forms the ghouls would take as they snuck into my room under the cover of darkness, and I've never forgotten it.

Fortunately we didn't stay in Witchwood Crescent too long. We soon moved to Kingsmuir Crescent, an altogether more regal and less distressingly named street. Although my next bedroom was painted entirely blood red so that didn't exactly help with my already shaken frame of mind.

I mention my past terrors because I can sympathize with anyone who has grown up in the Highland village of Tomatin where it is said that the legendary Cù Bòcan stalks their woods. A ghostly specter resembling a massive wolf with smoke whisping out of its nostrils, the Cù Bòcan wanders the woods close to the village, striking fear into even the bravest of hearts. I had it easy living in Witchwood Crescent. At least witches melt when you throw water on them. Or so the movies tell me.

As many of you may be aware, Tomatin distillery has embraced the legend of the Cù Bòcan and even lent the name to a new expression of their whisky—one with a big smoky flavor.

Following the success of that we find a limited edition vintage release from 1989 bearing the same name and with an addition to the story—and it is an addition that I take with a substantial pinch of salt.

It pains me to say but one of the things that has developed in me over those years since I hid under the covers is a mild case of cynicism. Vampires, werewolves and witches are now consigned to fairy tale and I can't but help find the story of the 1989 Cù Bòcan a little bit of the same.

It claims that an "accidental" batch of peaty whisky was made and has been slumbering in their warehouse ever since. It's a nice thought... but I just can't buy it.

I'm in no way writing off this whisky—let's set that right straight away. The close to 28 years I have had

walking the plains of this Earth have just made me a tad skeptical.

I'll happily embrace the idea of a ghost dog roaming the woods of Tomatin but I find it hard to believe a peated batch of barley managed to get past a mash-man, wash-man, still-man, and distillery manager in order to get to cask and then those same casks being allowed to mature for close to 23 years without being sold or bottled. It's too long a process for this to be an accident. I might be wrong (and usually am) but my gut just tells me different.

So, anyway, the Cù Bòcan 1989. It is vatted from only three casks and is pretty darn limited so it might not be too easy to get a hold of.

Nose: It's initially sweet, much sweeter than I anticipated it was going to be. Pear juice (perry?) and heather come whisping on through. The smokiness reminds me of the mossy campfires that we would make back home in my youth. The alcohol certainly grabs you. You can tell it's at full cask strength. There is a little bit of melon coming through as well as vanilla and cream.

Palate: It's so much fruitier than I ever would have thought. Fresh fruit too—peaches, pineapple and apricots. The hefty smoke then sneaks to the forefront and clobbers everything else into submission. If you're a fan of peat and you're looking to treat yourself, get one of these now! It's lingering but subtle. Like a good Terrence Malick film.

A very good whisky. A tad pricey but certainly not unfair in today's market. I'd try to acquire a bottle myself but then I would have to face my biggest fear since I've become a fully-fledged adult: My bank manager.

I'm not quite ready for that. In fact I think I'll just go hide under the covers for a minute or two.

JT

TOMATIN CUATRO SERIES

BY CARLO DEVITO

In September of 2014, Tomatin released its Cuatro Series. The word "Cuatro" is the Spanish word for "four." The concept was to highlight four unique limited edition expressions of Tomatin Highland single malt Scotch whisky. All four whiskies began the same way. All of the whisky was matured for nine years in traditional American oak casks. Then each was finished in different types of Spanish sherry casks, resulting in four connected, but different expressions: Fino, Manzanilla, Oloroso, and Pedro Ximenez.

TOMATIN FINO 46%

Aged in ex-Bourbon barrels and finished in Fino sherry casks.

Nose: Very fruit forward with citrus burst of orange and lime zest. Also some stone fruit with green apple and pears. A nice note of nuttiness tooo.

Palate: The citrus and stone fruits come through as promised. Bitterness balances with light creaminess. Light, with great balance. Smooth, dry finish.

TOMATIN MANZANILLA 46%

Aged in ex-Bourbon barrels and finished in Manzanilla sherry casks.

Nose: Dates and figs come across immediately with a creamy texture. A hint of citrus. There is almost the smell of bread or pastry.

Palate: Pears and apples mix with dates, and a hint of citrus. There's almost a slightly briny thing going on. Nice spice at the end. A little heavier than the Fino and slightly sweeter.

TOMATIN OLOROSO 46%

Aged in ex-Bourbon barrels and finished in Oloroso sherry casks.

Nose: A big chewy mouth full of fruitcake—candied fruits, bread, brown sugar, caramel, cocoa, and bits of orange and lemon zest. Slight smokiness.

Palate: Fruitcake comes through as marmalade and pastry, with subtle hints of nuts, cocoa, and caramel. Big and chewy, with slightly sweet finish. But just enough bitterness to keep it honest. Very nice!

TOMATIN PEDRO XIMENEZ 46%

Aged in ex-Bourbon barrels and finished in Pedro Ximenez sherry casks.

Nose: Dates, prunes, dried apricots, honey, almonds, and crème brûlée.

Palate: A big mouthful of semi-sweet orange marmalade, with hints of black tea, ginger, and licorice. Sweet marmalade with ginger fills the mouth and lingers for a long time.

WEMYSS SIZZLING CHARCOAL (BUNNAHABHAIN 1997) SINGLE CASK 46%

My first crack at the 2016 Single Cask line from Wemyss Malts is a doozy: a Bunnahabhain from a hogshead, distilled in 1997 (bottled 2015). For those of you not hip to the Scotch talk, a hogshead is the origin point for the 53-gallon American standardized bourbon barrel. Hogsheads are slightly larger, and these days it is not uncommon to use American bourbon barrel staves and re-cooper them into hogsheads, creating bigger ex-bourbon barrels.

This particular hogshead yielded 216 bottles of Islay whisky, bottled at the customary 46% ABV. Wemyss named it Sizzling Charcoal, and for good reason.

This whisky has two flavorful and particularly well-balanced sides. The "sizzle" comes from the spicy character, and the "charcoal" from the Islay smokiness. However, you would get none of that to just look at the whisky in the glass. The coloring is of a yellow so pale as to be very nearly clear. There is nothing in the appearance to suggest that this is a 18 year old single malt or that it is so flavorful.

The nose is more in tune with what awaits in the glass: predominately oily and ashy, with notes of ginger cookie spices. The flavor is charred and woody, with an oily feel to it, very much like a resiny spin on charcoal. Yet in almost equal measure, it is also honeyed and seasoned with spices like nutmeg, cinnamon, and ginger. A dash of pepper rounds the picture, and the balance, out nicely. The finish packs just as much currency, with its ashy, spicy aftertaste and long, warm conclusion.

Sizzling Charcoal is brimming with character, yet also very approachable and an easy sipper.

RT

WEMYSS LEMON ZEST
(AUCHENTOSHAN)
SINGLE CASK 46%

Lemon Zest is another of Wemyss' single cask bottlings. Although part of the first single cask batch of 2014, the run was actually bottled in 2013, so the 1998 distillation date makes this Auchentoshan whisky a Lowland, ex-bourbon barrel-aged 15 year old. As is the norm for Wemyss single casks, the whisky was bottled at 46% ABV. A limited edition, Lemon Zest came out as a 342 bottle run.

In the glass, Lemon Zest has a very Scotchy pale straw coloring. The nose is restrained but distinctly akin to a lemon meringue pie, what with the core citrus and cake spice notes. Add in a little toffee and a slight woodiness and you have what makes for a low-key, moderately complex scent.

The flavor is front-loaded with pepper and wood, and as that fades the honeyed lemon flavor comes up and takes over. Despite having a full-bodied mouthfeel, the whisky retains the fundamentally understated nature of the nose. The finish starts with a peppery afterglow, and as it winds down, a tobacco aftertaste remains.

RT

SOUTH AFRICA

BY CARLO DEVITO

There is no question that South Africa has firmly established itself as one of the major new world wine regions in the industry. South Africa has produced an impressive line-up of white wines made from Chenin Blanc and Chardonnay, and reds such as Pinotage, Shiraz, Cabernet Sauvignon, Merlot, Petit Verdot, and Tannat. Whiskey is also a popular drink in South Africa. And now, in the new world of craft distilling, there is a small but quality-focused industry budding on this tip of the African continent. Big strides from small producers are being made. From blends to single malts, South African distillers are studying and experimenting. And they are doing a pretty decent job! More to come from this small corner of the world! Industry insiders point to their impressive strides in the wine industry and think South Africa is a region, long-term, to watch.

DRAYMAN'S DISTILLERY

BY MARC PENDLEBURY

Drayman's distillery started off as many of its Scots counterparts did: as a brewery. This craft brewery has been making quality German-style beers since 1997, but in 2006 the master brewer, owner, and manager of Drayman's, Moritz Kallmeyer, followed another passion of his by donning a master distiller's cap and began plying the South African angels with their due share. After discovering Drayman's provides tours to the public, I arranged for the whisky club members and some interested friends to tour the distillery.

A tour of Drayman's features more as a-day-in-the-life-of-a-distiller than what you may expect from a traditional distillery tour. For those brave enough to bear the early mornings,

we joined Moritz at 5:30 a.m. in the morning to begin the day mashing proudly South African-grown barley that he mills himself. For those more sensible, distillery visitors who joined up with the dreary-eyed at 9 a.m. arrived just in time to catch the first droplets of new-make trickling off Moritz's homemade still.

The brewery-come-distillery at first appears somewhat haphazard. Moritz's undertaking has clearly outgrown his expectations more than once, with the building visibly having multiple additions bolted on as demand, and ambition, grew. Walking through the premises, which is small by any distillery's measure, has a sort of junkyard feel to it (apart from the fact that every item is spotless). Multiple stainless steel tanks, washbacks, mash tuns, heat exchangers, control valves, and all the interconnecting pipes and tubing lies naked and exposed like Leonardo's dissected cadavers. Although some may not find the scene pretty, those who find beauty in functionality and authenticity will appreciate what Moritz has created—and in most instances what he has created with his own hands.

It would be easy to label the distillery's operation simple, due to its small size. The truth is it's as complex as any distillery you'll find in Scotland, perhaps even more so due to the complete lack of automation; every temperature reading, valve, knob and lever acquiring adjusting gets the full attention of Moritz and his small team of two.

Drayman's has two whiskies available: a blended Solera whisky that is composed of his single malt, single malt Scotch, and blended Scotch, vatted together using an authentic solera system; and his recently released Highveld Single Malt. In addition, he produces a wide range and variety of beer, schnapps, liqueurs, and even some fiery mampoer/witblits (the SA equivalent of moonshine).

The tour includes one 75cl bottle of Drayman's Solera Whisky, as much whisky and beer as you can drink while touring, German sausages for lunch, and a branded nosing glass, all for the meager price of R230 (the price at the time of my visit). For me, however, and I suspect for most visitors, the real value is not material (although complementary whisky is usually a sure winner) but is rather the fantastic opportunity to see a craft working distillery in action with narration from the man who created it. No question, no matter how complex or intricate, is not promptly and precisely answered.

Whether you've toured other distilleries or not, if you're in the Johannesburg-Pretoria vicinity, as a resident or traveler, and vaguely interested in whisky, do the right thing and support a man who's realizing his dreams.

DRAYMAN'S HIGHVELD SINGLE MALT WHISKY 43%

Drayman's is the only single malt whisky distilled by Moritz Kallmeyer in 2006. It was the first single malt ever to be made on the South African Highveld. Drayman's Highveld was first released in 2010 in a batch of 1,000 bottles.

The nose is sweet cereal, with raisins, spice, honey, peaches, and apricot. Like a peach/apricot party. Sexy spices also linger in the air. Hints of vanilla and ginger. The palate puts marmalade, and apricot jam up front, with vanilla and caramel not far behind. Hints of cocoa in the background. This dram has a long finish with the marmalade hanging on with hints of oak and spice. Lovely.

THE JAMES SEDGWICK DISTILLERY

BY DAVE WORTHINGTON

The James Sedgwick Distillery has a long history in South Africa, being founded in 1886 when Captain James Sedgwick, captain of the clipper *Undine*, purchased the distillery that would go on to become the oldest on the African continent. It's set in the picturesque region of Wellington, about 45 minutes' drive from Cape Town, best known for the spectacular Bainskloof Pass, and an economy centered on agriculture such as wine, table grapes, deciduous fruit, and a brandy industry. The Distell Group Ltd now owns the James Sedgwick Distillery after the merger between Stellenbosch Farmer's Winery and Distillers Corporation in 2000. The company produces a huge range of wines and spirits including the popular cream liqueur Amarula Cream.

The whisky distillery produces both malt and grain whiskies on the same site and handles the entire whisky-making process—from mill-ing the raw ingredients through to maturation and blending. Our latest copy of *The Malt Whisky Yearbook* informs us that the distillery has undergone major expansion recently and is now equipped with one still with two columns for their grain whisky production, two pot stills for their malt whisky production, two mash tuns, and twenty-three stainless steel washbacks.

Malt whisky is only produced during the winter months, just two months of the year, in July and August. Fermentation is approximately 72 hours yielding a wash for distilling in the copper pot stills of approximately 9% ABV. Grain whisky is produced for nine months (one month of the year is for annual maintenance) and the wash is continuously fed into the column still, which results in a lightly flavored spirit of 94.3% ABV, which is reduced to around the industry standard of 65% before being filled into oak casks.

THREE SHIPS WHISKY CASK STRENGTH 10 YEAR OLD 46.4%

With more than 150,000 casks of whisky in maturation at any given time, the James Sedgwick Distillery has been the home of South African whisky since 1990, but the Three Ships story starts some thirteen years earlier.

The Three Ships brand of South Africa was launched in 1977, the brainchild of Irish marketing guru

Francis Naughton. It couldn't be called a whisky at that time as the initial product was a blend of South African-grain spirit and Scotch malt whisky, but in 1981, when the South African grain had been matured for three years, Three Ships Whisky was born. It was certainly a bold and pioneering move to create a South African whisky to compete against the iconic Scotch whisky blends that were available at that time, especially when the spirit of choice was still brandy.

We first met their sixth and current Distillery Manager Andy Watts at Whisky Live London a couple of years ago and we've kept in touch via Twitter and email ever since. We bumped into him again at this year's show and asked him how he came to be involved with Three Ships Whisky, as well as why we weren't able to find it in the UK yet.

Andy's involvement started when he was appointed as the Spirits Blending Manager for the Stellenbosch Farmers Winery (SFW). At that time, they were still receiving Scotch Malt Whisky in bulk and blending it with their own grain whisky distilled at the Robertson & Buxton (R&B) distillery.

A technical relationship had been established with Morrison Bowmore Distillers, and Andy volunteered to be sent to their distilleries to learn from them, with the aim of improving the quality of South African whisky going forward. Andy was promptly packed off to Scotland and spent the next four years regularly traveling back and forth with extended experience working at all three of their distilleries—Auchentoshan, Glen Garioch,

and Islay's Bowmore, which was then under the leadership of now legendary Jim McEwan.

Following a trip to Scotland in 1989, Andy was tasked with closing down operations at the R&B Distillery in Stellenbosch and moving the business across to the James Sedgwick Distillery, which up until then had been a brandy distillery. By 1991 the transfer was complete and Andy was given the manager's role at the James Sedgwick Distillery, holding total responsibility for all whisky-related activity, excluding bottling.

It wasn't an easy start though: Andy had inherited stocks of both South African malt and grain, which were a bit hit and miss. There had been no "wood policy" back then, and Andy had been given all of the casks nobody else wanted. He had red wine casks, brandy barrels, and some very old American whiskey barrels—blending was still a major challenge! However, Andy remained positive and began a program of change, making small enhancements to their processes and equipment, and the quality of the new make spirit started improving.

During Andy's last spell with Morrison Bowmore, he spent time on Islay and fell in love with the island, the people, and their whiskies, and returned to South Africa wanting to make his own peat blend. Allowing some South African grain whisky to age a further two years, and purchasing 5 year old Bowmore malt whiskies in bulk, he created the Three Ships 5 Year Old Premium Select. However, when Suntory took over Morrison Bowmore in 1994, the bulk purchases

were no longer an option and Andy had to find replacement components in order to continue the range.

Andy had already set up their own malt program, importing British barley each year, peated to his specifications for the different styles of malt whisky produced. Over the years he has been slowly replacing the Scottish malt content of the blends with South African malt whisky, but there still is a slight Scottish component to both the Select and 5 Year Old Premium Select—probably a marketing decision with a nod to the history of the brand.

When Distell was formed following the merger, quality improved significantly, a wood procurement policy was put in place, controls on fermentation were completely revamped (a necessity due to their high ambient temperatures), and in 2009, completely revamped and installed new equipment throughout the distillery was the next step in their young whisky-making history. It is no coincidence that since the mid-2000s and after all of the major improvements had started making their impact on the maturing spirit that the international awards started to come.

Although the malted barley is imported, it is where the product is distilled and matured that gives it its origin, and Andy tells us that they have some amazing work in the maturation warehouses just waiting for the chance to be released to the market. The Three Ships Single Malt, Bourbon Cask Finish, and Bain's Cape Mountain Whisky are 100% South African. All of the new releases going forward will also be 100% South African.

Andy is now into·his 24th year in charge of the distillery and blending, and says that it's been an amazing journey with no two years being the same. While Andy is in the twilight of his career, South African whisky is only at the dawn of theirs.

South Africa's first single malt whisky was another pioneering first for The James Sedgwick Distillery. First launched in 2003 as a limited release, it wasn't until autumn 2010 that the next batch was released. It sold out quickly and a further 8,000 bottles were released in October 2011, and a fourth batch followed in December 2012. These three releases commemorated the pioneering voyages of Bartholomeu Diaz, Vasco da Gama, and Jan van Riebeeck in a special collectors' series.

At Whisky Live London, Andy slipped us a sample of the next release of their limited edition 10 Year Old. The success of the first release took the distillery by complete surprise and there was no stock for single malt bottlings as the production all went into their blends. It wasn't until 2005 that planning for future releases was started and this should be the first release from this forethought.

The "'Angels Share'" in South Africa is around 4% to 5% a year, which is over double that of Scottish single malts. At 5% loss after 10 years, 40% of the original spirit laid down has been lost to the Angels, but due to the warm dry South African climate, the Angels sip more water than alcohol, and the alcohol content actually increases over the period. This cask sample was at a whopping 66.4% abv ABV but the final release will be a quirky 46.4%.

With such a high loss through evaporation, the casks are re-vatted after a period of time under Customs and excise supervision.

SO WHAT DID WE THINK?

Kat says: Because of the very high ABV, I've had to add a good slug of water to this dram. The others have had no water added.

Nose: Initially there are lots of fresh apples and pears on the nose. Next darker notes start to come through. Notes of damp wood, black and white pepper also present similar to the other drams but a lot spicier. Fresh chili heat is there too, with the fruitiness it's reminiscent of habanero chilies, however might not be detectable depending on how much water you add. Lastly towards the end, there are dry straw notes, citrus zest, cinnamon, and cloves.

Taste: Completely different beast to the nose. It's full-on high-impact flavors. It begins with some sweetness—dark honey, chili spice, as well as those cinnamon and clove notes (leaning more on the clove end for me). Next, toasted oak/wood notes then starts to come through, turning into a mahogany note, with some bitter dark chocolate and dark dried fruits—dates and prunes. Similar to the drams before, the dram doesn't feel heavy even though there are plenty of richer darker notes, and all of the flavors are still fairly balanced after aging.

Finish: Toasted oak/mahogany notes, dark chocolate, cloves and cinnamon, and dark fruit notes linger.

Dave says: Initial nosing revealed a citrus burst with lime tangerine and sherbet lemons. With water creamy vanilla notes develop.

This was quite challenging to sip at cask strength but very enjoyable with water added. I probably took it to below 50% and closer to its final bottling strength, and it came across as a perfect summer dram, very refreshing! This has a long lingering finish with sweetened limes.

DW & KP

SPAIN

BY CARLO DEVITO

When most people think of Spain, they immediately think of wine. Their wine growing regions are legendary and with good reason. However, Spain has also been known for its diversity and quality of spirits and liquors. Spain produces some of the best and most unique brandy, rum, and gin in the world.

When the Moors invaded Spain many, many years ago, they brought various and new innovations in distilling with them, like copper stills called alambiques. While the Moors primarily distilled Spanish wines for medicines and perfumes (due to their religious practices), over the centuries, a whole slew of Spanish spirits were born.

Anís, a spirit made from distilling aniseed, is a Spanish staple. The area surrounding Jerez produced the best sherry in the world, and the famous Brandy de Jerez soon followed. There is also the highly sought-after Gin de Menorca, which was inspired by the British. Brandy from wine, and Licor de Orujo which is distilled spirits made from grape skins. And of course, there is the famous Ron Montero, the coveted rum crafted in Granada.

So there was a rich tradition of distilling in Spain when the Destilerías y Crianza del Whisky S.A. (DYC) was originally established in 1958 to make whisky. By 1963, the first Spanish whisky was released, a popular and inexpensive brand distinctively produced for the domestic market. Today, DYC is a subsidiary of Beam Suntory, and produces high quality products for domestic consumption as well as for export.

DESTILERIAS Y CRIANZA DEL WHISKY S.A.(KNOWN AS WHISKY DYC)

BY RICHARD THOMAS

For decades, one of the largest distilleries in the world limited itself to producing only a few average types of whisky. The Spanish Destilerías y Crianza del Whisky (DYC) is a huge, two-plant complex with a staggering annual capacity of 20 million liters of whisky, although the last statistics I saw listed DYC's actual output at 2.3 million liters. Putting that in perspective, Glenfiddich is the world's best-selling single malt, and they produce about 10 million liters a year (and not a drop of it is grain whisky).

Yet for several decades, this big-but-obscure distillery in Spain limited itself mostly to producing two or three labels of inexpensive, scotch-inspired whisky with a light enough character to go well with ice, an important consideration for drinking whisky in Spain's sun-blasted summer months. Or at least they so limited themselves until the day their 10 Year Old Single Malt came along.

Released in 2010 and billed as the first installment of a collection of limited edition whiskies, for the time being the DYC 10 Year Old stands as the distillery's sole premium expression, as the distillery has no current plans to produce a second installment in the collection.

DYC SINGLE MALT 10 YEAR OLD 40%

The DYC 10 Year Old Single Malt comes in packaging worthy of a fine whisky. The squat, rounded, clear glass bottle shows off the whisky's light amber color, and comes with stylish inked labeling and a proper wood-and-cork stopper.

In addition to being older than anything else in the DYC line, this 10 Year Old single malt was distilled from specially chosen Castilian-Leonese barley, and aged in old American oak bourbon barrels.

Nose: In the glass, the DYC Single Malt has a fine, heavy gold color. The whisky has a woody scent with thick, semi-sweet vanilla notes. The effect is leathery and somewhat smoky, as one might expect from an older whisky. At this stage, I was left wondering if the climate of the Iberian Plateau has the same pseudo-accelerating effect on whisky maturation as the steamy summers and freezing winters of Kentucky, because it smelled older than comparable Irish and Scottish 10 Year Olds.

Palate: On the palate, this whiskey is malty and silky, retaining the semi-sweet vanilla notes from the nose, and with a hint of spiciness coming on at the end. That latter point makes the flavor of this single malt, turning what would be merely pleasant into a liquor of moderate complexity. The finish is short and light, with a little lingering spice and a touch of fruitiness.

The care and extra aging of the DYC 10 Year Old really shows vis-à-vis the other DYC whiskies I have experienced thus far. While this single malt is only two years older than the DYC's blended 8 Year Old, it strikes a nice sipper's balance between DYC's characteristic lightness and the heft of possessing a decent age. I would described DYC 8 Year Old as the whisky you buy to stock your Spanish holiday rental. If you can find it, DYC 10 Year Old is the stuff you bring home from that vacation as a liquor shelf conversation piece and sipping whisky.

RT

SWEDEN

BY CARLO DEVITO

Like Norway, Finland, and Denmark, Sweden has had a long association with akvavit (aquavit) dating back to the Middle Ages; akvavit of course stems from the Latin aqua vitae. If Swedish distilling is known for any other distilled spirit, it is for vodka, especially such brands as Absolut and Renat. Absolut is an international juggernaut, sold in more than 126 nations worldwide. Behind Bacardi and Smirnoff, Absolut is the third bestselling alcoholic spirit brand in the world.

But in the last almost 20 years, something had changed. In the mid- to late-1990s several groups of Swedish whisky and distilling enthusiasts wondered why there wasn't a Swedish single malt whisky. And since then, Sweden has produced, in a steady stream, some of the most impressive single malt whiskies in the world. And industry insiders can only see more good things happening.

According to Thomas Ohrbom, the Scandinavian whisky writer, no appreciation of Swedish whisky can take place without including Box Distilleri. A relative newcomer to the scene, their first four expressions were homeruns. And people, whose expectations were already high, are even more excited now. Many are expecting great things from Box Distilleri.

BOX WHISKY THE PIONEER
3 YEAR OLD 48.1%

This is the first whisky release from Box Whisky in Sweden. This relatively small distillery has been subject to a lot of well-earned praise and positive commentary over the past couple of years. Many looked forward to this release, and expectations were high. Box Whisky had presented their work-in-progress at festivals and whisky tastings for a while, and often to rave reviews. Box Whisky The Pioneer is the first of four whiskies in a series called The Early Days Collection.

A total of 5,000 bottles were made available through the state-owned Systembolaget at 10am on June 5, and by that same afternoon it was sold out! The total number of bottles produced of The Pioneer is 6508 bottles. The 1508 not sold through Systembolaget were reserved for stock holders and the distillery itself.

Box Whisky The Pioneer is composed of 50% unpeated whisky matured for three years in 40 liter bourbon casks ("Ankare"), 35% peated (31 ppm) whisky matured for three years in 40 liter bourbon casks, and 15% unpeated whisky matured for two years in 200 liter bourbon casks from Jack Daniels, which was finished for a year in 100 liter casks made from new roasted Swedish oak. The end result is a non-chill filtered whisky at 48.1% with no added coloring. Box has made all the technical details, and I do mean all, available on their website.

Nose: Oaky spices, peppermint, malt, a bit of salt and some caramel. The young age does show itself, but it is a vibrant and fresh-faced youth we have here, not a brash and unwashed scoundrel. After the initial nosing, I left the whisky in the glass for about 45 minutes and then dove in for seconds [Box Whisky does recommend that you leave this whisky in the glass for a minimum of 30 minutes to let it open up]. Vanilla, mild fruits (apples, pears and citrus), leather, soft smoke and cereals. The nose turns quite delicate; soft and almost creamy. With water: The young notes go hiding, and it becomes more fruity. The smoke morphs into a smoking beach fire.

Palate: Very soft, almost silken mouthfeel. Dry wood smoke, pepper, licorice. With water: Surprisingly, adding water makes it richer and a bit peatier, with added notes of honey and ginger. Warm, with medium length. Oaky spices and soft caramel. A bit dry. Dark chocolate and mocha on the finish. With water: The finish is longer now, and not as dry. Chocolate and ginger, with some citrusy notes. An impressive feat! This is a vibrant dessert of a whisky. The young age certainly does show, especially on the nose, before water is added. Normally I shy away from adding water, but for very young whiskies with a higher ABV it is always well worth trying. In this case it really did improve on the nose, taste, and finish.

TO

BOX WHISKY THE FESTIVAL 2015 3 YEAR OLD 54.5%

Box Whisky The Festival 2015 was made available exclusively to attendees at the Box Whisky Festival, summer 2015. The festival saw mad queuing for this special bottling here. As per usual the distillery provided a ton of detailed facts on this bottling: Phenol level: 24 ppm; Age is 3 years 8 months; total bottles produced: 700; Casks used: spirit from 10 bourbon barrels (100-130 liter) were finished in two fresh American oak casks and in two fresh Swedish oak casks, in addition one fresh American oak cask (100 liter) was also used.

Nose: Quite sweet, with lots of bourbon influence. I also find a lot of oak—the relatively fresh kind. The oak never gets over-powering, and although it gives a clear indication that we are nosing a young whisky, it is still well-balanced and rich. The peat is more a teasing tickle that a slap in the face. A bit of fudge, and mild fruit notes. I will assume this dram needs to sit in the glass for a while... (time passes)...Yep, I was right, and what a positive difference it makes! The bourbon and oak notes are now a lot more harmonious, and the peat is slowly stepping out of the shadows. The tempered sweetness on the nose is sublime.

Palate: Super smooth initially,

then it quickly turns more chewy and rambunctious (yes, it is a word—look it up). Pepper bordering on chili, rich vanilla flavored fudge, and a touch of oak. Chili-licorice hard candy dancing on my tongue, and super-rich caramel sauce that is just on the right side of the getting burnt. So, so rich! Medium to long finish. Vanilla ice-cream covered in said caramel sauce right up to the end. What a lovely dram! This is a dessert in itself. In fact, you might even get away with skipping dinner altogether! This is the best official bottling I have tried from Box so far.

TO

BOX WHISKY THE MESSENGER
3 YEAR OLD 48.4%

Box Whisky The Messenger was the fourth and final release in the Early Days Collection from Swedish distillery Box Whisky.

The details about this expression is, in short, as follows: 76% of the whisky in this vatting was matured in 130 liter ex-bourbon casks; 24% of the whisky was matured in 100 liter ex-Oloroso sherry casks; 7% of the whisky was peated, the rest unpeated; Distilled in 2011 and bottled in 2015; Total outturn was 8,169 bottles, and 8,004 of these were made available to the public.

Nose: Delicate and aromatic nose, with vanilla and light wood notes appearing first. I also find almonds, caramel, and hints of fruit. The peat is hardly noticeable here. I have a hard time believing this whisky is a mere three years old. It is very well integrated and mature for its age. You can bury your nose in the glass and there's only pleasant aromas to pick up—no

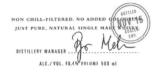

alcohol, no off notes. Given time, and you should of course give a young whisky time in the glass, especially if you do not add water. Anyways, given time I also pick up soft herbal notes. I am thinking mint and eucalyptus, maybe also a hint of aniseed. There is a whiff of smoke here, in the end, sweet and soft wood smoke.

Palate: Oily and a bit cool. There's eucalyptus and mint here. A bit of a green-ish feel. Roger the gardener? Spices are more present on the palate than on the nose. There's honey and caramel as well. Medium long finish. The peat is slowly coming to the fore on the finish. Slow burning embers that build a solid base for the lighter notes of vanilla and summer fruits. Aniseed and oak make an appearance, and it all becomes a little bit youthful. Another impressive release from Box.

TO

BY CHRIS HOBAN

Mackmyra began as an idea eight friends had on a ski holiday in 1998. They were a talented bunch of engineers and chemists who had met at Uni and were going on a ski holiday to blow off steam. They had gone to a lodge in the North of Sweden, and they had each taken a bottle of Scotch as a gift for the host. Soon drinking ensued and the conversation turned to the valid question: "Why was there no whisky made in Sweden?" It's a good question to ask, and they talked about it all through the night. The next day, they all woke with pretty sore heads, but the idea was still there. "Why don't we use our skills and make a Swedish single malt!" and that's what they did.

From 1998 to 2002, they spent their time trying out different recipes. Different barley strains, different oaks and different cuts of spirit. Their original, homemade still made 30 liter batches of spirit, hence why 30 liter casks were experimented with.

They also visited several distilleries in Scotland to garner some useful production information and to gain an insight into their ethos and philosophy when it comes to making whisky.

This is why I like Mackmyra so much. From looking at Scotland, they vowed to make whisky in their own style—a Swedish style. And by that I mean:

- 30 liter barrels for some of the spirit, 100 liter barrels for other spirit, 200 liter barrels for other spirit.

- Swedish oak, ex-sherry European oak and ex-bourbon American oak.

- Local peated barley, with the peat mixed with local juniper.

- Whisky matured in disused mines to regulate temperature and keep the whisky safe from the warehouse roof collapse we have to deal with in Scotland.

All of these different variables create their house style and their ethos. Similar to Scotland, but also completely different. Quite refreshing from my point of view.

In 2002, they purchased stills from Forsyth's in Speyside, and since then production, availability, and (as a consequence) popularity has gone through the roof. So much so that they have built a second distillery and they are looking to invest in a potential third distillery, although this is some time in the future. The new distillery is a gravity distillery, which I will try to endeavor to explain, once I fully understand it!

MACKMYRA SVENSK EK NAS 46.1%

Mackmyra Svensk Ek (Swedish Oak) is surrounded with a bit of controversy. This is in fact a re-launch of the previous product Mackmyra Första Utgåvan (The First Edition), although the composition of the whisky has also been slightly adjusted (so not simply a name change).

The controversy stems from the name "Swedish Oak," as only a small portion of Swedish oak has been used in the maturation. Since Swedish oak casks are a lot more expensive, and exclusive, than American oak bourbon barrels, and there is little use of Swedish oak in this case, the protesters feel

the name is misleading. The claim is that the name will mislead consumers to believe 100% Swedish oak has been used, and that this is in fact a more exclusive product than it really is.

10% of the casks used to mature this whisky have been Swedish oak (30 liter fresh oak casks), the remaining 90% of casks used have been bourbon casks of various sizes (full barrels, quarter casks, and 30 liter casks). Mackmyra states that a total of 5.4% of the whisky used to compose the Mackmyra Svensk Ek has been matured in Swedish oak casks.

The age of the whisky used to compose the Mackmyra Svensk Ek is in the range of four to seven years old.

Nose: Fresh, fruity and a bit earthy. Vanilla, apples, pears, licorice, honey, nuts, pepper, menthol, and light herbal or grassy notes.

Palate: Oaky, sugary, fizzy, and spicy. There's a clear cereal-like note to it, and the mouthfeel is medium rich. More spicy now, with pepper and a pinch of chili. Fizzy still. Ginger, camphor (old-style hard candy), menthol, and a bit of Tiger Balm. Medium long and warm finish.

Well-balanced, with lots of fresh oakiness. The Swedish fresh oak does seem to have had an influence on the end product.

TO

MACKMYRA PRELUDIUM:01 - DE FÖRSTA DROPPARNA 3 YEAR OLD 55.6%

The Mackmyra Preludium:01—De första dropparna ("The First Drops") is made up from whisky distilled at their first pilot distillery (1999-2002) and the very first casks of whisky distilled at their first real distillery, Mackmyra Bruk. The whisky is 3 years old, and bottled in 2006. This was a limited release of 4,000 numbered bottles.

Nose: A bit shy on the nose. Notes of oak and tropical fruit appear first, along with vanilla. It does seem a bit young-ish at first, but there are no off-notes here. I am starting to wonder why the Preludium series from Mackmyra got so many negative reviews. Let's dive deeper and find out...With time the nose turns a little bit perfume-y. Wet sawdust. Pineapple and lemons. Red berries in the next room.

Taste: Smooth and spicy. Quite spicy, in fact. Pepper, chili, acetone (yeah, that was not a plus), and perfume. Relatively short finish.

OK, the nose was pretty promising, but the finish really killed it. Still very exciting to finally have had a chance to try it properly. I also think it is very commendable of Mackmyra to invite its fans to follow their journey like this. This is naked, raw, and uncompromising. They never tried to sell this as the perfect whisky. They merely wanted to let us all know what was in the works. Kudos!

TO

MACKMYRA PRELUDIUM:04 - GRUVLAGRAD ELEGANS 53.3%

Mackmyra Preludium:04—Gruvlagrad elegans (gruvlagrad means stored in a mine, elegans means elegance) was vatted from spirit distilled both at the initial pilot distillery (1999-2002) and at the first proper distillery at Mackmyra. It was bottled in 2007.

The Mackmyra Preludium:04—Gruvlagrad elegans was mainly matured in first fill ex-bourbon casks. A number of ex-champagne casks and ex-sherry casks were also used in the vatting. The casks were stored in the Bodås mine, fifty meters below ground.

Nose: Vanilla mixed with youngish spices. Medium oakiness, and a touch of cereal. The fruits detected include baked apples and ripe banana. There's a touch of alcohol and perfume in the back.

Palate: Very soft and elegant mouthfeel. To taste it is quite spicy, and the perfume comes through a lot heavier now than on the nose. Soft spices now, mixed with heather honey. The sweetness is thick and pleasant. The perfume gives way to peppermint, eucalyptus, and fresh oak notes. The herbal touch is a bit heavy-handed.

Quite good, I would say. A bit too much perfume, and a bit raw, but considering what this actually is, moderately impressed.

TO

MACKMYRA TIO 10 YEAR OLD 46.1%

In late autumn 2013, Mackmyra invited customers to order what would be their, and Sweden's, first ever 10 year old whisky. Customers wanting this whisky had to order a minimum of 12 bottles each, out of a total outturn of 9,000 bottles. In addition the customers had to wait until late November 2014 to receive their bottles. A rather special and roundabout way of releasing their first 10 year old, but we imagine they had their reasons.

The whisky has been matured exclusively in bourbon casks, and is unpeated.

Nose: Sweet, with lots of vanilla. Camphor, eucalyptus, oak, nuts and pears. A bit floral and herbal.

Palate: White and black pepper, hints of chili. Caramel, vanilla, pears, and licorice. Medium body. Quite sweet to taste. Warm and medium long. Honey and hints of mint. Slightly metallic finish. Right at the end there's some dark chocolate and cocoa.

A fine effort from Mackmyra. Impressive to have reached the significant milestone of having released a 10 year old.

TO

MACKMYRA ISKRISTALL NAS 46.1%

Mackmyra Iskristall (Ice Crystal) is the third release in their new Season Series, which took over from the Mackmyra Special series.

This whisky has been matured on a mix of American oak, ex-bourbon casks, and Swedish oak. It has also been given a finish in Pedro Ximénez sherry casks, and the finish has been a bit longer than what Mackmyra has used for previous releases (we are still talking months though). The average age of the content in the bottle is about seven years, but there will be both older and younger elements.

Nose: Quite warm and spicy. There are some oaky spices here, as well as warm fruity notes. Underneath this there is a cooler element, mint or menthol. Quite like this nose.

Palate: Caramel flavored popcorn! A bit more spicy now – peppery. The sherry notes are very mild, but again I find the cool elements. More towards oaky coolness now – eucalyptus. With water it is more peppery still. Rich and fruity. The sherry influence more pronounced. Honey, raisins, dark fruits, slightly grassy or herbal.

Quite like the contrast between the warmer sherry influence and the cooler eucalyptus notes. Certainly thinking of winter, cold nights in front of a warm fireplace. Well done!

TO

MACKMYRA MIDNATTSSOL
NAS 46.1%

Mackmyra Midnattssol (Midnight Sun) has a rather special finish. We do not think we have seen this variant anywhere else. Here's how Mackmyra described the maturation of this whisky:

"Matured in sherry and bourbon casks, as well as combination casks made from American and Swedish oak, the finishing touch comes from casks which previously stored wine made from birch sap."

Master Blender at Mackmyra, Angela D'Orazio, says, about half the whisky that went into Midnattssol had the birch sap wine cask finish. It was left in these casks for about five months. The spirit used in this whisky has an average age of about seven to eight years.

Nose: Sweet, well-rounded, quite rich on the nose. Some oaky notes, fruits (summer fruits) and mild spices. A bit "green" on the nose, herbal or grassy or some such.

Palate: Quite spicy! There's some menthol and mint here, and on the second sip more mint. The main spice is pepper I would say. A bit oaky, but these are soft and mild oaky notes—is that the birch sap making an appear-ance maybe? Sweeter now. You'll find honey and citrus, warm apples. The spice returns towards the end of a medium long finish. Peppermint and white pepper; a cool finish!

This is a fun dram, and I like the fact that they dare have fun with finishes and try new approaches. Just don't release too many versions, please, you'll only end up confusing us!

TO

MACKMYRA SOMMARTID NAS 46.1%

The Mackmyra Sommartid (Summertime) is the fourth release in the Seasons series from Mackmyra. Previous installments in the series are Midvinter (Midwinter), Midnattssol (Midnight Sun) and Iskristall (Ice Crystal). These releases from Mackmyra often have a special finish, or include some unusual casks in the vatting.

This is the case here as well. Three types of casks have been used to create Mackmyra Sommartid: Swedish oak, American oak, and Cloudberry saturated barrels.

Nose: Fresh and light. The American oak is at the front upon first sniff. Vanilla and marshmallows are clearly present. It is also very fruity: green apples, pears, and grapes. Given a few more minutes in the glass, we can detect the influence of new Swedish oak as well: spicy oakiness and hints of fresh sawdust. I do detect some fresh berries here as well—not quite sure they are cloudberries, more red berries of some sort. Raspberries per-

haps…Going back to it when the glass is empty pick up on floral honey and camphor-flavored hard candy.

Palate: Smooth mouthfeel, with medium body. Quite light and fruity. Diluted honey, white pepper, ginger, caramel, and canned pears. Medium to short finish, medium warmth. Caramel, raspberries, oak, and moist sawdust.

I really liked the nose on this one, but it is a bit too light and volatile to taste.

TO

MACKMYRA MIDVINTER NAS 46.1%

Mackmyra Midvinter (Midwinter) is the third of the whiskies in the Season Series from Mackmyra.

Mackmyra Midvinter has received a finish from French Bordeaux casks, glühwine (mulled wine) casks, and sherry casks. A rather unique combination, and I am very curious about the glühwine influence here. It should be spicy, but could also be a bit too different from what you expect from a whisky.

Nose: Vanilla, Christmas spices, gingerbread, dark fruits. After a while in the glass it takes on a very pleasant, soft sweetness. I imagine it is the wine casks that contribute to this.

Palate: Pepper, ginger and cinnamon. Quite spicy. There is a clear wine influence here as well, soft and sweet. Pepper and mild caramel. The spices are certainly present all the way, and added to the mix I now find herbs. It is cool and dry on the finish.

A strange one this—not quite my cup of whisky, but it certainly is interesting. There is a boldness to Mackmyra that I like. They do push the boundaries, sometimes a bit too much maybe?

TO

Richard Jansson and Kristina Aner-fält-Jansson founded Norrtelje Brenneri AB in 2001. The farm has been in their family for more than five generations. The extensive renovation and refurbishment of the farm's barn, which is now the distillery, was completed in 2002. Anerfält-Jansson produces a number of fine craft distillates, including one of Sweden's most well-regarded punches, Roslags Punsch, and the Grisslehamnsbrennvin buckthorn schnapps (which was a gold-medal winner at Destillata in Austria, the world's largest fruit distillates competition).

ROSLAGSWHISKY EKO NO. 1 3 YEAR OLD 46%

This whisky was made by Norrtelje Brenneri AB, Sweden. This is their second release. It differs from the first batch, in that this one is matured in an ex-bourbon cask from Heaven Hill, whereas the first batch was matured in an ex-sherry Oloroso cask. Both were single cask releases.

The whisky is certified organic. The total outturn was 263 bottles. Of those, 200 bottles will be sold through Viking Line.

The bottle this whisky comes in is very nice. Also like the fact that they have decided on bottling this at 70cl, where most everyone starting out in the Nordics now release 50cl bottles.

Nose: Fresh and young-ish. No off-notes, mind you. There is plenty of malty notes, mixed with apples, pears, red berries, vanilla, and wet sawdust.

Palate: Very soft mouthfeel, almost too soft. It takes a couple of sips to distinguish any specific aromas here. Pepper, oak, vanilla and ginger. Medium to short finish, but it develops nicely. It has a nice, lingering and spicy sweetness to it. Runny honey with a touch of cinnamon, nutmeg, hazelnuts, unsalted peanuts, dark chocolate, and ginger.

The finish took me by surprise— and it was a positive surprise. It was relatively short, but very appealing. This is the first whisky sampled from Norrtelje Brenneri, and you certainly won't mind trying another few when you get the chance.

TO

BY THOMAS OHRBOM

Smögen Whisky is located in Hunnebostrand, Sweden. Pär Caldenby is the guy running the whole thing—literally. He is the only employee of the company as of yet. He started the company back in the summer of 2009, and distilling started in earnest in 2010. The whisky he produces is powerful, with a big, peaty character.

SMÖGEN PRIMÖR 3 YEAR OLD 63.7%

Smögen Primör is from the craft distillery Smögen Whisky. This is the first whisky to market from Smögen, and as such this is a great occasion! It is released in a limited batch of 2,188 50cl bottles. The content is pulled from eight 110-liter barrels, made of European new oak, and one 225-liter barrique that previously held Bordeaux wine. The barrique is also made of European oak. The cask numbers used are 5, and 14–21, and the spirit was distilled between September and November of 2010. Bottling was performed on November 15, 2013. I imagine that must have been a great day for Pär. Finally he had his own whisky, in bottles!

Nose: On one hand, this whisky strikes you as very well balanced, quite sweet, and with quite a lot of peat. On the other hand, given a bit more time in the glass, it is fresh and spicy, with a fair bit of oakiness. You can clearly tell that this is a young whisky; fruity maltiness, cereals. But there are no off-notes at all; it is well-rounded and pleasant. The peatiness is sort of Islay-ish, quite maritime. There's a hint of saltiness to it, and I love it when sweetness and peat combines well as it does here. The peat is not overwhelming at all; it just enhances and envelops the other aromas.

Palate: Quite fruity and very spicy. I find handfuls of pepper, chili pepper, and peat, peat, peat. It's almost so you can chew the peat—it is near solid! You may feel that you are close to some primal forces here—darkness lurks very close, but yet you feel safe. It's not all darkness though; you will also find some refreshing ginger and ripe berries. Wow! There is a Midsummer bonfire burning in the chest now! This whisky gives off an incredible warmth. It could prob-

ably be utilized to end winter in icy Norway! The finish is relatively short, as you would expect, but the warmth lingers long after the aromas have wandered off. Really like the ginger sweetness that accompanies the warmth for a brief period.

So, is this a good product? Yes, definitely! It is quite mature, well balanced and full for such a young age. As a first release from a new distillery it bodes really well for the future. Bring it on, Pär!

TO

SMÖGEN SHERRY PROJECT 1:1
3 YEAR OLD 51.8%

The whisky was distilled in July 2011, and bottled on September 5, 2014. It was matured in casks 32-34/2011, European oak 100-liter virgin feuillettes, before the finish in the sherry butt. The malt type used is Optic, peated at 50+ ppm phenols.

Nose: Warm ashes, glowing embers, coal, dark fruits, raisins, baked apples, and some citrus notes. Quite rich.

Palate: Fresh, sweet and peaty. Creamy vanilla, caramel, citrus, pepper-flavored dark chocolate. Still creamy and rich, fruity, with a more pronounced oaky presence now. Medium length on the finish, warm.

A very nice start to a new series of bottlings from this young distillery on the Swedish west coast. Stay tuned for more!

TO

Interview with Pär Caldenby, Smögen Distiller

BY THOMAS OHRBOM

Up until the winter of 2014, this young distillery had only released one expression, the Smögen Primör. One of the new bottlings is called Smögen Sherry Project 1:1, a name that does raise a few questions. We therefore sat down with Pär Caldenby, the owner and master distiller at Smögen Whisky, to find out more:

TO: The "Smögen Sherry Project," what is the idea behind that?

PC: As we are driven by the love both of whisky and for exploring new variations on known themes, the idea of a number of projects on the influence of Sherry cask maturation came about. Now, the name for the bottling (-s) may not be the most evocative ever, but it is certainly to the point: "Sherry Project."

TO: And why sherry casks specifically?

PC: Sherry matured malt whisky is – quite rightly – one of the classical expressions any whisky can be presented in and one which is also typically very popular. As the casks tend to be quite active when compared to ex-Bourbon casks, not every malt whisky would be suited for the use of fresh Sherry casks. However, our fairly heavy and decidedly peaty whisky can bear just about any cask type you can find, with former Sherry casks being an obvious choice and one which is common in our warehouse, from 30 liters volume (a.k.a. "Bloodtub") all the way up to 600 liters for the massive "Gorda" casks. Obviously, the projected maturation time will differ wildly between the extremes.

TO: You say "bottlings" plural, so this will be a series?

PC: "The "Sherry Project 1:1," [is] the first installment of four in the initial group of the project. The focus is here on the successive increase in influence from the Sherry casks, with the installments 1–3 being given four, eight and twelve months of finishing period in one fresh Sherry butt each.

The fourth installment will be a 4 year old full term maturation in fresh Oloroso Sherry quarter casks, and this is also the common denominator for all four installments, the maturation in quarter casks made from European oak. The installments 1–3 matured for two years and ten months in virgin European oak quarter casks, prior to their aforementioned finishing period, while installment 4 will get the full term maturation in them, although those particular quarters are fresh Sherry casks to start with.

TO: Can you tell us a little bit more about the first release of the series?

PC: The 1:1 is bottled at 51.8 % ABV, and is peated at 50+ ppm phenols. The total outturn is 932 bottles, and 600 of these bottles will be released for sale through Systembolaget. In our view, the 1:1 is excellent in its very own right, just as the second to fourth installments show excellent promise. But to get the full impact of the Sherry Project 1, all four bottlings should be secured and tasted side by side. It will be an interesting exercise for any whisky enthusiast and one that we can all learn from.

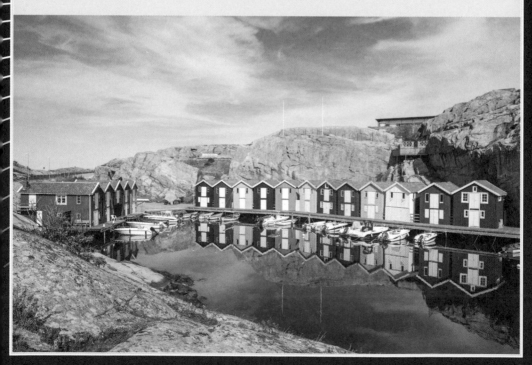

SPIRIT OF HVEN

BY THOMAS OHRBOM

The Spirit of Hven Distillery is on the small island of Hven, in the middle of the Øresund strait, between Sweden and Denmark. The island of Hven is only 2.9 square miles, and is home to 371 inhabitants.

The island was historically under Danish rule, until the ownership of the island transferred from Denmark to Sweden in 1660 with the Treaty of Copenhagen.

The Danish astronomer Tycho Brahe built two observatories here, Uraniborg and Stjerneborg, which have inspired the names of all whiskies released by Spirit of Hven so far. In 1988 the resort Spirit of Hven Backafallsbyn was established. In 1998, Anja and Henric Molin bought the resort, and slowly started expanding. They established the very impressive whisky bar on site, and built the restaurant. They soon started planning the distillery. In 2008, the distillery was opened and production started.

In 2009, they launched their first products: Spirit of Hven Organic Oak Matured Aqua Vitae and Organic Winter Spirit. In 2010, they released the Spirit of Hven Organic Summer Spirit. Then in 2012, they launched their first single malt, the Spirit of Hven Urania.

Since the distillery is located on an island, you have to take the boat. There are no bridges connecting it to the mainland, and it is a bit too far to swim. The easiest way to get to Spirit of Hven Distillery is to fly to Kastrup (Copenhagen Airport), then take the train from the airport over to Landskrona, Sweden, where you take the boat out to Hven. Once you are on the island, you take the local bus from Bäckviken to Backafallsbyn where the distillery is located.

At the distillery, gin is the main product. They also produce a lot of aqua vitae, vodka and other spirit drinks. Whisky makes up about 15% of their sales. All production is ecological. They focus a lot on traceability in all processes, from the oak, to the barrel, to the barley (and other grain), the yeast, the

maturation, and each individual bottle sold.

They will typically source the oak, and have casks made to order. The fresh oak casks are then brought to the distillery where they are filled with neutral spirit, which will subsequently become their vodka and gin etc., for two years. The casks will then be emptied and filled with the new make that will mature into whisky.

Henric Molin, the owner and Master Distiller is a professor type. He has an impressive laboratory set up at the distillery, and a growing part of their business is actually performing analysis and research on behalf of other companies.

In production, they use different types of malt, playing around with different roasting levels. They mainly use lager malt, as most distilleries do, but there are typically always two or three different types of malt in their whiskies (types of malted barley).

About 5% of the malt is malted at the distillery, and the ambition is to increase this to 100% over time. All the barley is sourced from the local area.

The distillery holds a 2,000 liter wash still and a 1,500 liter spirit still. The water used in production is always filtered and distilled, then have the desired minerals added and pH value set. Yeast is another area in which Henric pays a lot of attention to. He always uses a minimum of two yeast types in whisky production, where the second yeast type is typically added after the first 24 hours of fermentation. On occasion a third yeast type will be added after 60 hours of fermentation. All this to build a very specific flavor profile of the resulting new make. Typical fermentation at Spirit of Hven Distillery is 90–120 hours.

There is also a small pot still for experimentation. There is always a lot of experimentation going on. They are playing around with rye, bourbon, wheated whisky, and rum. In the warehouse I got a taste of an 8 year old wheated whisky that was really impressive! I do hope this will be released as a product soon.

They have their own bottling plant on site as well, with a capacity of 600–1,200 bottles per hour. Another area where the attention to detail comes to light is when you hear that they will always "wash" the bottle with the spirit they will fill the bottle with. Sort of a Richard Patterson "washing" procedure on an industrial scale.

The resort and distillery includes conference facilities with eight conference rooms, a fantastic whisky bar, and a very good restaurant. I had two impressive three-course dinners at the restaurant, as well as lunch and breakfast. Everything that was served was of high quality, and the price was at a reasonable level.

The whisky bar at any time holds about 500 different whiskies, as well as thirty to fifty different beers. It was absolutely no problem getting lost in this bar for hours on end. I enjoyed a lot of the local products, of course, but also some great whiskies from the Hanyu Card Series. Again the prices were quite reasonable.

It can be a bit windy, but it is really beautiful. Take the trip to the nearby Tycho Brahe Obervatory, or visit the very old St. Ibb's Church. There are few cars and many bikes on the island of Hven.

Spirit of Hven Distillery is one of my best distillery trips ever. They have the complete package with the distillery, the cottages to stay in, the restaurant and the whisky bar. Strongly recommend taking the trip out to Hven. You will not regret it.

SPIRIT OF HVEN
TYCHO'S STAR NAS 41.8%

The Spirit of Hven Tycho's Star is named in tribute to the astronomer Tycho Brahe (1546-1601), who lived on the island for many years. This whisky was launched at The Whisky Exchange Whisky Show in London.

Just love the level of detail given for the products from Spirit of Hven. Here are the details on Tycho's Star box:

"Tycho's Star is made from a mash bill based on three types of barley, pale ale malt for the grassy base notes, chocolate malt for the enticing caramel notes and heavy peated whisky malt to create the leather, liqourice and tar scents.

The carefully distilled spirit has matured on casks made of air-dried oak. The casks are 58.20% heavy char *Quercus muehlenbergii* from Missouri, 33.44% heavy toast *Quercus petraea* from Allier and 8.36% medium toast *Quercus robur* from Bourgogne.

"Tycho's Star is bottled at site on Hven at 41.8% without carbon- or chill filtering, no coloring, or additives. It is organic certified, completely natural, as should be. Every bottle is individually numbered and controlled before being waxed by hand."

It is very interesting that Spirit of Hven is actively experimenting with different types of malt, for example by using chocolate malt in this release.

Nose: Quite spicy yet very soft at the same time. Milk chocolate, vanilla, bananas, licorice, malt and soft wood smoke. Relatively sweet, you might say, and quite fruity. Give it time and it will also show off mild coffee notes and an herbal touch.

Palate: The peat is more pronounced to taste. The spices are a bit more aggressive; pepper, ginger, and chili up front. Still very fruity; bananas and pineapple. Oily and rich mouthfeel. Milk chocolate, bananas, oak, and a touch of ashes. Almost minty—certainly a touch of the herbal that I found on the nose. Feels a bit thin on the finish, and tapers off a bit too quickly.

It is intended as an entry-level whisky, and for that it works very well.

TO

SPIRIT OF HVEN SANKT IBB
3 YEAR OLD 51.4%

The Spirit of Hven Sankt Ibb was distilled in 2011, bottled in 2014, and the total outturn was 273 bottles. It was first matured in a fresh oak cask, before receiving a finish in an ex-wine cask previously used for an Italian Cabernet Sauvignon/Merlot wine.

Here is what the distillery has to say about the Spirit of Hven Sankt Ibb:

"Sankt Ibb, cask 11-217, is made from barley grown on the coordinates 55°91'N, 12°69'S just outside the distillery. The barley was malted in our pilot plant and the kilning was done with Chinquapin oak from old casks and locally harvested seaweed.

After 120 hours fermentation with two different yeast strains, specifically grown to embrace the fruity phenolic character, the wash was gently distilled and the heart was carefully collected. The spirit was laid to rest on a high toast, high char cask made of air dried *Quercus muehlenbergii* harvested on the shores of Meramec river.

After given its initial character the spirit was transferred to a cask made from air dried *Quercus petraea* harvested outside Moulin's (Allier). This cask was previously used to enhance one of the most rewarded Cabernet Sauvignon/Merlot wines from Italy."

Nose: Honey and spices. Dried fruits. More spices. Soft and delicate. Baked apples with cinnamon and leather. Found a lot of medicinal notes here, and something metallic—a wet steel sword perhaps. There is a very soft, almost delicate, smokiness to it. A bit difficult to get a grasp on this one, but it is a fun challenge. There's a lot going on here, mainly in the domains of fruit and spices.

Palate: Very spicy and quite dry. Pepper, cinnamon, liquid smoke, and caramel. Warm and long finish. Quite minty and fresh. Still with some pepper and other spices, but the mint dominates. "After Eight" mint chocolate! Vademecum mouthwash and fresh oak.

The nose is very complex, and the finish surprisingly long. The very minty finish is slightly at odds with the nose, but it is a good dram.

TO

SPIRIT OF HVEN SANKT CLAUS CASK #11-229, 3 YEAR OLD 53.2%

The Swedish distiller Spirit of Hven released three single cask expressions just before Christmas 2014. They were aptly named Sankt Claus. One release was for the Swedish market (cask #11-222), one was bottled for Juul's in Denmark (cask #11-224), and finally this cask (cask #11-229) that was for the rest of the world.

Spirit of Hven Sankt Claus Cask #11-229 was matured in a French oak cask for three years. The cask had previously held a wine of 100% Merlot. The total outturn was 294 bottles (50cl).

This is what the distillery says about the naming of this whisky:

"This release named Sankt Claus, pays tribute to Saint Nicholas, patron over amongst others sailors and fishermen. With the winter storms just around the corner and as we see the waves whip up frisky foam around our island, we would like to send some thought and warmth to the ones sailing the seven seas and narrow straits bringing us delights from far away."

Nose: Warm and peppery up front. There is definitely a lot of oak, and berries here. Mild sweetness that does resemble wine.

Palate: More spicy to taste. Oaky spices and mild pepper. It has a round and slightly dry mouth-feel. Even drier on the finish. The spices remain all the way, tempered by a mild sweetness. A bit short.

Definitely still a young whisky, but we like the sweetness and spices that it has picked up from the cask.

TO

SPIRIT OF HVEN SEVEN STARS NO. 1 DUBHE NAS 45%

Spirit of Hven Seven Stars No. 1 Dubhe was released in March 2013. This is the first of seven annual releases that will be named after the stars in the asterism Big Dipper (or The Plough, or in Scandinavia, Karlsvognen). This first release is named after the star Dubhe. The releases will continue for seven years, until 2019, and each will have a special character differentiating them from previous expressions.

Dubhe is about 4.5 years old, but there is no age statement on the bottle. It is medium peated (about 12–15 ppm). It has mainly been matured in American oak, but there are a few barrels of both French and Spanish oak in the mix. All barrels are initially new oak, but the distillery then initially used to mature their "generic" grain spirit on these barrels for a year, before using the barrels for maturing whisky. The grain spirit is subsequently sold as gin, vodka, and aquavit. The gin and aquavit are actually very nice products, well worth seeking out.

Nose: Fruity, well-rounded. There is a thin and welcoming layer of smoke covering the aromas here. I find leather (quite a lot), vanilla, honey, orange, strawberries, and a hint of licorice. It is very soft and appealing.

Palate: Mild and friendly smoke. Lots of fruit, especially oranges, and some vanilla and a dollop of runny honey. Medium long, still quite fruity. The oranges keep dominating, but they are now accompanied by lemons. The finish is peppery as well.

A very nice, young whisky. It shall be very interesting to continue following the Seven Stars series in the coming years.

TO

SPIRIT OF HVEN SEVEN STARS NO. 2 MERAK NAS 45%

This whisky takes its name from the star Merak in the asterism Ursa Major (Big Dipper, the Plough). It has been matured in a mix of American, French, and Spanish oak. A total of twenty-five casks were blended together to create Merak.

Nose: Quite rich and creamy on the nose. Light spices and a thin veil of smoke. Citrus, lemon peel, malt, honey, and oranges. It is a fresh whisky, revealing its youth, but there are no off-notes here.

Palate: A light touch of smoke and licorice is the first to hit the palate. Then you detect creamy caramel, simple syrup, malt, and vanilla. Medium long, cool rather than warming, and a bit more spicy towards the end.

Compared to the Dubhe, Merak can be slightly richer and creamier, where Dubhe was more fresh. Supposedly, Merak is slightly older, at around five years.

TO

SPIRIT OF HVEN SEVEN STARS NO. 3 PHECDA NAS 45%

Spirit of Hven Seven Stars No. 3 Phecda is the third star in the Seven Stars project.

The Spirit of Hven Seven Stars No. 3 Phecda is an even more limited release than the previous releases. Where the Merak was made from twenty-five casks, the Phecda is limited to only twelve casks. The whisky was matured in a mix of American oak (Quercus muehlenbergii from Missouri) and French oak (Quercus petraea from Allier). As always, there is no chill filtering and no coloring.

The names of the whiskies in this series are taken from the stars in the asterism Ursa Major (Big Dipper / The Plough). Here is what the distillery says about the name Phecda:

"The name Phecda derives from the Arabic fakhð ad-dubb (الا ب د ف ذخ) meaning "thigh of the bear" referring to the star's position in the asterism. Since 1943 the spectrum of Phecda has been used to classify all other stars. Phecda is reminiscent of our sun but somewhat hotter and bigger."

This is medium peated whisky. It

was distilled in 2008, which makes it around 6–6.5 years old. This whisky is sold in 50cl bottles.

Nose: Soft peat and light oakiness hits the nose at first sniff. Slightly salty, a bit of chocolate. Give it more time in the glass and you also detect salt licorice, and a bit more spiciness. It does have a bit of sweetness to it, but you will be hard pressed to be very specific here—maybe we'll leave it at sweet licorice and soft oaky notes. Given even more time in the glass it picks up a whiff of perfume, something floral or herbal.

Palate: Pepper, diluted orange juice, floral notes, and a very pleasant soft smokiness. The mouthfeel is quite rich, and a bit chewy. Medium-long finish that becomes a bit dry towards the end. Lightly fruity, with some salt licorice and pepper added. Slightly oaky and herbal right at the end. Cool rather than warm.

A bit similar to Merak, but slightly more "narrow" in character.

TO

SWITZERLAND

BY CARLO DEVITO

Like its inhabitants, Switzerland is a very diverse country. With Italian, German, and French influences, Switzerland is a crossroads of taste and integration. For example, did you know that this country of 7.25 million people has somewhere in the neighborhood of 90 small breweries and brewpubs, according to the Association des Buveurs d'Orges (ABO)?

Switzerland also has 15,000 hectares of vineyard planted: 42% is white grapes, and the remaining is red. Less than 2% of Swiss wines are exported. That's supporting local! Their tradition dates back to Roman times. Pinot Noir is the dominant grape and wine.

The Swiss drink 1.6 liters of spirits per year, per person. That's just distilled products. That doesn't include wine or beer. Switzerland's whisky production began when the laws regarding distilling were relaxed. Now the whisky industry in this small European country is exploding. No one is sure where it will go. To say the least, there are some very serious practitioners in this country. Whisky is making quite an impact!

BRENNERIE HOLLEN

HOLLEN SINGLE MALT WHISKY 10 YEAR OLD 49.9%
HOLLEN SINGLE MALT WHISKY 12 YEAR OLD 43.7%

The Hollen whiskey distillery can be found in an idyllic farmhouse in Baselbieter village Lauwil. For the last 90 years, it has primarily been a working dairy farm but also grows fruits and farms more than 500 fruit trees as well. Like in many other countries, recent laws made it possible for small farms to augment their earnings by opening up ancillary distilleries to make whisky.

Hollen put in a distillery and drew the first drops of distillate on July 1, 1999, and never looked back. Their still has been in constant use ever since. Over the years, the quality improved, and they increased the number of and types of products and spirits they offered. Fruit brandies, spirits-based beverages. They've even been making absinthe since 2005.

As far as whisky was concerned, they had started making their own beer back in the 1990s. The story went that they came back from working in the fields and found out there was no beer. "Then we just brewed our beer ourselves," came the retort. So making the jump to whisky was not that big a stretch. They now offer numerous whiskies. Today Brennerie Hollen holds 90 barrels aging in their cellars.

Hollen offers several different bottlings of their whiskies. They offer typical Hollen Single Malt Whisky 10 Year Old 49.9%. They also offer Hollen Single Malt Whisky 12 Year Old 43.7%. Hollen touts this as "The first Swiss whisky with 12 years of barrel aging." The whisky was produced from pure barley malt and aged in American white oak. It was then expanded into two barrels of French oak.

Hollen Single Malt Whisky 9 Year Old Doublewood 52.5% is another special bottling. According to the distillery, this whisky was produced from barley malt *ungeräuchertem* (unsmoked) and expanded in two used wine French oak barrels after primary aging in American white oak. "Fruity, slightly bread crust, well-measured timber. Much pressure, lush, slightly dry, interesting flavor fullness, long, slightly rougher finish," reported Swiss wine Zeitung (09/2012). "A characterful whisky with a lot of power."

JOHNETT SINGLE MALT WHISKY
6 YEAR OLD 44%

Paul Etter founded Etter Distillery in Zug, Switzerland in 1870. Today, Etter is considered one of the premiere producers of fine-quality fruit brandies in Europe. Zug is a picturesque region in central Switzerland. Farmland, lakes, and forests give way here to the Alps. Etter began producing whisky on July 1, 1999 when the government allowed distillers to start making whisky. Etter Söhne AG finally added whiskey to their repertoire after 140 years of being in business.

Master Distiller John Etter wanted to produce a product that conveyed his passion and desire for a top-quality whisky. This became a personal mission for him. John knew where the base of his great whisky would come from—a neighbor. The Uster family owns the Baar Brewery, founded in 1862. They were the perfect partner. They were local, and they could produce the 100% malted barley necessary for the whisky. And they too were a family-run business. Made with spring water from the local Höllgrotten (Baar Hell Caves) owned by the Schmid family for generations. Not only does John draw from the spring in these caves, but JOHNETT whisky is aged in the Baar Hell Caves as well.

The whisky is stored in special oak barrels from the Weingut Rosenau of the Ottiger family in the Kastanien-baum region of Lucerne. The young whisky produces a special flavor unique to JOHNETT, giving it a further distinctive appeal.

According to Swiss food journalist Christian Langenegger, "Johnett has dried-fruit notes, is lightly spicy and nutty."

LANGATUN OLD BEAR 5 YEAR OLD 2009 64%

Langatun is a Swiss whisky with a long history. In 1857, Jakob Baumberger took over a small brewery in Langenthal (a village formerly known as Langatun). He started brewing and distilling there, quite a successful business that was taken over by his sons. They also ran a malting plant and a peat cutting activity.

Unclear as to why there was a gap after that, but in 2007, Jakob's grandson Hans reignited the family tradition and started producing unpeated whisky (Langatun Old Deer), peated whisky (Langatun Old Bear), whisky liqueur, rum, vodka, rye, bourbon, and fruit spirits. While Old Deer is matured in Chardonnay and Sherry casks, the peated Old Bear is aged in Châteauneuf-du-Pape red wine casks. We're trying the cask strength version.

Nose: Fresh wood, young but nice. Berry fruits and candied oranges. Honey. Clear smoke, but well integrated. A faint spiciness too.

Palate: Powerful, very sugary, and very smoky now. Lots of caramel and candy sugar sweetness. Red berries, raspberry candy from the red wine casks, but also less impressive, plain winey notes. Sweet grape juice. Some tannins too. The peat stays stronger than on the nose. Long, a tad more bitter and herbal now, but still sweet and deeply smoked.

This Langatun Old Bear is a fairly simple, very sweet but enjoyable whisky. The wine influence is just right.

RL

LOCHER BREWERY

SÄNTIS MALT EDITION DREIFALTIGKEIT 52%

Säntis Malt Edition Dreifaltigkeit is a cask strength peated whisky from Switzerland. This beauty has been matured in old (60-130 years old) oak beer casks that were smoked with oak wood by the "Swiss Highlander." Säntis whisky is a product of Locher brewery—famous for making a wide range of beers in Appenzell, Switzerland. They take their water from the Alpstein Mountains and peat from the Upland Moor.

Edition Dreifaltigkeit (The Trinity) gets its name from a local mountain peak. This dram is stated to be lightly peated. Still, strongly peaty and smoky, it gets it all from various stages of smoke treatment in the process. The malt is smoked in three different ways: beech-smoked, oak-smoked and peat-smoked (done in two stages). Smoked in two woods, the barley is then resmoked with peat from the local Appenzell Highmoor.

The brewery started distilling whisky in 1999 and ever since then they've released a limited 2,000 bottle output per year-limited because of the casks that are being used for maturation. Before maturing whisky in them, the casks have been used for maturing beer for a century in a process called lagering. Very unique, but not exhaustless.

Säntis Single Malt Edition Trinity is a Swiss not to miss!

So unique and bit weird, but very good and well acknowledged, award-winning single malt whisky—if this was a movie, it would be "Birdman."

Nose: Very fascinating nose for a whisky—reminds me of Schlenkerla Rauchbier, German smoke beer. With the exception, that Schlenkerla has more ham and Säntis is more like mettwurst (uncooked German sausage). Though, there's cold-smoked ham as well. Sweet and spicy, like a mix of cinnamon and spicy sherry with peat on the back. And what felt like spicy sherry turns out to be more like malted dark bread.

Palate: Delicate and warm spices with soft oiliness. Sweet and bit dry. Ham and mettwurst, malted barley, ale, and peat. Bit fruity as well, with oranges. All in a strong but smooth way. Great palate. Mildly dry, like bitter ale. Some caramel sweetness. Red grapefruits, when given time in the glass. This single malt whisky from Switzerland is truly amazing. One of a kind at the moment. Like Dominic Roskrow put it in his book *1001 Whiskies You Must Taste Before You Die*, "If you like smoke in abundance, you don't want to miss this Swiss." Jim Murray chose Säntis Malt Edition Drei-faltigkeit, aka The Trinity, as *Whisky Bible 2010's* "European Whisky of the Year" with a score of 96.5.

JL

ÖUFI SINGLE MALT WHISKY
11 YEAR OLD 42%

Öufi Braui Beiz is a micro-brewery and restaurant. They make their beer from scratch, even harvesting their own grains. Öufi Single Malt Whisky starts out as beer made at the micro-brewery. This is a collaboration product. The beer was shipped to Hugo Grogg distillery in Altreu the southern Jura. In 1974, the then 20 year old Hugo Crogg bought a mobile still from the previous owner, Walter Kocher, with the idea of making it stationary. Hugo and Astrid Grogg founded their commercial distillery in 1975. Hugo and Alex Künzle (from Öufi Brewery) have been working on Öufi whisky since 2001.

The temperate climate of the area between the Jura and Aare is consistent. The whisky is laid down for 11 years. Why 11 years? Because *Öufi* is a German dialect meaning "eleven." The 2004 vintage was sold out. The second release will be late 2016. The whisky is aged in Marsala barriques. Marsala is a sweet Sicilian wine, known for its unctuous body, much like port or sherry. It is available only by special order from the brewery.

BREWERY RUGENBRAU AG

High up in the Berner Oberland are the Bernese Alps (which are located in western Switzerland), and part of the higher Canton of Bern. Lake Thun and Lake Brienz are two beautiful natural wonders there. In prehistoric times, hunters and traders crisscrossed these mountains. Later, the Romans established the first known settlements on the banks of the river and the lakes. The Bernese Mountain dog was originally bred in this and other nearby regions, as a rugged, all-purpose farm dog to work on the plains and mountains of this region. It was first shown at the large dog show in Bern in the early 1900s.

It is in this region, in Matten bei Interlaken, Switzerland, that the Brewery Rugenbräu AG of Interlaken was established in 1866. Swiss High-

land Single Malt Whisky is produced there. Like other distillers, Rugenbräu began distilling whisky once the laws were enacted on July 1, 1999, allowing them to make the famous brown spirit. They released their first single malt, Mountain High, in 2003.

Famed Islay Master Distiller Jim McEwan, who retired from Bruichladdich, has been consulting here since 2008. And later that year on March 14, 2008, McEwan was on hand as they launched the rebranding of the line as Swiss Highlands Single Malt.

In 2010, the company installed a new still just above the old brew house. Rugenbräu brews its own beer, using fresh, pure Alpine water, and then distills it, aging it in American white oak and old sherry casks in deep caves called Felsenkeller, which were carved out underground in 1875.

SWISS HIGHLAND FORTY THREE 43%

This bottling is named for the ABV at which it is bottled. Rugenbräu positions this as their entry single malt whisky. Whisky is

aged for at least three years in selected oak barrels, including American white oak and former sherry casks. The color is amber. Tasting notes include,

"Slightly woody notes are combined with coffee and chocolate tones for a soft gentleness. A slight maltiness is felt at the beginning, which then rises wonderfully in caramel and fermented vanilla pod. The good balance between sweetness and rigor...."

SWISS HIGHLAND CLASSIC 46%

This bottling is twice distilled, aged in American white oak and finished in Oloroso sherry casks. The Swiss Highland Classic received a shockingly wonderful score of 95 points in *Jim Murray's Whisky Bible 2012*. The color is golden. "Good nose with winey sweet

sherry notes, malty Karamelaspekten but the fruitiness of apricot and peach, and honey notes are visible. The complex aroma of the nose is confirmed on the palate. Slightly woody, astringent flavors are combined with vanilla and caramel... impressive balance."

SWISS HIGHLAND ICE LABEL EDITION II 2015 56.7%

Twice distilled, and aged in American white oak and then finished in Oloroso sherry casks. This is a cask strength single malt whisky,

single barrel. The color is light gold. "Strong nose with fresh fruit. Notes of apricot, pear and raisins and sweet sherry notes, malty Karamelaspekten

and honey notes are visible. Elderflower. Subtle smokiness and an accent of light wood, augmented by vanilla. On the palate the subtle combination of wood and spicy flavors with vanilla and caramel... impressive balance."

BERGSTURZ 10 YEAR OLD
SINGLE MALT WHISKY 40%

On September 2, 1806, one of Switzerland's worst national natural disasters occurred. In what was called the Goldau Landslide, more than 40 million cubic meters of rock and rubble slid 1,000 meters down the southern face of Rossberg Mountain. In a matter of a few short minutes, to 20-meter high tsunami of dirt and stone wiped out four miles of the valley below! The villages of Goldau and Rothen were completely erased from the earth. Parts of neighboring towns, such as Buosingen and Lauerz, were also hit hard. The citizens of the country came together to help save the victims and brought on a new sense of nationalism in Switzerland. *Bergsturz* means landslide. That landslide is the illustration on the label of Bergsturz single malt whisky.

Bergsturz ("landslide") is produced by Schaubrennerei Z'Graggen. In 1948, Anton Z'Graggen established a small distillery to complement his income from his farming. By 1953 he moved his distilling base to a larger facility in the mountains to accommodate his growing business. There he also built an apartment house with a petrol station and a kiosk. His businesses all grew. He eventually diversified, making wine and other beverages. Anton's sons Tony and Andrew now operate this business. In 1994 they did a major upgrade of the distillery and reopened it. They currently produce more than 55 spirits, beers, and other beverages. If you go there, the tasting room is beautifully situated on the shore of a lake. Beautiful!

Z'Graggen touts Bergsturz as "Switzerland's first-ever 10 year old single malt."

Color: Deep amber.

Nose and palate: "oak, figs, prunes, fresh fruit of orange and citrus, slight hints of tea and leather. Oily and lingering aftertaste."

CD

TERRENI ALLA MAGGIA SA

ASCONA SINGLE MALT WHISKY
3 YEAR OLD 43%

The Terreni alla Maggia SA was established in the 1930s. They are a small agricultural company that makes numerous handcrafted, artisanal products. They have been making whisky since 2007. They grow their own barley. Of their 150 hectares, 130 are planted for agriculture and are located in the Tessin region, the municipalities of Ascona, Locarno and Gordola. They are 198 meters above sea level, making it the lowest lying land in Switzerland. Their operation is divided into farming, viticulture, fruit growing, and poultry farming. The Brauerei Locher AG brew five to six barrels of beer for new spirits each year. The barrels are warehoused in a building they call Stallone Rusca, which dates back to the seventeenth century. The whisky is stored in French oak barrique barrels and aged three years. Amber in color. Tasting notes: "A refined sweet and at the same time full-bodied single malt... slightly fruity with a hint of vanilla."

CD

LAKELAND 3 YEAR OLD
SINGLE MALT WHISKY 42%

In 1954, Willy Zürcher returned to his parents' small farmhouse on Nägeligässli 7, after his parents had died. Willy had a mobile distilling line and wheeled it from village to village. In 1968, Willy installed a new still in the former goat barn, but a year later, Willy died and his eldest son, Heinz Zürcher, continued the distillery for the next thirty-five years. Heinz built the business up slowly, offering new products, eventually requiring more space, which resulted in building an addition in 1988. The family then, as now, distilled numerous products, including fruit brandies (apples, cherries, plums, apricots, quince), grappa, absinthe, and whisky, as well as other things. It was a successful micro-distillery. Heinz and his family considered the making of their own Lakeland single malt whisky in 2003 a crowning achievement.

On July 1, 2004, nephew Daniel Zürcher (lead distiller) with his wife Ursula, and their children Matthias, Natalia, Sven and Sina, continued operations, the third generation of the family to run Zürcher distillery. Daniel trained as a wine technologist.

But uncle Heinz Zürcher taught Daniel the other finesses of working with a still. Continuity is everything, and there has been consistency in staff. Alain Pascal has worked at Zürcher for twenty years working the still and production.

Heinz distilled his first whisky in 2000. He let the whisky rest for three years in Oloroso sherry casks. Released in 2003, it sold out immediately. Since then, Zürcher lays down at least one barrel of whisky annually, usually more. They use mostly Oloroso sherry casks. Over time, Zürcher has experimented with ex-bourbon, port, and Swiss Sauternes oak barrels. They even have a few hogsheads (oak barrels with 250 liter capacity). Now Zürcher bottles at least one barrel of Lakeland Single Malt Whisky every year. Distinctive sherry, malt, and oak.

In August 2014, Zürcher bottled their first Anniversary Edition, an 8 year old single malt aged in Oloroso sherry casks. It was the 10th anniversary of Daniel and Ursula Zürcher running the distillery. More special bottlings are planned.

TAIWAN

BY RICHARD AUFFREY

During the last approximately one hundred years, Japanese whisky has taken the world by storm, winning plenty of international awards and thrilling the palates of whisky lovers everywhere. But it isn't the only Asian country involved in whisky, and you will likely soon hear more and more about an island in Asia that is producing world quality whisky: the island of Taiwan.

Probably the oldest alcohol produced on the island of Taiwan is millet wine, which was made by the aboriginal peoples and was an element of many of their rituals and festivals. Eventually, they started producing rice wine, though nowadays it is used far more often in cooking than for drinking. Currently, Taiwan's most famous spirit is Kaoliang, a clear alcohol made from fermented sorghum that commonly ranges from 76 to 120 proof.

Besides these wines and spirits, and because of the country's hotter temperatures, beer is extremely popular, and many people enjoy drinking their beer over ice. Most bars serve beer in a bottle, and taps are uncommon. One of the most popular local beers is Taiwan Beer, an amber lager that is brewed with barley and fragrant penglai rice.

In the last twenty years or so, international spirits from all around the world, including whisky, have begun to appear on store shelves in Taiwan. As such, whisky gained some popularity there, and eventually led one local entrepreneur to construct his very own whisky distillery, the first of its kind on the island.

At the beginning of the twentieth century, there were over 2,600 commercial producers of alcohol on Taiwan; however, that all changed when the Japanese seized control of Taiwan after the First Sino-Japanese War. The Japanese established the Monopoly Bureau of the Taiwan Governor's Office, which became responsible for all liquor, tobacco, opium, salt, and camphor products in the country. However, even when Japan was defeated in World War II, the government monopoly on alcohol remained in place, though it was soon after renamed the Taiwan Tobacco and Wine Monopoly Bureau.

Significant change would not arrive until January 1, 2002, when Taiwan officially became the 144th member of the World Trade Organization (WTO). The Monopoly Bureau was renamed as the Taiwan Tobacco and Liquor Corporation, and new laws were enacted that permitted private companies to open distilleries and produce alcohol. This opening quickly led to aa number of wineries and micro-breweries and one whisky distillery opening up in recent years.

The Taiwanese have a healthy appetite for whisky, and the market has been growing significantly in recent years. Taiwan is around the fifth or sixth largest export market for Scotch whisky, though they are around only twentieth place for whiskey consumption per capita. The King Car Food Industrial Company, founded in 1956 by Tian Tsai Lee, has been involved in numerous businesses, including beverages, food, biotechnology and aquaculture. It is known for such products as Green Time Natural Drinking Water and Mr. Brown Coffee. With the breaking of the government alcohol monopoly in 2002, the path was opened for the company to construct a distillery, and they were interested in producing whisky, though many people were skeptical that the plan would work. They went forward with their plans anyway, assembling a research and development team to explore the possibility, and traveling to Scotland to study their options.

Tian Tsai Lee had been born in Yilan County, located in the northeastern region of Taiwan, and chose to build his distillery there, in the township of Yuanshan. As homage to the aboriginal people of the Yilan, he decided to name his whisky Kavalan. The word *Kavalan* roughly means "the people of the plains" and is also the name of the people who once inhabited this area. Yilan was partially chosen because it possesses excellent natural water sources that flow down from the Central and Snow Mountain ranges. This is also the source of the Green Time Natural Drinking Water that King Car bottles. In addition, the Yilan is close to the Pacific Ocean, so the distillery benefits from that climate.

In 2005, construction of the distillery began and, surprisingly, it was completed in only nine months, when this task usually takes five years. The facility is quite substantial and has even grown since its initial construction. Originally, it had the capability of producing 3 million bottles annually, which has grown to about 9 million bottles. There are approximately 46,000 casks in storage. The distillery has a large visitor center, and over one million people visit each year. In comparison, that is roughly the same amount of tourists to visit all of the whisky distilleries in Scotland!

Whisky consultant Dr. Jim Swan worked with the people at Kavalan, including Master Blender Ian Chang, to set up the distillery and overcome the potential problems and obstacles with producing whiskey in Taiwan. Ian

Chang is also the whisky producer's brand ambassador, director of global business development, and head of research and development.

The primary problem is the hotter temperatures in Taiwan, which result in a more rapid maturation. For example, what might take 8–15 years of aging in Scotland only takes three years, or even less, in Taiwan. On average, Taiwan is about 27 degrees warmer than Scotland. The higher temperatures also mean that the whiskey barrels lose much more to evaporation, the "angel's share," than they would elsewhere. The angel's share might be 2% to 3% in Scotland, but in Taiwan, it is more like 10% to 15%—a huge difference. In addition, these higher temperatures can lead to increased bacterial growth. As such Dr. Swan and Chang worked together to handle these issues. For example, they use stainless steel fermenting containers, instead of wood, to prevent bacteria. (By the way, their barley is imported from Europe.) Much of their work is directed toward the maturation of the whisky, including the creation of a five-story warehouse. The higher levels are hotter so larger 500–700 liter barrels are used on that floor, while smaller barrels, 18–250 liters, are used on the lower and cooler floors. Experimentation and research into other methods of slowing maturation are ongoing.

The first whisky from Kavalan was produced in March 2006, and the first bottles sold in December 2008. Initially, to cater to the taste of Taiwanese consumers, their whiskies presented with a fruity flavor profile. All of their whiskies are also cask strength, non-chill filtered, and natural in color. The squared-off design of the single malt bottle was inspired by the Taipei 101, one of the tallest buildings in the world. Kavalan now produces about ten different whiskies, with at least six available in the United States.

The Kavalan whiskies have received a number of accolades and awards and are being taken very seriously. They have proven that world-class whisky can be made in Taiwan, despite the higher temperatures, which should be interesting news to other countries that have considered making their own whisky. In time, maybe additional distilleries will open in Taiwan. Right now, the Taiwan Tobacco and Liquor Corporation bottles some other whiskies under labels such as Yutai Golden Whisky and Jade Supremacy Taiwan Whisky, though that is actually distilled in Scotland (they merely blend the whisky in Taiwan).

The distillery is part of a substantial site on the plains at Yilan, with many acres of company-owned ground at its disposal for expansion. A steep range of heavily wooded hills and mountains lie just behind the distillery, and their lush, green slopes suggest that water shortages are unlikely to represent a future problem. The parent group is well financed and, as a family-owned company, capable of taking the long-term decisions essential for success in the whisky business.

KAVALAN

BY RICHARD THOMAS

Founded in 2005, Kavalan, the first whisky distillery built in Taiwan, caused quite a stir in the whisky circles when it beat traditional Scottish brands at a blind tasting held on Burns Night in 2010. Even noted whisky expert Jim Murray named one of Kavalan's products "Best New World Whisky" in his 2012 edition of *The Whisky Bible*. Now a wider circle of American palates can sample Taiwanese whisky, as Anchor Distilling put seven Kavalan expressions into US distribution in April 2014.

Those expressions include the Kavalan Classic, Kavalan Concertmaster, Kavalan King Car Conductor, Kavalan Fino Sherry Cask, Kavalan Ex-Bourbon Cask, Kavalan Sherry Cask, and Kavalan Vinho Barrique.

Accounting for the tastes of Taiwanese drinkers, Master Blender Ian Chang and Dr. Jim Swan, an international whisky expert and consultant to Kavalan, aimed at creating fruitier flavor profiles. All Kavalan whiskies are cask strength, non-chill filtered, and natural in color.

"The world of whisk(e)y is evolving quickly and we at Anchor are extremely honored and excited to bring arguably the most interesting range of whiskies to discerning American consumers," says Anchor Distilling Company President David King. "The Kavalan range of whiskies is truly world class and stands shoulder to shoulder with the best products out there."

KAVALAN SINGLE MALT WHISKY 43%

It is easy understand why Kavalan is receiving so many accolades. This whisky was tasted without and with the addition of a little water. The water generally brought out more fruit flavors in the whiskies, especially in the Solist line. If you are a whisky lover, you need to put these on your radar and see why so many are raving about Kavalan.

The Kavalan Single Malt Whisky was the first whisky produced by Kavalan and has an ABV of 43%. With a light amber color, it has a fruity and floral nose. On the palate, it is silky, with a lush blend of flavors, including tropical fruit, honey, vanilla, orange peel, and coconut, with chocolate notes on the lengthy finish. Clean and complex, this should appeal to most whisky lovers.

RA

KAVALAN CONCERTMASTER WHISKY 43%

The Kavalan Concertmaster Whisky is a single malt whiskey that was finished in port casks and has an ABV of 43%. The port casks include ruby, tawny, and vintage port. With a slightly darker amber color, the nose is more chocolate and savory notes. However, on the palate, there is more fruit, including red berries, along with vanilla, chocolate, and a bit of leather. A little heavier in the mouthfeel than the basic Single Malt. It was also silky and complex, clean and with a lengthy, satisfying finish.

RA

KAVALAN SOLIST CASK STRENGTH 57%

Solist Ex-Bourbon Cask is a single cask release and apparently only 3 years old. The reason why they don't have to mature their whiskies for several years is the climate, depending on the local temperature and the wood to imbue the spirit with unique character. I have to admit, the young age doesn't show that much in Kavalan Solist, at least in this bourbon cask-matured version. And I guess it doesn't show in their sherry cask-matured Soloists either, because they are well praised too.

King Car, the large Taiwanese group, was established in 1956 and has several business fields under its name. They have production in food, biotechnology, aquaculture, and beverages.

Wo hu cang long AKA Crouching Tiger, Hidden Dragon is a movie combining intelligent storytelling with goodlooking special effects and martial arts. The movie came to my mind while sipping this bourbon cask-matured Kavalan Solist. Both are kicking it hard, but with complexity. And doing it good. Kavalan is truly a rare whisky experience—a single malt so young, offering so much character in aromas and taste. Good dram indeed.

Color: Pale gold.

Nose: Without water, pine was the first aroma that hit me. With water and lime in the glass, vanilla and bananas start to dominate. The vanilla feels toasted at first but turns sugary with time. Hints of creamy coconut. Tropical and fruity.

Palate: Amazing taste, starts with peppery, salty licorice (salmiac). The palate turns into sugary and tropical quite fast, though. Sprinkly, like gin and tonic. Carbonated berries with vanilla butter and toast. The body isn't buttery thick, more like a light vanilla butter. Great length, peppery hot with oak. As the hot notes fade away, tropical fruits and bananas in doughy form start to rise in the aftertaste.

Amazing whisky, now I know what all the fuss is about. I am amazed for scoring whisky so young so high. Single cask and cask strength with climate helping to make rapid maturation. Those are the ingredients for this great single malt whisky. Complex, powerful, and tropical whisky.

JL

UNITED STATES

AMERICAN SINGLE MALT WHISKEYS SERVE NOTICE

BY CLAY RISEN

The humid streets of Waco, Texas, may not have much in common with the misty glens of Scotland, home to some of the world's best malt whiskeys.

Not much, that is, [until a single] malt whiskey from the Balcones Distillery in Waco (see pages 500-505) bested nine others, including storied Scottish names like the Balvenie and the Macallan, in a blind panel of British spirits experts.

It was the first time an American whiskey won the Best in Glass, a 5 year old competition to find the best whiskey released in a given year.

Balcones, said Neil Ridley, one of the organizers, is everything you'd expect from a young American: brash, robust and full of flavor. "It was like putting a New World wine against an Old World chateau," he said.

This wasn't supposed to happen. American whiskey is all about corn and rye; malted barley, the primary grain in the Scotch variety, traditionally plays a minor role in bourbon recipes. And single malts have long been considered an exclusive province of Scotland.

But suddenly, American malted whiskeys—most of them single malts—are popping up, some to loud acclaim.

[Years] ago, just a few oddball American single malts were available. The [next] year's arrivals included Pine Barrens, a whiskey made by Long Island Spirits, on the island's

North Fork, and Leviathan, produced by the Lost Spirits Distillery outside Salinas, California. "They're pushing the convention forward about what American whiskey is."

In a way, the surprising thing about American malt whiskey is not that it exists, but that it took so long to come around. Corn and rye may be the traditional American whiskey grains, but most of today's craft distillers come from a brewing background, in which working with malted barley is the core of the business.

"I've been studying beer since I was 16 years old," said Chip Tate, the master distiller at Balcones (pronounced bal-CONE-ays), who worked as a brewmaster before co-founding the distillery. "I woke up one day and realized I wasn't a beer lover who liked whiskey, but a whiskey lover who liked beer."

The American malt whiskey trend is also a recognition that in a global market thirsty for new spirits, the national love affair with corn- and rye-based brown liquor is hardly the only story. Indeed, distillers say the bulk of the interest in their single malts comes from overseas.

"The malt whiskey thing is something you're seeing around the world," with great new whiskeys appearing from unexpected locales like India and Taiwan, said Lew Bryson, managing editor of the magazine *Whisky Advocate.* "Malt whiskey is huge."

Most of the American whiskeys are single malts—that is, produced entirely at one distillery, from the same type of barley—by default; distillers here, unlike their Scottish counterparts, do little blending. But while many embrace their single-maltedness, and the inevitable comparison with their Scotch cousins, some shy away, preferring to pitch themselves as another drink entirely.

The American whiskeys tend to fall roughly into two categories. Some, like Balcones, Leviathan, and St. George, a well-regarded single malt from Alameda, Calif., use Scotch as a model, with some even importing peat-smoked malt directly from Scotland.

Steve McCarthy, who makes the heavily peated McCarthy's Single Malt, alongside a range of eaux-de-vie, at the Clear Creek Distillery in Portland, Oregon, said he was inspired to create a Scotch-style whiskey after tasting a 16 year old Lagavulin on a trip around Ireland in 1992. "I thought, 'I would like to go home and make that,'" he said.

Some fifteen years after Mr. McCarthy's first release, even many hardcore Scotch drinkers say he succeeded.

"I was skeptical at first," said Nathan Keeney, a computer programmer and Scotch devotee from San Jose, California. "But if I were in a blind tasting, I wouldn't have been able to tell you it didn't come from Islay," the Scottish island home of world-famous peat monsters like Ardbeg and Laphroaig.

Unlike those Scottish distillers, however, American whiskey makers face few limits on what they can call "single malt"—a freedom that many have grabbed with both hands. Theirs is the second category of American single malts: a catchall grouping where the sole defining characteristic is aggressive innovation.

Wasmund's, a whiskey from Sperryville, Virginia, gets some of its signature fruit notes from a bag of apple wood chips that steeps in the barrel along with the aging whiskey, a process that might cause a Highlands distiller to jump out of his kilt.

To create its Pine Barrens Single Malt, Long Island Spirits, in Baiting Hollow, New York, starts by distilling a commercial beer—Old Howling Bastard, a barley wine from the nearby Blue Point Brewing Company—and then aging it in oak barrels.

The result is hoppy and bready, with strong citrus notes, a world away from the mellow smokiness of a typical Scotch. And that, said Richard Stabile, the owner of Long Island Spirits, is the point. "It's part of the pioneer spirit to try to do something by putting your own signature on it," he said. "I'm not trying to make someone else's product."

Innovation isn't just about putting one's mark on a style, though. One of the few rules governing American malt whiskeys is a federal law, enacted in 1938, requiring that they be at least partly aged in previously unused oak barrels. Unfortunately, malted barley is delicate and prone to lose its flavor in new oak, which is why Scottish distillers prefer barrels that once held sherry, port, or bourbon.

To compensate, American distillers often start with a more robust, flavorful mash than a typical Scotch, which can better stand up to new oak, flavor that continues to shine through after the whiskey is bottled.

They also rely on America's higher temperatures, and bigger temperature swings, to speed the aging process. "A hot day in Scotland is 75 degrees," said Mr. Tate, of Balcones. "Seventy-five degrees isn't even a hot day in January here."

As a result, even Balcones, despite its peat and smoky notes, is unlikely to be confused with an Islay Scotch. "A lot of what we do is riffing on old traditions in new ways," Mr. Tate said. "It's like fusion cooking."

In this way, American craft distilling is following the same path trod by wine making and craft brewing. What started with a close adherence to Old World styles — Bordeaux, Vienna lager — gave way in time to new categories like California cabernets and American Pale Ale.

And it's that relentless creativity, as much as the quality, that is winning worldwide adherents for American single malts.

Mr. McCarthy, who says he plans to expand production in the next year, is pleasantly frustrated with his whiskey's growing global following. "I get calls from Japan for my entire inventory," he said. "I labor over my eaux de vie, but the product they all want is whiskey."

Seattle, WA

3 HOWLS SINGLE MALT WHISKEY 44%

3 Howls Distillery was established in 2013 in the heart of Seattle's SoDo neighborhood. They gained almost instant notoriety for their 3 Howls Navy Strength Gin. A small batch distillery, they produce 12 unique products, including various styles of rum, vodka, whiskey, gin, and a line of flavor-infused vodkas. Their whiskies have started to turn heads. 3 Howls Single Malt Whiskey is Scottish in inspiration, but with a local twist. This Seattle-based distiller starts off with beer brewed using Northwest specialty grains and is smoked with traditional Scottish peat. This amber liquid has a nose of cocoa, toast, honey, apricot, and caramel, all topped with vanilla and smoke. Smokey, rich, and hot. Nice spiciness lingers.

CD

San Francisco, CA

OLD POTRERO SINGLE MALT RYE WHISKEY 45%

The story of this whiskey starts with beer.

Anchor Steam is San Francisco's beer. It is as much a symbol of that city as cable cars and sourdough bread. Some have called it the first microbrew, but that's not really accurate. It dates from 1896, when microbrews were really all there were. There were more than two dozen breweries in San Francisco at that time, but only Anchor survived. It survived and thrived until 100 years later, when there was another microbrewery movement.

In 1993, the folks from Anchor, ahead of the curve again, founded Anchor Distilling Company to make small batches of premium spirits. Anchor Distilling makes Junípero Gin, which has gotten good reviews, but we are here to talk about Old Potrero Single Malt Rye.

Unlike most ryes, which are cut with corn or wheat, Old Potrero is made from 100% malted rye (hence the single malt designation). They currently have three offerings: (1) 19th century style; (2) 18th century style; and (3) Hotaling's, which they bill as the style of whiskey from the time of the 1906 San Francisco earthquake. In addition, I had previously tasted a version with no age statement or other designation, but that does not seem to be available any longer. Prices for these whiskies seem to range from $55 to $70.

I love the spiciness of rye, and it comes out in full force in Old Potrero. Be warned, if you are used to Kentucky ryes cut with corn and wheat, you may be knocked down by the strong rye statement in these whiskies. I loved both the versions of Old Potrero I tried and was impressed at the boldness and flavor intensity of OP's whiskies.

To sum up: I highly recommend these rye monsters for anyone who craves the spiciness of rye.

SU

BALCONES

Waco, TX

BY CARLO DEVITO

Balcones is one of most storied and wildest rides in American distilling in the last half century. The distillery in Waco, Texas was founded by the mercurial and talented Chip Tate. He was a maniac, experimenting with whiskeys in anything that would hold the liquid, from 5 gallons to 60 gallons and more. He was a mad scientist, for whom distillation wasn't just a business but a mad creative world wherein he could concoct amazing things. He made amazing potions with great passion, using ingredients like blue corn and fig, just to name two. Everything he touched seemed to turn out just right.

He started the company, and slowly, he built Balcones up into a powerhouse. Tate brought on Allison Patel as his brand ambassador, and the two made American distilling history. Tate made award-winning products, and the beautiful and brilliant Patel spread the gospel of Balcones. It all ended in triumph as Balcones was named the best whiskey in the world in 2013, defeating some of the world's great single malt Scotches in a competition akin to the great Paris wine tasting of 1973.

Success brought on opportunities... and investors. But that is where the tale turned crazy. Tate and his investors spent millions expanding Balcones, ready to build it into a world super power of distilling. Only problem was, they didn't get along. Eventually, through legal wranglings, Tate lost control of the business he made famous, and after much public infighting, and court filings, Tate left his beloved mad genius lab with a buy-out, a bag of cash, and a dream to build a new business.

In the meantime, Balcones moves forward. Balcones Distillery continues with Keith Bellinger as president. Longtime Balcones hand Jared Himstedt, who had been with the company since 2008 (and a former brewing partner of Tate's), was named head distiller and distillery manager. Balcones won American Craft Distillery of the Year in 2015. They continue to make excellent whiskey.

BALCONES "1" SPECIAL RELEASE TEXAS SINGLE MALT WHISKY BATCH SM 14.2 53%

Color: Gosh this stuff looks amazing. Amber and then some. Elegant short bottle, textured black label with a nice wax seal. No chill-filtration and no colorant so that is nice. Batch and date clearly marked on the back in what looks like pen. Actual hands were needed to get this out the door. You can really feel the passion they have for their whisky at Balcones.

Nose: Marzipan, tangerines, hazelnuts, caramel, raw honey, cereal grains, rising dough, vanilla, sandalwood, poached pears, and homemade whipped cream. This smells great. Here you are on a wonderful tour of all the great bourbon and single malt scents. As soon as this bottle is opened you know you are in for a treat. Every time I pour a dram of this fine liquid I get excited as these wonderful fragrances waft up from the glass.

Palate: Honeyed malt with rich creamy nuttiness, sherried sweetness, figs, and dark chocolate. Big, bold, powerful and rich. Firing on all cylinders. There is a real vibrancy to the flavors here. They are urgent and direct. You are out visiting your uncle, who is a little bit of a black sheep in your family. He tells you he has been distilling and aging his own whisky. As you take a sip you see a glimmer in his eye. He winks at you as the amazing liquid destroys your sense of what is possible in this life. Long and lip smacking. The finish reveals some sherry and oak. Drying out now but urgently requesting another sip. Candied nuts served from a street vendor in a paper cone while the gentle late summer evening chill is bested by a sip of this honeyed liquid. Gentle chest warming heat but very little burn. Lingering thoughts of this stuff can haunt your memories for days.

Serious American craft whisky that can hang with much older single malts. There is no age statement, and it is possibly very, very young but there is no way you could know that as you drink it. Being at nearly cask strength really enhances this malt. Its raw boldness echoes bourbon, but its underlying flavors lean more toward a Speyside malt. This is a good place to be. I love malts that exhibit creamy nuttiness and this has it in spades. There is so much hype around Balcones, and this expression in particu-lar, but it is so nice when the liquid in the bottle exceeds even your hyped-up ideal of what to expect. Fact: if you get a bottle of this you will not be dis-appointed. I find myself already trying to hold back my excitement to make the bottle last longer. Given Chip's level of extreme whisky geekery and unbridled passion for tinkering we can expect this stuff to just get better and better. If he can make this amaz-ing of a whisky with so few years in barrel, imagine what he could do with a 12 year old—the ceiling may have to be raised.

JM

Chip Tate's Mad Geeky Genius

BY JOSH FELDMAN

Editorial Note: Chip Tate is no longer associated with Balcones, but his spirit, work, and influence within the American whiskey scene are undeniable. Here is an interview while he was still with Balcones, but it gives you a sense of what drove Balcones to be considered one of the best single malts in the world. Allison Patel, of course, now has her own brand.

Balcones Distillery is doing wonderful work lately. Its core expressions of Baby Blue, True Blue, Brimstone, Texas Whisky, Rumble, and Rumble Cask Reserve are among the best craft spirits being made in the vibrant and effusive US craft whisky movement. It's a group of spirits marked by tremendous innovation in terms of mash bill, barrel management, and production methods. More importantly, it's a group of spirits with a shocking level of maturity and refinement given their young bottling age.

I had a wonderful opportunity to meet with Chip Tate of Balcones Distillery and, as Chip calls it, "geek out" about whisky. "Geeking out" means getting into the technical details of the artistry of whisky-making, including the empirical science behind some of the concepts. For example, I asked about the design of Balcone's famous handmade copper pot stills and what criteria he used. Chip said he did a mathematical analysis: to determine turbulence versus laminar flow he calculated the Reynold's number for the shapes he was considering. We discussed flavors and the chemistry behind them. For example, while tasting a fine craft East Coast bourbon from a different distiller (geeking out involves drinking a range of interesting spirits and discussing them), I commented on an acetone flavor note. Chip identified this note—often found in bourbon—as ethyl acetate, a primary ester composed by the chemical bonding of alcohol plus organic acids. The acetate from acetic acid and ethyl from ethyl alcohol. And while every bourbon has Ethyl acetate to some extent—the degree to which it appears emphasized has to do with the richness of other flavor compounds to balance it. The conversation ranged over other chemical compounds, which appear as flavor components. For example: butyric acid (a sort of baby puke note in some bourbons), acetic acid (the vinegar in bourbon), or nitrosamines with a characteristic flavor formed of sulfur and peat combined via heating.

I asked about water, and Chip made clear that Balcones uses filtered municipal water prior to distillation and spring water post distillation. We talked yeast, and Chip discussed how careful yeast selection at Balcones gives stonefruit, peach, ripe pineapple, and banana notes. The discussion of yeast lead to a discussion of the life and work of Jean De Clerck (Belgian brewer scientist/monk).

Following Chip in a conversation like this is dizzying and exhilarating. Allison Patel, The Whisky Woman (who works with Chip as a brand ambassador as one of her many hats), had warned me to bring a notepad when hanging out with Chip. Man, she wasn't kidding.

We discussed barrel management and rapid maturation. The use of small barrels is a big trend in craft distilling that has become a controversial topic lately. Buffalo Trace released the results of an experiment with small barrels where they found the spirit over-oaked and declared small barrels a failure. Chuck Cowdery wrote an article, which he expanded into a book, reiterating the argument and concludes that rapid maturation tricks can make interesting spirits but not good bourbon. In the book he looks at some (not any Balcones products however) and damns them with faint praise. Others, such as "In With Baccus," have ridiculed the experiment as so obviously flawed that its clear intent is marketing against craft distillers. Balcones uses small 20 liter (5 gallon) yard-aged white oak casks to accelerate wood extraction. The yard-aged part is important because kiln drying harshes the wood. Yard-aged wood has more sweetness of the wood sugar left in the wood—and this shows clearly all over the Balcones line. Small barrels such as these are, according to Chip, hard to use. He likens managing maturation in them to "trying to gently and carefully cook a steak on an extremely hot fire. You have to pay attention or they'll burn." Among the really exciting things Chip is doing is empirically testing the differences in flavor in maturation in small barrels versus large barrels. The differences are apparent but are far smaller than you might believe. Balcones succeeds in making very polished finished spirits using small barrels, which appears to blow the argument out of the water—but to be fair to Cowdery, nothing Chip makes is quite "bourbon" in either the legal or traditional sense. What Chip is doing is unique to Balcones.

Chip uses both small 5 gallon and large 60 gallon barrels in his production process, but he uses special yard-aged American white oak casks that have been exposed to freezing cycles in Missouri winters to condition the wood. A number of the experiments that Chip is currently doing involve bespoke barrels with special woods to achieve special flavor signatures. Among casks aging now are ones made of a spicy Eastern European oak, Quercus robur. In the future, Chip informed me, watch for Texas Live Oak bespoke casks. Staves of this wild wood that has never been used for whisky production are yard drying on the roof of the distillery in Waco and will be transported by car roof to Reynold's cooperage in Missouri where winter freezes and strong seasonal changes can properly cure the wood according to Tate's specifications.

Chip is a fertile intellect and has thought, researched, and calculated intensively in building his stills, developing his barrel management techniques, and honing his mash bills and expressions. As I quickly discovered, Chip hasn't stopped or even slowed down in any of these domains. He is continuing to experiment with materials and tweaks to his existing expressions and he is ambitiously developing new ones. On a trip to New York, Chip brought a rockstar roadie's custom travel case loaded with bottles of samples from single casks selected for awesome flavors and examples of in-process experiments that illustrate his thought and creative process. Chip has been traversing the country doing this. In fact, I've written about his previous trip to New York before where he poured many of these special experiments and selected casks. Chip is a scientist, and he's an artist too. But he doesn't seem to have an insecure bone in his body and he doesn't suffer from the "you can't see it til it's finished" affliction of some artists. Among the things he brought was a bottle of his new rum experiment— just under a scant 2 months old. All over town Chip poured this for everyone—eager for feedback. The immature rum is incredible, BTW. A nose full of buttered toffeed popcorn, intense confectioner's sugar on the entry and a lush mid-palate bloom of Maillard reaction butter-cream-cane-sugar caramel cooking in the pan.

I think part of the reason Chip is so easy pouring with this very young experimental liquor is that it's good and he's proud of it. But another part of it is that Chip is evangelizing why it's good. It's no accident that Balcones' spirits taste so good so young. It's no accident that they have big, bright, sweet openings full of confectioner's powdered sugar—seemingly no matter what's in the mash. It's no accident that so many are loaded with rich oak vanilla flavors and oak perfume and incense filigree at an age where many other distilleries' products are weak, insipid, rough and raw. Chip wants to explain, scientifically, to you why it's no accident—but even more he wants to show you, empirically. My experience showed me that Chip has a scientific rationale for each phase of the process and is deliberately crafting his spirits to hit a flavor profile he desires. My first instinct is to look for holes in any attempt at applied science in such a complex topic. There were moments (particularly when the conversation was going over my head) when I wondered to myself whether maybe Chip might be a fast-talking con man. Yet, the proof is in the glass and Balcones has achieved extraordinary success. I'm not just talking about awards (of which there have been many— including Gold at SF and the first Icons of Whisky in the category of Craft Distillery). I'm talking about the unmistakable presence of a clear house style to Balcones' products—a sense of balance and a flavor signature that spans disparate mash bills. Even more convincing, there is a progression over time. What I'm tasting in these new special casks and experiments is a movement toward greater refinement and even greater fidelity to Chip's aesthetic and vision. In a nutshell, and very broadly, the house flavor signature of Balcones runs something like this: a nice nose but the main action is on the palate where you always get a sweet and explosive opening with a powdered confectioner's sugar palate entry and plenty of vanilla floral notes. The mid-palate expansion is richly flavored with the aspects of whatever is in the mash but is generally off-dry. This balances the sweet of the entry. This is where the august quality comes in—where the best Balcones spirits drink like high-end cognac or top-tier Scotch. The finish has plenty of oak, with sandalwood incense perfume and sometimes the full-blown patchouli you see in cognac.

The fact that Chip regularly gets this flavor profile and is getting it more and more dialed in as he hones his craft proves, to me, that his science is real. A con man can fake out your mind but not your palate. What's happening in the glass here is incredible and real. The fact that he achieves all this with spirits that are under 3 years old in the wood shows me that, in addition to being an artist and a scientist, he is, effectively, a genius.

BALLAST POINT

San Diego, CA

Ballast Point is one of the most celebrated breweries on the west coast. Like several other famous breweries, they too are getting in on the distilling act. It follows that whiskey will be a big item for many of these. Head distiller Yuseff Cherney and his staff have been very successful.

DEVIL'S SHARE 3 YEAR OLD 50%

Ballast Point's Devil's Share starts, of course, with the beer made from brewer's malt. They distilled it in small batches and then it was left to mature in new, heavy toasted American oak barrels. The first batch was two barrels. The whiskey has won numerous awards. Ballast Point was named California Distiller of the Year in 2013. This single malt won a gold medal for Best Single Malt at the ninth annual American Distilling Institute Conference in Louisville, Kentucky. "Being recognized here in Kentucky, by people who have been doing this for generations, means the world to us," Cherney said after the victory.

CD

Roseville, MN

KURSED SINGLE MALT WHISKEY
42% (FUTURE)

Auburn University grad Bartley Blume has had an interesting career, working at NASA and then working in Australia, Southeast Asia, and South America. His hobby then became an obsession. Today, Bent is the only brewery-distillery in Minnesota. The 7,500 square foot brewery uses a 2-vessel, 20-barrel system that fills four 40-barrel conical fermenters and more. The brewery produces washes for the distillery. The distillery features a 500-gallon MegaStill, and a 26-gallon spirit still for creating new product. Their whiskey is made from cherry wood- and oak-smoked malts. They filter their single malt through charred oak and charred apple wood.

CD

Green Mountain Falls, CO

BLACK BEAR IRISH STYLE UN-PEATED 45%

This is one of the most unique whiskey-making stories in the industry.

"I did not set out to re-define craft. I actually did not even think about those words when I first began plans for a distillery back in 2013," states owner Victor Matthews.

It's farm to glass, and all done in-house from the malting to the grinding of the barley. The whiskey is made from locally grown corn. It's bagged and soaked in the stream near the distillery and then floor-malted in the distillery. It's dried in the

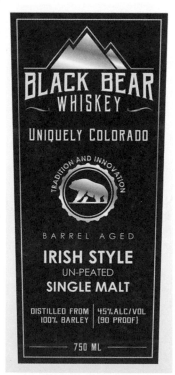

brewery's fireplace and then ground by a massive old-fashioned 1,000-pound stone wheel driven by rescued donkeys. Then they distill in a hand-hammered 400-gallon oldstyle pot still. That's not all. They actually have their own cooper, and make a small amount of their own barrels, so even the oak is local!

"Some say insane. I say: you want "craft"? You got it. No one else in the world that I have ever encountered can claim this level of absolute commitment to ancient artisan techniques," says Matthews.

CD

BLUE RIDGE DISTILLING CO, INC.

Bostic, NC

BY JAKE EMEN

As craft distilleries continue to explode onto the scene across the United States, each

brand has to find its way past a common obstacle. How do we produce a mature, refined spirit when we want our product on shelves and atop home bars, not years from now, and not even today, but yesterday? Small barrel aging is the norm, and a variety of other techniques and subtle shifts have been developed as well.

At Blue Ridge Distilling Co., in Bostic, North Carolina, which is located in a region—the Golden Valley—famous for its moonshiners, they say to hell with barrels, and to hell with the norm. Their tag line is "unbound by barrels or convention" but what exactly does that mean?

Blue Ridge takes great pride in their process but perhaps even more in their ingredients: their carefully selected and cultured strain of yeast; the 100% two-row premium malted brewer's barley; their pure below-ground water source. That covers three of their four listed ingredients. Last up, toasted American white oak, which is actually both ingredient and process. A video on Defiant's website explains:

"It's not about aging whiskey, it's about imparting the qualities that are

in the oak, in the whiskey, in a way which marries those two together and complements the whiskey. And barrels are such an inefficient way of doing that."

The solution Defiant sees as more efficient essentially turns the tables by putting the barrel into the whiskey. That means that they put spiral cuts of that toasted American white oak and insert that into the spirit itself.

Aging time? Just 60 days. It's a proprietary process, which the mad scientists at Defiant developed in part thanks to their experience as an international salvage diving team—Defiant Marine. In some ways, the idea is similar to the use of barrel inserts to impart certain desired flavors, such as Maker's Mark 46 does with French oak, but that is just trim whereas what Blue Ridge is doing goes to the core. In others, it's similar to the way small barrel aging increases surface contact with the whiskey.

All that is fine and good, but how does it actually turn out? Keep reading.

DEFIANT AMERICAN SINGLE MALT WHISKY 41%

In the glass, Defiant is a coppery amber offering cereal grain, honey and oak on the nose.

DEFIANT
AMERICAN SINGLE MALT
WHISKY
Distilled from 100% Malted Barley & Pure Mountain Spring Water
BY
BLUE RIDGE DISTILLING CO.
GOLDEN VALLEY, NC

Take a sip and you'll find a chewy spirit, with that cereal grain coming strong in tandem with the malt. The finish is very long, and while mostly pleasant, it's also a bit hot and offers a lasting note of black pepper and spice

in front of a slight backdrop of caramel sweetness. Add some ice if you're so inclined, and a vanilla caramel sweetness takes center stage with malt and honey, offering a very smooth sip.

For a single malt whisky aged for only 60 days, Defiant is indeed revolutionary. Still, I'd love to see what they came up with if they utilized that proprietary process for a longer time, perhaps a year, allowing those flavors to become even richer and more nuanced.

JE

Reno, NV

BRANDED HEARTS SINGLE MALT WHISKEY 60%

Joshua Nichol and Ryan Cherrick both had careers in Nevada law enforcement, in the Ventura Sheriff's office, when they finally decided to start a distillery. "The science behind it is quite romantic," Ryan explains, "but that's not what the name implies."

In an effort to increase the complexity and flavor profile of Branded Hearts Single Malt Whiskey, they make the whiskey using two different yeast strains. They take the distillate and age it in new charred American oak barrels, but they also age their whiskey in the same barrels that previously used to age their superlative dark rum made from pure dark panela. The angels drink fast in the Nevada desert, so the resulting whiskey has a richness and denseness that is magnified. Nellie Day and Eric Cachinero wrote in *Nevada Magazine* that Branded Hearts Single Malt was "revered for its complex characteristics and chocolate and toffee flavors."

CD

Bloomington, IN

WHITE OAK SINGLE MALT WHISKEY 40%

Cardinal Spirits, based in Bloomington, Indiana, released a white, unaged single malt distilled spirit, made from 100% pale malted barley. The barley was local, coming from Sugar Creek Malt Co. in Lebanon, Indiana. Now most white whiskey is made from corn, but Cardinal Spirits wants to make a true blue single malt whiskey, so they also came up with a fascinating idea. Release some of the white single malt, and offer it in kits to do your own aging at home! One of the most innovative marketing ideas in single malt whiskey in the last few years. Gimmick? Maybe. Brilliant marketing? Absolutely! Geek out, and try this!

CD

AGE YOUR OWN WHISKEY KITS:
LET'S DO IT TOGETHER

BY ERICA SAGON

Our Age Your Own Whiskey kits are for those geek-out moments, and they come with a built-in crowd of fellow DIYers. We're all going to do it together. Here's what we mean...

First: what's in a kit? A bottle of our White Oak Whiskey (our unaged single malt barley whiskey), a toasted American oak stave and an instruction card. It's $25, and available through the holidays at the distillery (oh, hey there, perfect gift). You're in the driver's seat with this kit and get to decide just how much color and flavor you want.

The idea is that everyone with a kit starts aging their bottle at the same time and uses social media to do this thing together.

Here's how it works:

1. Drop the stave in the bottle on 12/26.

2. Snap a photo each week and post it to social media with #whiskeymyway. Use the hashtag to see who else is aging, how it's going, and how their whiskey tastes. And let's share tips: are you agitating? Keeping it warm? Adding an extra stave? (We sell extra staves for $2.50 a pop.)

3. Each week, we'll post a summary of the bottles so we can see each other's progress. Follow along on Instagram, Twitter, Facebook, and on the blog.

It's all on the instruction card that comes with the kit.

We've seen great color and flavor right around five weeks, but the fun part is that you get to decide when your whiskey is ready.

And that's how you age whiskey without filing for a federal distiller's permit. Hurray!

Swisher, IA

CEDAR RIDGE SINGLE MALT WHISKEY 49%

Cedar Ridge Single Malt was one of the standout whiskeys at the 2014 Whisky Live LA. Hailing from Cedar Ridge Winery in Cedar Ridge, Iowa, this single malt is part of an ongoing experimentation by this scrappy little distillery. A distillery who is one of the few craft distilleries out there doing things the right way and is putting out some really good whiskey.

The bottle tried is Batch #13, which is a marriage of batches 9-12 that are then given an additional maturation in 15-gallon ex-bourbon barrels. For their single malt Cedar Ridge only uses 2-row barley aged in 15-gallon ex-bourbon barrels and then finished in various other casks. The exception is their peated batches, which utilizes peated malt, from Scotland. Batch 9 was peated and finished in ex-bourbon (53 gallon), Batch 10 was finished in ex-Sauternes, Batch 11 was finished in French oak, and Batch 12 was finished in new American oak. Aged five years.

Color: Light yellow.

Nose: Lovely fruity and malty sweet nose with notes of vanilla taffy, honey, and spice. It reminds me of the nice fruity nose that's found in Glenmorangie 10.

Palate: Same lovely fruity and malty notes as the nose; even the vanilla taffy and honey transition here. What differs though are the light touches of toffee, nuts, and wood. Buttery fruit, wood, and malty sweetness fade out at a medium pace. Nicely balanced, round body, and a smooth buttery texture.

I really enjoyed trying the Cedar Ridge Single Malt. It's warm and flavorful and ended up being one of the bottles from the night that I wanted to walk away with. It's a relaxing and approachable whiskey that almost any whisk(e)y fan could enjoy. I'd love to try all of the components individually, side by side, and see how much influence each have... but nonetheless it was enjoyable. It's one of those nice-to-find gems from the current craft-distilling boom in America.

JP

Portland, OR

MCCARTHY'S OREGON SINGLE MALT 3 YEAR OLD 40%

McCarthy's is distilled at Clear Creek Distillery in Portland, Oregon. Owner Steve McCarthy buys peated barley malt from the Port Ellen maltings on Islay and has it shipped to Oregon. After it arrives, the malt is fermented by the Widmer Brothers Brewery. The resulting wash is distilled only once in Clear Creek's Holstein pot still. According to their site, the spirit spends some time in old sherry casks (though these casks may have been discontinued several years ago) as well as casks made from Oregon oak. They age it for three years. If you've ever tried to buy a bottle of McCarthy's, you'll know why they don't age it any longer: each batch sells out quickly. For more details on their processes, please the Clear Creek site, which has a lot of good info.

Uncertain which batch this was from. It may be somewhere between 2006 and 2008. Many batches have been at 42.5% ABV, one was "cask strength" at 49% ABV. This one was bottled at 40% ABV.

NEAT

The color is gold. The first thing I notice in the nose is the ocean. Is it the Atlantic or Pacific?! Then bacon, well charred bacon. Then cinnamon, brown sugar, and kirsch. The peat is rich, clean, and bright (if that makes any sense) as opposed to dirty or ashy. There's a nice vanilla bean note, maybe from the Oregon oak? Also some plum brandy (Slivovitz) to go with the kirsch. After being aired out for over 30 minutes, the whiskey releases a scent that reminds me of the white plastic siding on the house I grew up in. The palate is loaded with applewood-smoked bacon. The peat gets ashy here, though it gets brightened up by sweet mint. Sweetness grows with time, but it is kept in check by an IPA-style bitterness. More bacon in the finish. The beer that goes with the palate's bitterness shows up here. Then sugary cigar ash. And—to continue the personal notes—the air on Inis Mór, the rocky Irish island I got lost on eleven years ago.

WITH WATER

Some fresh fruits (apricots and apples) peek out into the nose. Lots of bourbon-like American oak notes too, caramel specifically. Then candied peat, apple mint, and tangerines. The palate gets sugary, toasty, and mossy. Maybe a little bit of green herbs and yeast. The finish is sweet and smoky.

It's been a while since I've experienced multiple sense memory connections with a single whiskey. Putting aside these emotional connections for a moment, I have no issue with this single malt's very young age. While there are distillate characteristics in the nose, they work very well with the big ocean, bacon, and beer notes. The sweetness stays mellow until water is added, the oak doesn't get too big, and the peat lingers at a medium level. While I prefer it neat, water doesn't wreck it, which is impressive considering the low ABV.

Hard to ignore those sense memories. I realize that you won't have the same connections, but they draw me more deeply into the drinking experience. Maybe you'll have your own. Or maybe you'll see this as a decent alternative to the other (imported) whiskies created from the Port Ellen maltings. In any case, McCarthy's shouldn't be dismissed by you peat fans. If young Taliskers and Caol Ilas ever get out of your price range, maybe you should look to Oregon next.

MK

Hiding Out in
the Single Malt Scotch Section

BY CARLO DEVITO

The next time you go into a store, check out the single malt Scotch section. You know, that section where they have all the single malt whiskey from Scotland. Usually hidden there, among all the whiskies from the Highlands and from Islay, is McCarthy's. Mistake? Maybe. Maybe not.

Firstly, McCarthy's make great peated single malt whiskey. It is so dead on that many people have mistaken it for Scotch! And its labeling doesn't hurt. It fits right in with the Scotches on the shelf, so much so that most liquor store owners and stock people easily slip it into the single malt Scotch section without realizing what they've done.

That's OK, because their customers don't notice it either. In several recent conversations with enthusiasts, in asking for their favorite Scotches, McCarthy's has come up time and again. When I inform them that's it's not Scotch, but malt whiskey, they bristle, and tell me to "check your facts."

McCarthy's Single Malt Whiskey is hiding in plain sight. And people love it! Let's be honest, that's the highest compliment!

Sperryville, VA

WASMUND'S RAPPAHANNOCK SINGLE MALT 48%

Even with new micro-distilleries opening every day, there are only a handful of micro-distilled whiskeys that are available on local liquor store shelves. Rick Wasmund's Copper Fox Distillery in Sperryville, Virginia, was one of the earlier micro start-ups and has been producing one of the more available and more unique American whiskies. Copper Fox's Wasmund's Rappahannock Single Malt (Rappahannock is the county where Sperryville is located) is a four-month-old, pot distilled, non-chill-filtered malt aged with apple and cherrywood chips. The use of these alternative woods is unusual in whisky. But at four months old, can there really be any impact on the flavor? We'll see.

On the nose it actually smells a bit more Scotch-like than other American single malts I've had. There is sweetness, fruit, and a bit of smoke, though not a peaty smoke that you would encounter in Scotch. The flavor is a bit harsh, more so than it should be at this alcohol level. There is some interesting stuff going on in here though, with the continuing intertwined dance of the fruit and smoke, which may come from the use of fruit wood in the kiln that dries the malted barley. And in the back of the palate, there is still a clear malt that links it to Scotland.

This is a fascinating and unique malt with a lot of character for something so young. There is an intriguing flavor profile here that could really be amazing, perhaps with more time in the barrel.

Copper Fox is definitely a micro-distillery to watch.

SU

Seattle, WA

COPPERWORKS AMERICAN SINGLE MALT WHISKEY BATCH #1 (FUTURE)

The first batch of Copperworks American Single Malt Whiskey is made from 100% pale malted barley. Owners Jason Parker and Micah Nutt double-distilled their whiskey in a handmade still from the Scottish highlands. The whiskey is then piped into brand-new, charred 53-gallon American barrels made from Missouri oak made in Kentucky. Many fans of the distillery have clamored to reserve a bottle, so Jason and Micah created the Copper Ticket, which guarantees the holder can buy one bottle when Batch #1 is released.

Nashville, TN and Bowling Green, KY

CORSAIR TRIPLE SMOKE 40%

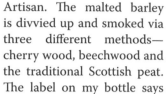

Good ol' fashioned American whiskey produced in the rolling Kentucky hills isn't typically associated with the intense, peaty smokiness and maltiness of Scotch, but many trends have sprung up in the whiskey craze of modern times, and one of them is the American malt whiskey. Imagine the malt whiskey base of the Scottish style, but liberated from Scottish traditions, leaving the distillery free to do whatever it damn well pleases with their whiskey, and you have an American malt.

So, when you make an American malt whiskey and call it "Triple Smoke," you're hinting at that spirit of American experimentation. Kentucky-made whiskey as this may be, it draws its character from American charred new oak aging and three different sources of fire-malted barley, making a unique cross for your palette, as well as an intriguing experiment that any whiskey lover should be eager to approach.

Corsair Triple Smoke is an American single malt whiskey, distilled by Corsair Artisan. The malted barley is divvied up and smoked via three different methods—cherry wood, beechwood and the traditional Scottish peat. The label on my bottle says "small batch," although there is also a single barrel expression of this whiskey as well.

The whiskey falls back into the American pattern with its new charred oak barrel aging, and is produced and hand-bottled at the Bowling Green, Kentucky distillery (the company also has a Tennessee distillery, but all the whiskey for this product comes from the Bowling Green facility, making it a single malt instead of a vatted malt). From batch to batch you may, of course, notice subtle differences in both taste and aroma. The bottle I happened upon was labeled as Batch 57, bottle 11/296, with a standard 40% alcohol content by volume.

The reason I initially tried Corsair Triple Smoke is that I wanted to see how these two divergent halves of one product would mesh. Which would win out: the Kentucky or the Scottish side?

Take a sip either neat or on the rocks, and either way it's the smoke that dominates. Is that a bottle of Islay single malt Scotch you're sampling? No, but a double take is certainly

warranted. Corsair Triple Smoke has exceedingly deep and complex flavors. While the peat sticks out the most, you'll notice the caramel undertones of new oak, highlighted by the cherry wood, and overall a thick, rich quality.

However, if you're one for mixing your whiskey, prepare yourself for the best "Scotch" and soda you've ever had. Corsair Triple Smoke mixes wonderfully with a tonic or soda water, and suddenly the sweetness comes parading out at the forefront of each taste. The smokiness is left as a faint afterthought, keeping the beverage from straying too far into the land of honey and caramel. I'd imagine it would work quite well in a variety of modern, smoky cocktails, and the distillery recommends it for Manhattans.

Corsair Triple Smoke has picked up several awards in the past few years, including golds at the 2010 San Francisco World Spirits Competition, 2010 International Review of Spirits Awards, BTI, and 2011 MicroLiquor Spirits Awards.

JE

La Vista, NE

CUT SPIKE SINGLE MALT WHISKEY 43%

Scotch style single malt is not only made in Scotland. High quality single malts rivaling the best of Scotland have been made for years in Japan, and more recently, quality single malts have come to us from India and Taiwan, but not the United States.

Why can't American distilleries make high quality single malts in the Scotch style? Part of the answer is in our regulations. While Scotch-style single malts are aged in used barrels, American malt whiskey, like bourbon and rye, is required to be aged in new, charred oak barrels. The problem is that barley is much less bold than sweet corn or spicy rye, and its flavors tend to be buried by the new wood. Add to that the fact that Scotland (and most other jurisdictions making single malt) requires three years of aging whereas the United States has no minimum, and you can start to understand why most American malt whiskeys tastes nothing like Scotch, even when the producers are trying to mimic it. (Americans could age malt in used barrels and call it "whiskey distilled from malt mash" but that designation somehow seems less appealing than "single malt whiskey.")

Knowing all of this, I was a bit skeptical when K&L spirits buyer David Driscoll told me there was a distillery in Nebraska making single malt whiskey that tasted like Scotch. David is a great guy and one of my favorite retailers, but let's face it, he is a bit excitable. This is a guy who sources some of the best spirits on the market, but his talents are such that he could probably unload Seagram's 7 by the caseload as the latest budget retro-fad. (And if he ever goes into political advertising, watch out!)

A few days later, I received a sample of Cut Spike Single Malt, a 2 year old whiskey made outside of Omaha. Cut Spike is made from barley that comes from Rahr Malting in Minnesota, one of the largest malting companies in the United States. Like many craft distillers, Cut Spike gets their fermented wash from a brewery, in this case, their sister company, the Lucky Bucket Brewing Company. Their stills are made by Forsythes in Scotland, and they use a variety of casks ranging from lightly to heavily charred.

I've never heard anyone compare Omaha to the Scottish Highlands, but I figured I'd give it a try. Wow! This was by far the best American single malt I'd ever tasted, and the only one that could pass for Scotch. In fact, I certainly would have guessed it was Scotch in a blind tasting. It was fruity and perfumey on the nose with a touch of milk chocolate. The palate was sweet, if a bit thin, with bubblegum that faded to malt, and it had a light, fruity finish. The flavor was reminiscent of Balvenie with its light, fruity nose and slight chocolate note. I had no idea how they tamped down on the raw wood notes.

While this was great for an American malt, it wasn't great Scotch. It was too sweet and thin on the palate, so while Cut Spike had successfully made a Scotch-like whiskey, it was a decent one, not a great one.

After my initial tasting, I got an email from Driscoll. The bottles had arrived, but they weren't quite the same. Cut Spike had changed their filtration method. He still liked it, but I told him I wasn't able to review a sample that was different than the product being offered, so he kindly sent me a bottle of the new stuff.

The nose is malty. The palate comes on a bit raw with some alcohol notes, then it turns nicely malty with some floral/perfume notes and some sweetness. The finish is sweet and floral with malt in the background. Overall, it's nicely balanced between sweet and malty notes.

Interestingly, this new batch is a very different from the previous one, though it's of comparable quality. It's less sweet and less thin on the palate, which is an improvement, but it also has some of those raw notes that are typical of young American whiskeys. Those are the notes that I was surprised were absent from the earlier sample. In this batch, they aren't pres-

ent in an amount that is off putting, but they are there.

Overall, I think I like this batch better, though unlike the previous sample, I would be unlikely to mistake this for a single malt Scotch. Tasting blind, I might guess that it was a good Scotch single grain whisky. And both samples are better than any other American malt I've had (excluding the hopped malt whiskeys as that's a whole different category).

I have to hand it to Cut Spike. They are clearly on to something, though they haven't nailed it yet. Much like the 2 year old Willett Rye, this was good, not great, but it made me very excited to try it at 5 or 10 years old.

SU

TRADE MARK

CUT SPIKE

SINGLE MALT

WHISKEY

The distinguished taste of Cut Spike Single Malt Whiskey comes from premium grains and limestone-filtered water from the Sandhills of Nebraska. Aged for two years in charred American oak barrels for an exceptional finish.

43% ALC./VOL.
750 ML

DAMNATION ALLEY DISTILLERY

Belmont, MA

MASSACHUSETTS SINGLE MALT WHISKEY 42%

Damnation Alley Distillery, based in Belmont, Massachusetts, was founded in 2011, and they make whiskey and vodka from all local ingredients. They are a very small distillery, though that also gives them the ability to experiment frequently, to make small batches of whatever they desire. I tasted four of their products—a bourbon, rye, single malt and vodka—basically all which have been aged for less than six months in small barrels. They do have future plans to release some whiskey that has been aged longer. The Single Malt Whiskey, made from 100% barley, has some baking spices notes with hints of chocolate.

RA

DEERHAMMER DISTILLING COMPANY

Buena Vista, CO

DOWNTIME SINGLE MALT WHISKEY 44%

Distilled from 100% malted barley, this is definitely a different whiskey than most you will try. It is also aged in smaller barrels, giving it more influence from the oak for how young it is.

The nose on this is definitely an oaky one. There are some sweet smells, maybe a bit of honey, and a little bit from the barley, but that oak is the most prevalent.

Taking the sip, the palate starts with some sweetness, honey, and vanilla flavors. The mid-palate has the sweetness open up a little more and the oak start to comes through, with a little bit of smoke, making the mid-palate a bit more complex. The finish is a lot of toasted oak flavors that goes quick.

After letting an ice cube melt slightly into the glass a little bit, this whiskey opens up a lot. The sweetness on the start opens up a bit, and the Deerhammer becomes more complex. The honey and vanilla become much more prevalent and then mix into spice, smoke, and a lot of oak. It is smoothed out, but opens up a lot. I usually prefer to have whiskey straight, but this one needs just a little bit of water, or a melted ice cube, to really let you enjoy all the flavors and nuances it has to offer.

Great whiskey. Overall, it is really fun and unique.

ZP & AP

THE DEPOT CRAFT BREWERY

Reno, NV

DEPOT SINGLE MALT WHISKEY (FUTURE)

Depot is a well-regarded brewhouse that, like others across the country, is finding its way into the craft distilling market. But these folks are doing it farm to glass. Their whiskey begins on local farms in nearby communities. Depot works with the farmers to select the best crops for their purpose. The grains are milled on site, cooked in there, and poured into traditional open-style fermenters. The fermented juice is double-distilled. Their bourbons and their single malt whiskey are aged on the third floor of their operation, "where the western sun of the summer and the cold winters of the Sierra Nevada Mountains move the spirit in and out of the small wooden barrels." The anticipation for this one is great!

CD

DJINN SPIRITS

Nashua, NH

BEAT SINGLE MALT WHISKEY 50%

Djinn Spirits (pronounced "gin" spirits) is a craft distillery located in Nashua, New Hampshire. It was established in December 2013 by Andy and Cindy Harthcock. Djinn's gin was an instant hit, and they followed up with a series of white and aged whiskeys. Andy and Cindy were thrilled to release the first single malt whiskey in the state's history. Micro-batch fermentation, double distilled, and aged in small 15-gallon high-char oak barrels resulted a very smooth, spicy, new spirit. The first bottling was very small, and available only at the distillery tasting room. More expressions are on the way.

CD

Evanston, IL

FEW SINGLE MALT WHISKEY 46.5%

The FEW Single Malt Whisky is a seasonal release from those crafty lads in Illinois and is the third member of their whiskey trio. The occasional sibling of the FEW Bourbon and FEW Rye, it doesn't get nearly the attention that the others get not because it isn't good but because it's not as widely distributed.

To make this single malt the folks at FEW took an undisclosed percentage of their malted barley and smoked it with cherry wood, which is supposed to give a subtle smoky flavor to the whiskey, but I honestly didn't pick any of it up in this sample. It came across as bold and earthy with very little sweetness peaking its head out, but no real smokiness that I could find. It reminds me a lot of the Roughstock Montana Pure Malt and if it behaves like it too, then I'm sure it would open up and expand more in the bottle over time, but since I'm going off of this sample, no chance to find out if that indeed would be the case.

Color: Dark straw.

Nose: Barley and hay start things out with some nice notes of butterscotch fudge and mushrooms. Raw sugar and dusty grains mix in the background and help create a pleasant earthy aroma with a touch of sweetness.

Palate: I sense a theme here with the barley and hay now dominating the palate. Subtle notes of wood, raw grains, citrus, and ambiguous sweetness combine with a touch of astringency in a flavor that's rich but a tad one-dimensional. Long and full of barley, alfalfa, hay, raw grains, and a warm earthy undertone that rides out for the entirety of the finish. Feels a bit unbalanced with almost no sweetness on the palate and finish to even out the grainy earthy notes. Medium body with an easy texture that carries only a light amount of burn. I really enjoy the rich fudgy grain on the nose and the rustic grainy flavor, but it all comes across a bit one-dimensional. It would be nice if there was a bit more sweetness in there to help balance things out, and if I could pick up some of that smoked malt they talk about it having, but all things considered it's still pretty good. A fun little American single malt that's worth a taste if you get the chance.

JP

Bow, WA

GOLDEN SAMISH BAY SINGLE MALT WHISKEY 40%

Two retirees, Jim Caudill and Bob Stillnovich, founded Golden Distillery, the first small-scale distillery to open in Skagit County in Washington State. The two men met after their wives there introduced them on Samish Island. Between the two men, they have more than 50 years of combined hospitality experience. That, and they are both spirit enthusiasts. After two years of research, development, testing, and refining, Golden Distillery opened its doors for business in Octobe2010. Their whiskies are craft-distilled in small batches. They use only local, hand-selected ingredients.

They make three whiskies: Samish Bay Single Malt, Samish Bay Single Malt Reserve, and Samish Bay Peated Single Malt. All have won medals in various competitions. All the reviews have been very favorable, including from whiskey expert Jim Murray. They make some very nice sipping whiskies.

Samish Bay Single Malt won the Gold Medal, Best in Class at the 2012 American Distilling Institute 6th Annual Judging of Artisan American Spirits. It is aged in white American oak and similar in profile to a good Irish whiskey.

Nose: Bread, apple, pear, malt, honey, caramel corn, hay, vanilla, spices.

Palate: Brown sugar and butter, apple, maple, toast, vanilla and honey. Toffee, honey, and vanilla stay with you. Clean finish. Very nice.

CD

Tucson, AZ

WHISKEY DEL BAC DORADO
MESQUITE SMOKED 45%

In keeping with being from the Southwest, Whiskey Del Bac from Hamilton Distillers is all about the mesquite. They use mesquite wood to smoke their floor-malted barley rather than peat, making a Southwestern single malt with a Scottish heritage. Of the three varieties in its lineup, Whiskey Del Bac Dorado is the aged, mesquite-smoked version, making it the true core of their offerings.

Whiskey Del Bac Dorado is aged in 15-gallon barrels obtained from The Barrel Mill in Minnesota. Hamilton will be continuing to use those, but will eventually move up to 30-gallon barrels and then standard, full-sized 53-gallon barrels. It's one of many upgrades they're intending, in addition to the usage of a system that will allow them to malt 5,000-pound batches as opposed to tiny 70 pound batches.

Owner and distiller Stephen Paul jokes that he chose the 15-gallon barrels because, "I'm old and in a hurry." He wants to figure out the process and make good whiskey as quickly as he can, while understanding that down the line, when its feasible, larger barrels and more substantial aging will likely improve the outcome. Currently, they age the whiskey in those small barrels for roughly five-and-a-half to six months.

In the glass, Whiskey Del Bac Dorado, bottled at 90 proof (45% ABV), is a copper brown color. On the nose, you'll notice much more depth than was apparent in the Clear unaged variety, which blasted you with all smoke. The wood gives it more character and balances out the mesquite smoke, transforming it into more of a chipotle pepper smokiness.

On the palate, the whiskey is dry, with tastes of mesquite jerky, and chipotle and ancho chile. You'll find notes of black pepper, spice, and cereal grain. There's a lurking hint of sweetness with vanilla and caramel. The finish is warm, and lasting; it lingers and tingles, and leaves you notes of with cracked pepper.

Add an ice cube, and Whiskey Del Bac Dorado

becomes more mellowed. A sweetness and creaminess emerges from its depths, masking some of the deep smoke omnipresent when tasting neat.

If you close your eyes and knew nothing of what was to come, your first impression of Whiskey Del Bac Dorado would likely be that it was indeed a Scotch. It is, after all, a smoked single malt. But as you dive in and find that deep mesquite, it's clear that this whiskey calls the American Southwest home. Certainly less refined than say, Corsair Triple Smoke, but if you want powerful, hearty, American mesquite smoke, this is for you, and with improvements and upgrades to come in the future, it's definitely one to watch.

JE

Monroe, OR

ELEVENTH HOUR SINGLE MALT WHISKEY 45%

James Stegall and Dudley Clark started Hard Times Distillery back in 2009, in Monroe, Oregon. Both happened to be in publishing. James (a long time Army veteran) as a publishing executive, and Dudley wrote novels. Starting the distillery, the whole thing was done by hand. The stainless steel hand-made double boilers were made by James and Dudley themselves. Mike McCaw of the Amphora Society designed the distillation column. The best way is to let friend Joel Johnson describe the rest, "Copper tubing coils around the front, and a radiator ripped from a Ford Explorer sits in front of a box fan, keeping the still heads cool when they need to be."

They started with a vodka made from molasses named Sweet Baby Vodka. It was a solid hit. Then they introduced Green Geisha, an infused vodka made with fresh wasabi! Each year brought one new product. They introduced six labels in six years, the last one of which was Hard Times Eleventh Hour Single Malt Whiskey. Success was so good, they opened a second tasting room in Eugene, Oregon.

"One of the things that was mentioned to us early in this process is that a great spirit tells a story: about how it was made, and who made it," James Stegall said. "That made a lot of sense to me. As I've progressed with the business, the storytelling aspect of every part of it becomes more and more important."

They small-batch ferment single malt barley in a pot still—twice. The whiskey is then aged in hand-charred Oregon white oak. A small, hand-made, single malt whiskey delivered, according to them, in the eleventh hour. Which is how it got its name. Tasting notes include deep-toasted notes of caramel with a touch of raisin and vanilla overtones.

CD

HARVEST SPIRITS

Valatie, NY

Harvest Spirits is owned by Derek Grout and Ashley Hartka. It is a small, fruit-based distillery located on a centenary family farm in Valatie, New York. Harvest Spirits first made a splash making Core Vodka, an apple-based Vodka that was wildly popular.

But their Cornelius Applejack brought back classic, American applejack in a big way. This small, family-owned enterprise recently started producing single malt whiskey and is at work on bourbon as well.

JOHN HENRY
SINGLE MALT WHISKEY 42%

Firstly, John Henry is named after a long tenured and trusted worker at Golden Harvest Orchards for more than four decades, who also doubles at Harvest Spirits, a sister company. That tells you something right off about the people who run this place. The whiskey itself reflects the Master

Distiller's desire for authenticity. It's made in small batches and distilled twice using 2-row malted barley, then the new make is matured in new oak and aged in Harvest Spirits' own Applejack barrels for 2 years. This lends a lovely fruit note and some very nice spices.

Derek Grout and Peter Upstill (and their team) have done it! Harvest Spirits released their first Single Malt Whiskey from Harvest Spirits! Oh, boy!

OK, now let's talk about Harvest Spirits' John Henry Single Malt Whiskey. It's made using a beer made by Adirondack Brewing, which is made from 75% New York smoky 2-row malted barley. It's double distilled. Then aged for two years. Approximately one month in new barrels, and then the rest in older applejack and bourbon barrels, or what they refer to as re-fill barrels.

Now, before I go into my review, I want to state out right that I am a bourbon guy. Generally I am not a huge fan of single malt. But I do like some.

That said, I like this whiskey for everything it is not. If you are looking for a big, smoky, mossy, peat monster, you will absolutely be disappointed. If you are looking for a big, bitter, biting, hot-going-down-your-throat single malt, then this is not for you.

On the other hand, if you're looking for a light, lovely, floral nose with sourdough bread, caramel apple, and lots of spiced fruit, then this is your whiskey. It's a lovely, elegant, complex spirit, with layers of delicate flavors and no sense of grain alcohol or anything like that.

If I've heard anything about brown spirits coming out of the Hudson Valley and the rest of the northeast, it's that they are not allowed to age long enough in the cask to acquire the complexity to compete with other spirits from Tennessee or Kentucky. I think the point with John Henry is twofold: 1. This is, in Derek Grout's wheelhouse, a more delicate and complex whiskey, instead of the caveman-ish club some would prefer. 2. Derek and Pete's palates across the board have always been to the more refined, elegant, delicate side, and this take on Scotch whisky is more than admirable. It's downright lovely!! Strike that! It's damned good!

CD

Pipersville, PA

HEWN RECLAMATION SINGLE MALT CHESTNUT FINISH 45%

Sean Tracy loves wood. Especially old wood. White oak, hickory, black birch, cherry, sycamore. For over 15 years, his company, Bucks County Timber Craft, has reclaimed antique barns and given them new life in the form of custom homes, commercial buildings and, even, new barns. He has access to wood hundreds of years old, some from trees that are even extinct, like the chestnut.

Several years ago, Tracy started getting intrigued by micro-distilling. He wondered if there was a way to use this unique, old wood in a new way. After much research, including a workshop in the Catskills, he decided it was time to give it a try.

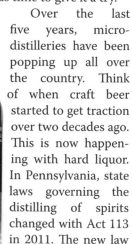

Over the last five years, micro-distilleries have been popping up all over the country. Think of when craft beer started to get traction over two decades ago. This is now happening with hard liquor. In Pennsylvania, state laws governing the distilling of spirits changed with Act 113 in 2011. The new law allows for a limited distillery license, lowering fees for a company that produces less than 100,000 gallons of spirits per year. The distillery can also have a tasting room on the production premises. This opens the playing field to small producers.

For Pennsylvania consumers, this is wonderful news. Bucks County got its first distillery in 2010 when Mountain Laurel Spirits started making rye whiskey in Bristol, Pennsylvania, bringing back a very old Pennsylvania industry. Now Bucks County has its second distillery, Hewn Spirits, which opened in March 2014 in Pipersville.

Hewn Spirits is currently distilling rum, rye, single malt whiskey, and moonshine (which is just the pure distillate with no aging). Their Dark Hollow bourbon was recently released and is made from local heirloom Bucks County corn. Look for their gin to release soon!

The distillery produces two types of rum: a golden rum that is aged in white oak barrels, and a white rum. Come to the tasting room, and you can not only sample it but also purchase some interesting rum cocktails, like a White Squall (rum, ginger ale, and lime). Or try one of the moonshine-inspired cocktails: Ain't That

a Peach (moonshine, peach tea, and lemonade) or a Moon Julep (moonshine, spearmint, and sugar). It's a very nice way to pass an evening.

I've done the Bourbon Trail in Kentucky, visiting such venerable distilleries as Maker's Mark, Four Roses, and Jim Beam. The distillate goes into 53-gallon barrels of new white oak, briefly charred on the inside (by law, all American whiskey must be aged in charred white oak barrels) and is aged four years or more. Of course, each of the distilleries stores and ages their bourbon a little differently and swears their way is the best way.

So when Tracy said he was making whiskey in 5-gallon barrels and aging them for only months, I was wary. But then I thought, where is innovation going to happen if not in micro-distilleries? The big spirit producers have a good thing going (and powerful marketing organizations behind them). Why would they change?

Let me step back a moment. Whiskey science—or lore—says as the distillate ages in the charred oak barrels, and as it expands and contracts over time due to temperature, it "picks up" both taste and color from the barrel. Traditionalists say you don't mess with that and insist you have to give the whiskey time.

Others—like many of the new micro-distilleries—say, why not try something new and see what happens? A smaller barrel, scored or honeycombed on the inside, provides more surface area for the distillate to interact with the charred surface and might quicken the aging process. Some say it gives the whiskey a more "woody" taste. You be the judge.

This is how Hewn Spirits is doing it. Tracy distills the spirit five times in his 130-gallon copper still and then puts it into the barrels for one to four months. The time varies due to the proof of the specific spirits as well as the time of the year. The summer definitely speeds the aging up as warmer temps move the spirits in and out of the barrel staves much quicker.

After aging the whiskey in the barrels, Tracy does a secondary aging in stainless steel vats—with a twist. He puts charred staves from his collection of antique woods into the whiskey and lets it sit for no more than two weeks. "More than that overwhelms the oak," he explains. "I want just a taste."

One shelf in the distillery is filled with small bottles of brown liquid. This is Tracy's "laboratory" where he tests different kinds of woods in the whiskey. I was privileged to taste one of those experiments and it definitely got my attention. The whiskey was complex and surprising. Traditionalists say what you will, this is fun.

Hewn has just released their single malt whiskey, Reclamation American Single Malt Whiskey, available in two releases. The first uses 300-year-old, reclaimed hickory that imparts a buttery and subtle maple character to the whiskey. "It's very smooth, with a touch of sweetness," says Tracy, and it packs a 90 proof (45% alcohol) punch.

The second release uses very old American chestnut for the secondary aging. Tracy describes this 86 proof whiskey as having hints of lemon, pepper and vanilla. The first limited release of the Chestnut Reclamation sold out quickly but the second release is already laid up in barrels. Other unique and rare woods Reclamation Single Malt Whiskeys are in the works. "We're getting incredible feedback and reviews," he says, "And we're trying to ramp up production to keep up with that demand."

A big part of what both Tracy and Andrew Knechel at Bucks County Brewery (who shares the building with Hewn) are about is a love of local community. For instance, Hewn Spirits sources its rye and corn from local farmer Nevada Meese of Meadow Brook Farm in Springtown. Tracy's old friend Mark Fischer grinds the grains at his mill in Doylestown, Castle Valley Mill. The spent mash goes to Dave Johnson at Beech Tree Farm in New Hope, who feeds it to his cows and pigs (which you may see one day at one of the barbecues being planned at the distillery).

LG

HILLROCK ESTATE DISTILLERY

Ancram, NY

BY RICHARD AUFFERY

While in the Hudson Valley, I sampled a peated single malt that was impressive. The story and philosophy behind this whiskey is fascinating and compelling, an intriguing tale of "field to glass" and terroir. Tradition is respected and emulated in a number of respects. This is not a simple craft distillery but one seriously dedicated to producing a special type of whiskey. And there is clear passion at work. This is a distillery that all whiskey lovers need to know.

We toured the Hillrock Estate Distillery, located in Ancram, New York, and our host was Jeff Baker, the owner of the estate. He was personable and earnest, leading us through the malt house and distillery, telling us the history of the estate as well as explaining their production process. It was a fascinating insight into this craft distillery, and my respect for their operation increased through the tour.

In 1995, Jeff purchased the land, which would become the Hillrock estate and now encompasses over 250 tillable acres. Initially, he began the region's first pasture-raised, sustainable beef operation. He moved an 1806 Georgian house to the property that once had been owned by a Revolutionary War Captain who was also a grain farmer and Freemason. Eventually, Jeff decided he wanted to produce whiskey, so he constructed a distillery,

malt house, granary, and barrel house, locating all of them at the center of the estate. About four years ago, they started making whiskey.

It is important to Jeff that they try to produce "field to glass" whiskey, which is reflective of the terroir of their estate. As such, they grow all of their own grains organically, including winter rye, barley, and corn. As about 90% of US corn is GMO, Jeff has ensured that they grow sufficient non-GMO corn for their purposes. That is an important factor to numerous people. Harvesting is conducted from individual fields and the amount

of the yield takes second place to the quality of the yield.

As they began to produce whiskey from their grains, they soon learned that their whiskies possessed distinctive notes of clove and cinnamon, indicative of the terroir of their estate. This is exactly what Jeff hoped for, that their products would be reflective of the land, water, and climate of their estate. He didn't know what flavor profile that might entail until their whiskey production begun. As such, you should detect clove and cinnamon in all of their whiskies.

Most people are familiar with hearing about terroir and wine and may also have heard the term used with certain foods too, such as cheese and tomatoes. However, some spirits can evidence terroir. It has been said that terroir is an opportunity and the choices that are made in the production process can obscure and eliminate terroir. Not all spirits show terroir, but Hillrock is making positive choices intended to lead to their whiskies reflecting the terroir of their estate.

For their peated whiskey, Jeff has been importing Scotch peat, but he has been actively seeking a local source. Unfortunately, what he has found so far have been part of protected wetlands, so inaccessible to him, but his search continues. Finding local peat sources is an issue for other whiskey distilleries in the United States too. I recently wrote about the Westland Distillery in Washington who were able to purchase a 60 acre peat bog though they haven't yet produced any whiskies using this peat. If Hillrock can find a local source of peat, they can enhance the terroir of their whiskey.

HILLROCK ESTATE SINGLE MALT WHISKEY 43%

The Single Malt Whiskey ($100) is a peated whiskey made in a Speyside style, meaning it is intended to be a lighter whiskey. Interestingly, Dave Pickerell usually makes bold whiskies and this may be the softest one he has ever produced, but he still really enjoys it. This whiskey spent about 8 hours with the peat, though Dave mentioned they have produced another whiskey, a "smokebomb," which spent 18–20 hours with peat. No caramel color is added to this whiskey, and all of its beautiful color is natural. I found this whiskey to be smoky and intense, with strong spicy notes, a pleasant nuttiness, some citrus notes, and more noticeable clove and cinnamon flavors. Complex and intriguing, this was an excellent peated whiskey, perfect for the fall and winter. I had to buy a bottle of this whiskey too, and it is also highly recommended.

RA

TERROIR IN WHISKEY? INSIDE THE QUEST FOR INDIVIDUALITY AT THE HUDSON VALLEY'S HILLROCK ESTATE DISTILLERY

BY EVAN DAWSON

It wasn't yet midnight, but it was long past sunset in the peat marsh. Two men who looked like deep-sea divers were prepared to use their wetsuits for a new purpose: they would be diving for peat. The decayed vegetation is an attractive part of the process of making single-malt whiskey — it's smoked, adding a classic aromatic texture the likes of which can be found in Lagavulin and Laphroaig — but there's one problem. The New York State Department of Environmental Conversation protects the marshlands, so the peat can't be extracted legally. That's why the men were prepared to obtain it under the cover of night.

The preceding paragraph is only an idea, for now. But don't think the ambitious minds behind the Hudson Valley's Hillrock Estate Distillery haven't thought about it.

"The local peat tends to be in the DEC wetlands," said Jeffrey Baker, the owner and financial muscle leading the remarkable new facility. "We want to stay above board."

That's the last hurdle, it would seem, in the hunt for single malt terroir.

The notion of terroir tends to live in the wine world, where enthusiasts debate the impact of soil, place, and more. Baker is convinced that there is terroir in whiskey, and to show it, he constructed the only purpose-built malthouse at a distillery in the country. It's a throwback. Baker studied malthouses in the United Kingdom and decided to create what have been called, in seventeenth century Europe, a "one-man malthouse."

On your visit, you'll see the grain on the floor, but you'll want to resist the urge to pick it up or lay down and do grain angels. "That's $60,000 worth of whiskey on the floor," Baker explained. The grain will stay on the floor of the malthouse for three days; it needs to be aerated every six to eight hours, which is what the crew was doing when we visited. After three days, the grain slides through the floor hatch and down into the kiln. It's on its way, part of the process now celebrated as "field to glass."

Most Scotch is aged in used bourbon barrels for at least six years. Hillrock puts 80% of their production away for longer-term aging, but they've created a shortcut for the rest: by using smaller barrels, Baker thinks he can achieve the same effect in less than three years.

The Hillrock team has considered every detail, from the barrels, to the barley fields rolling off the hills, to the view of the distant Berkshires. Baker proudly pointed to the land he bought in 1999 and said, "The water is different here. That might be the most significant factor. The grain is going to pick up different characteristics here. The grain won't be the same here that it is in Scotland."

If Baker chose the land and equipment carefully, he made the obvious choice in his Master Distiller. Well, it was only obvious if he could convince Dave Pickerell to take the job. The notion of searching for terroir in American whiskey was appealing to Pickerell, who has become an industry titan. He worked as the Master Distiller for Makers Mark, earning respect across the distilling world.

"Our fields write their name in clove and cinnamon," Pickerell said when our group visited the tasting room. "We knew it the first batch. There were contractors hammering nails in, and everyone stopped. Everyone knew, before we even had everything built. This is what terroir is in whiskey."

Pickerell is not only a highly regarded distiller, he is a master entertainer when he's in front of a crowd. Gesturing for emphasis, he declared that there were only three differences between Hillrock's peat-smoked single malt and Scotch.

"One, we're not in Scotland," he said. "Two, the law says the barrels must be new here. And three, we don't add caramel coloring. That's it."

When the group fell silent to taste the whiskey, Pickerell announced, "We do have a smoke bomb coming." By that he means: the current single malt includes eight hours of peat smoking. Hillrock will soon release a single malt with 20 hours of peat smoking. Ask Pickerell what he thinks and he doesn't need to say anything; his eyes go wide and his mouth curls into a broad smile.

Eventually there will be a fourth difference between Hillrock and Scotch: the peat. Hillrock continues to bring in peat from Scotland a couple pallets at a time, as needed. Baker is patient but eager to learn what Hudson Valley peat will do to his product.

"The local peat will taste different," he said. "Remember that a lot of the peat in Scotland has seaweed, which gives it an iodine, salty flavor. We won't have that here. It will be interesting."

Hillrock makes one 30-gallon barrel per day. By comparison, Maker's Mark produces roughly 2,000 barrels per day. That leaves Hillrock with the relatively small production of 60,000 bottles annually. For now, most of the Hillrock allocation goes to Northeast markets. Eventually, Baker expects to hit the West Coast, then Europe.

The single malt sells for $100. Baker knows that customers can find Scotch for less, but he expects the quality to compete. Hillrock also offers what might be the only true solera-aged American whiskey.

But a visit to Hillrock seems to melt the concerns over the price tags. The quality is unimpeachable, the aromas addictive. Terroir in whiskey? Come to Hillrock a cynic, you might leave with an open mind.

"Just as pinot noir is not the same in Burgundy as it is in Napa Valley, we'll offer something different, something that is our own," Baker said to a room filled with writers and critics. They are accustomed to rolling their eyes, but on this day, no one seemed to be doubting him.

WESTWARD OREGON STRAIGHT MALT WHISKEY 2 YEAR OLD 45%

I have to admit I had never heard of this distillery before my whisky buddy Shai sent me this sample. Not hearing of the distillery automatically means never hearing about the whiskey either. I even had to look up what Straight Malt Whiskey meant.

In this case, it's a malt whiskey. Just like Scottish single malt but just 2 years old. I find these indicators in the United States rather confusing, since in this case they could have called it single malt. The straight indicator is used similarly to bourbon, since it's 2 years old.

The distillery is located in Portland, Oregon, smack in the middle of American suburbia. I wish we had more distilleries in cities like this. Or at least, in my vicinity like in Zaandam, or Alkmaar or so. It would be even better if they actually made some good stuff there, but let's keep the wishful thinking for another time and see what those folks in Portland are up to.

Nose: It's very gentle, with soft oak notes on the nose. Quite a bit of vanilla too. No surprises so far. Some cinnamon and clove for spices, and behind that you get a whiff of the raw spirit. It's very smooth, but not completely tamed. I have to admit, so far, so good; it's better than I expected/hoped for.

Palate: The palate is dry and slightly peppery with crushed black pepper. It's sharper than I expected with a bit of character. Thick syrupy sugars and vanilla. Some spices again, the cinnamon and clove. Maybe some dried ginger too. The vanilla is almost

custard-like but never overpowering. The pepper keeps building up and getting more intense. Rather oaky again, more so than on the palate. The spices are still here, and there's a slight burn in my throat, but in a good, masculine way. The finish isn't too long but the stickiness remains longer than the flavors.

I love tasting whiskies like this. It's reminiscent of a Scotch, but also has some American bits, like the oakiness and big vanilla notes. And, in this case, contrary to a lot of those really young distilleries and whiskeys, this isn't all bad. I actually quite like it, although it's a fairly simple dram.

But, compared to some others I've tried that were this young, this is recommendable. Getting back to me wanting more distilleries around, if a local still house produced stuff like this around here, I'd be a fan. Now, since it's small batches and from across the world, it'd be way too expensive to get hold of here. But, still, if you're in the area there, go try it out!

SHK

Opelika, AL

JOHN'S ALABAMA SINGLE MALT WHISKEY 40%

In the loosely defined category of American single malt whiskey, almost anything goes at this point it seems like. While it is hopeful there will eventually be a clearer understanding of what this category of whiskey actually should be, for now it is interesting to see innovation at work as different craft distillers take a swipe at it. One of the latest comes from Alabama in the form of the John Emerald Distilling Company.

This start-up distillery, according to a locally published report, plans to launch what very likely is Ala-

bama's first single malt expression. It is being called a "hybrid between a Scotch and a bourbon" in that it will be made like the former and barreled like the latter.

You know how Alabama is known for its peaches, right? That apparently is an influence in what's coined at this point as "John's Alabama Single Malt Whiskey." The spirit will be distilled from its own blend of Southern "pecan and peach wood smoked malted barley" that reportedly give it "an excellent mouthfeel with refined and well-rounded smoke notes."

As the distillers tell the tale, the single malt "will be matured first in new charred white oak barrels then finished with Alabama Norton wine staves to add a slight fruit finish to the spirit. A sip will reveal a slight upfront sweetness developing into vanilla notes from the oak barrel followed by a fruity finish from the wine staves while a backdrop of Alabama smoke flavor binds all the flavor notes together to make a true southern spirit experience."

The aging statement for this whiskey looks to be 4 to 6 months of age in smaller 5-gallon barrels, which is said to be "roughly equivalent to 3 years in the standard 53 gallon barrel."

NM

JOURNEYMAN THREE OAKS SINGLE MALT 45%

Journeyman Distillery is, satisfyingly, located in a 130-year-old warehouse that once housed a buggy whip and corset bone factory owned by an ardent Prohibitionist named E. K. Warren. Now that buggies, corsets, and Prohibition have all long gone out of style, the historic building is quietly churning out some of the tastiest craft spirits in the Midwest.

Based in Three Oaks, Michigan, Journeyman Distillery is right on the northern edge of the grain-fed American heartland, so it seems fitting that whiskey is their largest product category. In addition to the second annual release of the Three Oaks Single Malt, their portfolio includes rye, bourbon, and Silver Cross, a four-grain whiskey. They also have an extensive lineup of gin, rum, brandy, vodka, and liqueurs, if you're into that sort of thing. Notably, all of their spirits are certified organic.

This American single malt expression sold out fast. In 2015, Journeyman released its second batch. Made from 100% malted two-row barley, the 2015 Three Oaks Single Malt has seen the inside of three different types of barrels: one year in Featherbone bourbon barrels, nearly 18 months in Road's End rum barrels and two final months in imported Port casks. That's a total of 32 months in the barrel, which puts Three Oaks Single Malt on the older side for a craft whiskey.

This is a real gourmand of a spirit. The nose is heavy, syrupy, and a little musty, with strong notes of praline, marzipan, blackberry, mushroom, and potpourri. With water, the fruitier elements of the nose like green apple and grape come through more strongly.

In the mouth, the flavor is less intense than you'd expect from that powerful aroma. Caramel, butterscotch, and brown sugar provide a sweet counterpoint to a pleasingly bitter, cocoa-like finish. There's also something a bit vaporous about the spirit; if I didn't know it was bottled at 90 proof, I'd guess it was stronger.

This is a very dessert-y whiskey that tastes older than it is. Though the flavor doesn't quite follow through on the epic promises of the nose, the Journeyman Three Oaks Single Malt is so easy to like, especially if you prefer a less oak-forward spirit.

MW

Baiting Hollow, NY

PINE BARRENS SINGLE MALT WHISKY 47.5%

From rumor to first taste at the Long Island Spirits (LIS) tasting room, I wanted a bottle of Pine Barrens single malt whisky. It's got a Long Island pedigree, from the distiller to the choice of malt, which is made from Blue Point Old Howling Bastard, a local barleywine, and aged for less than four years in oak casks. I'd like to be more of a whiskey (or whisky as LIS spells it) fan, but I don't know much about them as singularly, and I know even less about single malts. That's because I'm much more of a cocktail kind of guy. But I know what I enjoy, and Pine Barrens is downright enjoyable.

A bottle of Pine Barrens Single Malt Whisky, batch 3. Some bottles I own for years. I went through this one in a month. It's a bit pricy, though, and notoriously hard to find. I've been looking for a bottle for over a year and finally found one at the excellent Empire State Cellars out in Riverhead. They sell liquor, wine, and beer from New York State, and the 375 ml bottle of Pine Barrens, batch three, was just under $50. Of course, that is around the same price of other artisanal, regional whiskeys, but for a schlub like me, it's just a bit beyond my price range, especially since I ended up treating most of the bottle as an ingredient for cocktails. Still, I wasn't going to pass up this rare opportunity.

Pine Barrens is highly sippable on its own. It brings a lot of heat and a lot of sweet. Cooled down with a nice large ice cube, it's a tasty unwinder.

I can't help but experiment; so, I made some expensive, top-shelf cocktails.It makes a great Manhattan. It keeps the heat, but works well with the sweet port I combined it with. The recipe I used was a bit different, so I'm including it here:

THE PINE BARRENS MANHATTAN

1½ oz. ruby port
4 oz. Pine Barrens Single Malt
    Whisky
dash of bitters
two frozen cherries
fill ⅓ shaker with ice cubes

Put cherries in old-fashioned glass. Combine rest of ingredients in a shaker cup, and shake until the outer cup gets frosty. Strain into the glass what with the cherries.

Pine Barrens makes an amazing, simply super whisk(e)y sour. The vanilla notes in the whisky weren't too strong for the lemon in the sour, and the sweetness inherent in the whisky just sent the cocktail into orbit. I could make one of these to drink every night, if I worked on Wall Street or something.

I'll have to update my research into the Old Fashioned, which at this time, I hadn't quite gotten the hang of. I think I've got it down, but Pine Barrens brought a bit too much heat in my new and improved recipe. While the whisky sour worked perfectly, the Old Fashioned had some elements that tasted out of place, so I'll stick to the blended whiskeys with that one.

Nose: Oak and sweet esters.

Palate: Hot! Sweet with vanilla tones. That fire spreads out. Warm and malty.

LIS has done a great job with its first whisky, and everyone who is interested deserves a bottle. Plus, the more people who demand it, the more likely it is that Long Island Spirits will update their website! Sadly, I'm down to my last drops of Pine Barrens, and I can't see how I can talk Mrs. Ferment in buying me another bottle, so if anyone gets hold of a bottle, let me know, and I'll make the happy owner a killer whisky sour, for two.

JR

MAINE CRAFT DISTILLING

Portland, ME

FIFTY STONE SINGLE MALT WHISKEY 45%

The drink scene in the greater Portland area has expanded exponentially in the past few years with a number of breweries and a handful of distilleries opening to add a beautiful complement to our top-notch food. Maine Craft Distilling (MCD) is one of those leading the charge. Look around at local restaurants and liquor stores and you'll spot their liquid loveliness at every turn. I had been to their tasting room briefly once before but had the opportunity to go again and really sit down to enjoy the "Farm to Flask" spirits they produce. With nine bottles currently offered, tasting all of them will keep you occupied for a while and, if you're coming in from out of town as many patrons seem to be, they're a great stop on your boozy tours of Portland.

MCD is a really stellar part of Portland's drink scene. Their variety, obsessive use of local ingredients, and really cool tasting room are more than enough reason to visit. However, I think patrons will find in their time there that MCD's biggest asset is their ability to suit any taste in spirits. From the relatively simple rums and near vodka—always with a touch of Maine Craft's own style—to the complex botanical spirit and one-of-a-kind gin aged in whiskey barrels, you can drive down the highway or stumble down the path less traveled. It's all up to you. Either way, they put so much work and so many flavors into their processes, you might find yourself with new tasting notes every time you try a sip.

I was really excited to see what was in store at MCD so I immediately grabbed one of the available bar seats on a Saturday afternoon and got ready to try some of what was in front of me. I reviewed the list of spirits I had been given and decided I definitely wanted to taste all the available options. The bartender noted that the ingredients the distillery used were essentially all from Maine, which only added to my enthusiasm. I settled on starting my tasting with their whiskey—Fifty Stone Single Malt. A sip of the small pour revealed the oak from the barrels in which it's aged and a background of the flavor of grains smoked in peat and seaweed, though there wasn't enough smoke to be confused with a Scotch. I found it to be a solid, smooth whiskey that would fit well on my liquor shelf.

PB

NASHOBA VALLEY WINERY

Bolton, MA

BY CARLO DEVITO

Located in the heart of Massachusetts' apple country, Nashoba Valley Winery is a stunning hilltop orchard overlooking the charming town of Bolton. They first started producing fruit wines in 1978, and since then have gone on to produce fine food wines, beers, and fine spirits. The family-owned orchard and farm not only boasts all of those but also a restaurant as well.

Nashoba Valley Winery has won more than 100 national and international medals and has received accolades from such noteworthy publications as *Boston Magazine, Wine Enthusiast, Cooking Light, Food & Wine,* and *Yankee Magazine.*

"I remember sitting down with my wife and saying, 'We'll spend $60- or $70,000 and after 10 years we might start getting some of it back,'" owner Richard Pelletier told Eric Felton of *The Wall Street Journal.* "At least the kids are young," he joked with his wife, "so at the very least, years from now we can have an open bar at their weddings." Felton noted that Mr. Pelletier kept "the oldest barrel in his living room, where he [could] easily steal tastes and keep tabs on its progress."

STIMULUS SINGLE MALT WHISKEY 42%

Nashoba started distilling in 2003. They laid down their first two casks of whiskey in 2004. They laid down five in 2005. And they've been laying down 20 barrels a year since 2006. They released their Stimulus Single Malt Whiskey for the first time on November 14, 2009. The first two batches produced 600 bottles. They use barley, and the batch sizes have fluctuated, as is normally the case with small micro-batch distilleries.

"It's paranoia (about hard liquor). There are no books about how to make rum, but thousands on how to make beer and wine. Distilleries have to glean information on their own and learn it themselves," Pelletier told *The Telegram* (Worcester, MA). "For all intents and purposes, the process of making beer, and the whiskey wash (a byproduct of beer) are the same processes. The temperature is different, and some of the grains are different. The whiskey wash is distilled after that."

The thing you have to love about Stimulus is that it is absolutely a product of place, like few others in the nation. Their malt whiskey is produced, aged, and bottled at their distillery in Bolton, Massachusetts. They make the wash for distilling. They distill it right there behind the tasting

was originally named for the stimulus packages that were given out in the early 2000s, which was partly how the still was funded. As a tongue-in-cheek homage, the distillery first submitted the name to a partisan, conservative governmental board, which rejected it, saying that "Stimulus" sounded more like a drug than a whiskey. Disheartened, Pelletier and his team regrouped and came up with a whole new name and package for approval. But just before presenting it for the second time, he realized that there were new names on the approval board who had never seen or heard about the old package. They submitted the old package again, and this time it came through with flying colors, proving that all politics is local... and timely.

Color: Rich golden.

Nose: Lots of fruit up front. Apple. Pear. Red fruits. Slightly floral. Spices. Toast. Vanilla.

Palate: Medium bodied. Apple, pear, and light red fruits all come through. Hints of honey, apricot, and spice all come through with lovely mouthfeel. Smooth, easy finish. Lingers nicely, lightly. Fine.

CD

room bar. It is aged in new whiskey barrels as well as in their own previously used wine barrels for cask finishing. Then, they have several of their whiskey barrels cut up, and the small chucks are used as the stopper in the bottle! That's intense!

There is a funny story about the origins of the packaging. The whiskey

NEW ENGLAND SWEETWATER
FARM & DISTILLERY

Winchester, NH

New England Sweetwater Farm & Distillery was established by Robert Spruill, his wife Patti, and his brother Joshua Spruill in Winchester, New Hampshire. They are in the Southwest corner of New Hampshire's Monadnock region. The farm is nestled on more than 50 acres near

the slopes of Mt. Pisgah. It is a family-run operation, both farm and distillery, and according to them, it's conveniently located within a 200-mile radius of Portland, ME; Manchester, NH; Boston, MA; Providence, RI; Hartford, CT; and New York City.

CLARK & CHESTERFIELD SOLERA AGED SINGLE MALT (FUTURE)

Clark & Chesterfield Solera Aged Single Malt Whiskey is a single malt barley-based whiskey. Using the solera method, often associated with port and sherry but being used by a number of American distilleries now, they age the whiskey in a combination of new and used

American oak barrels. Robert and Joshua explain that their barrel aging rooms are right next to the river, which helps to modulate the temperatures, making for "constant year-round temperature for perfect aging."

CD

ORANGE COUNTY DISTILLERY

Goshen, NY

ORANGE COUNTY SINGLE MALT WHISKEY 45.6%

What happens when a fifth generation farmer meets an owner of a lawn care franchise? That's simple. They open a distillery! Orange County Distillery was founded by John Glebocki and Bryan Ensall. Co-owner and Co-founder John Glebocki is the owner of J. Glebocki Farms, a fifth-generation farm in Goshen, New York. Co-owner and co-founder Bryan Ensall is the owner of a lawn care franchise that services all of Orange County, New York.

There is a clear division of labor. John works the dirt. Bryan does the paper and reporting. Then of course, they both get to have fun—distilling, from mashing to fermenting, distilling, aging and bottling. The whole operation fits into a small 1,600-square-foot barn.

This is a real farm-to-bottle craft distillery. They plant and grow everything on their farm they need. Their mantra is quality ingredients and small batches.

They grow their own beets and make vodka. They grow their own corn and make bourbon. They grow their own botanicals for their gin!.You can step outside their barn and see where it is all grown right there.

They make five types of whiskey. They handcraft a corn whiskey, a bourbon whiskey, an aged rye whiskey, an unaged single malt whiskey, and an aged version of the single malt. The Orange County Single Malt is aged in the same charred barrels previously used for the bourbon. And it is peated.

CD

RANGER CREEK BREWING & DISTILLING

San Antonio, TX

RIMFIRE MESQUITE SMOKED TEXAS SINGLE MALT WHISKEY 43%

"Instead of using Scottish peat, we used Texas mesquite," says the label on Ranger Creek's Rimfire, a single malt whiskey made in San Antonio, Texas, and the second release of Ranger Creek's Small Caliber Series, following their .36 Texas Bourbon.

It's a catchy phrase, but more than that it speaks to the intent of Rimfire, a Texas-born, Scottish-bred, mesquite-smoked single malt whiskey. After a much-delayed legal labeling and classification process, spurred along in a small way by a helpful hand from Richard Thomas, Rimfire was released in 2013, with a limited run of less than 500 cases of hand-numbered 375ml bottles. This review was based on batch #1, bottle #2953, Spring 2013.

Rimfire is actually based on Ranger Creek's Mesquite Smoked Porter—Ranger Creek is both a brewery and a distillery, or a "brewdistillery" in their preferred jargon. They basically brewed the same recipe as that beer, minus the hops, distilled it, and then aged it for six months in small barrels. The mesquite single malt is bottled at 43% ABV.

The mesquite used for smoking purposes with Rimfire is sourced from a local farm, and Ranger Creek then takes the mesquite and places it into a converted 20-foot shipping container, using it as a huge smoker.

Having seen its billing as "a smooth, sweet, sipping single malt with just a touch of smoke," I found it to be heavier on the smoke and drier than advertised, although still certainly suitable for sipping purposes.

The nose offered a molasses sweetness, hints of vanilla, and a sweet, charred aroma. A light, golden-amber in the glass, Rimfire is intense, smoky and sharp.

Rimfire has a biting, long finish, which is felt not only in your throat and stomach but also resonates in your mouth as well. A bit of water or ice will highlight more of the flavor of that smoke, its mesquite backbone, while dulling its bite and allowing its sweetness to linger through a warm, smooth finish.

While Rimfire pegs its ancestry from Scotland, I tend to think its roots are a bit closer to home, in Kentucky, at least in terms of what's delivered versus what was conceived. Its sweetness and char called to mind more of a sharper bourbon than a sweeter single malt, to my taste at least.

JE

Akron, OH

KING'S CUT SINGLE MALT WHISKEY 43%

Grape and Granary has been supplying home-brewers and winemakers as well as small industry folks for many years. They also have a very active Internet business. Their name is well known in both small-batch industries. Renaissance Artisan Distillers is an outgrowth of that business. John M. Pastor, Jim Pastor Jr., and Ron Petrosky, all familiar with the techniques involving brewing and vinting, are taking their combined interest to a new level.

"The name Renaissance comes from a resurgence of interest in artisan spirits," John Pastor said to Brittany Nader of The Devil Strip. "People's tastes are changing. They prefer local and quality over the mass-produced. Mass-produced products just don't have a lot of character."

As the guys like to point out, most of the small breweries, wineries, and distilleries in America were wiped out by Prohibition, never to return. "Today, there is a renewed interest in artisan distilled products. These spirits tend to be unique and flavorful. Welcome to the Renaissance!"

Renaissance Artisan's King's Cut Single Malt Whiskey is their flagship whiskey brand. It was launched in October 2014. John, Jim, and Ron use imported English-grown barley and specialty malts in order to emulate the taste of fine single malt Scotch. The whiskey is barrel aged in 5, 10, and 15 gallon charred whiskey barrels. Small barrels are more intense and offer more wood to liquid interaction, shortening the aging process.

Nose: Toffee, cocoa, honey and vanilla, along with apple and hints of spice.

Palate: Toffee and apples come across, with a hint of cereal. Spices and honey linger. Nice clean finish.

CD

Newport, OR

CHATOE ROGUE OREGON SINGLE MALT WHISKEY 40%

There is a new trend in the way whiskey is aged—it's called ocean aging. Ocean aging is when the whiskey is placed in oak barrels and those oak barrels are placed on large ships where they will age for a period of just a few months up to a few years. The idea behind ocean aging is that the salt air, oceanic pressure, extreme heat, and rolling movement of the waves will age the whiskey much faster than it would if it were aged on land.

I recently picked up a bottle of Rogue Oregon Single Malt Whiskey, which happens to have been ocean aged for three months. This was my first experience with an ocean-aged whiskey. This whiskey has a surprisingly dark color for being aged for only three months. It has kind of a hazy appearance to it. The nose has a strong aroma of cinnamon with a salty ocean smell to it also. The salty ocean smell kind of scared me, to be honest. I wasn't sure what to expect when I tasted it. The flavor is similar to the aroma, with a hint of sweet cinnamon combined with a salty ocean taste. This whiskey also has the flavor of a Scotch whiskey with a mild smoky taste, which comes from 12% of the malt used in this whiskey being hand-smoked using alder and maple chips.

Overall, Rogue Oregon Single Malt Whiskey was an interesting drink, but the salty ocean aroma and flavor are not what I'm looking for in my whiskey. The ocean-aging concept is an interesting idea, but the end result is not very appealing to me anyway. I've read some reviews on another brands of whiskey that was ocean aged for three and a half years and the reviews were all positive and didn't mention the salty brine taste that I noticed in the Rogue Oregon Single Malt Whiskey. It seems that aging it longer, even on the ocean, reduces the salty taste and imparts plenty of the flavors from the oak.

VA

Santa Fe, NM

COLKEGAN SINGLE MALT WHISKEY
46%

Colkegan Single Malt Whiskey is the "aged" version of one of the two Scotch-style whiskeys distilled by Santa Fe Spirits—and another fine example of an inde-

pendent distiller making good things happen to whiskey in the twenty-first century.

An American distillery, set against a backdrop of Rocky Mountain peaks and Rio Grande basin vistas, established in 2010 by an English architect who arrives in Santa Fe via the British Virgin Islands, and producing a Southwestern variation of Scotch-style whiskey? Could this be part of a CM for a new character in another critically-acclaimed TV drama set in New Mexico? Santa Fe Distillery's hometown of Tesuque, New Mexico, was one of the last places visited by Walter "Heisenberg" White in the 2014 season finale of *Breaking Bad,* but a fictional distiller named Colin Keegan wasn't the person Mr. White visited.

Colin's story is very real, as is that of Santa Fe's distiller John Jeffery. His choice of craft, though rooted in the high tradition of Scottish distilling, is a singular refinement attuned to Willa Cather's wind-swept immigrants (she mentions Tesuque in the 1927 novel, *Death Comes to the Archbishop*), an ironically life-affirming desert still life of Georgia O'Keefe, or the novels of Cormac McCarthy (who also resides in Tesuque).

Colkegan Single Malt Whiskey is distilled from 100% malted barley and bottled at 92 proof (46% ABV). That mashbill, the base of traditional Scotch and Irish whiskeys, distinguishes Colkegan from most American whiskies, which are traditionally corn and/or rye-based. As Colkegan's website says, however, "this whiskey... wouldn't want to be called Scotch even if it could be."

It's one of a unique breed of American single malt whiskeys that are adapting the Celtic traditions in new and exciting ways. Early American distillers imported the basics of their craft from Scotland but initially took to the more durable rye grain in practice as a substitute for barley.

Now independent American distillers are returning to malted barley and refining the traditional method at the malting level. Santa Fe Spirits isn't the first—Rick Wasmund's Copper Fox Distillery, in Sperryville, Virginia, has been distilling its Wasmund's

Single Malt Whiskey since 2005—but like its peers, it stands apart from them and other American whiskeys.

The barley base of Colkegan Single Malt Whiskey employs a smoked malt that substitutes Southwestern mesquite for peat, an idea now prevalent in Southwestern craft circles. The whiskey is aged in various oak casks, at the Santa Fe elevation of 7,000 feet above sea level, in the high desert.

In the glass, Colkegan has the mellow golden glow of a classic Scotch or Irish whiskey, and a woody scent of smoky vanilla bean with caramel stripes gives way to a pleasant hint of sliced star fruit and strawberry.

The body is warm and relaxing, with a moderate sweetness at first, commanded by the flavors that filled the nose, but grows more earthy with a dash of mown grass and lemon zest.

The result of the malt's smokiness is uniquely revealed in a mellow finish, where a moderate mix of bark, leather, and tobacco harden around a soft, lingering taste of vanilla ice cream laden with fresh black raspberries. Although Colkegan Single Malt Whiskey is rooted in the Scotch tradition, its lasting finish is much closer to the triple-distilled velvet of an Irish malt whiskey.

SDP

SEATTLE DISTILLING COMPANY

Vashon, WA

"We're a little family-owned, small batch distillery. We make all our spirits by hand from scratch in the old-school methods that are slow, but create a really delicious spirit," said Tami Brockway Joyce, co-owner of Seattle Distilling, told the local Channel 5 news.

Seattle Distilling is actually made on Vashon Island, which is the largest island in Puget Sound. It is owned by two families. The distillers became famous for their coffee liqueur, but their single malt whiskey has been an impressive hit. It's small batch and hard to get because it sells quickly.

IDLE HOUR SINGLE MALT WHISKEY 44%

Seattle Distilling Idle Hour Whiskey is a single malt whiskey crafted from barley grown in the Palouse. This is some of the richest farmland in the state, which has enjoyed an excellent reputation among foodies since the late 1800s. Seattle Distilling adds a few new extra little touches. During fermentation, they add just a wee bit of local wildflower honey. They also take old Sauvignon Blanc wine barrels and re-char them, them-selves, by hand, before aging their whiskey.

Brett Konen, a local journalist wrote in *Sip Northwest*, "Having tied the malted Palouse Valley barley spirit together with a hint of wildflower honey, the richness of the grain is balanced by the lightest bit of sweetness, and united they stand up to dark charcoaly smoke and woodsy spice that comes from aging in reclaimed and house-charred Sauvignon Blanc barrels before bottling at a solid 88 proof."

CD

SONS OF LIBERTY SPIRITS CO.

South Kingstown, RI

UPRISING AMERICAN SINGLE MALT WHISKEY 40%

I first tasted Sons of Liberty at a massive whiskey tasting show in Manhattan before I ever knew anything about them. I didn't know where they were from or who they were. And out of more than 100 whiskies that day, their products stood out! Done!

Now, having lived in New England, I loved that they were located in South Kingstown, near Charlestown, Exeter and Narragansett. So that cemented it for me. I have been going to those towns since I was a kid. I've been writing about wines, beers, and spirits from the region for more than a decade. So the rest was easy.

Sons of Liberty, of course, were a secret society of citizens in the American Colonies that organized in an attempt to protect the rights of colonists and to oppose unfair taxation. Their's was the famed motto "No taxation without representation." Enter Mike Reppucci who thought it would be a good idea to try to make world-class whiskey in New England. He founded Sons of Liberty Distilling.

"A little-known fact, even among regular whiskey drinkers, is that all whiskey starts as beer," says Mike. "For years, craft brewers have been producing outstanding seasonal brews, and we saw the opportunity to advance the trend to American craft whiskey."

That's when Mike turned to the famed master distiller Dave Pickerell to begin experimenting with recipes using different beers. They finally settled on a stout, which featured 100% barley malts such as Chocolate Malt, Crystal 45, and Biscuit malts among others. They double-distilled the beer

after it was finished. They aged the distillate in a combination of new, charred American oak and toasted French oak barrels to give it added complexity.

Nose: Cocoa and coffee come through, along with apples and figs, vanilla, and caramel.

Palate: Apple, cocoa, vanilla, caramel, and honey all come through. A hint of spice comes through at the end. The finish, though, is surprisingly vanilla and cream and finishes dry and clean. To me, this whiskey finishes lighter and drier than it smells. Maybe because the roasts suggest it, I was expecting a bit more brown sugar? But that is being picky. This is a wonderful whiskey. Well executed. Beautifully done. Like me when I first tasted it, it will open your eyes! Strike another blow for the Sons of Liberty and for Rhode Island!

CD

BATTLE CRY SINGLE MALT WHISKEY 40%

Despite the title, this isn't about a *Game of Thrones* or *Ice Road Truckers* episode, and it's certainly not a patriotic Braveheart-esque call to arms about Scottish independence. Having said that, what I am going to write about is an American distillery that sees itself as a bit of a revolutionary, which is pretty apt. From what I can gather, it thinks of itself as the American whiskey equivalent to Brewdog's ruffling-of-feathers in the beer scene over here. Sons of Liberty is a distillery based in the state of Rhode Island who see themselves as leading the craft spirit revolution in the United States and redefining the American single malt whiskey category. That's a pretty bold statement by anyone's standards.

Their main focus is on the fermentation process, with the thought that awesome beer gives rise to awesome whiskey. Battle Cry consists of 100% malted grain, with a mash bill of 80% malted barley and 20% malted rye. This is then fermented with a Belgian Trappist yeast strain, creating a flavor profile with notes reminiscent of a classic Belgian ale. The wash is then double-distilled and matured in a mix of freshly charred American oak barrels and lightly toasted French oak casks. Got all that? I have to admit, I'm a sucker for attention to detail and love the fact these guys are experimenting with the fermentation process. I often feel, in Scotland, a disproportionate amount of emphasis is placed on the cask. As important as cask selection is, it's great to see people tinkering with other parts of the production process.

The Sons of Liberty whiskeys (they also have a bottling called Uprising that is born from an Imperial Stout) are produced in rather small volumes, as you'd expect from a craft distiller, so they're only really available in and around Rhode Island and New England. If you're in the neighborhood, you should look them up.

Nose: Orange marmalade on toast, rich butterscotch, manuka honey, cinder toffee, sweet malt, treacle cake, coffee cream chocolates and charred oak. Pretty big!

Palate: Caramel fudge, buttered popcorn, pancakes with Nutella, cloves, maple syrup on bacon, BBQ steak flavored crisps, smoked rack of ribs. Big, sweet and chewy with plenty of depth. Long, with sweet caramel and charred wood.

Considering you can get a bottle of this for the equivalent of about £20, it's an absolute must buy if you live on, or visit, the northern end of the US East Coast. It reminds me quite a bit of the Balcones expressions that I've tried (and really enjoyed), but it's a bit more subtle and slightly more on the lighter side compared those whiskeys. Aside from this whiskey they also do Uprising, as I've mentioned, and seasonal whiskies, which currently consists of hop-flavored whiskey and pumpkin spice whiskey. I'm actually heading over to the United States soon, but I'm California-bound. Coast-to-coast road trip, anyone…?

TW

PEREGRINE ROCK CALIFORNIA PURE SINGLE MALT WHISKY 40%

Jim Busutti founded Saint James Distillery in 1995. The distillery is situated near Irwindale, California. Jim's family tradition in the wine and spirits business dates back generations. The family has been making wine on the farm for two generations. The distillery produces fruit brandies, rum, vodka, tequila, and other spirits. Jim makes sure that at the Saint James factory, all the spirits are stored and aged in French oak barrels.

"It takes a substantial investment to get started in the distillation business. And after years of saving, I was fortunate enough to be able to purchase an Alambic copper pot still from Germany. It is only with the use of a pot still that the flavors of the fruit came through."

This single malt is made from peated Highland Scottish Barley and local mountain spring water. Peregrine is aged in American bourbon casks. "Connoisseurs say, however, that the raw product shows promise," *Newsweek* wrote of the "southern California single malt." "'I think it's ready to go,' says the enterprising [Jim] Busutti (who also makes an agave liquor that he can't officially call tequila). To make sure, he'll let his malt age another year before releasing it nationally."

CD

Alameda, CA

ST. GEORGE SINGLE MALT WHISKEY, LOT 15

While much of the buzz around American whiskey releases during the fall focuses upon the rush of all things bourbon, American single malt drinkers in the know quietly queue up for the release of St. George Single Malt Whiskey. It is now in its 15th iteration, known also as Lot 15.

St. George Single Malt Whiskey, Lot 15, is produced by St. George Spirits of California. One of the pio-

neers in the craft spirits movement, they've been making their whiskey and other spirits since 1982. The whiskey in particular is a big deal to them, as master distiller Lance Winters reportedly first got into the business of craft distilling to produce just such a fine bottling as you are reading about now.

The Lot 15 batch, like those before it, is limited in release. This time

around there are only 3,000 bottles making their way to retail. It will likely be a highly sought-after expression by those who are fans of this brand, especially given the fact Lot 14 was named Craft Whiskey of the Year in 2014 by Whisky Advocate.

Information on Lot 15 from St. George indicates it is a blend of whiskeys drawn from barrels aging between 4 and 16 years, with the cask types including Tennessee whiskey cask, used Kentucky bourbon cask, used French and American oak wine cask, used port cask, used apple brandy cask, and used late-harvest Semillon wine cask. The mash bill is 100% barley malt.

Official tasting notes for this American single malt are below, courtesy of the distillery. It is set to price at around $90 per bottle.

Nose: Lavender honey, tangerines, watermelon, and an undercurrent of sandalwood. Evolves into jackfruit, pineapple, and the bright-ness of apple cider. Eventually these fruitier aromatics give way to chocolate and butterscotch. Further time in glass will show lighter cocoa, Saigon cinnamon, salted pecans, cream, coffee, flint, and soil all as parts of the classic St. George chocolate heartstring. As your glass dries, the salty saline aromatics give a sense of drying fennel.

Palate: Pale and crystal malts broadly show across the palate and are soon deepened by dusty cocoa and bittersweet chocolate notes that go towards molé (cinnamon and nutmeg). The spice on the back palate expands with further impressions of cream, butter, clover honey, honey-roasted peanuts, and the sweet citrus Semillon wine. The malts continue to show throughout, and after a few sips the sweetness of licorice and chocolate mint give a cooling sensation as the long finish goes toward gunpowder tea and ale.

NM

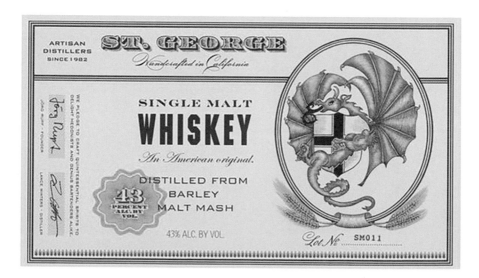

STILLTHEONE DISTILLERY

Port Chester, NY

BY CARLO DEVITO

I finally caught up with Ed and Laura Tiedge at the Hudson Berkshire Wine & Food Festival 2014 back on Memorial Day weekend. I had wanted to taste their spirits for some time, and I have not been able to get in front of them. The weekend gave me the opportunity...and what an opportunity! And I realized after talking with them, and reading about them, that I have as much affinity for them as I do their line of products!

StilltheOne Distillery is located along the banks of the Byram River in Port Chester, New York. This is the first reason I have an affinity for them. I have fond memories of Port Chester, which lies in the part of Westchester County that abuts Connecticut. My parents lived in Greenwich and

now back-country Stamford. I went to school at Stamford UConn for six months, and went to school with Moby and then used to go to The Beat (a club) to hear him spin records. He was awesome even back then. There was also a home center there wherein I spent a lot of time. Ed and Laura's distillery is situated in a manufacturing district, surrounded by welders, metal fabricators, and commercial fishing vessels.

Master Distiller Ed Tiedge is a former officer of Marines and Wall Street bond trader who decided to pursue his passion for unique and excellent spirits. According to their website, "After leaving Corporate America, Ed began his journey into crafting spirits by studying distillation and vinification (wine making) techniques in California and working at a small winery and distillery in Cognac, France. He then began researching the production of mead, a honey wine that has been made since ancient times. Thinking back on his experience in distilling wine into brandy, Ed began to formulate a process to distill honey wine into spirits. Through much research and hard work, he found the right varietal honey and yeast combinations and the precise distillation technique to create an incredible honey-based vodka we call Comb. Nowadays, Ed works hands-on every day with his crew to make world class spirits at StilltheOne Distillery—the name of which is inspired by his wife and Chief Tasting Officer Laura, who, after all these years, is Still the One."

287 SINGLE MALT WHISKEY 45%

I have an unabashed love for this whiskey. No, full disclosure, I am a bourbon guy. I love bourbon, I hate the peaty-ness of single malts, etc. I like the smoky, slightly sweet bourbons with lots of character—Whistle Pig, Hillrock Estate, Rebellion, etc. But this is whiskey. This is a big drink for sure. And I loved it!

Ed approached Captain Lawrence's owner, Scott Vacarro. Ed wanted to make a whiskey from one of Scott's beers. In December 2013, Vaccaro shipped him thousands of gallons of his Freshchester Pale Ale. Ed distilled it and 287 Single Malt Whiskey was born. The name comes

from the Westchester highway (that I myself have driven maybe a couple thousand times) that connects StilltheOne Distillery and the Captain Lawrence Brewery.

The idea was that Ed wanted to capture the nuance of the malted barley. He then aged it in new oak barrels to give it more depth and flavor as all good whiskey should be. The first batch of 287 Single Malt Whiskey is in limited production, with only the First Taste edition bottles released after a 10-month aging time. Each bottle is filled and labeled by hand, with our master distiller's signature on every single one. I bought myself one of these bad boys.

Firstly, I love that this is a collaboration effort here in the valley. There needs to be more of this kind of conversation going on! Secondly, this whiskey was amazing. Yes, it is completely dry and I like a slightly sweeter brown spirit generally, but this was smooooth. I was absolutely shocked. Great nose. Cereal. Vanilla. There were hints of soft fruit, spice, nuts, and maybe a sherry-like quality to it? I really liked it. Who knows, maybe Ed is starting me down the road to a greater appreciation of whiskey. Regardless, this was outstanding!

Still the One is the one you should be looking for.

CD

STILLWATER SPIRITS

Petaluma, CA

Stillwater is first and foremost about its team, a group of remarkably accomplished people. Don Payne, the founder and distiller, graduated from distilling school in 2001 and has been a journeyman distiller ever since. Paddy Griffen, Stillwater co-founder, is a brewer at Lagunitas Brewing Co. and has been brewing beer for more than 25 years. He too graduated from distilling school in 2001. Retired Business Agent for Plasterers Union Local #66 in San Francisco, and also a four-time member of the Golden Gate Bridge Board, John Moylan is also a founder and Director of Sales. Brendan Moylan, the General Manager, is also a well-regarded Bay Area brewer. Tim Welch is also a distiller here and works on the whiskeys. One immediately begins to understand that these people will accomplish something impressive.

Now, the second thing you need to know is that Stillwater Spirits has been producing award-winning brandy, grappa, and eaux-de-vie since 2004. They have already proven their stripes as distillers. They are not waiting for your approval.

The cool thing about Stillwater Spirits is that not only do they make amazing spirits for commercial sale, but also companies and private citizens may come here and distill! Stillwater Spirits is also a custom distillation facility. They have a 500-gallon Vendome copper column pot still, a 40-gallon Jacob Carl stainless steel/copper bottom column pot still, and a 550-gallon Yabuta stainless steel vacuum still, one of the few vacuum stills in the United States.

MOYLAN'S AMERICAN SINGLE MALT WHISKY 43%

In this release, 100% two-row barley is fermented and put through the copper pot still. The white whisky is aged for four years in 100% American white oak charred bourbon barrels and former beer barrels. The whisky is then finished for an additional six months by aging in orange brandy barrels, adding a layer of citrusy, dried candy to the caramel and malt notes.

MOYLAN'S AMERICAN CASK STRENGTH SINGLE MALT WHISKY 58.7%

This is the same whisky released in a Cask Strength expression. The alcohol is higher, but the intense layers of flavor from the barrels matches it. Impressive.

MOYLAN'S DOUBLE-BARREL CASK STRENGTH SINGLE MALT WHISKY 58.1%

This whisky is made the same way as the American Single Malt, but instead the 100% two-row barley is smoked with cherry wood, to give it a smoky, fruit finish. Then it is aged eight years in 100% American white oak charred bourbon barrels and former beer barrels.

This is an incredible line-up of American-styled single malt whiskies with high quality, integrity, and taste!

CD

STRANAHAN'S COLORADO WHISKEY 47%

The tale of Stanahan's Colorado Whiskey goes something like this. George Stranahan (who also owns Flying Dog brewery) had a barn that caught on fire. Jess Graber was a volunteer firefighter who responded to the fire. They decided to let it burn itself out and so while watching the fire they got to talking and discovered they both loved making alcohol. Stranahan brewed beer, and Garber was a fan of distilling.

After the fire George offered Jess his other barn to set up a still and distill some of his old beer in. A while after that George gave Jess a spot by his brewery, and that's when Jess brought on Jake Norris to help with the distilling and they began distilling the Flying Dog four-barley mash. In 2011 the brand was sold to Proximo spirits and the rest is history. Mashbill is 100% malted barley, with four different kinds used in mash.

Color: Caramel.

Nose: A cavalcade of complex dark dessert notes move this whiskey forward. Notes like toffee, caramel, brown sugar, brittle, and butterscotch are the engine pumping this down the tracks with sweet malty and light nondescript fruity notes in tow.

Palate: Malt and citrus are pushed across the palate by that same complex dark dessert engine, but this time it's towing cherries, coconut, and a toasted nutty quality that works as a nice counterpoint to the sweet notes. Dark sweetness fades to dark fruit, which fades to toasted nuts and caramel on a long finish. Despite the wave of sweet notes there's a nice balance to it with the fruity, malty, and toasty notes helping to even things out. A medium body works well here and the enjoyably smooth texture adds to the experience. Stranahan's is a craft distillery doing it right. There is a lot to like about what they're doing and how they're doing it. Everything from the comments on the side of the bottle by the labeler to the use of new charred oak and four-barley mash bill make this something that's a unique and tasty American whiskey that deserves the cult like following it's picked up. I enjoy the darkly sweet nose that moves to the palate where it picks up some toasted notes before fading out with some dark fruit on the finish. Definitely a keeper.

JP

SWIFT SINGLE MALT WHISKEY 43%

Located in evocatively named Dripping Springs, Texas, Swift Distillery is a new single-product distillery taking the craft ethos to heart. Founded by Nick and Amanda Swift in 2012 and focusing entirely on the production of Swift Single Malt, a Scotch-inspired single malt, this grain-to-glass distillery mills, ferments, distills, and ages on-site. The single malt focus helps set them apart from other Texas distilleries like Balcones, Ranger Creek, or Garrison Brothers, who are more honed-in on American whiskey styles.

Swift Single Malt is made from 100% malted barley and fermented with a single malt yeast the distillers purportedly source from the Speyside region of Scotland. After fermentation, the spirit is distilled in copper Portuguese pot stills before being aged for a bit less than a year in used charred Kentucky bourbon barrels. It's then transferred to Oloroso sherry casks from Spain, a move inspired by the fine sherry-casked whiskeys of Scotland.

With its stylish hand-numbered label and classic dropper-shaped bottle, Swift Single Malt would have a lot of shelf appeal if it weren't for the murkiness of the contents. Swift Single Malt is not chill filtered, a step that involves freezing and then filtering a spirit to remove the oils that contribute haziness—and add flavor—to a distillate. It's normal for non-chill filtered spirits to cloud when diluted with water or ice, but it's unusual to see a whiskey so cloudy in the bottle, and not particularly appealing.

Color: Cloudy yellow in color with a thin texture.

Nose: Tart and funky, with a lemony acidity that unfortunately reads as bilious alongside cut grass, mint, and a peanut-like earthy bass note.

Palate: Thin at first, the mid-palate is decidedly more robust with notes of peanut skins, walnut, and char as well as citrus juice and white pepper. Quite long and dry with a distinct acrid astringency. Swift is obviously dedicated to doing things right, but they still seem to be pulling all the pieces together. This single malt has some interesting nutty notes and a lot of character that might translate to complexity with more aging...

MW

THUMB BUTTE DISTILLERY

Prescott, AZ

CENTRAL HIGHLANDS SINGLE MALT 46%

When the good folks at Thumb Butte Distilling named their new American single malt whisky Central Highlands, they weren't trying to be misleading. The distillery is located in the Central Highlands of Arizona! As self-described by them, "On a side street, in a semi-industrial area, across from the Holiday Laundromat, which is not open on holidays, sits the home of Prescott's own Thumb Butte Distillery." Not exactly the Scottish highlands. But it's very, very down to earth, and very real.

Thumb Butte is led by Dana Murdock and Jim Bacigaupi. Dana was an artisan baker in Santa Barbara and Ventura, California, an importer of goods from Central American to Alaska, a management engineer in health care, a bartender, a home builder, and a potter. Her knowledge of wild and exotic yeasts comes in handy in the fermenting of their whiskeys and other products. Jim has made furniture for the Pope! He went to business school, has a BA in Psychology, and has an MA in Creative Arts. Jim is also an active participant in Big Brothers, Big Sisters. Other partners in this award-winning distillery include Scott Holderness and Mario Passalacqua. These are creative people.

This is a relatively new, small batch single malt. Each bottle is numbered by hand. The quantities are very small and can mostly only be obtained directly from the distillery. The response so far has been good, with folks offering notes of honey, chocolate, and light smoke.

CD

TRADER JOE'S IRISH SINGLE MALT 40%

When we lived in Maryland, I was disappointed to discover that their Trader Joe's (TJ's) grocers were not allowed to sell alcohol. It was difficult to describe to Marylanders how agreeable TJ's booze pricing can be. And I am not talking about Two Buck Chuck. That doesn't count.

TJ's now has a well-chosen selection of whiskeys—Dalwhinnie 15, Balvenie Doublewood, Glenfiddich 12 & 15, Macallan 10 Fine Oak, Laphroaig 10, etc. They also have their own label of Scotch whisky, though the quality of those have been mixed at best.

Recently, much to my (and many others') surprise, a Trader Joe's Irish Single Malt suddenly appeared on the shelves. Somehow TJ's had successfully contracted with Cooley Distillery to bottle some of their 4-year-old juice under the store's label. At a price of $19.99.

New whiskey at that price is difficult to pass up. In LA, $19.99 is less than two glasses of mid-shelf booze at a bar. For a whole bottle of some-

thing new, an Irish single malt no less...

It was a bold move by TJ's to go with an Irish single malt, something not very familiar with the average drinker in the States. And I use the word "was" because now that Beam Inc. has taken over Cooley and announced that most of their independent contracts will not be renewed, we may not see this whiskey for much longer.

It's also a bold choice because the nose and palate of this whiskey is quite different from the usual Irish blend or Scotch single malt. It's sort of its own soup. Though the bottle says this is only matured in bourbon casks, there is undoubtedly sherry stuff in here.

At first sips, this one was a puzzler. I couldn't get my mind around it. But with some oxygen and time, it has improved and I've had better luck cracking the malt.

NEAT

Color: Light amber.

Nose: Sandy and/or dusty, teeny bit of smoke, smoky butter?, old notebook paper, winey tannins, hints of a sweet sherry and dried fruit.

Palate: Lots of cocoa, cloves, sweet malt, oak tannins, very drying. Still very drying, mildly flat, cocoa.

WITH WATER (near 33% ABV)

Nose: Gets sugarier, some coconut oak stuff, starts to sniff more like a good blend.

Palate: Less cocoa but more vanilla, a little smoke, very oily and silky texture, still quite drying. Goes weird here, a brief bitter vegetal vanilla puff.

Though I don't recommend adding a few drips of water, this whiskey actually makes for a pretty good highball as the club soda brings out the palate's sweetness.

To be honest, I haven't been the biggest fan of Cooley's Irish single malts. I do like the Knappogue Castle 12 Year and the Tyrconnell finishes, but their Connemara bottlings and indie spinoffs have underwhelmed me. This one sits somewhere in the middle. On one hand: I won't go back for a second bottle of this TJ's malt. It makes me yearn for Irish single pot stills. On the other hand: Some people are enjoying it quite a bit. If you like the Cooley malts, then this may be your jam. And at the price, it's a rarity and not much of a risk.

MK

Nantucket, MA

THE NOTCH 10 YEAR OLD SINGLE MALT WHISKY 46%

As someone who covers the East Coast scene for wines, beers, ciders, and spirits, I have been following Nantucket for almost a decade. Their triple threat operation has been an inspiration for the entire Eastern seaboard. I have reviewed their Nantucket Vineyards wines, their Cisco Brewery beers, and their Triple Eight Distillery spirits!

Triple Eight, and their sister labels, can be found in the pastoral heart of Nantucket on the way to Cisco Beach. Nantucket Vineyard was founded in 1981 by Dean and Melissa Long. Dean and Melissa have always felt that a part of their mission was to educate consumers about the production process involved in all three products.

Cisco Brewers was founded by Randy and Wendy Hudson. The two couples joined forces to make Triple Eight. Visitors can now in a single afternoon learn how beer, wine, and spirits are made and the commonalities between them.

The building complex at Cisco Brewing/Nantucket Vineyards/Triple Eight Distillery is a popular Nantucket destination for locals and tourists.

Triple Eight Distilling became extremely popular for their Triple 8 Vodka, which featured three Eight Balls on its label. Its popularity spawned a whole run of flavored vodkas as well, the sales of which form the backbone of the distillery's success.

They also established a line of high-quality spirits like Gale Force Gin, Hurricane Rum (aged in ex-bourbon casks like a good, classic rum), and Nor'easter Bourbon aged in charred American oak for four to eight years. The rum and the bourbon are both very good.

But for years there were shouts and murmurs about a single malt. Triple Eight even went to so as to offer futures in their single malt. That's how they financed this whisky (it is a

cash-flow technique previously used by Scottish start-ups across the big pond). Well, for those who gambled, their investment paid off in the winter of 2015, when Triple Eight's newest product, The Notch Single Malt Scotch was named best American Single Malt!

Lead distiller Randy Hudson and the gang called it Notch because, it's "Not Scotch!" Dean and Randy started working on The Notch in 2000. They contacted George McClements, former production manager at Islay's Bowmore Distillery, to advise on technique for batch distillation. It is the only US single malt whiskey made on an island. The 8 year old whisky was released on 8/8/08.

The Notch Single Malt Whisky is crafted from an heirloom malted barley called Maris Otter. The grain is milled and mashed in their own Cisco Brewery. After the wort is separated, it is then transferred to Triple Eight. Triple Eight ferments the wort and batch distills it through their Arnold Holstein copper still.

The Notch has been aged in a number of different barrels. They were procured from Buffalo Trace, Woodford Reserve, Heaven Hill, Jim Beam, and Jack Daniels. To provide more layers of complexity, they also sourced barrels that previously held cognac, Sauternes, and various other types of wine, port, and sherry.

They are convinced their maritime climate plays an important role in the whisky's maturation, especially since it is so similar to the western isles of Scotland. The whisky is stored in a ventilated warehouse, allowing ocean breezes to wash over the stored spirits. The whisky is also double-barreled (or finished) in former sherry casks. They also age some of whisky in ex-Nantucket Vineyards wine barrels, adding to their sense of place or somewhereness (as wine essayist Matt Kramer might say).

There are several expressions of Notch. They have released 8 Year Old, 10 Year Old, and 12 Year Old editions of this fine single malt. The Notch has gone on to become one of the most decorated of American whiskeys, winning award after award, and even receiving raves from press and experts abroad. Head distiller Randy Hudson celebrated when The Notch 12 Year Old was named Best American Single Malt Whiskey by the American Craft Spirits Association. He was so excited, he dove into the icy waters of Lake Michigan in the first week of March! An incredible, complex whisky.

Color: Amber maple syrup

Nose: Layers of cereal, granola, Cap'n Crunch, figs, dates, caramel, apples, vanilla, and honey.

Palate: Figs, dates, apples, and vanilla all come through with almost gingery hint. There's some farmyard? Bramble? Caramel and honey and apples linger with hint of vanilla. Smooth, smooth finish.

CD

Hillsboro, OR

OREGON SINGLE MALT AMERICAN WHISKEY BATCH #5 46%

Located in Hillsboro, a suburb of Portland, Tualatin Valley Distillery is a small craft distillery focused on single malt whiskey. They released a single malt whiskey made entirely from Oregon-grown and Oregon-malted barley, made by Mecca Grade Estate Malt, one of Oregon's first malteries.

That whiskey, called Tualatin Valley Oregon Single Malt American Whiskey (Batch #5), has finally hit the market. The spirit was distilled from 100% Oregon-grown and malted barley, and then aged for six months in a mix of small charred American oak and toasted Hungarian oak barrels. While the small barrel, short duration aging approach isn't always successful, in this case, I wondered if that tactic would help showcase the qualities of the grain itself, unobscured by maturation.

Mecca Grade Estate Malt, Tualatin Valley's source for Oregon barley malt, is one of a handful of new craft malteries popping up around the United States. Mecca Grade is unique in that they grow all of their own barley on an eighth-generation family farm in central Oregon. In partnership with Oregon State University's barley breeding program, Mecca Grade grows a unique variety of barley called Full Pint, which was specifically designed for the craft brewing industry. While their malts have been adopted with enthusiasm by West Coast craft brewers, this might be the first whiskey made entirely with Mecca Grade's Full Pint malt.

Color: Bright yellow-gold.

Nose: A meaty, almost savory nose with earthy notes of mushroom, earth, and salt. Underneath, there are sweeter suggestions of peanut brittle, candied nuts, and a hint of red fruit.

Palate: Sweet, toasty, and nutty, very reminiscent of toasted white bread. There's a richness that reminds me, again, of peanuts, as well as a nice sweet-tart quality evoking lemon zest, apple skins, cinnamon, and nutmeg. On the short side, as to be expected from such a young whiskey, but pleasantly sweet and toasty. Jason O'Donnell described Mecca Grade's malt as "peanutty," and I definitely agree. This is a surprisingly rich spirit for its young age. While it won't fool you into thinking that it's a 10 year old Scotch, for fans of the American single malt category, this is an interesting release and a fascinating window into the new world of craft malting.

MW

HUDSON SINGLE MALT WHISKEY 46%

Tuthilltown's Hudson line is arguably the most successful craft or micro whiskey in the United States over the last decade. Started in 2001 by Ralph Erenzo and Brian Lee, the Tuthilltown Distillery has been cranking out whiskey consistently for the last six to seven years. Hudson has been one of the biggest success stories and trailblazers in this micro movement. As a result, the distillery got the attention of one of the largest beverage alcohol companies in the world in William Grant and Sons (Grant). The Hudson line was purchased by Grant in 2010, but the distillery still makes the product in their Gardiner, New York facility.

Gable Erenzo, Ralph's son, has taken a big step forward in running the operation since his father's serious auto accident in December 2010. I am glad that Ralph is doing much better and back, involved day to day. According to Gable, the partnership with Grant has allowed Tuthilltown to benefit from resources they didn't have prior. Most notably, the distillery can now rely on Grant to assist with tricky distillation problems, technological, and production advances they wouldn't have access to this quickly under more organic growth conditions.

In recent years, Tuthilltown has moved from using only small 3-gallon barrels to aging their products in both 3-gallon (for around six months) and 14-gallon barrels (for 18–24 months). All of their whiskeys are aged in this manner. Tuthilltown then blends a combination of these barrels to get the desired flavor profile. Gable informed me the distillery is continuing to increase the age of their products while making sure production stays consistent.

Always looking to grow and expand the Hudson whiskey line, Tuthilltown debuted a single malt whiskey about three years ago. Barley is one grain the distillery has had difficulty obtaining locally due to the region's poor barley growing conditions. What's interesting is in spite of the fact that it's a single grain whiskey the malt does not emerge easily through the oak-forward aromas and flavors. The result is an intensely spiced, cinnamon-bomb of a whiskey. But honestly it kind of works in a strange way. In addition to the cinnamon explosion, nutmeg, black pepper, and honeysuckle are present on the nose. A sweet fruitiness on the palate makes a brief appearance before being choked out by oak and spices. This one is not without its moments, but very one dimensional.

JP

Tuthilltown Spirits:
More Than a Distillery—
An Experience

BY CARLO DEVITO

Ralph Erenzo was not the first to distill in New York State, nor was he the first to distill in the Hudson Valley. But he was the first to take it to a whole new level. Brandies and eaux-de-vie had been distilled in the valley for years. But Ralph secured a distilling license and blew the lid off the distilling industry by breaking one wall down after another. He distilled rye, which hadn't been done in New York State for who knows how many years. He distilled bourbon. It was preposterous at the time he did it—who did he think he was kidding distilling bourbon outside of the sacred grounds of Kentucky and Tennessee? And he got so big, so fat, that UK whiskey giant Grants offered him a partnership deal that was too sweet to turn down! Today, no one talks about distilling in New York State without seeking his opinion or advice. Ralph is an impressive guy!

Before Prohibition, more than 1,000 farm distillers produced alcohol from New York grains and fruits. In 2005, Tuthilltown Spirits brought the tradition of small batch spirits production back to the Hudson Valley.

For 220 years Tuthilltown Gristmill, a landmark that is listed on the National Register of Historic Places, used waterpower to render local grains to flour. In 2001 Ralph Erenzo and Vicki Morgan acquired the riverfront property. In 2003, Ralph Erenzo and Brian Lee created Tuthilltown Spirits LLC. They converted one of the mill granaries to a micro-distillery. Two and a half years later, Tuthilltown Spirits produced their first batches of vodka from scraps they collected at a local apple slicing plant.

Today, Tuthilltown Spirits distills vodka from apples grown at orchards less than five miles away and the highly awarded Hudson Whiskey line, using grain harvested by farmers less than ten miles away. The Visitor Center offers guests the opportunity to taste the collection of whiskeys, vodkas, gins, liqueurs, and other unique, hand-made spirits. Tours illustrate how Tuthilltown's spirits are made by hand, one batch at a time. Guests are encouraged to stay for the day and enjoy the family-friendly environment. The on-site restaurant, The Gristmill at Tuthilltown, serves homemade American cuisine, featuring prime steaks, grass-fed beef, seafood, and locally grown produce in the historic 1788 gristmill. Executive Chef Jared Krom's menu is inspired by modern American cooking, showcasing fresh, local artisan products and ingredients of the Hudson Valley.

Innovation at Tuthilltown is snowballing thanks to the input of over 50 hardworking and creative team members. New products, cocktails, dishes, and tour improvements are brought to fruition each week. Tuthilltown Spirits is proud to have been the early bird in the post-Prohibition New York distilling scene. The team is now at the forefront of the craft distilling movement and is quickly building legacy of sustainable growth.

"[In] 2006...an entrepreneurial man named Ralph Erenzo, who had moved from Manhattan to the Hudson Valley, was researching the possibility of booze-making and discovered a little-known 2000 law on the books that allowed locavore micro-distilling at a greatly reduced licensing rate. The state had slashed the $65,000 distilling permit to just $1,500—so long as the producer was a little guy, making less than 35,000 gallons a year," wrote Amy E. Zavatto in *Edible Manhattan.* "This became the precursor for Erenzo's grand opus: helping to create a new law that would become the 2007 Farm Distillery Act, which would let farms become full-on distilleries with doors flung open to tourist-friendly tasting rooms. When Erenzo founded Tuthilltown Spirits in 2003, he was the only farm-based distiller in the state. Thanks to the changes in those laws and a new atti-

tude in Albany, just a few years later New York boasts over 40, with many more fermenting."

To cap off its success and to signal the rest of the world that American whiskey distilling had finally arrived, British whiskey giant W. Grant & Sons made a distribution deal for the rights to the Hudson line of whiskey products for millions of dollars. American brown spirits were now being taken seriously around the globe, especially those located in Scotland (a major compliment in and of itself).

Strange as it was, going to Ralph's place was a must but a little redundant. I'd already tasted most of his line before I even got there. They called the tasting room the Visitor's Center. To call it a tasting room is mundane. To undergo the Tuthilltown experience was another thing. The first thing I tried was the Noble Handcrafted Tonic 1 Barrel Aged Maple Syrup. Rich, multi-layer, and absolutely fantastic! Brought home a bottle of this ASAP! Tuthilltown sends used Hudson Whiskey barrels to Woods Syrup, a Vermont maple producer that ages syrup in those same barrels, decants them, then sends them back to Tuthilltown. At that point Tuthilltown finishes off a small selection of rye in these used casks. Brilliant!

The tasting room is spacious but never isolating, as sometimes large ones can be. Instead it is very well merchandised and full of very fun bric-a-brac. Many fun souvenirs to take home. And plenty of nooks and crannies that one never feels like they are in a giant, cavern-like room. And the service at the bar was excellent. The visitor center has a large deck outside. The weather was not cooperative when I was there, so no deck for me, but in the summer and fall it must be absolutely gorgeous.

However...I was drawn to their on-site restaurant. I walked into a lovely greeting room and was told I could have a table or sit at the bar. I absolutely chose the bar. I sat at the well-stocked bar and had a Manhattan made with Tuthilltown rye. Absolutely superb. And I had it with a side order of fries and a dipping sauce. Very nice. Going to Tuthilltown isn't just going to another tasting room. I understand why they call it a visitor center. It's fun, exciting, and it's an experience.... it's not just a tasting bar. And I really appreciated that. And you will too. It's a must go.

VAN BRUNT STILLHOUSE

Brooklyn, NY

VAN BRUNT STILLHOUSE MALT WHISKEY 40%

I met Daric Schlesselman at Whisky Live NYC. It was a mob scene. But with everything going on around him, Daric had an easy temperament and enjoyed the conversations. He never appeared harried. It might be

his northern Midwest background (his father was a farm banker), or maybe it's the whiskey. Regardless, a thoroughly entertaining, rough-hewn gentleman.

Daric partnered with his wife, Sarah Ludington, to establish this small, artisan, unique distillery in Red Hook, Brooklyn. To top it off, they named their operation after one of the original Dutch settlers of Breuckelen, Cornelius Van Brunt. In only a few, short years, they are gathering attention in a crowded market. Make no mistake, they are as hip as it gets, but it's not posing. Daric is genuine for his love of process and product, even in a charming, eccentric way. Nothing phony here. A very real guy.

"Van Brunt Stillhouse first distinguished itself in the fast-growing Brooklyn distilling world early on by rolling out, as its first product, a rum called Due North. That was original; at the time, no one in Kings County was making rum," wrote cocktail authority Robert Simonson in *Edible Manhattan*. "In its short life, Van Brunt Stillhouse has produced enough varieties of grain spirit for Schlesselman to be able to refer to the distillery's 'family of whiskeys.'"

"...They're giving their whiskey cousins across the pond a run for their money," wrote Chris Erikson in the *New York Post*.

Indeed, they make five different whiskeys, despite being an artsy, handmade, small-batch operation. This is extremely limited production. Van Brunt Stillhouse Single Malt Whiskey is made from 100% malted barley. It is unpeated. Daric turned to Master Brewer Ian McConnell for a beer wash made at the local Six Point Brewery. Daric ages his whiskey in small kegs of new American oak for nine months. The small barriques give more wood-on-liquid contact and shorten the aging process. It gives it flavor and color bigger and faster.

Nose: Roasty barley, cocoa, cereal, apples, vanilla, and spice. Hint of honey.

Palate: Chocolate malt, honey, and cereal all come through. A nice dose of apple and honey as well. Caramel. Some spice comes through at the end for a nice, smooth, clean finish. Lots of layers here that one does not expect, especially out of something so young. And the flavor lingers on the palate nicely. No whiskey face sipping this stuff. A very good sipper.

CD

Santa Cruz, CA

WAYWARD WHISKEY SINGLE MALT 46%

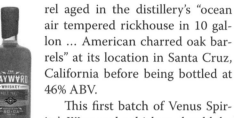

Venus Spirits is one of those interesting craft distilleries formed on the idea of a single individual with a lot of drive. One Sean Venus, long having an interest in craft brewing and organic foods, moved into distilling in 2012 with the idea to produce a range of organic spirits, including small batch whiskeys. Having successfully crowd sourced funds to help build his tasting room, and already having released a gin and blue agave spirit, Venus has now moved into his first batch of whiskey in the form of a single malt.

Wayward Single Malt Whiskey, as it is called, was double-distilled on Venus Spirits' hand-pounded, copper Alembic still imported from Spain from a mash bill of organic two-row, organic crystal malt. It was then bar-rel aged in the distillery's "ocean air tempered rickhouse in 10 gallon … American charred oak barrels" at its location in Santa Cruz, California before being bottled at 46% ABV.

This first batch of Venus Spirits' Wayward whiskey should be available in limited supply at least in the San Francisco Bay Area for the moment until it sells out. I know, for example, that the retailer Bitters + Bottles recently had some 750ml bottles in stock for around $50. Further whiskey releases, including a bourbon and a rye, are planned for later this year. I'm predicting great things for the folks over at Venus and look forward to seeing their other craft whiskey unveilings.

NM

WESTLAND DISTILLERY

Seattle, WA

BY RICHARD AUFFREY

It's an exciting time for whiskey lovers as excellent whiskey is now being produced all over the world. Some of these new distilleries have been making their mark, impressing everyone with world-class whiskey that can compete with the best.

In 2008, the state of Washington passed a new law, creating a "craft distillery" license, allowing small distilleries to open tasting rooms and sell their product. Since that time, additional laws have passed, expanding the advantages granted to these craft distilleries. The production limit has been raised to 150,000 gallons per year and there are no limits as to how much they can sell from their tasting rooms. In addition, in 2012, a law was passed eliminating the state monopoly on liquor sales and opening up thousands of new markets for craft spirits. All of these changes have led to a boom in distilleries so that there are now over 85 in the state, with about 30 more on the way.

One of these new distilleries, Westland Distillery, located in Seattle, was established in 2010 by two high school friends, Matt Hofmann and Emerson Lamb. I think Westland is standing out as distinctive and unique,

and their future looks bright. Before they opened their distillery, and rather than just jump into the distilling game, they toured the world, visiting about 130 distilleries. It was an educational journey and they learned much about whiskey production. Their lofty objective is to put Washington on the map for single malt whiskey, and I think they might just accomplish their goal.

Recently, I attended a Westland Distillery dinner event, hosted by Anchor Distilling Company, at Grill 23 & Bar, and had the chance to meet and converse with Emerson Lamb. It was a fascinating evening, and Emerson is very serious about whiskey. As we talked, I found reflections of Scotland, Japan, and Spain in all that he said. And when I got to taste his whiskeys, a single malt and a peated version, I was thoroughly impressed. These are whiskeys that you are going to hear more and more about, and I'm intrigued about the future products they will be creating.

Despite possessing a craft distillery license, Emerson was adamant that they were not really a "craft distillery," or at least that they were very different from nearly all other craft distilleries. An important distinction is their size, as he said that most craft distilleries may have only 50 or 100 barrels, yet Westland possesses about 3,000 barrels, stored in two different rooms, and produces about 2,500 bottles each day.

This size difference is significant, allowing them far more choices for blending. For example, they typically use whiskey from 50 different barrels to make their Single Malt. He feels that a distillery needs at least 1,000 barrels to be able to properly blend whiskey. The smaller craft distilleries have far less options available to them, making it much harder to make a consistent product. The greater amount of barrels does give an advantage to Westland for blending, allowing them an opportunity for greater complexity and depth to their whiskey.

An interesting element of Washington's craft distillery law is the requirement that distilleries must use at least 50% ingredients that are sourced from Washington. So why does Emerson believe Washington is a good place to create whiskey? He has three major reasons why it is an excellent environment for such.

First, the state is home to two great barley growing areas, mostly organic, and Westland doesn't use any GMO barley. Malted barley isn't really cheap either, typically selling for 50–60 cents a pound, while you could find corn for under 10 cents a pound. Second, Washington has excellent water and Westland's source is the Cedar River Watershed, one of the last sources in any major US city of unfiltered water. Third, the climate in Washington is fairly steady year round, unlike the big diurnal swings that occur in Kentucky, and that consistency allows their whiskey to retain its balance.

During my conversation with Emerson, comparisons to Japan arose frequently. For example, a Junmai Sake is made from only four ingredients, yet those four are still able to create a great diversity of aromas and flavors. And it is the skill of the brewers that transforms those basic ingredients into the wonder of sake. Westland Single Malt Whiskey is also made from only four ingredients, three similar to sake. They include a grain (barley rather than rice), water, and yeast. Their Single Malt uses a grain bill of five different roasted and kilned malts.

The main difference with the whiskey is that their fourth ingredient is oak, most of which is currently new US oak. However, they are currently experimenting with maturation in various sherry barrels, from Fino to Pedro Ximénez, and not just as a finishing element. Their yeast, nicknamed Jean-Claude Van Damme, is a French-Belgian yeast that was isolated for flavor and its strong fermentation ability. In addition, it provides a fruity aspect to their whiskey.

And like sake, it is the distillation process that transforms those four simple ingredients into the wonders of whiskey. Emerson likes to use the Japanese term *Jizake* to describe their aim, to create a house style for their whiskey. Jizake, which roughly translates as "local or regional Sake," usually refers to small, artisan breweries that possess their own style. Westland describes their house style as "a sweetness and ease on the palate accompanied by a fruity and complex but ultimately grain-focused finish."

In addition, in Japan blending is considered an art form, as it also is in Champagne. Emerson is a big advocate that blending of whiskey is also an art, and they seek consistency in their products, with the ability of using many barrels to create their own blends, far more than the average craft distillery can use. I definitely agree that blending is a specialized skill and art, especially when you are mixing so many different whiskeys together. As I mentioned before, it usually takes a blend of 50 barrels to make their Single Malt and it takes about 25 for their Peated. It should also be noted that they have a large single cask program as well.

Though other whiskey distilleries won't reveal certain secrets about their production methods, such as the nature of the grain bill, Westland has no secrets. They publish a small booklet about the distillery, which contains two pages of detailed Distillery Specifications, including Mashing, Fermentation, and Distilling. They don't see any reason to hide anything and want to be fully transparent.

What is the taste of Westland Whiskey? Emerson stated that "good is not a tasting note." He wants consumers to have a better vocabulary to explain what they taste in whiskey, and to that end they have an extensive Tasting Wheel, which is also in their small booklet. For Emerson, he wants to "find the emotional button," to connect with consumers through the whiskey. In addition, he feels people can drink whiskey any way they want, whether neat or in a cocktail, and also notes that a little addition of water to their Single Malt will bring out the fruit flavors more.

On the label of their products, you will see a diamond-shaped symbol at the top, which is the symbol of their company. The diamond has long been the Lamb family symbol, and Emerson's family was also involved in lumber for many years, and thus the tree inside the diamond. The coil refers to the distilling equipment.

Their two main products are the Single Malt and the Peated; both will sell in the local area for around $78.99. Westland Whiskey is a whiskey you need to seek out, whether for a cocktail or to drink neat. The future for Westland looks bright, and I am excited to see what future products they create.

WESTLAND AMERICAN SINGLE MALT WHISKEY 46%

The Westland American Single Malt Whiskey reminded me of one of those alcohol-filled chocolates you find at a high-end chocolatier. Co-founder Emerson Lamb mentioned that chocolate notes help to define the taste of Westland, and I found those chocolate flavors to pervade the taste of this whiskey. It was a balanced taste though, which complemented the other flavors of the whiskey rather than overpowering them. I added a little water to the whiskey, and it seemed to bring out fruity flavors of citrus and cherries, which were part of a mélange including vanilla, caramel, and coconut. There was a silky texture to the whiskey and a pleasant heat, perfect for a chill autumn day. An impressive whiskey, with plenty of complexity and a nice depth of flavor. Highly recommended.

RA

WESTLAND PEATED AMERICAN SINGLE MALT WHISKEY 46%

Of the Westland whiskeys, my personal preference was the Westland Peated Whiskey. It uses imported peated barley from Scotland, which they combine with 50% Washington barley. They mature the whiskey in 80% used bourbon casks and 20% Oloroso and Pedro Ximénez sherry barrels. As an aside, they recently purchased a peat bog, about 60 acres, in Washington, the only one that can be legally harvested in the state. They won't sell any of their peat, and considering their proposed future use, the peat should last for about 10,000 years.

This Peated Whiskey reminded me of barbecued dirt, a smoky and earthy mix that I found especially compelling. Once again, the flavors were well-balanced, and the smokiness didn't overpower the whiskey. And like the Single Malt, this whiskey was silky smooth and delicious, with a complex blend of intriguing flavors, including vanilla, caramel, salted nuts, and subtle red fruit flavors. There were hints of chocolate, coffee, and citrus, but to a much lesser degree than the Single Malt. The aroma alone in this whiskey delighted me, and it was tempting to simply smell it and not even drink it, though I would love savoring a bottle with friends over a long fall afternoon. Highly recommended and one of the best spirits I have tasted this year.

RA

WESTLAND SHERRY WOOD AMERICAN SINGLE MALT WHISKEY 46%

Westland Distillery of Seattle, Washington has been distilling a small handful of American single malt whiskeys since 2010. We visited them to tell their story, noting they are another of the growing number of American craft whiskey producers pushing to make American whiskeys of single malt status akin to their Scottish industry forbearers.

The distillery makes a flagship single malt, a lightly peated expression, and a sherry wood expression. The Westland Sherry Wood American Single Malt is the dram visited here. In true Scottish tradition, the mash bill is purely 100% barley, relatively uncommon for American-style whiskeys. Those hoping to find a friendly alternative to their usual bourbon may shy away from Westland's expressions. Those hoping to find whiskeys with a nod and wink to Scotland may be pleased with these local expressions.

The Westland Sherry Wood American Single Malt presents in the glass a light golden, just barely orange from yellow. Very obviously barley-forward from the first sniff, the dram displays no vaporosity or bite. Very honeyed on the nose, reminiscent of an apiary smack-dab in the middle of a barley field. Overlaying these is a light layer of candied sweetness not unlike the traditional kitsch Easter ham toppings of pineapple and maraschino cherry.

The ham topping element of the nose couldn't help but make me miss some of the smokiness of peated expressions and the lack of leathery, chewiness of some tougher American bourbons. After opening entirely, the candy and sweetness on the nose give way to a darker, woodier note—finally making the sherry cask element obvious. Further, the quality and age of the sherry casks shines through almost unbelievably clearly.

The first impression on the pal-

ate, as on the nose, is a barley-packed punch. After the initial barley impression wears off, black licorice and fresh anise appear, backed very lightly by spice. The integrity of the sherry cask comes into play mid-taste, making room for candied fruit notes once again. Plums in heavy syrup and stewed red currant round out the palate.

The finish at first is subtle and sweet, slightly candied, but not so heavily as on the nose. Herbal enough to be refreshing, but as the finish stretches out becoming more akin to a gob of sugar syrup on the tongue.

Very typically a barley-forward expression at first blush, the dram transforms with the addition of the sherry cask-aging period, transforming it from basic to nuanced. Although in many ways, barley-forward mash bills make for whiskeys that taste naked, Westland rose above that feeling for me. Westland Sherry Wood does not achieve American single malt perfection in my eyes but may to many others. An incredibly solid dram, with the taste of clear intention in production.

SW

Lewisville, TX

WITHERSPOON'S
SINGLE MALT WHISKEY 40%

Witherspoon Distillery makes its home in a 15,000-square-foot former Piggly Wiggly on Charles St. in Lewisville, Texas. Witherspoon gets its name from Quentin Witherspoon, founder and master distiller. Cofounders Ryan DeHart (chief financial officer) and Natasha DeHart (revenue, business development, and customer operations) help make sure the place runs properly. Witherspoon's has a distillery, a bar, and a whiskey garden! And it is a popular destination among the distilleries in Texas.

But distilling is at the heart of what they do. And they do it well. Their Texas Straight Bourbon is among the most popular of the state-based bourbons in Texas. "The artistic part of distilling is learning how to keep in good flavors and get rid of bad flavors," Witherspoon said. "There's a trial and error process, and it takes a lot of time to create the best spirit."

Witherspoon's Single Malt Whisky has a small legion of fans as well. That group might be larger, but this is a small-batch distillery. It's won numerous medals. The unpeated whiskey is smooth and silky.

Tasting notes include: "Witherspoon's approach to Malt Whiskey showcases the subtle and delicate flavors and aromas that are found only in obscure Lowland and Speyside regions of Scotland. In this fine liquor are traditional scents of earth and grass. Each moment in the glass reveals layer after complex layer of floral jasmine and honey sweetness. This delicious spirit is best enjoyed neat or on the rocks."

CD

WOOD'S HIGH MOUNTAIN DISTILLERY

Salida, CO

TENDERFOOT COLORADO SINGLE MALT WHISKEY 45%

Wood's High Mountain Distillery is fairly new to the spirits industry, part of the burgeoning Colorado whiskey gang, and the hard work in spirits production it takes to build a successful business is a true passion for the brothers who founded it. This makes the whiskey all the more likeable, as it displays true American sensibility and spirit (pun intended).

The brothers, PT and Lee Wood, were first attracted to spirit-making in 1999, but only in 2012 acted upon their idea. Prior to opening Wood's distillery, PT was a river guide and homebuilder, while Lee organized tech events (he still does). The brothers financed the distillery with savings and home loans and opened up shop in an old auto repair garage in Salida, Colorado. The distillery currently hosts tastings and tours, and these are all very well received according to the stellar Yelp and TripAdvisor reviews. Clearly, the brothers want to share their passion and personally connect with their community.

The brothers first started with distilling gin and then moved on to whiskey liqueur. Tenderfoot is their single malt offering. It is distilled twice in their antique German pot still, named "Ashley." It is aged in new oak, and bottled, unfiltered, in batches of 350 bottles. Specs for the bottle I sampled: Age: 1 year; Batch number 16, Bottle 140.

What is notable about this whiskey is that it is made from a blend of five malted grains, including two-row barley malt, smoked barley malt, chocolate barley malt, malted rye, and malted wheat (so in this case, single "malt" does not mean 100% malted

barley). This blend makes this whiskey unique and memorable. It is unbelievably oaky, yet its oakiness does not destroy subtly lingering flavors.

Tenderfoot is burnt orange in the glass. The bottle labeling and finishing is thoughtful and adorable. The label includes a small depiction of Ashley at the top and manages to squeeze in a moustache under the word "Wood's," presumably a nod to one of the brothers' moustaches that looks almost identical to this one. A paper square of literature about the whiskey is hung from a string that includes a mini-carabiner. Mountain climbing, anyone?

The name "Wood's" is fitting for this whiskey, as wood is a reference point for Tenderfoot. The immediate nose is oak, oak, oak. Images that come to mind when smelling it are a woodworking shop (think freshly felled trees with wood polish, wood oils, and light chemicals), a wood house being built atop a breezy mountain, and watching the sun rise on the Rockies as you lie in your cabin. Surprisingly, with the heavy charred oak scent, there is no nasal burn. This whiskey is meant to evoke the essence of Colorado (specifically, a "passion for the outdoor adventures…with the essence of the mountains of Colorado"), and it certainly does.

The mouthfeel is initially slightly creamy with an insistent spiciness that lingers on the top of the tongue for quite a while. It tastes just as one would expect from the nose: oak. The taste thins out as the finish endures and heavy salivation helps it on its way. The tail end of the finish is very dry. It is clear that this is a young whiskey, but this does not do it a disservice. In order to keep that bright oakiness and bold spiciness, its youth is necessary. There is also a subtle smokiness that comes from the charring and the taste of a citrusy dark chocolate.

EE

Cincinnati, OH

WOODSTONE MICROSPIRIT MURRAY CASK PEATED SINGLE MALT WHISKEY 46.5%

You've gotta love Don Outterson. His self-proclaimed title is CFO—Chief Fermenting Officer. He and his wife Linda oversee an operation in Cincinnati, Ohio, that produces whiskey, wine, gin, mead, rum, and port.

Whatever their reputation in the other areas, when it comes to whiskies, small as they are, they excel. Their bourbon is highly rated, and hard to come by, as is their single malt whiskey. Woodstone Creek only turns out three barrels a year. It's all done by hand. "We have no production lines—no automated equipment, no computers, no bottling line, and no employees." The output could be small. One batch consisted of just 192 numbered bottles. The whiskey is distilled in a 238 gallon pot still, designed by Don himself. Don insists they make whiskey the old-fashioned way. The story goes that Don and Linda carried a sample all the way to Islay, in Scotland, and brought their 10 year old first sample with them. They got famed master distiller Jim McEwan of Bruichladdich try it! And he liked it! The whiskey is aged in a former sherry barrel, a bottling called the Murray Cask. It's working: Woodstone Creek Microdistillery Murray Cask Peated Single Malt received a rating of 92 in Jim Murray's 2009 Whisky Bible, calling it "Glorious!" 'Nough said!

CD

WALES

BY CARLO DEVITO

Located in the southwestern corner of Great Britain, Wales is famous for its craggy coastline, rugged mountain terrain, and unique native language. The people have been known for centuries for their beautiful lilting singing voices. Up until now, Wales was most famous as a region for its coal mining and production. It was also known for iron works and slate quarries, the most well-known of which being Penryhn.

Wales has also produced numerous famous people including Laura Ashley, T.E. Lawrence, Bertrand Russell, Ken Follett, Dick Francis, Tom Jones, Richard Burton, Anthony Hopkins, Christian Bale, and Timothy Dalton among others.

Whisky distilled in Wales is known as Welsh whisky. Whisky has been distilled and aged in Wales since Medieval times. Reaullt Hir, known as "The Great Welsh Warrior," supposedly distilled whisky in AD 356 with the help of the monks of Bardsey Island. However, the commercial tradition of distilling in Wales slowly waned, until the last producers seemed to have died out in the late 1800s.

It was not until 2000 when the Welsh Whisky Company established a distillery at Penderyn in the Brecon Beacons National Park, a popular mountain range in South Wales. The Old Red Sandstone peaks play host to countless hikers every year. The highest mountain in the region is Pen y Fan. According to Arthurian legend, two peaks of the Brecon Beacons together are also known as "Arthur's Seat." Penderyn released its first whisky in 2004, and remains the sole purveyor of single malt in the region.

BY GAVIN D. SMITH

The Welsh Whisky Company Ltd. has been making Penderyn single malt in its purpose-built distillery in the Brecon Beacons National Park since September 14, 2000. Penderyn is produced in a unique still, designed by David Faraday, and unlike most malt whisky, which is processed in both a wash still and a spirit still, here the entire business of distillation takes place in the one vessel. Penderyn also differs from Scotch single malts in that while in Scotland mashing and fermenting on site is a legal requirement, in this case wash is transported from the brewery of SA Brain & Co. in Cardiff once a week for distillation. A youthful Penderyn was launched on St David's Day in March 2004, and the spirit is usually finished in Madeira casks after initial maturation in Bourbon barrels. There have also been limited edition releases of whisky made using peated malt and some matured in ex-Oloroso Sherry butts.

PENDERYN SINGLE MALT WELSH WHISKY 46.0%

On the nose, intense, peachy sweetness overlays grainy, gummy, young spirit. The palate is spicy and fruity, with a suggestion of custard powder towards the end, which finishes with raisins and vanilla. Better balanced now than some of the earlier releases sampled, but there remains a nagging doubt that the full-bodied Madeira finish is masking what is essentially rather immature spirit.

GS

PENDERYN SHERRYWOOD 46.0%

Following on from its initial release of spirit matured in ex-Madeira cask, the Welsh distillery of Penderyn proceeded to offer a Sherry cask-finished expression and a variant made with peated malt. The Sherrywood version was initially matured in Buffalo Trace ex-Bourbon casks before spending time in casks that had formerly held Oloroso sherry. The result is a nose of sweet sherry, almonds, and peanuts. Caramel and ginger emerge, along with notes of vanilla. Clearly quite youthful on the palate, somewhat sharp-edged, fruity, with developing nuttiness and more caramel, both of which last through the lengthy and slightly metallic finish.

GS

PENDERYN PEATED 46.0%

This variant of the Welsh single malt has not been made using peated malt, as might be supposed, but was matured initially in ex-Buffalo Trace Bourbon casks before being finished in second-fill casks from the Scotch whisky industry that had previously held heavily-peated spirit. Quite refined, sweet smokiness on the nose. Vanilla and apple notes develop and the smoke fades. As with the Sherry-wood, obviously relatively young and a little assertive, with wood smoke, ginger and nuts. Smokiness lingers, along with a mildly citric note.

GS

— ACKNOWLEDGMENTS —

The editor would like to begin by thanking Clay Risen of *The New York Times* and Chip Tate from Tate and Company for their participation. A thanks also goes to Lew Bryson, who reviewed these pages with the sword of Damocles hanging over his head. Special thanks are also due to Alex Ward of *The New York Times* for his help and guidance.

More special thanks belongs to Angelo Capuano, Thomas Ohrbom, Richard Thomas, Davin de Kergommeaux, Stefan Van Eycken, Nino Marchetti, Tabarak Razvi, Josh Feldman, Steffen Brauner, the writers from the Edinburgh Whisky blog, and the rest of the writers who participated in this adventure. Thank you all!

Special thanks to those who worked on the book goes to Jaime Christopher for her incredible design work, and the rest of the Cider Mill Press team: Brittany Wason, Amy Paradysz, Alex Lewis, Kelly Gauthier, Emma Kantola, Charlotte Sawyer, and, of course, publisher John Whalen, who gave us the resources to do this thing right.

A final thank you goes to the many distillers and bottlers who donated their photography and time to help this book come to fruition.

GLOSSARY

BY MATT CHAMBERS & KAREN TAYLOR

Angel's share: This is the name given to the alcohol that evaporates from a cask as the whiskey is maturing in a warehouse. In Scotland and Ireland, this is approximately 2% of the contents of each cask each year, although this amount is higher in other countries with warmer climates.

ABV: The abbreviation for Alcohol By Volume—the term used to describe the percentage alcohol level in spirits.

Blended whiskey: A whiskey made by blending together any number of single malt whiskies and grain whiskies to create the required flavor and characteristics. These whiskies can be from different distilleries and be of different ages.

Campbeltown: The once bustling Scottish whiskey producing region that is now home to just a couple of distilleries. It lies on a spit of land called the Campbeltown Peninsula on the western coast of Scotland.

Cask: The wooden barrel used to mature the whiskey. These are traditionally made from oak. The most used types of oak are American, European or Japanese.

Cask strength: The strength of whiskey as it comes from the cask. It is not diluted further before bottling and the strength can be anything between 40% and 65% ABV, depending on age. The younger a whiskey is, the higher its ABV will generally be.

Charring: The process of burning the inside of a cask. This blackens the inside of the cask, accelerating the natural compounds in the wood to come out once the cask is filled with spirit. The level of charring can be controlled so as to control the amount of flavor compounds that pass from the wood to the whiskey during maturation.

Chill filtration: The process by which natural substances that make whiskey go cloudy when cold or diluted with water are removed before bottling. The whiskey is chilled, the natural substances coagulate and are then removed by being passed through a series of metal meshes.

Column still: A large industrial still that allows for continuous, mechanized distillation. Column stills are mostly used in the production of grain whiskey and are modern and cost effective. May also be called a Coffey still, continuous still or a patent still.

Condensation: The process where the alcohol vapors turn into the liquid spirit, with the help of cooling apparatus that form part of the still.

Cooper: A highly skilled person who makes the casks for whiskey maturation by perfectly locking staves of wood together to make a watertight container. This art is called coopering and it takes place in a building called a cooperage.

Distillation: The process of turning the mildly alcoholic wash into highly alcoholic spirit. The wash is heated in a still and the alcohol vapors evaporate and rise up the neck of the still and travel along the lyne arm, where they are condensed to form a liquid again.

Draff: The residue from the mashing process. It consists of barley husks and other bits of the grain that are then collected, dried and compressed in to pellets and sold as animal feed.

Dram: The traditional Scottish name for a glass of whiskey.

Drum malting: This modern method is used to produce malted barley in most malting facilities. The barley is put in to a large drum and soaked with water. It is then turned consistently for a number of days until the barley starts to germinate and becomes 'malt'.

Fermentation: The process of turning sugar in to alcohol. In whiskey production, a sugary liquid called wort is put into a container called a washback and yeast is added. This triggers the start of fermentation and after a couple of days, all the sugar has turned to alcohol and is called wash. The liquid has a strength of between 5-8% ABV.

Floor malting: A traditional method of producing malted barley that is only still practiced in very few distilleries. The barley is soaked in water and then laid out on a wooden floor for about a week until germination starts to take place. This is very labor intensive as the barley has to be regularly turned by hand so as to ensure even germination.

Grist: Malted barley that has been ground up into a powder, so that it can be added to water to become mash and the natural sugars present will dissolve.

Highlands: The Scottish whiskey producing region, which covers the large geographical area roughly from just north of Glasgow and Edinburgh up to the far north coast. This region includes the sub-region of Speyside, which lies roughly between the cities of Inverness and Aberdeen.

Islands: The Scottish whiskey region that covers all whiskey produced on an island. Most of these lie off the west coast of Scotland, plus the Orkneys, which lie to the north of the far northern coast. Most are well known for their peaty, smoky characters as peat was traditionally the only fuel available.

Islay: The most famous of the Scottish island for whiskey production. The whis-kies from Islay are famous for their peaty, smoky qualities and the island is home to eight whiskey distilleries—more than any other island.

Kiln: The large room where malted barley is heated to stop the germination process and to remove moisture so that the barley is ready for milling. Traditionally, these were fired by peat but now most are powered by coal or oil. A number of the island distilleries still use peat to give their traditional smoky flavor characteristics.

Lowlands: The Scottish whiskey producing region that covers the Central Belt between the major cities of Glasgow and Edinburgh and everywhere south of that. Once a traditional powerhouse region, now just a few distilleries remain.

Lyne arm: The part of the still where the spirit vapors are transported to be condensed back in to a liquid. This arm is normally horizontal or close to horizontal, although some distilleries have odd shapes or steeper angles for the arm and this allows some liquid spirit to travel back down into the still to be redistilled.

Malt: Barley grains that have been through the malting process (see Malting below).

Malting: The process where the starch in barley is converted to sugar, which in turn can then be turned in to alcohol during fermentation. Malting is achieved by soaking the barley grains in warm water and then allowing them to germinate, which turns the starch present in to natural sugars. This takes place in a drum or on a malting floor. The malted barley is then dried and ground up, with the resulting substance being called grist.

Mashing: The procedure where grist is added to warm water and the natural sugars are dissolved to form a sugary solution. This takes place in a large tank called a mash tun. The solution is then called wort and is passed to a washback tank for fermentation to take place. Any grain husks and other residue are known as graff and are collected, dried and formed into animal feed.

Mash tun: A large tank or vessel that is made from cast iron, stainless steel or wood, where the mashing process takes place. The mash tun is filled with a mixture of grist and warm water and the soluble sugars in the grist dissolve to form a sugary solution. This is then passed through the perforated floor of the mash tun to go to the washback tank to under go fermentation.

Master blender: The person working for a company or distillery that scientifically selects and then mixes whiskies of different ages or origins together to form the required final flavor profile of the whiskey.

Maturation: The time taken for the whiskey to gain the optimum amount of character from the wooden cask in which it is being stored. The whiskey spirit draws natural oils and substances from the wood over time and the cask also pulls in air from the surrounding environment, as wood is a porous material.

Milling: The process where the dried malted barley grains are ground down in to grist.

Neck: The section of a still between the pot at the bottom and the lyne arm at the top. The width and height of the neck control the amount and type of alcohol vapours that are allowed to reach the top in order to be condensed back in to a liquid spirit.

Pagoda: The pyramid shaped roof that provides ventilation from the kiln where the malted barley is dried. Invented by architect Charles Doig, who drew inspiration from the similarly shaped designs used in Japanese architecture for centuries.

Peat: A layer of earth that lays below the topsoil and consists of grasses, plants, tree roots and mosses that have been compressed over thousands of years. It is a very dense substance that when dried is used as a fuel. The peat burns with a very consistent, high temperature with a thick acrid blue smoke. Used in the whiskey industry to dry malted barley, with the thick smoke being absorbed in to the grains and the flavor getting carried through the rest of the whiskey making process.

Pot still: A style of still that is the most common to be used in the production of single malt whiskey. They are made of copper due to its excellent conductive qualities and is formed of the pot at the base (where the alcoholic wash is heated), the neck (where the alcohol vapors rise up) and the lyne arm/ condenser (where the vapours begin returning to the liquid form).

PPM: The abbreviation of Parts Per Million—the scientific measurement for showing the amount of phenols present in a whiskey, that have been absorbed from the burning of peat.

Purifier: A device connected to the lyne arm that condenses heavier alcohol vapors that are not useful in the whiskey making process. It leads the liquids back down to the base, where they undergo further distillation.

Quaich: A traditional Scottish whiskey-drinking cup that consists of a bowl with a short vertical handle on either side. They are associated with friendship and ancient Celtic stories say that if you share a drink from a quaich with someone, then you will be friends forever.

Reflux: The name given to the re-condensing of alcohol that then runs back in to the still and gets re-distilled. The amount of reflux is determined by the shape and size of the still and the angle to which the lyne arm is set.

Saladin box: An old method of malting barley, named after its inventor Charles Saladin. The box is a large automated trough that has a perforated floor through which air is blown. The germination process of the barley is controlled in the Saladin box by regulating the airflow and temperature between the grains.

Shell and tube condenser: A copper tubing that surrounds the lyne arm on a still. Cold water is fed through the tubing and this process cools the alcohol vapors and condenses them in to liquid spirit. It is the most common type of condenser used in distilleries today.

Single malt: Whiskey that is made of 100% malted barley and is from just one single distillery location. They generally contain slightly different ages of whiskey from numerous different casks within the distillery's warehouse. These are then married together in a larger container to establish the required consistent flavor profile. The age stated on the bottle is the youngest age of any whiskey included.

Speyside: The largest Scottish whiskey-producing region in terms of amount of distilleries. There are approximately 40 of the 90+ Scottish distilleries operating in this area. The area stretches roughly between the cities of Inverness and Aberdeen, and is named after the famous River Spey that runs through it.

Spirit safe: A brass framed box with glass walls that is attached to the spirit still. It is used to analyze the spirit when it leaves the still. By law, the operator cannot come in to contact with the spirit and as a result the spirit safe is padlocked with a Customs & Excise officer keeping the key.

Spirit still: The second and usually smallest in a pair of stills. The 'low wines' from the wash still are re-distilled in the spirit still—this raises the alcohol level to between 64-69% ABV and clears the alcohol of unwanted impurities. Only the middle section of this distillate is collected for maturation. This section is called the cut.

Vatted malt: A whiskey that consists two or more single malts that are blended together. Unlike a blended whiskey, vatted malts contain no grain whiskey and only single malts. These can be from the same or different distilleries and be of differing ages.

Warehouse: The area where whiskey is stored during its maturation. There are two main types. The first is the dunnage or traditional warehouse which have earth floors and stone walls where casks are stacked no more than three high. The other is the racked warehouse, which is a modern facility with temperature and humidity control and where casks are stacked on racks up to 12 high.

Washback: A large deep tub or vat in which the fermentation process takes place in a distillery. Traditionally made of wood, they are now commonly made of stainless steel.

Wash still: Stills normally operate in pairs and the wash still is the first and usually largest of the two. The fermented wash is heated and the alcohol vapors evaporate and are then cooled and reformed in to a liquid by a condenser. The resulting liquid has an alcohol level of 20-22% ABV and are called the low wines. These then move to the spirit still.

Worm tub: An older form of apparatus used for cooling alcohol vapors back to a liquid spirit. The worm tub is connected to the lyne arm of a still and is formed of a long downward spiraling copper pipe that is submerged in a wooden tub full of cold water. The tub is usually positioned outside and was traditionally filled with rainwater. Under ten distilleries in Scotland still have this system in operation. Most others use shell and tube condensers.

Wort: A warm and sugary solution that contains the soluble sugars from the malted barley dissolved in warm water. Wort is the liquid that goes forward to the fermentation process, where the sugars are changed to alcohol.

Tun   Pipe, Butt 1/2 tun   Puncheon, Tertian 1/3 tun   Hogshead 1/4 tun   Tierce 1/6 tun   Barrel 1/8 tun   Rundlet 1/14 tun

ENGLISH WINE CASK UNITS

BY CARLO DEVITO

The idea of standardizing barrel quantities and measurements was first introduced in the 15th century in the Parliament. As international trade increased, reliable, standard measurements that could be negotiated on a dependable basis were necessary to insure good commerce within the nation and across borders. These quantities came into being, and have stood the test of time. They came to be used for wine, beer, and spirits over the years. These vessels were used in the trade of wine, spirits, beer, honey, or other liquid commodities. Barrel, cask, or tun were traditionally known as a hollow cylindrical container.

Rundlet – 18 gallons – The rundlet was a seventh of a butt, or a fourteenth of a tun.

Barrel – 31.5 gallons – The word "barrel" was thought to come from the medieval French word *baril,* and is still in use, both in French and as derivations in many other languages, such as Italian, Polish, and Spanish. The "drum" is also commonly interchangeable for this quantity. It is commonly referred to as a "barrique Bordelaise," which became popular more than a century ago.

Tierce – 42 gallons – Tierce casks were roughly 20.5 inches across. They were originally created to hold numerous liquids, but dry barrels were also produced and were used to transport everything from rum to salted beef and fish.

Hogshead – 63 gallons – The hogshead was first standardized in 1423. During the nineteenth century, the hogshead was used to measure sugar in Louisiana. According to English philologist Walter William Skeat (1835–1912), the origin is to be found in the name for a cask or liquid measure in several Teutonic languages, such as Dutch oxhooft (modern okshoofd), Danish oxehoved, Old Swedish oxhufvod, etc. The word should therefore be "oxhead," "hogshead" being a corruption of that name.

Puncheon (Tertian) – 84 gallons – The puncheon was a third of a tun. The term "puncheon" is thought to derive from being marked by a punch to denote its contents. The unit was also known as a "tertian" (Latin for "third").

Butt (Pipe) – 126 gallons – The butt (from the mediæval French word botte) or pipe was half a tun, or 1,008 pints. Tradition has it that George, Duke of Clarence, was drowned in a butt of malmsey. In Edgar Allan Poe's short story "The Cask of Amontillado," the narrator claims he has received "a pipe of what passes for Amontillado."

Tun – 252 gallons – The tun (Old English: tunne, Latin: tunellus, Middle Latin: tunna) is an English unit of liquid volume (not weight), used for measuring liquid commodities. Typically a tun held 252 gallons but occasionally other sizes were available. Of course, a tun weighs approximately 2,000 pounds with wine or spirits or beer in it, which, of course, also approximately equals the weight of one ton.

CONTRIBUTORS

Keith Allison is a writer based in New York, where he's spent nearly two decades in the wilds of south Brooklyn. He was born in Kentucky, educated at the University of Florida, and writes about spirits, travel, film, history, and when he can, the intersection of all of the above.

Vance Alm graduated from Business Management School at University of Nevada, Reno. His blog, Vance Alm's Thoughts, covers wines, beer, and whiskey, and he is liquor connoisseur and aficionado.

Eric Asimov is the chief wine critic for *The New York Times* and the author of *How to Love Wine: A Memoir and Manifesto*, and co-author with Florence Fabricant of *Wine With Food: Pairing Notes and Recipes from The New York Times.*

Richard Auffrey is a life-long resident of Massachusetts, a licensed attorney, and has been involved in food and wine writing for more than nine years. Beside his food, wine, saké & spirits blog, *The Passionate Foodie*, he's also written a food & wine column for the *Stoneham Sun* newspaper, and his work has been published in such periodicals as *Beverage Media, Drink Me, Boston Scene, North End Scene, the Valley Patriot, the Medford Patch* and *Melrose Patch*. He is a Certified Spanish Wine Educator and a Certified Sake Professional. He has been inducted as a Cavaleiro in the Confraria do Vinho do Porto, a Knight in the Brotherhood of Port Wine. He is also on the Board of Directors of Drink Local Wine, Inc., and has written the *Tipsy Sensei* novel series.

Michael Bendavid blogs about (mostly single malt) whisky at maltandoak.com, and is head of whisky content for the Hebrew language tastewhisky.co.il. An international attorney by training and ex military judge, he owns one of Israel's premier business and management coaching companies, Forlife Coaching. He lives and works in Tel Aviv, Israel.

Peter Blanchette is the editor of Eating Portland, Me., and better known by his nom de plume Peter Peter Portland Eater. His reviews cover wines, beers, spirits, and restaurants of the region. (www.peterpeterportlandeater.com).

Steffen Brauner has been a whisky enthusiast for more than 20 years. He has been a beer enthusiast for 15 years. He is a member of PLOWED. He has visited more than 140 breweries and 140 distilleries. He writes and edits his own blog: Danish Whisky Blog. He is obsessed with maps. He lives in Aarhus, Denmark.

Angelo Capuano is an Australian lawyer and whisk(e)y enthusiast, whose passion for whisk(e)y was ignited while he lived in the United Kingdom as a masters student at Oxford University. He has since tasted over 2,000 spirits and whiskies from all over the world. He writes regularly for his blog maltmileage.com. MaltMileage.com has been online since March 2013. It has over 10,000 followers and 9,000 Facebook fans from all over the world.

Matt Chambers & Karen Taylor started Whisky For Everyone in March 2008 and have been writing and blogging about whisky and the whisky industry ever since. Between them they have written for and featured in the newspapers such as the *London Evening Standard* and *The Sun*, magazines such as *Shortlist* and *The Spirits Business*, online for various websites including The Huffington Post UK and across various social media platforms. Both are judges for The Scotch Whisky Masters awards and both were inducted as Keepers of the Quaich in April 2015.

Diana Kaoru Cheang is an irreverent resident of the Washington, DC area, and a contributing writer to The Whiskey Reviewer.

Evan Dawson is the Managing Editor and Finger Lakes Editor of the New York Cork Report, the two-time winner of the award for Best Single-Subject Wine Blog. He is also the Roderer award-winning author of *Summer in a Glass: The Coming of Age of Winemaking in the Finger Lakes.* Formerly the 13WHAM-TV, morning news anchor, he now hosts the NPR affiliated radio talk show Connections, which originates at WXXI in Rochester, NY. He has written freelance articles on topics including politics, wine, travel, and Major League Baseball for many publications. He lives with his wife, Morgan, and their child, in Rochester, NY.

Davin de Kergommeaux is the author of the award-winning book *Canadian Whisky: The Portable Expert* and has contributed to three other books about whisky, and two about spirits and cocktails. An independent whisky expert, de Kergommeaux has been writing about, talking about, and teaching about whisky for nearly two decades. He is the founder, head judge, and master of ceremonies for the Canadian Whisky Awards, and publishes comprehensive notes about Canadian whiskies on canadianwhisky.org. His writing and tasting notes appear regularly in *Whisky Magazine, Whisky Advocate* magazine, and various lifestyle publications. De Kergommeaux lives in Canada and writes full time. Follow him on twitter and instagram @Davindek.

Carlo DeVito is one of the most experienced wine, beers, and spirits editors in the world whose list of authors has included *The Wine Spectator, The New York Times,* Michael Jackson, Kevin Zraly, Clay Risen, Matt Kramer, Oz Clarke, Tom Stevenson, Howard G. Goldberg, Josh M. Bernstein, Stephen Beaumont, Ben McFarland, Jim Meehan, Salvatore Calabrase, William Dowd, and many others. His books and authors over the years have won James Beard, Gourmand, and IAACP awards. He has traveled to wine regions in California, Canada, up and down the east coast, France, Spain, and Chile. He is the author of *Jiggers and Drams: A Whiskey Journal*, and is the publisher of East Coast Wineries website which covers wines, beer, whisky, and ciders from Maine to Virginia.

Jake Emen is a freelance writer based outside of Washington, D.C., and a lover of all types of whiskey. He's passionate about food, drink and travel, and lucky enough to write such topics as he explores both newly burgeoning regions around the United States, and others across the globe. For whiskey and spirits coverage, he has been published in *Whisky Advocate, Eater Drinks, Tasting Table, The Washington Post Express, Distiller,* and various other outlets. He also runs his own site, ManTalkFood.com, and can be followed on Twitter @ManTalkFood. His piece is from Whiskey Wash.

Elizabeth Emmons is the second member of the New York team for the website The Whiskey Reviewer. Elizabeth is well-rounded and -grounded in whisk(e)y, as fond of a shot of bourbon as a dram of single malt whisky.

Josh Feldman is the Network Administrator of The Morgan Library & Museum, a cultural landmark in Midtown Manhattan. He is also a well-regarded whisky blogger known for detailed historical essays at The Coopered Tot. A fixture in the New York whisky scene, Feldman also leads tasting events and participates in the community of bloggers as a co-administrator of the Whisky Bloggers Facebook group. Originally from Berkeley, CA, he has lived in New York for over 30 years. He has two kids, 13 and 15. His blog is The Coopered Tot.

Graeme Gardiner writes for the Edinburgh Whisky Blog and was brought up in the sparkling seaside resort of Aberdeen. In 2007, Graeme decided to run away and make his fortune in Edinburgh where he emerged with a degree in English and Journalism four years later. He is an editor by trade.

Lynne Goldman has written over 1400 articles about local food in Bucks County, PA and nearby since starting her blog, Bucks County Taste, in 2008. In the past year, Bucks County Taste has received more than half a million page views from readers all over Bucks County, Philadelphia and New York City.

Sjoerd de Haan-Kramer focuses on whisk(e)y mostly on his blog Malt Fascination (www.maltfascination.com), but also covers many different kinds of distillates and brews. Since 2014 he has been chief-editor of the club magazine of the Usquebaugh Society (*De Kiln*), a quarterly magazine by and for members of the club. He also hosts whiskey tastings.

Chris Hoban has been a guest contributor to Grant's Whisky Blog, quoted in the *Metro*, interviewed for *Whisky Magazine* and even bottled his own Glenfarclas for Movember (with Master of Malt). He is co-founder of the Edinburgh Whisky Blog, has been a tour guide for The Scotch Whisky Experience, and been a web person for Drinkmonger HQ.

Johan Johansen is a passionate eater and a connoisseur of fine wines and spirits. He started johanjohansen.dk as a creative outlet for his greatest passions: gastronomy, home cooking, fine wines and spirits. Since 2013, it has served as his virtual soapbox for thoughts and opinions on everything from classic recipes over Michelin-starred dinners to niche wines and artisan spirits.

Tobias Johnsson is a whisky fan and occasional contributor to Whisky Saga (www.whiskysaga.com).

Sebastian Kelbassa is a spirits blogger from Dortmund, Germany. During his university studies he started bartending as a hobby in the year of 2008. He is now hosting Galumbi - Drinks & More (www.galumbi.com), a blog mainly about mixed drinks, beers and spirits. He is very passionate about whisk(e)y.

Michael Kravitz, a spirits connoisseur, provides reviews and industry commentary on his popular whisky blog, Diving for Pearls (www.divingforpearlsblog.com). The co-president of the Orange County Scotch Club, Michael designs and leads public and private tasting events as well as consults for whisky enthusiasts, helping curate their collections.

Lukas Kreft writes and edits Luk LovesWhisky.com. He is passionate about single malt whiskey. His adventure with this type of drink started when he got a gift of strongly peated single malt whiskey. It was his conscious malt. Conscious, because when he drank it he knew more or less what single malt was. With each glass of it he began to see the beauty of the whiskey. It became his guide at the entrance to the World of Whisky.

Ragnhild S. Lervik is the author/editor of drikkelig.no (drikkelig means drinkable in Norwegian) where they write about things you can drink, with the main focus being malt whisky, cider and beer. Ragnhild (known by English speaking friends as Robin since his given name is too difficult to pronounce) has been blogging since 2002. He has been a malt whisky enthusiast for more than fifteen years, beginning with his first sip of Talisker 10. He has also been one of the main contributors to the prize-winning Whiskywiki.

Johannes Lindblom is a professional writer and a whisky lover from Finland

and is the author of the popular Whisky Rant website (www.whiskyrant.com) which mostly features whisky reviews, and industry news and information. You might also know Johannes as Rantavahti in different social medias, in Whisky Connosr for instance. He is a SEO friendly marketing man and decathlete in the dangerous world of advertising.

Mic Lowther has been a computer systems analyst since 1962, working for companies in New York, Arizona, Alaska, and now at his own business in Minnesota. He has backpacked 5,000 miles of long distance trails and written two books about those adventures. He took a course at bartender school at age 70 to become more familiar with cocktails and spirits which led to writing 53 blog articles at www.awhiskeyjournal.com.

Ruben Luyten is the editor of one of the longest running blogs about whisky (www.whiskynotes.be, since 2008), publishing daily tasting notes and news. He was elected IWC Whisky Blogger of the Year 2015 and is also writing about sherry on www.sherrynotes.com.

Kurt Maitland, born in Brooklyn, was one of the earliest contributors to The Whiskey Reviewer, and now serves as Deputy Editor. He is also one of the best-known faces in New York City's hyperactive whiskey circuit, and when not there might be found prowling for "dusties" in the Eastern United States or on the distillery trail in Scotland.

John Malatino aka "Smoky Peat" is a North County San Diego whisky blogger and enthusiast. He enjoys whisky of every style and is a strong believer that every cask is unique. Get out there and explore the wonderfully diverse world of whisky.

Nino Marchetti is a writer and journalist by trade and an Internet dot-com veteran prior to that. He has written extensively about whiskey, particularly bourbon and the American craft whiskey movement, both for The Whiskey Wash and also other publications. Nino also has an extensive collection of whiskies from both start up distilleries and centuries old operations in Scotland alike, sprinkled with some other odds and ends from around the world, that have provided him with a unique picture of what's going on with this wonderful spirit.

Luke McCarthy's writing on whisky and spirits has been published in numerous Australian and international publications. A drinks columnist for Fairfax Media's *Executive Style*, and a bartender at one of Australia's finest whisky establishments, Luke's first book, *The Australian Spirits Guide* – a comprehensive and irreverent exploration of distilling Down Under – will be published in 2016.

Harold McGee is the author of *On Food & Cooking: The Science & Lore of the Kitchen*, and wrote The Curious Cook column for *The Times*.

Jonathan Miles wrote the Shaken and Stirred column for *The New York Times* from 2006 to 2010. He is the author of two novels, *Dear American Airlines* and *Want Not*.

Thomas Ohrbom discovered whisky back in 1997, and over time his interest grew quite significantly. In January 2012 he started the blog Whisky Saga, where his aim is to share his passion for this golden liquid. Where he wants to be different, and perhaps add something new, is by focusing on Nordic Whisky, while still covering the whisky world in general. He tries to publish new articles every weekday, every week.

Zach Pearson and **Angela Poetzl** are a couple of whiskey lovers living in Denver, Colorado. When not working, spending time with Angela's daughter, or going to Avalanche and Bronco games, they love to visit different distilleries and breweries throughout the state. The idea for their website came when both were sampling different Colorado made whiskeys, and finding out just how much they both enjoy the spirit. One day, they hope to own a distillery and produce their own whiskey.

Marc Pendlebury is the founder and owner of Whisky Brother, a whiskey retailer. His interest in whisky grew and turned into a no-nonsense, games-aside, passion. He actively seeks out new and old whiskies, reads the latest news from the industry, distilleries, publications and fellow bloggers, tastes whiskies from around the world, swap samples, plan trips to whisky destinations, et cetera.

Josh S. Peters is an Los Angeles based whiskey blogger who spends an absurd amount of time reading, writing and talking about whisk(e)y of every variety. When he's not at a tasting, whiskey club meeting or writing up tasting notes he can be found either guzzling green tea in a L.A. coffee shop, hanging out in a museum or relaxing at home with his 2 dogs. . . during which he's usually thinking about whiskey.

S.D. Peters is one of the original contributors to The Whiskey Reviewer, and has served from the beginning as it's main "rye guy." Although his tastes include all forms of whiskey, he is one of that handful of people who was seriously into rye whiskey years before it became fashionable.

Jason M Pyle is a whiskey enthusiast who edits and oversees one of the more popular whiskey-related websites on the internet, Sour Mash Manifesto. Sour Mash Manifesto focuses predominantly on various styles of whiskey produced in the United States, including micro-distillers. Over the last six years Jason has contributed on many publications, books, and websites across the globe.

Father John Rayls was born and raised in central and southern Indiana, but moved to San Antonio, TX 12 years ago to be an Anglican Priest. He began an enthusiastic journey into all things whiskey at the same time and began writing about these experiences ten years later, at first for The Whiskey Wash and now for The Whiskey Reviewer.

Tabarak Razvi aka Malt Activist is all things whisky: founder of his club, a blogger, a YouTuber, an Instagrammer, a critic but above all a geek. He is happiest when discussing the finer nuances of whisky and has been known to go to great lengths to discover hidden gems. His motto in life: drink it any way you like.

Maria Buteux Reade transitioned from 27 years as a boarding school teacher and dean to become a working partner at Someday Farm in East Dorset. When not on her tractor turning compost, she writes in an old sugarhouse, happy to share that space with a few cows, some wandering geese and bales of sweet hay. Maria has a home along the Battenkill River in Arlington, Vermont.

Philip Reim founded the online magazine Eye for Spirits (eyeforspirits.com) in April 2010. He studied biology and chemistry at the University of Regensburg and Friedrich Schiller University in Jena, where he completed a thesis on "Chemistry of whiskey". Besides working as a bartender he published then in numerous print media of cash and spirits scene as *Mixolog* magazine and *Fizz* magazine. He currently advises spirits companies in product development and writes the majority of the EFS articles.

Clay Risen is a senior staff editor for *The New York Times* opinion pages, the drinks columnist for *Garden & Gun* magazine and the author of *American Whiskey, Bourbon and Rye: A Guide to the Nation's Favorite Spirit* and *A Nation on Fire: America in the Wake of the King Assassination.*

Jason Rowan has written for *The New York Times, Men's Journal, Wine Enthusiast* and the website Embury Cocktails.

Jonathan Russell is the publisher and editor of Drink and Unemployed, a blog devoted to cocktails, wine, beers, and spirits. He is a mixology hobbyist, an amateur oenophile, and a whisky aficionado. Armed with his Boston shaker, his bottle opener, and citrus fruit, he covers regional beverage and food events.

Catherine Saint Louis is a reporter for *The New York Times,* covering health and medicine. She has contributed to the Dining and Wine column for *The New York Times* as well.

Rosie Schaap has written the Drink column for *The New York Times Magazine* since 2011. She is the author of the memoir *Drinking With Men,* and tends bar in Brooklyn.

Amanda Schuster is a freelance writer, consultant and marketer. She is the Editor in Chief of online drinks site The Alcohol Professor https://www.alcohol-professor.com/ and writes for several other publications. With advanced training in both wine and spirits, she likes to think of herself as "bi-spiritual." She also makes jewelry and strives to find at least one weekday afternoon a month to play hooky and see a movie. She thinks the worst thing to happen to whiskey is the Pickle Back. Follow her on Twitter and Instagram @winenshine

Robert Simonson began writing about cocktails, spirits, bars and bartenders for *The New York Times* in 2009. He also writes for *Saveur, Lucky Peach, Imbibe* and *Whiskey Advocate,* among other publications, and is the author of *The Old-Fashioned: The World's First Classic Cocktail.*

Gavin D. Smith is one of the world's leading whisky writers and authorities on the subject. Editor, author and journalist, he contributes feature material to a wide range of specialist and general interest publications. He is also the author of more than 20 books, including *The A-Z of Whisky, Worts, Worms & Washbacks, Whisky Wit & Wisdom, The Secret Still, The Scottish Smuggler, The Whisky Men, Whisky: A Brief History,* and *Ardbeg: A Peaty Provenance and Goodness Nose* (with Richard Paterson). Gavin provided tasting notes and editorial material for the 6th edition of Michael Jackson's *Malt Whisky Companion* (2010), and his book *Discovering Scotland's Distilleries* was published in the spring of 2010 by GWP. Gavin is proud to be a Keeper of the Quaich, and he is in demand for consultancy work, hosting of whisky-related talks and tutored tastings. See www.whiskytasting.co.uk.

Chip Tate is an acknowledged leader in the craft distilling industry, having received more than 150 national and international awards, including US Craft Distillery of the Year and Global Distillery of the Year from the Wizards of Whisky International Competition in 2012. In recognition of his contributions to the development of the craft spirits industry, *Whisky Magazine* awarded him their inaugural Craft Whiskey Distillery of the Year Icon award in 2012, a category which he won again in 2014. In 2013, *The Spirits Business* named him a Grand Master of World Whisky. In 2014, at the prestigious World Whisky Awards in London, he won the Best Overall American Whisky category. At the end of 2014, Chip embarked in a new strategic and creative direction, establishing Tate & Company Distillery and Chip Tate Craft Copperworks in Waco, Texas.

Femke Tijtsma Sijtsma is 37 years old and a whisky enthusiast. In 2012 Femke started her blog whiskygirl.nl to find out more about the wonderful world of whisky. What started as a hobby, whiskygirl has grown into a well-known and respected blog.

Richard Thomas is a Kentucky native who lives and drinks in Europe. Thomas applies that transatlantic perspective as the owner and managing editor of The Whiskey Reviewer. He is also the spirits beat writer for Inside Hook, as well as the author of *Port: Beginners Guide To Wine* and two novels. In addition to writing about whiskey and travel, Thomas is working on his third novel and researching coopering and whiskey wood issues.

Jason Thomson writes for the Edinburgh Whisky Blog. Finding his feet in the world of fine alcoholic beverages he started to turn up in one of the capital's fantastic whisky shops on a day to day basis. This resulted in them having to offer him a full time job. He can be found here most days peddling his wares. Jason also writes the blog for his work place and has had work featured in national newspapers. He also once ate four quarter pounder cheese burgers in one sitting.

Nick Turner and **Alex 'Ted' Matthews** are two young(ish) men who share a love for whisky. In particular, whisky made in their home state of Tasmania. By day Nick is a teacher in a little town called Penguin on the North West coast of Tasmania. Ted is a Biosecurity Inspector based in Burnie. Together with a team of writers they publish WhiskyWaffle.com.

Steve Ury is an attorney by day. He is also the writer/editor of SKU's Recent Eats a blog highlighting eating and drinking in the Koreatown neighborhood of Los Angeles and beyond. He had judged at several whiskey competitions and has been interviewed by Audie Cornish on NPR's All Things Considered, and has been featured in the *New York Times*.

Serge Valentin lives in Turckheim, France near Colmar in the Alsace Region. Since 2002 he has been a member of the Malt Maniacs and updates the enormous Malt Monitor. He founded his website Whisky Fun (www.whiskyfun. com) where he has been publishing tasting notes and scores since 2002. Oliver Klimet of Dramming.com once wrote, "Serge Valentin's site has become one of the premier sources for whisky reviews on the internet. His ratings are quoted in countless forum posts and blog articles. It seems that also whisky makers read Serge's reviews very carefully . . .Serge's passion for Jazz, off-beat rock and world music becomes obvious by browsing whiskyfun.com. Another hobby of his is hitting the Alsatian roads with one of his motorcycles." Despite his reputation for his world famous palate, his has a mantra: "Do not take all this too seriously!"

Jan Van Den Ende was born in Rotterdam, Netherlands, where he attended Marten Luther High School, and at the age of 42 moved to Sao Paulo, Brazil in 1994. He has published regularly on his website Best Shot Whisky Reviews (www.bestshotwhiskyreviews.com). He reviews and publishes tasting notes on whiskies from all over the world.

Stefan Van Eycken grew up in Belgium and Scotland and moved to Japan in 2000. He's the editor of Nonjatta (www. nonjatta.com), the foremost online resource on Japanese whisky, regional editor (Japan) of *Whisky Magazine* UK, and regular contributor to *Whisky Magazine* Japan and France. He's also the man behind the 'Ghost Series', an ongoing series of bottlings of rare Japanese whiskies, and 'Spirits for Small Change', a bi-annual whisky charity event. He's been on the Japanese panel of the World Whiskies Awards since 2012.

Margarett Waterbury writes about food and drink for magazines and newspapers. She lives in Portland, Oregon, where her home is steadily filling with whiskey bottles.

Savannah Weinstock is a Portland, OR based whisk(e)y writer. She is currently working in the industry getting up-close and personal with whisk(e)y, spirits, and cocktails every day.

Tiger White grew up in the hills of the Scottish Borders before studying at the University of Edinburgh. He has been a full time contributor to the Edinburgh Whisky Blog in the autumn of 2011. As a budding whisky consultant Tiger has lead tastings, masterclasses, talks, staff training, and generally any whisky-related event.

David Wondrich is the longtime Drinks Correspondent for *Esquire* and the author of the James Beard Award-winning *Imbibe*, which examines the life and drinks of the legendary bartender Jerry Thomas, as well as four other books.

Dave Worthington and **Kat Presley** are a father-and-daughter team who love whisky! They write about their whisky journey on the Whisky Discovery blog, which has been recognized in the *Malt Whisky Yearbook*. Dave has also written for magazines *Whisky Quarterly* and *UK Cigar Scene*. They have founded the Bedford Whisky Club and were invited to judge Cognac, Brandy and Whisky at the Spirits Masters Competitions held by the *Spirits Business* Magazine. They're now independent Whisky Ambassadors and currently working with Douglas Laing, Wemyss Malts, and Maverick Drinks amongst others.

ADDITIONAL RESOURCES

BOOKS:

Michael Jackson's Complete Guide to Single Malt Scotch, 7th Edition by Dominic Roskrow and Gavin D. Smith

American Whiskey, Bourbon & Rye: A Guide to the Nation's Favorite Spirit by Clay Risen

Tasting Whiskey: An Insider's Guide to the Unique Pleasures of the World's Finest Spirits by Lew Bryson and David Wondrich

Jiggers and Drams: A Whisky Journal by Carlo DeVito

Whiskey Cocktails: Rediscovered Classics and Contemporary Craft Drinks Using the World's Most Popular Spirit by Warren Bobrow

Jim Murray's Whisky Bible by Jim Murray

Whiskey Women: The Untold Story of How Women Saved Bourbon, Scotch, and Irish Whiskey by Fred Minnick

Whisky: The Manual by Dave Broom

MAGAZINES:

Whisky Advocate

Whisky Magazine

— CREDITS AND PERMISSIONS —

PHOTO CREDITS

CONTRIBUTORS

Photos used hereunder are reprinted by permission of the authors, contributors, and other photographers and publications. Copyright © 2016. All rights reserved.

Malt Mileage p. 16, 81, 82, 89, 91, 96, 106, 118, 120, 122, 338, 339, 341, 344, 345 (bottom), 396

Whisky Waffle p. 93, 97

Whisky Saga p. 168, 174, 238, 250 (both), 252, 348, 349, 350, 352 (both), 355, 448, 452 (both), 454 (both), 455, 456 (top), 457, 458 (top), 460, 462, 465 (both), 466 (both), 467, 468, 469, 470, 471 (both)

Stefan Van Eycken p. 60

Brent Harrewyn p. 39–44

WhiskyDK p. 171

Johan Johansen p. 186

Finnish Malt Society p. 211

Whisky Rant p. 212, 213, 214, 492

Nonjatta p. 60, 313 (top), 366

LukLovesWhisky p. 358

Edinburgh Whisky Blog p. 416 (top) and 432

Whisky Brother p. 438 and 440

Todd Godbout p. 539 (left)

Vance Alm p. 555

Sandy Wasserman p. 574

Elizabeth Emmons p. 589

Shutterstock/ YMZK-Photo p. 321, 322

Odd Society Distillery/ R.D. Cane p. 147

COPYRIGHT PERMISSION

The following articles appear courtesy of *The New York Times*: Eric Asimov p. 13, Harold McGee p. 53, Catherine St. Louis p. 59, Robert Simonson p. 64 & 70, Rosie Schaap p. 66-68, Jonathan Miles p. 69, Jason Rowan p. 72-74, and David Wondrich p. 75. Reprinted by permission of *The New York Times*. Copyright © 2016. All rights reserved.

"Bob Hockert and His Old School Cooperage" by Maria Buteux Reade, Photos by Brent Harrewyn appear courtesy of *Edible Capital Region* magazine, p. 39. Reprinted by permission of *Edible Capital Region* magazine. Copyright © 2016. All rights reserved.

The following articles appear courtesy of the Alcohol Professor.com: Amanda Schuster p. 45 and Keith Allison p. 145. Reprinted by permission of the Alcohol Professor. Copyright © 2016. All rights reserved.

Lynne Goldman's article on Hewn Spirits (p. 534) is reprinted by courtesy of *Bucks County Taste* magazine. Reprinted by permission of *Bucks County Taste*. Copyright © 2016. All rights reserved.

Luke McCarthy articles on p. 84, 86, 94, and 99 appear courtesy of Steve Calhoun, *Executive Style* and Fairfax Media. Reprinted by permission of *Executive Style* and Fairfax Media. Copyright © 2016. All rights reserved.

— INDEX —

ABOUT
Cider Mill Press
BOOK PUBLISHERS

Good ideas ripen with time. From seed to harvest, Cider Mill Press brings fine reading, information, and entertainment together between the covers of its creatively crafted books. Our Cider Mill bears fruit twice a year, publishing a new crop of titles each spring and fall.

"WHERE GOOD BOOKS ARE READY FOR PRESS"

Visit us on the Web at
WWW.CIDERMILLPRESS.COM

or write to us at
PO BOX 454
KENNEBUNKPORT, MAINE 04046